The Erotics of S

The Erotics of Sovereignty

Queer Native Writing in the Era of Self-Determination

MARK RIFKIN

 University of Minnesota Press
Minneapolis
London

Portions of chapter 1 were previously published as "The Erotics of Sovereignty," in *Queer Indigenous Studies: Critical Interventions in Theory, Politics, and Literature,* edited by Qwo-Li Driskill, Chris Finley, Brian Joseph Gilley, and Scott Morgensen (Tucson: University of Arizona Press, 2011), 172–89.

Chrystos's poetry reprinted by permission of the author. Copyright 1988, 1993, 1995. Qwo-Li Driskill's and Deborah Miranda's poetry reprinted by permission of the authors and by Salt Publishing.

Published by the University of Minnesota Press
111 Third Avenue South, Suite 290
Minneapolis, MN 55401-2520
http://www.upress.umn.edu

Library of Congress Cataloging-in-Publication Data

Rifkin, Mark.
   The erotics of sovereignty : queer native writing in the era of self-determination / Mark Rifkin.
   Includes bibliographical references and index.
   ISBN 978-0-8166-7782-5 (hc : acid-free paper)
   ISBN 978-0-8166-7783-2 (pbk : acid-free paper)
 1. American literature—Indian authors—History and criticism.
 2. Gays' writings, American—History and criticism. I. Title.
   PS153.I52R54   2012
   810.9'897—dc23

                                        2011044240

Printed in the United States of America on acid-free paper

The University of Minnesota is an equal-opportunity educator and employer.

20 19 18 17 16 15 14 13 12   10 9 8 7 6 5 4 3 2 1

Contents

Acknowledgments

This book began life as an effort to invent something in response to an invitation. The editors of what would become *Queer Indigenous Studies: Critical Interventions in Theory, Politics, and Literature* asked if I wanted to write something for their incipient project. I recently had read Qwo-Li Driskill's *Walking with Ghosts* and was excited about the possibility of doing something with it. In thinking about where I wanted to go, I started playing around with hir notion of a Sovereign Erotic, and I began to think about what difference it would make to flip around the terms—to think of an erotics of sovereignty. At the same time, I was wrapping up *When Did Indians Become Straight?* and was thinking about where I wanted to go next. I thought that I would like to keep working at the intersection of Native and queer studies, but I wasn't sure what form that desire could, would, or should take. While considering my essay for the prospective collection, I began to wonder if maybe that idea could be stretched into an entire book, taking up the work of a series of contemporary writers. First and foremost, then, I would like to thank Scott Morgensen, Chris Finley, and Brian Joseph Gilley for inviting me to participate in their excellent endeavor, and to Qwo-Li I owe an inestimable debt not only as another coeditor of that volume and a friend but as the inspiration for this project.

No act of any kind, scholarly or otherwise, happens in a vacuum. For this project I have had a number of wonderful interlocutors. For reading parts of the manuscript, I owe a debt to Jen Feather, Mary Ellis Gibson, Malea Powell, and Bethany Schneider. In this vein I would particularly like to express my deep appreciation to Mishuana Goeman, whose work on mapping and nonstatist spatialities in contemporary Native women's writing first suggested to me the idea of approaching Native literature as a vital source of political theory in dialogue with and dissent from existing frameworks in Indian policy. Also, as a friend and a reader for a number of years now, she has

< vii >

provided support and feedback, a gift for which I am immensely grateful. I have often said that when I grow up, I would like to be Daniel Heath Justice. His encouragement and critical engagement have been unflagging. In addition, conversations with Nancy Bentley, Chris Bracken, Kevin Bruyneel, Jessica Cattelino, Eric Cheyfitz, Jennifer Denetdale, Jean Dennison, Tol Foster, Alyosha Goldstein, Lisa Kahaleole Hall, Shona Jackson, Scott Morgensen, Beth Piatote, Audra Simpson, Andy Smith, and Craig Womack have been invaluable.

The University of North Carolina at Greensboro has provided me with a rich and endlessly rewarding community of scholars and friends, including Risa Applegarth, Danielle Bouchard, Liz Bucar, Sarah Cervenak, Tony Cuda, Michelle Dowd, Asa Eger, Jen Feather, Mary Ellis Gibson, Greg Grieve, Ellen Haskel, Jennifer Keith, Karen Kilcup, Sarah Krive, Derek Krueger, Christian Moraru, Noelle Morrisette, Kelly Ritter, Gene Rogers, Scott Romine, Hepsie Roskelly, María Sánchez, Ali Schultheis, Amy Vines, Anne Wallace, and Karen Weyler. I also owe a great debt to my graduate students, especially those who took part in the courses Queerness, Race, and Empire in the U.S. Context and Citizenship, Diaspora, Indigeneity.

Parts of the book were presented at the American Studies Association, Duke University, the MERGE Making and Remaking Subjects workshop at UNCG, the Native American and Indigenous Studies Association, Vanderbilt University, the University of California at Berkeley, and the University of North Carolina at Chapel Hill, and I would like to thank those who invited me to give talks or participate in workshops and everyone who attended for their excellent feedback.

Working with University of Minnesota Press has been a fabulous experience, due to the outstanding work of my wonderful editor, Jason Weidemann, and his assistant Danielle Kasprzak.

I owe my continued sanity, and sense of an extra-academic lifeworld, to Erika Lin, Geoff Wall, Christian Hansen, Jon Dichter, Tammy Sears, Sheila and Alex Avelin, Craig Bruns, Keith Brand, Albo Jeavons, Kent Latimer, JJ McArdle, Jon Van Gieson, Paul Caparotta, and Ali Zweben. Love to Zivvy, Doodles, and Bugga.

My parents, Neal and Sharon Rifkin, and sister, Gail Dichter, serve as an endless source of comfort and laughter (as well as kvetching). Their sustaining love continues to make me possible.

Introduction

> Self-determination among the Indian people can and
> must be encouraged without the threat of eventual
> termination. . . .
>
> This, then, must be the goal of any new national policy
> toward the Indian people: to strengthen the Indian's sense
> of autonomy without threatening his sense of community.
> We must assure the Indian he can assume control of his
> own life without being separated involuntarily from the
> tribal group.
>
> —*Richard Nixon, Special Message on Indian Affairs, 1970*

I N HIS STATEMENT OF HIS ADMINISTRATION'S POSITION ON federal Indian policy, Richard Nixon repudiated the logic of termination, inaugurating what has come to be known as the era of self-determination.[1] Termination sought to eliminate federal aid to and recognition of Native peoples, dismantle Native governments, and increase settler access to Native land and resources.[2] Nixon's commitment to ending this policy officially inaugurated a new kind of relationship between tribes and the federal government, suggesting the potential for a more substantive engagement between the United States and Native peoples premised on mutual respect. Couched in a performance of national shame for previous mistakes, the expression of support for self-determination promises autonomy, but its meaning seems to inhere primarily in the government's no longer actively seeking to destroy the "tribal group" as such.[3] In other words, this rubric seems less to offer a sustained reconceptualization of the jurisdictional presumptions previously undergirding U.S. Indian policy than simply to remove the "threat of eventual termination." If "autonomy" functions as a catachrestic figure for the absence of a direct assault

< 1 >

on the existence of Native nations, then what are the legal dimensions of peoplehood? Or perhaps more to the point, what aspects of peoplehood remain unintelligible within U.S. policy frameworks despite the promise to attend to Indigenous formulations of collective selfhood? Aileen Moreton-Robinson's description of contemporary policy in Australia is quite apt: "While it is often argued that self-determination has been the dominant policy framework since the late 1960s, a closer analysis of government processes and practices would reveal that self-management has occupied center stage."[4]

While offering a form of recognition that appears to redeem the history of settler violence, the administrative discourses and structures of state-managed self-determination tend to disable the acknowledgment of persistent legacies of violence and trauma while also enacting new modes of displacement and erasure. How does the experience of indigeneity in the contemporary moment exceed these ways of acknowledging tribal identity? This study addresses how contemporary queer Native writers use the representation of bodily, emotional, and psychological sensation to challenge U.S. formulations of political subjectivity by highlighting the limits of the portrait of tribal identity contained in official discourses. In approaching poetry and fiction in this way, I treat them as forms of political theory, as efforts to trace the contours of contemporary peoplehood that remain unaddressed in and even constitutively excluded from the field of U.S. and tribal politics. These texts seek to reimagine what counts as sovereignty, and rather than merely supplementing or providing metaphors for "real" political claims, these authors provide alternative ways of figuring Native experience, not simply describing it differently but indexing collective modes of being effaced in current administrative discourses. The writings I address explore the ways histories of settler dispossession, exploitation, and attempted genocide and their ongoing effects and current trajectories are embedded in the dynamics of everyday life. Reciprocally, attending to such experiences reveals forms of survival amid catastrophe, registering the quotidian ways peoplehood is lived and the complex relation between persistence and change in the face of an imperial occupation that has not ended.

How might individual sensation register aspects of collective memory and belonging occluded by the federal government's apparently affirmative narration of Native community? Such a dynamic, in which affective configurations bespeak the presence of unacknowledged political negotiations, historical trajectories, and social formations, can be characterized as a "structure of feeling." In *Marxism and Literature* Raymond Williams develops this concept to address the ways that "practical consciousness is almost always different from official consciousness," registering "experiences to which the fixed forms do not speak at all, which indeed they do not recognize" (130). He further observes, "All that is present and moving, all that escapes or seems to escape from the fixed and the explicit and the known is grasped and defined as the personal" (128), and he notes of "modes of domination" that "what they exclude may often be seen as the personal or the private, or as the natural or even the metaphysical" (125). The kinds of feeling characterized as personal can refer not only to forms of experience that lie at the edge of conscious awareness but also to those associated with entire social configurations that lie outside or challenge the parameters of existing structures of domination. In this way, an Indigenous structure of feeling can refer to sensations of belonging to place and peoplehood excluded from settler governance but that remain present, most viscerally in the affective lives of Native people. Structure of feeling, then, has a dual reference: (1) to the continuing presence of Native sociopolitical formations that are not reducible to or substantively recognizable within settler ideologies and administrative networks and (2) to the effects of living under that regime for Native people(s), registered as emotive and physical responses that can be dismissed by narrating them as private. Although U.S. Indian policy formally circulates the topos of self-determination, portraying the federal government as engaging with tribes' lived sense of landedness and representations of themselves, it continues to foreclose forms of indigeneity, as a residual geopolitics predicated on principles other than those of the liberal state and as the collective memory of an ongoing history of violence. The force and consequences of that foreclosure are experienced as *feeling* and can be captured within other discourses, such as poetry and fiction.

The effort to deny the relevance of individual and collective feeling for political identification and decision making by categorizing it as merely personal depends on an a priori segregation of sensation from what constitutes the polity as such. Those whose supposedly nonnormative sexual and gender identities are denigrated as personal pathology, then, are in a particularly good position to articulate the potential damage done by the acceptance of settler notions of social life, including what properly constitutes politics. The development of alternative visions of peoplehood and sovereignty through the representation of an Indigenous erotics takes up the most seemingly apolitical, or personal, aspects of individual experience and insists on their collective character so as to challenge the obviousness of models and mappings inherited from and imposed by the United States. In the texts I discuss, the supposedly self-evident continuity of *Indianness* gives way to genealogies of sensation, varied for different peoples, that trace how peoplehood inheres in forms of feeling. From this perspective sovereignty is less the construction and operation of a bureaucratic apparatus than it is the changing force field of lived relations through which collectivity is (re)constituted in everyday ways. Or put another way, by attending to quotidian kinds of embodiment and feeling, the writers I address theorize dynamics of Indigenous sociality and spatiality that are not recognized as sovereignty within the administrative grid that shapes the meaning of self-determination under settler rule. In this way, these texts open up possibilities for conceptualizing and realizing alternative versions of collective identity and indigeneity to those enshrined in U.S. Indian law and policy while illustrating the ongoing effects of efforts to displace, regulate, translate, and erase Native peoples.

Determining Indigenous Selfhood

With reference to U.S. Indian policy, the understanding of self-determination as local management of existing federal programs appears in statements prior to Nixon's speech and in the legislation enacted under this rubric. A government task force on American Indians created during the Johnson administration noted in its 1967 report that the executive branch, within the existing legislative framework, could and should put in place "measures that put a premium on Indian self help, self growth, and self determination," a goal that "stresses self determination rather than termination of Federal support," and this language and sentiment is echoed in President Johnson's message to Congress on Indian affairs, which advocates for "programs of self-help, self-development, self-determination."[5] Although not necessarily aware of the articulation of this language and position, Nixon promised on the campaign trail in 1968 that under his leadership "the Right of self-determination of the Indian people would be respected" and that "local programs and Federal budgets [would be] operated with minimum bureaucratic restraint and in full consultation with the Indian people who should achieve increasing authority and responsibility over programs affecting them."[6] These statements present self-determination as a program of "self-help" in which forms of programming and services that were then overseen by the Bureau of Indian Affairs (BIA) could be administered by tribes themselves. The administrative orientation indicated by Johnson and Nixon was enacted as law in 1975 in the Indian Self-Determination and Education Assistance Act, which expresses Congress's "commitment to the maintenance of the Federal Government's unique and continuing relationship with and responsibility to the Indian people" and allows tribes to contract for federally funded services.[7] Though it acknowledges tribal governments' capacity to exert forms of "authority and responsibility" with respect to aspects of Indian affairs, this shift alters neither the structures for determining who or what gets to count as a tribe nor the perception of tribes as semimunicipal units within the scale structure of U.S. federalism.[8]

In light of the utterly stifling oversight of the BIA and the prior absence of investment and development on reservations due to the fear of termination, the change to an ethos of self-determination should not be minimized in its significance, but its limited scope also should be acknowledged.[9] Such limits become apparent if the policy discourse of self-determination is compared with the "Trail of Broken Treaties 20-Point Position Paper." Written in 1972 as part of a cross-country activist caravan to Washington, DC, to protest the state of Indian affairs, which resulted in a week-long occupation of the BIA just prior to the presidential election,[10] the document emphasizes not the local administrative capacity of tribes within the policy structure of existing U.S. Indian law but, instead, a wholesale revisioning of the terms and imagination of U.S. governance with respect to Native peoples.[11] It insists on a return to treaty making as the principal mode of Indian policy, the recognition of Native peoples' right to be interpreters of those treaties, the return of millions of acres of Native land lost due to allotment policy, and the removal of the states from all jurisdictional matters relative to Indian affairs. This vision emphasizes the international character of U.S. relationships with Native peoples, or at least its exemption from regular federal law and questions of federalism, and it forcefully challenges the legitimacy of all claims to superintendence by the United States and declares the illegitimacy of the settler-state's claims to Native lands, except via treaties as compacts declared by the Constitution to be the supreme law of the land. The kind of collective selfhood envisioned here highlights the constricting contours of tribal governance under the declared policy of self-determination.

In this vein, Vine Deloria Jr. and Clifford M. Lytle have suggested the need to mark a significant distinction between self-governance and self-determination. They observe, "Self-government . . . has come to mean those forms of government that the federal government deems acceptable and legitimate exercises of political power and that are recognizable by the executive and legislative branches"; "self-government is not and cannot be the same as self-determination so long as it exists at the whim of the controlling federal government" (18–19). From this perspective U.S. Indian law and policy manages the possibilities of Native peoplehood in ways that make it consistent with other government aims and interests, including when that very regulation is conducted under the rubric of self-determination. Deloria and Lytle gesture toward a more capacious conception of political autonomy and sovereignty, one that exceeds the terms of settler jurisdiction. That notion of self-determination can be traced back to Wilsonian and Leninist discourses of national independence and decolonization in the wake of World War I, a conversation in which Native (particularly Haudenosaunee) leaders participated,[12] but it began to take on greater meaning within discourses of international law and the UN system after World War II with the Declaration on the Granting of Independence to Colonial Countries and Peoples (1960) and the specific emergence of "indigenous" issues in the early 1980s.[13] The UN Working Group on Indigenous Populations was created in 1982, giving recognition to "indigenous" as a way of naming groups whose territory had been subsumed as "domestic" space within a state without their consent, and in 1985 they began drafting the Declaration on the Rights of Indigenous Peoples, completed in 1992 and adopted in modified form by the UN General Assembly in 2007.[14] The document recognizes "the urgent need to respect and promote the inherent rights of indigenous peoples which derive from their political, economic, and social structures and from their cultures, spiritual traditions, histories and philosophies, especially their rights to their lands, territories and resources," and it broadly defines "the right to self-determination" to include the authority not just to govern themselves but to do so through whatever means and traditions they see fit, as long as they do not violate "human rights and fundamental freedoms" as defined by other UN documents.[15] Such a vision clearly exceeds the kinds of local program development and management championed by the Nixon administration and made law in 1975.

The distinction between self-government and self-determination extends beyond the particular policy changes brought about in the 1970s and afterward, instead providing a lens through which to consider the totality of the legal and political status of Native nations in this new *era*.[16] Though clearly distinct from the goals of termination—or of the allotment period from 1887 to 1934, which sought to break up Native landholdings into privately held units and to dismantle all tribal governments—U.S. Indian policy in the current moment impinges on Native peoples and lands in a range of ways, bearing the legacies of earlier, more directly assaultive programs while also engaging in new incursions. Since *U.S. v. Kagama* (1886), the Supreme Court has consistently found that Congress has plenary power in Indian affairs, such that it can do virtually whatever it will without judicial check—including revoke treaties. In terms of their modes of governance, federally recognized tribes since the Indian Reorganization Act (1934) have been able to enact their own constitutions, but in many cases they and changes to them have needed the secretary of the interior's approval.[17] As a result of the passage of Public Law 280 during the termination period, tribes in certain states have been subject to state civil and criminal laws, leaving them at least partially under state jurisdiction. The courts have ruled that Native governments cannot prosecute non-Indians for violations of tribal laws on reservations, and they have cut back on the capacity of such governments to tax non-native businesses and have at times found non-Indian-owned lands to be outside tribal civil regulation—diminishing the boundaries of the reservation. The BIA continues to negotiate sweetheart deals for corporations that seek to extract natural resources from Native lands, as well as for those leasing allotted lands for grazing, agriculture, or logging, and the federal government not only has withheld information about the terms of such leases from those whose lands they are but also has misplaced and failed to account for billions of dollars due Native trustees. The courts have denied the right of tribes to extend sovereignty over lands they purchase (even if the territory previously was theirs and is ruled to have been taken illegally) unless such land is taken into trust for them by the Department of the Interior or by Congress, and Native peoples continue to be denied control over sacred sites and ceremonial grounds, particularly when they are located in national parks. Hazardous waste continues to be placed on or near Native lands. Any tribe that wants to offer Las Vegas–style gaming needs to negotiate a compact with the state, by which the latter can hold the former hostage to its demands. Peoples that are not currently federally recognized—because they never were in treaty relations with the United States, never had an Indian agent assigned to them, or simply were removed from the list of federally recognized tribes by bureaucratic whim or accident—have to go through a rigorous process of proving their existence and authenticity, a process in which gaps in the documentary record caused by U.S. government actions are still fatal to a people's claim and in which the current backlog is decades long. Though tribes can determine their own membership, they remain subject to assumptions about what properly constitutes *Indianness* (by Congress and the Department of the Interior), and some federal programs continue to use a blood quantum standard (a calculation of the percentage of Indian blood). Peoples whose territories straddle U.S. national boundaries have had their ability to move in their own homelands vastly decreased due to national security measures (including the building of the fence on the U.S.–Mexico border). Cumulatively, these means of regulating Native peoples and places indicate a wide gap between Indigenous self-determination as articulated in U.S. law and policy and as envisioned in international rights discourse.

However, marking the ways Native peoples are managed, exploited, and erased under the current policy regime is not equivalent to claiming either that they lack all agency or that current circumstances should be contrasted to a traditional standard that can be treated as the authentic basis for indigeneity. Among other initiatives, peoples have created their own judicial systems (many of which incorporate elements of older structures and principles of adjudication, mediation, and conflict resolution), developed economic infrastructures, engaged in forms of language rejuvenation and dissemination, built institutions of higher learning and funded tribal citizens' access to other colleges and universities, participated in political lobbying and advocacy, built museums and cultural centers, reclaimed some sacred sites, set up outreach relations with citizens living off-reservation, and undertaken meaningful constitutional reform. The taking of action within a system of settler constraints does not negate, though, the effectivity of those constraints as such, and the recognition of such coercive impositions does not require presenting the kinds of collective subjectivity to which such policies give rise as false—as a compromise of real Indigenous identity. In *X-Marks* Scott Richard Lyons refuses the narration of contemporary Native governance as inauthentic, insisting on the need to reckon with the diversity of Native life in the present and to address current institutionalized modes of Native nationhood as the result of Native choices (rather than just imperial imposition). He argues, "To address our historical moment honestly is not only to admit to our impurities but to connect ideas and events to the material conditions of daily life" (xii), and such "impurities" point toward the "intractable multiplicity of Indian space" in the present (21), opening onto investigation of the varied "*kinds* of Indian identities . . . in production during a given historical moment" and what is at stake in their making "rather than a limited focus on which of them appears best to fit a given definition of *tradition*" (60). As against the insistence on purity by what he terms "culture cops," Lyons emphasizes the openness to change suggested by the "x-mark," the signature on treaties by those who could not sign their names: "An x-mark is a sign of consent in a context of coercion; it is the agreement one makes when there seems to be little choice in the matter. To the extent that little choice isn't quite the same thing as no choice, it signifies Indian agency" (1). He later adds, "The original x-marks were pledges to adopt new ways of living" (10), "a commitment to living in new and perhaps unfamiliar ways" and to "work with what we have in order to make an x-mark that delivers something good" (169, 188).

Yet to what extent does "work[ing] with what we have" register and challenge the continuing "context of coercion"? If there is a choice to work within and through settler-imposed frameworks and doing so does not make a person or people less Native, how does that imposition continue to shape present possibilities? How is the imposition felt and lived as a form of force? And what options are there for instituting other "ways of living" that are not those sanctioned by the state—i.e., modes of Indigenous selfhood not determined by the United States to be part of self-determination? While noting that "American fingerprints can usually be found at the scene of Indian identity controversies," "reveal[ing] the impossibility of establishing definitions of Indian identity without taking into consideration the fact of American involvement" (47–48), Lyons tends to bracket U.S. "involvement" in shaping and regulating other aspects of contemporary Native sovereignty, casting the structuring of Indian nationhood under U.S. Indian policy as simply the "modern" form of sociopolitical order despite noting the problem of needing to "speak the language of nations" in order to achieve intelligibility as a polity (136).[18] In other words, the effort to multiply "*kinds* of Indian identities" leads toward a bracketing of the conditions of settler coercion through which some are privileged and, thus, are realized in official Native modes of governance, as against other potential formulations (individual and collective). In resisting a limiting model of authenticity, Lyons largely overlooks the implicit and sometimes explicit forms of authentication at play in federal Indian law and policy and the ways they shape and weight the options available for Native governance and forms of self-representation.

The problem of Native authenticity and its relation to the structures and legacies of Indian policy surround all of the authors in this study. Either they are not enrolled members of a federally recognized tribe (Qwo-Li Driskill and Chrystos) or their peoples were not federally recognized (Deborah Miranda and Greg Sarris, whose people was eventually officially acknowledged by a Congressional act in 2000). All of them, at one point or another, have had their claims of being Indigenous challenged. Are they *really* Indians? This question indirectly points to an "intractable multiplicity" that haunts the silences in Lyons's account—the histories, experiences, memories, and relations that do not fit into the U.S. frame of self-determined Native nationhood. In "'Go Away, Water!'" Daniel Heath Justice suggests that Native people's judgments about each other's realness tend to redeploy "rank ideologies of fragmentation" that can be traced back to U.S. legal and administrative logics (150), particularly blood quantum definitions of Native identity that were invented for and recorded as part of tribal censuses in the late nineteenth and early twentieth centuries and employed as a signifier of "competence" under the allotment system starting in the 1910s.[19] In response to charges by certain scholars (belonging to Native peoples farther west) that peoples in New England "are not Indians" (156), Justice observes, "Those communities from the eastern edge of the continent have a much longer history of dealing with the immediate effects of European invasion than do many of the communities in the northern U.S. and southern Canadian prairie," serving "as a buffer that protected many western communities from the full brunt of white expansion" such that "the bodies" read as non-Indian "are the living testaments to that legacy" (158). As against this kind of judgment, which according to Justice takes settler administrative structures as the naturalized frame, he suggests, "Indigenous intellectual traditions have survived not because they've conceded to fragmenting Eurowestern priorities, but because they've *challenged* those priorities," adopting "models of self-determination that speak to the survival and presence of indigenous *peoples*" instead of taking up state "priorities" (150). From this perspective gradients of authenticity through which the truth of Native personhood or peoplehood are assessed, including by other Native people(s), often follow from policies, categories, and principles instituted by the United States. Thus, choosing the legal terms of Native nationhood over those of "culture cops" still may take U.S. government definitions of Indian and tribal identity as given in ways that edit out other extant possibilities for Indigenous being. As Malea Powell asks in "The X-Blood Files,"

"Whose complicated histories and messy relationships to conquest and colonization simply become unimportant, unheard, absent?" (91). She adds, "What are our goals and responsibilities? Must they all be the same if we claim them as 'Native'?" (99). Rather than quelling questions of authenticity, the turn to legal matters of sovereignty and tribal citizenship can intensify such issues while displacing the struggle around the legacies of settler colonialism behind the notion of self-determination.

Who or what is the subject of self-determination? Of sovereignty? Of indigeneity? Are these the same question? All three could be treated as synonymously indicating the political entities recognized under U.S. federal Indian law. Alternately, self-determination could be defined in internationalist terms, drawing on the notion of indigeneity as exceeding the jurisdictional authority of the settler-state and looking to supranational documents and processes, like the UN Declaration on the Rights of Indigenous Peoples, as the standard. Further, such a shift in scale could be used to mark the limits of U.S. policy (the distinction between self-government and self-determination) in order to push the legal and administrative parameters of Native sovereignty toward potentially more capacious internationalist framings. As Bruce Miller notes with respect to such accounts, however, they largely fail "to adequately clarify who indigenous people are and what one might say regarding nonrecognized peoples. Attention is given to finding a way to describe various quite different communities whose identity as indigenous is not in question" (60–61).[20] How do we know which groups can or should count as Indigenous? What criteria do we use, and on what basis? Moreover, who is the "we" doing the knowing and choosing? And through what process do they become so? If indigeneity can name relations to place and modes of peoplehood that precede national and international acknowledgment, that term's content, scope, and contours still take shape within the changing, negotiated, and contested discursive and institutional matrices of policy, advocacy, and activism. Thus, not only does the designation of people(s) as Indigenous have variable meanings attached to it, but the set and kind of persons and groups included shift depending on the ways the term/concept is employed. From this perspective authenticity can be understood less as a matter of being a *real* Indian or tribe than as a matter of how well a person or group meshes with the (shifting) ensemble of attributes that explicitly or implicitly serves as the basis of categorization and intelligibility. The better the fit, the more authentic.

The Work of Metaphor

More than an issue of speech or consciousness, determinations of authenticity powerfully affect possibilities for being. Or rather, the apparatuses and procedures through which a particular account of authenticity is generated, circulated, and implemented help shape the effective reality—the actually existing options for and stakes of identification, articulation, and action—available to persons and groups.[21] This is not to say that Indigenous, Indian, tribe, people, sovereignty, and self-determination can only mean and be what existing institutions say they can mean and be. Rather, I am offering a caution, a hesitation that reflects the work performed by the creative writings I address. Treating such concepts as if they transparently referred to entities and processes completely separate from the institutional fields through which the terms themselves move brackets the effectivity of those institutions—the ways they influence possibilities for being in the world. Through their organizing/operative discourses, institutions speak as if their modes of apprehension and mapping simply reflected existing social relations while working to materialize that vision. The fact that they fail to do so, or to do so as completely as they would like to imagine or in fully coherent/unified ways, does not negate the influence of that process of actualization on those within its sphere. Whatever Indian, tribe, or Indigenous might mean, the possibilities for identifying and acting as such are contingent on, though not mechanically determined by, how those terms/concepts are deployed, implemented, regulated, and policed in U.S. Indian law and policy.[22] Thus, the question of who is really Indian or what is really a tribe cannot escape the problem that one's ability to realize one's claim to be Indian or a tribe and, thus, to exert self-determination remains affected in profound ways by the materiality endowed to its own official representations by the operation of the U.S. state. To what extent is the exercise of self-determination, then, a decision about how to employ the notions of Indian and tribe already at play in U.S. administrative discourses and practices?[23] In this vein, might we understand the operation of the institutions of the settler-state as a process of literalization—of making literal their terms and topoi? How might addressing literary texts enable such a perspective by drawing attention to the work of figuration—the relation between the act of representation and the making possible of thought and action? Reciprocally, how might fiction and poetry index and imagine forms of individual and collective being denied recognition as Indigenous or as peoplehood within settler institutions, which cast them as not "real" and deny them access to state processes of realization?[24]

The distinction between the literal and the figurative appears self-evident but can be understood as due to the political work of metaphor. In *The Poetics of Imperialism,* Eric Cheyfitz addresses the role of metaphor in the colonization of the Americas. He draws on Aristotle's definition of it as "the 'transference' of an 'alien name' into a familiar context"—a concept very much at play in early modern Europe and its imperial ventures that grounds metaphor "in a kind of territorial imperative, in a division, that is, between the domestic and the foreign" (36). What gets characterized as metaphor, then, depends on installing another contrasting vision as "the 'proper,' . . . the *national,* the *domestic,* the *familiar,* the *authoritative,* the *legitimate*" (90). From this perspective English understandings of the proper relation to land as property (fee simple ownership) are installed within discussion of jurisdiction and geopolitics in the New World as the paradigmatic form of land tenure, against which Indigenous modes of mapping and governance could be cast as improper, as figures rather than as reality—relations to "the same place" in which "this ground . . . was grounded on different grounds" (49). This process of enacting a particular kind of figuration of territory and political authority as if it were simply empirical truth works through "a strict economy of literalization" (38), which "represses the figurative basis of the literal—its constitution as an ideological or culturally specific formation" (14). Assertions of literality, including the definition of *real* Indian and tribal identity, then efface the ways such claims are acts of figuration backed by institutionalized authority and legitimacy. Simultaneously, such assertions of literality displace discussion of how those narratives of the real, actualized through the matrix of law and policy, work to dematerialize competing narratives—casting them as merely metaphors.

Accounts of the real depend upon drawing on while disavowing the power of metaphor. Moreover, as Chris Bracken argues in *Magical Criticism*, the ostensibly animistic belief in the ability of language to effect alterations in the material world has been repeatedly castigated in Euramerican intellectual work as "savage philosophy." "The theory of magic works on the premise that physical forces can be deployed by discursive means," yet "the more loudly scholars censure savage philosophers for positing a real, physical connection between signs and objects, the stronger is the desire to commit the same radical error" (3). To believe in such causal connection improperly accepts the efficacy of "metaphor, which effects an unnatural passage from potentiality to actuality": "Metaphor harbors a stock of actualizing energy" (82). In its "capacity to discover 'similarities' between things that are not manifestly 'the same'" (64), metaphor "enrich[es] signs with a principle of change," "traffic[ing] in signs that grow into things" (21). Thus, the "error" labeled "savage" lies in understanding language as exceeding representation, as not simply reflecting but helping constitute material phenomena. Bracken locates this distinction in two different conceptions of mimesis, both of which have been part of the term's use at various points: restricted (imitating "what already is") and general (projecting "an image of what is not yet, modeling a form for what cannot give form to itself"). He adds, "Restricted mimesis stands for reality; general mimesis takes part in the realization of a still unfinished reality" (18). The work of civilization supposedly lies in differentiating the actual from the imaginary, in recognizing the former as such and understanding metaphor as solely a linguistic effect (of depiction, commentary, ornamentation, etc.) rather than as related to being—as making possible a transit from potentiality to material presence. Reciprocally, Bracken suggests that the non-"savage" conception of "reality" as already existing concretion depends on a disowned—metaphoric—process of "realization": what seems "always right and necessary" appears as such due to forms of repetition, "solidifying what was [once] fresh into what is merely commonplace" (94). The nonmetaphoric, or literal, attains its status as such through reiteration and, one could add, institutionalization, "solidifying" its apparent distinction from the ethereal, immaterial, purely figurative qualities of metaphor or poiesis.[25]

While Bracken focuses on how metaphor offers "principles of change" (186), its ability "to affirm the being of nonbeing" (104), his account gestures toward the ways metaphor also indexes the presence of forms of being not recognized as reality within dominant discourses and institutions. In discussing the public representation of the land claims of the Nisga'a people against the Canadian government, he notes that their pursuit of new treaty negotiations was portrayed as excessive and ghostly, unsettling existing geographies through the reappearance of a presence thought gone: "Do they mean that the specter is 'unsett*ler*ing' or even 'unsettle*ment*ing'?" (202). Here, the issue can be seen less as the actualization of potentiality—of what does not yet materially exist—than as a recognition of a kind of existence (Nisga'a sovereignty over their traditional territory) heretofore unacknowledged as real by the government of the settler-state. In a different yet complementary vein, the situation could be described as the realization of a potential—Nisga'a sovereignty—that had material force previously and was dematerialized by the literalization of Canadian jurisdiction. Alternately, one might characterize the *specter* of Nisga'a sovereignty as a form of being that existed as Nisga'a collective memory, feeling, and aspiration awaiting an opportunity to more fully (re)actualize this vision. How does one decide among these options? Is there a need to do so?

Metaphor can designate the effort to articulate the presence of any of these options, as well as the productive transit/indeterminacy among them. At one point Bracken quotes Paul Ricoeur on the ways metaphor "has the 'power to make contact with being'" (87).[26] In *The Rule of Metaphor*, Ricoeur seeks to understand metaphor in relation to the referentiality of language—its "denotative purpose" to indicate the presence of things and relations in the world (125). He argues that metaphor works neither as decoration nor as substitution but as a process of redescribing reality (22), disorienting current modes of description and classification in order to reference "the polysemy of being" (307). Being presses against language ("something seeks to be said" [125]), and in registering that impression, metaphor disorders operative ways of narrating the real or the literal. "It could be that the everyday reference to the real must be abolished in order that another sort of reference to other dimensions of reality might be liberated" (145), and Ricoeur later adds that metaphor "opens [meaning] toward a dimension of reality that does not coincide with what ordinary language envisages under the name of natural reality" (211). The apparent incoherence of metaphor with respect to conventional modes of reference—in Ricoeur's terms, its "impertinence"—bespeaks a kind of reality that cannot be addressed in ordinary language. The designation of a statement as figurative, then, can indicate less its status as merely imaginary (as opposed to real) than its effort to register something in being that available discourses do not count as part of reality.[27] Ricoeur further suggests that those references treated as literal began life as metaphor, but "the metaphor has been lexicalized [and, one could add, institutionalized] to such an extent that it has become the proper word" (290). As in Cheyfitz's analysis, the "proper" indicates that which has naturalized itself as the real (and, in Bracken's terms, has realized itself as the actual), but it does not exclude the existence of forms of being—such as relations to place and peoplehood that precede the settler-state and exceed its law and policy—that do not coincide with literalized narratives and that, therefore, gain expression as metaphor.

Yet if metaphor can be seen both as magically transforming the immaterial into the material and as bearing the impression of what already exists but has remained unacknowledged in ordinary language, does it then mark the potential or the actual? The texts I address utilize metaphor to do both while suggesting the movement between them, expanding the possible meanings of indigeneity in ways that exceed the literalizations of settler policy. As Ricoeur observes, poetic discourse, due to its reliance on metaphor, puts into crisis "the distinction between discovering and creating and between finding and projecting," expressing "our primordial belonging to a world . . . which at once precedes us and receives the imprint of our works" (306). In this way, such discourse reflexively renders ambiguous the difference between expression (indexing and transmitting what already is) and action (a doing that changes what is). The political implications of this slippage with respect to indigeneity lie in conceptualizing it less as a self-evident presence, the apparently empirical obviousness of real Indian or tribal identity, than as bound up in contested and multi-vectored processes of realization. Settler institutions endow a solidity and concreteness to their operative categories (themselves shifting, uneven, and negotiated) that makes them into the literal basis for identification as Native—by those institutions, oneself, and others who identify as Native. That process materially affects possibilities for future action.

If dominant formations shape the contours of social life, they remain permeated by residual and emergent formations. Raymond Williams notes that "the residual, by definition, has been effectively formed in the past, but it is still active in the cultural process . . . as an effective element of the present"; it also "may have an alternative or even oppositional relation to the dominant culture" (122). "Emergent" refers to "new meanings and values, new practices, new relationships and kinds of relationships [that] are continually being created" (123). "Emergent" suggests bringing into being—actualizing—something that did not exist previously, whereas "residual" indicates what already is but is not incorporated into dominant accounts of reality. These terms speak to the dual work of metaphor I have been addressing, further suggesting the ways the use of metaphor within literary texts might be understood as part of the broader process of negotiating existing sociopolitical formations. Moreover, in articulating these differentiated concepts, Williams observes that "there is indeed regular confusion between the locally residual (as a form of resistance to incorporation) and the generally emergent" (125). Rather than taking such confusion as a failure to distinguish between them, it might be understood as indicating the ways the residual and the emergent theoretically and practically are enmeshed, the enduring past providing both existing and possible options that can be materialized further in social practice while also being altered in the process. If indigeneity minimally entails some claim to precede settler occupation, metaphor, in its bridging of the residual and the emergent, can provide a resource for uncoupling such continuity from dominant ways of narrating and regulating what constitutes Native being, opening up the possibility of recognizing other modes of being—other social formations—as *really* Indigenous.

The authors discussed in this study use metaphoric strategies that tie their visions of indigeneity to embodied experience, positioning sensation and affect as key in exploring the complex relations among the actual conditions of Native life, the presence and effects of memory, and the possibilities for altering existing circumstances. As noted, Williams's emphasis on feeling as indicative of shifting social patterns suggests that kinds of experience conventionally understood as personal can provide insight into collective phenomena, including ongoing struggles over what will get to count as properly political. He describes feeling as "an unease, a stress, a displacement" and as "impulse, restraint, and tone," "what is actually being lived" and that "which is still *in process*" (130–32). Feeling suggests both the tactile and the emotional, proximate physical presence and inchoate intimation, and as such, it productively renders indeterminate the boundary between the material and the mental, as they fold into and work through each other.[28]

Memory offers a powerful example of this *felt* threshold between the actual/residual and the potential/emergent. It confounds the distinctions between presence and absence, past and present, collective and personal, and physical and psychological. As Ricoeur observes in *Memory, History, Forgetting,* the embodied experience of memory works as both "debt" and "latency." The past bears on the present as "our dependence on the past in terms of heritage," suffusing the current moment with a "being-in-debt" to what has come before (363). The past lives on as a force in organizing the present, and memory functions as a mode of registering this material presence, "relat[ing] the being affected by the past to the potentiality-of-being turned toward the future" (381). Through discussion of the phenomena of forgetting, however, Ricoeur suggests that memory also can be thought of as a "reserve of forgetting" (417): it exists "virtually" in ways not present to consciousness but available for access by it (433–43). As an experience in the present, memory, like metaphor, both bears the impression of the materiality of the past as it animates the current moment and calls forth ways of engaging existing circumstances that were not materially present before but become efficacious in their employment now. Memory also pushes against the notion of self-possession common to dominant Euramerican accounts of personhood, as relations with others provide memory's substance, context, and conditions of relevance and recall (96–128). In this way, what appears as individual memory can be understood as a structure of feeling through which collective experiences are coded, are lived, and gain expression, and the articulation of memory can serve as a way of both marking the presence of and making present that collectivity.[29] From this perspective, personhood can be rethought as a *reserve of peoplehood,* possibly at odds with what currently is realized institutionally as peoplehood's "proper"—tribal—version. This process could take the form of seemingly individual stories of shamed subjectivity in diaspora in the wake of removal (chapter 1), impressions of denied belonging for a people bureaucratically declared "extinct" (chapter 2), familiar traditional stories refashioned in light of contemporary structures of "sadness" (chapter 3), or accounts of the labor of survival as an Indigenous person in a social landscape shaped around stereotype (chapter 4).

Against the terms of U.S. policy that require documentable continuity as the basis for Indian and tribal identity—in terms of racial genealogy, consistent self-government, and occupancy of the same territory—this approach to memory also acknowledges as part of collective experience the ruptures, dislocations, and dispersions produced by settler occupation and jurisdiction. As Veena Das argues, "The experience of world-annihilating violence" leads to "the failure of the grammar of the ordinary," such that "when the memory of such events is folded into ordinary relationships . . . a shared language [has] to be built" to capture that experience and what happens in its wake—the relation between the before and after (7–8). If processes of settlement fracture prior sociopolitical formations, they and the violence done to them live on in memory, and that memory as lived, refracted by, and passed on in "ordinary relationships" gives rise to collective experiences for which there is not "a shared language," especially as sanctioned by a state whose existence is made possible by and sustained through that violence and its official erasure (or sublation as redemptive *recognition*). Such memory is present both as a force in everyday experiences and as a virtual reserve that becomes active in moments in which, in Das's terms, "particular regions of the past are actualized" (102). Finding language to mark these dynamics and feelings and the *realization* of these dynamics through that process of finding language are the work of metaphor performed by the texts I address. Understanding feeling as, in Williams's terms, an index to formations that the "dominant social neglects, excludes, represses, or simply fails to recognize" casts it as necessarily exceeding isolated personhood (125). The very kinds of sensation often understood as embedded in individual selfhood bespeak collective experience and, by extension, potentially an experience of collectivity—of peoplehood. In this way, depictions of feeling in creative work can serve as metaphors for modes of indigeneity not counted as such within structures and practices consistent with settler policy: again, metaphor indicating not the figurative opposed to the literal but a relationship between unrecognized presence and possibilities that do not get to count as real within existing institutional discourses and the conditions such discourses materialize.

Positioning feeling as a way of contesting the terms of state-sanctioned literalizations, my account of the role of experience in contemporary queer Native writing differs notably from realist approaches, which have become increasingly prominent in Native literary studies. Sean Kicummah Teuton's *Red Land, Red Power* and Craig Womack's "Theorizing American Indian Experience" provide compelling examples of this trend. Situating itself within what has been termed *postpositivist realism*,[30] such work productively emphasizes the need to engage with the current conditions of Native people(s), taking them as the basis for conceptualizing Native identity against an idealized and static standard (as in Lyons's critique of the "culture cops"). Teuton suggests that scholarship needs, as the novels he interprets do, to avoid "longing for an impossibly timeless past" and "disconnecting Indians' stories from the political realities of their lives" (2), instead addressing the "ongoing encounter with the world" in ways that also promote "an honest engagement with the diversity" of contemporary Native communities (3, 198). This process involves, as Womack argues, both pluralizing the notion of experience, so that we do not present a singular "Native perspective" or "Native paradigm" as all inclusive (359), and more fully articulating and accounting for the sheer variability of Native lives and viewpoints in the present. Moreover, scholars such as Teuton and Womack insist on the need to move past a skepticism toward the possibility of truth claims, which they associate with postmodernism and/or poststructuralism, in favor of scholarly perspectives that allow for making "normative" judgments, evaluating available representations of Native people(s), and defending the existence and importance of sovereignty. As Womack notes, "We cannot simply descend into an impotent relativism where all cohesive claims are impossible" (361). Yet to what extent does a realist framework aid in pursuing these goals? How does it implicitly treat the real as a stable object—rather than as ongoing and potentially competing processes of realization—in ways that hamstring an ability to map extant social dynamics and to envision and theorize change?

At the center of realist methodology lies the notion of adequation, the idea that scholarship seeks to reflect as closely as possible existing material conditions.[31] In this vein Teuton often insists on the need for empirical forms of analysis that offer more accurate accounts of the facts of Native social life,[32] and similarly, Womack, while offering a far more qualified embrace of realism, suggests the need for a kind of knowledge that "would be measured in relation to how well it describes material conditions in the community of which it speaks" (386), adding that such scholarship would extend the "long tradition" in "Indian cultures" of "evaluating claims in reference to how well they describe the real world" (396). The idea that criticism should mirror the real world gives rise to the following set of conceptual and methodological impasses: treating accounts of Native peoples as propositional statements to be falsified rather than as materially effective in organizing Native lives; taking the scope of the category Native as itself stable rather than as a subject of contention and struggle; presenting empiricism as knowledge of what exists rather than as itself a process for regulating what will count as real (both discursively and institutionally);[33] and conflating the normative with the actual, rather than seeing the former as a reserve that could help actualize new possibilities.[34]

From within a realist frame, the problem with "a colonialist historiography and a white supremacist identification" is that they "inaccurately account for our colonial past," and the remedy is to offer alternative accounts "that adhere to the social facts of Native life."[35] Illustrating the logical fallacies of settler narratives or their failure to reflect conditions of Native life, both of which are legitimate and important intellectual endeavors, does not address the effectivity of such narratives and formulations as implemented through the apparatus of U.S. Indian policy and the consequences of that implementation in shaping material possibilities. As I have been arguing, the metaphorics of settler governance powerfully affect, while not wholly determining, "the social facts of Native life." Similarly, conceptualizing Native identity/community as "suppressed by the federal government" and presenting knowledge of the real world as having been simply ignored leaves aside how the federal government and other settler-dominated institutions can and do engender subjectivities, circumstances, and forms of knowledge production lived by Native people as the real.[36] Womack has cautioned against an "etymological approach to Native studies" that treats any concept, practice, or terminology supposedly originating from nonnatives as bearing the exact same meaning, trajectory, and implications when utilized by Native people(s) (301). Though his point is well taken about the ways such a perspective can reinforce prevalent notions of Indian stasis and authenticity, treating such adoptions as wholly free from the orbit of settler institutions not only leaves little room for considering the productive (rather than just repressive) dynamics of imperial jurisdiction but also provides few resources for addressing the meaning of Native governments' implementation of forms of authentication drawn from state-initiated logics—like blood quantum criteria, ejection of people of African descent from tribal membership, repudiation of homosexuality, and patterns of disenrollment—that Womack and Teuton critique. These dynamics are part of "the social facts of Native life," and as I suggest throughout, they can be understood as realizing particular visions of Native identification in a context overdetermined by the authority and discourses of state institutions. Moreover, although refusing the idea that "each tribal person . . . possesses an unchanging, self-evident tribal understanding" (12), Teuton refers back to "a community of experience" in which people draw "collectively on a shared tradition" (20, 194), and in a similar vein, as part of his effort to move away from reified conceptions of indigeneity, Womack insists, "A Native perspective is any perspective articulated by a Native person" (407). Who determines, however, the boundaries and contours of a given community? And what happens when there is not agreement over who counts as a Native person?

If realism seeks to engage the actual conditions faced by Native peoples, part of those conditions are ongoing debates, negotiations, and struggles over what counts as Native or as peoplehood. If part of the aim is to take Native politics seriously, doing so entails acknowledging the presence of disagreements and contentions over the shape of tribal identity, the proper aims of tribal policy, and the merits and effects of both—a process that is influenced by the ongoing legacy of settler regulation and superintendence. Presenting experience as a basis for knowledge, then, does not obviate the problem of addressing how it generates varied kinds of knowledge that are potentially at odds with each other and have differing abilities to be realized/materialized through existing institutional processes. In other words, taking the real as an empirical given that can serve as a ground for defining and defending indigeneity enacts a double disavowal. Doing so effaces the role of processes of literalization in shaping the conditions of Native life and of identification as Native (or as Indian or as of a certain tribe), and it overlooks the persistence of the past as feeling and memory that provide nonempirically verifiable—*virtual*—reserves for generating emergent formations (a point I address in the chapters as specters, melancholy, stories, and emotional labor, respectively).

The writers I address present forms of Indigenous continuity—such as connections to Native peoples, lands, and languages—as having been actively disrupted and foreclosed by the material consequences of settler literalizations (removal, the boarding school system, denial of treaty rights, termination). Through their use of metaphor, however, these texts index the survival of such continuity as residue and potential, as embodied feelings that are not separate from histories of settler occupation. These authors mark as Indigenous the effects and legacies of such disruption, as well as the possibilities for the wider (re)emergence and realization of relations to the past, to place, and to peoplehood narrated as lost—and, therefore, unreal and impossible—within settler discourses and institutions. In this way, the texts use figurative language and strategies to register forms of being—structures of feeling—rejected as a basis for legally cognizable Native identity. In the act of representing the presence and potential of such sensations *as* experiences of indigeneity, the texts work to shift the terms of public discourse so as to increase the possibilities for materializing these experiences as Native identity on a sociopolitical terrain dominated by U.S. Indian law and policy.[37]

The Ethics of Touch

If realist analysis characterizes accurate depictions of existing conditions as making possible a normative account of the social world, what room is there for thinking the disjunction between actual circumstances and desirable ones? If the real and the good are equivalent, what intellectual resources are there for determining what in existing social life is to be retained, deciding what should be changed, and envisioning possibilities and principles for the latter—except to declare that what one desires is more real than what one does not?[38] If one wants to critique the use of blood quantum as a means of defining Native identity or citizenship in Native nations (a point I address in particular in chapters 1 and 3), for example, on what basis does one do so? One could say it offers a version of indigeneity that is not what it really means to be Indigenous. Given that numerous Native nations utilize that criterion, however, it operates as the basis for citizenship in those polities, and it is effectively part of the "social facts of Native life" as a functional aspect of how some Native people(s) define membership, at least officially. Should this policy be treated as less real than beliefs or practices not institutionalized as part of the apparatus of governance? If so, how do we know when we've hit the really real, as opposed to the fake masquerading as the real? And how do we account for the material effectivity of the fake institutionalized identity? On what basis does one adjudicate among discrepant, equally real versions of Native identity? To be clear, I am not suggesting that such choices on the part of Native national governments are less authentically Indigenous, that they somehow result from being duped, or that they do not count as acts of sovereignty.[39] Instead, I am asking about the effects of such institutionalizations. Put simply, are they a good idea? Who gets to define what counts as good? How is that process affected by an uneven ability to determine and actualize what counts as real? Can normative questions—in terms of the good and the right—be settled through realist modes of analysis? To what extent does such an approach sidestep this problem by positing an already coherent tribal entity in which the contours of the tribal are not at issue? What discursive and institutional mechanisms help stabilize and give material shape to that entity? And can a realist account engage with that process of realization and the residual/potential formations that process disavows or repudiates as inauthentic?

Forms of discourse not directly connected to institutions of governance might offer alternative accounts of indigeneity, peoplehood, sovereignty, and self-determination while providing strategies for negotiating among and evaluating claims to Native reality—not in the sense of deciding which is more real but which should provide a means for moving forward and on what basis. In addition to highlighting the work of metaphor, as both a disowned part of how institutions generate/realize their mappings and a vehicle for registering possibilities for being that exceed such mappings, the writers examined in this study suggest normative principles that might guide the complex process of forging Indigenous futures. In his essay "Theorizing American Indian Experience," Womack, himself a queer Native creative writer and scholar, raises the question, "When the inevitability arises that one group is going to have to be privileged over another, how does one make those decisions?" adding, "We have to evaluate how competently those making the claims justify them" (396). At one point he suggests the criteria for such evaluation could entail "how well [a given set of claims] describes the real world" (396), but earlier, with respect to the use of tradition to legitimize present action, he asks, "Let us say that a group of elders could assert confidently that traditionally Blackfoot men *did* used to hit women, would that mean that Blackfoot men should continue to hit women today" (385)?[40] Similarly, if such abuse is part of the real world, does that make it a principle on which to build? How does one locate such principles? In a different vein, Womack emphasizes the importance of imagination in renewing and sustaining Native peoples, insisting that "imagining is a real event" and that "the way we understand our own experience in relation to collective experience is through a process of vision" (370, 374).[41] This conception of the real extends beyond the realist notion of an accurate reflection of what is, highlighting the generative power of imagination in ways that resonate with my discussion of metaphor in the previous section. Womack also argues that "the body itself is a site of theoretical knowledge," providing "experiences that turn into knowledge," specifically through the pathway of the erotic (390–92). While not posed as such, this conjunction invites the question, how might the erotic serve as a source for imagination? Considering and representing the nexus of emotional and bodily sensation both produces knowledge about survival under continuing settler occupation and articulates experiences that can serve as generative principles in negotiating among competing accounts of Native identity. Creative engagement with the erotic can function as residual and emergent, registering the largely unacknowledged presence of the past as well as opening heretofore (officially) unrecognized potentials for living indigeneity in the present.

In this way, the erotic bears on, and can redefine, the meaning of peoplehood. Over the past decade, scholars have begun to consider the relation between sexuality and sovereignty in sustained ways. They have developed a notion of the erotic as inextricably enmeshed in processes of settler colonialism.[42] In "Stolen from Our Bodies," Qwo-Li Driskill defines the "Sovereign Erotic" as "an erotic wholeness healed and/or healing from the historical trauma that First Nations people continue to survive, rooted within the histories, traditions, and resistance struggles of our nations" (51). Ze observes, "I do not see the erotic as a realm of personal consequence only. Our relationships with the erotic impact our larger communities, just as our communities impact our senses of the erotic" (52).[43] Similarly, in "Dildos, Hummingbirds, and Driving Her Crazy," Deborah Miranda argues, "Five hundred years of colonization and its many painful wounds have resulted in many Native women living basic survival-level emotional lives" (138). The erotic in these accounts speaks to a sense of embodied and emotional wholeness that includes but extends beyond the scenes and practices of physical pleasure and gratification usually termed "sexual." Instead, such interactions, usually deemed the most personal and intimate, serve as touchstones for a broader conception and narration of selfhood. They register legacies of imperial violence, which continue to have material effects in relations and spaces not usually considered political, while also functioning as a site through

which to understand the enmeshment of individual feelings in collective formations—participating in and affected by shared histories,
circumstances, challenges, and aspirations.

However, why make the experiences often segregated as the sexual
into a means of approaching the broader nexus of affect and sensation
toward which the erotic gestures, and why make such seemingly individual experience the index of the effects of colonization?[44] Does
such a focus not distract from the properly political issues and implications of sovereignty and self-determination? Dian Million implicitly replies to such questions by emphasizing that "to 'decolonize'
means to understand as fully as possible the forms colonialism takes
in our own times" (55). Moreover, as part of the process of enacting
settlement, state institutions seek to generate shame around certain
practices and relations as a "debilitating force of . . . social control"
(54), so publicly giving voice to improper topics, like those of sexual
life (including state-sanctioned rape in boarding schools), offers an
"alternative truth [that goes] against the same state that is the pro-
tector of the civil truth" (60). Put another way, attending to and rejuvenating the erotic as a basis for collective self-understanding and
mobilization functions as an important part of decolonization because
the mechanisms of settlement, of enacting settler control and literalizing settler frames, depends upon imposing interdependent logics of
personhood, property, and governance. Moreover, the traces of that
management, recoding, and erasure of Native peoplehood live on in
embodied sensation not only as trauma and wounding but also as the
survival of alternative possibilities for being in the world. In Kateri
Akiwenzie-Damm's terms, "To reclaim and express our sexuality is
part of the larger path to decolonization" precisely because the concept of sexuality points to a nexus of practices, desires, relations, and
pleasures in which one could locate the presence of modes of indigeneity that exceed the "oppressed, repressed, shamed, and *imposed* sense
of reality" generated through institutionalized processes of settlement
(151, 147). The articulation of indigeneity as an erotics takes the kinds
of physicality, intersubjectivity, and vulnerability categorized and cordoned off as "sexuality" within dominant discourses as a starting point
for mapping both the ongoing management of Indigenous polities

and the forms of collective perception and experience settler policy has sought to foreclose.

Yet, if *the erotic* in some sense seeks to name the entire matrix of bodily and emotional sensation, why use a term so closely associated with sexuality as a specific domain of experience? Following Michel Foucault's lead, one could say that sexuality refers less to a particular area of life than to an artificial unity in which a range of potentially discrepant phenomena (desire, particular physical acts, homemaking, procreation, family formation, etc.) are linked together through interwoven discursive and institutional formations.[45] Those formations realize that unity as if it were merely a self-evident fact of human nature, a cumulative effect that has been called *heteronormativity*. Turning again to the question of shame, one could suggest that a heteronormative understanding of proper sexuality (monogamous, marital, procreative, structured around the nuclear family) has been crucial in inserting Native peoples into structures of settlement, and privatizing shame has functioned as a central means of inculcating a sensibility that disciplines alternative social formations as dangerous aberrations.[46] The marking and policing of certain kinds of sexual identity as perverse, then, provides an important vehicle through which to track the realization of settler-instituted norms. In "Disobedience (in Language) in Texts by Lesbian Native Americans," Janice Gould notes, "I am aware that in speaking about a lesbian America Indian erotics . . . I am being disloyal and disobedient to the patriarchal injunction that demands our silence and invisibility" (32): "Disobedience—revealing the fact of my lesbianism, establishing in myself what it means to me to be Indian—led, when I was younger, to my being emotionally and psychically cast out from my family" (41). Notably, her lesbianism serves for her as a pathway to define what being Native means, but for her family it cannot mark a legitimate form of Native being due to its violation of patriarchal norms.[47] The pathologization and repudiation of those deemed queer illustrates the intimate ways settler-inspired logics inform everyday interactions among Native people.[48] As Beth Brant argues, "Perhaps this is the key to understanding homophobia in my Nation. The love that was natural in our world has become unnatural as we become consumed by the white world and the values therein. . . . When we fight amongst ourselves as to who is a better Indian, who is a more traditional Indian, we are linking arms with the ones who would just as soon see us dead. Homophobia has *no* justification within our Nations" (59–60). She adds that when she is rejected by Native people due to her lesbianism, she believes "what they are really saying is—you embarrass me with your sexuality, therefore you embarrass our people and *white* people will have even more ammunition to use against us" (76). Nonstraight sexuality serves as a particularly dense point for negotiating collective boundaries: who can be included; what counts as properly Indian; how do Native people engage with white expectations and ongoing forms of settler denigration and dispossession?

Sexuality registers current tensions around conceptualizing and experiencing indigeneity and addresses forms of lived affect and interpersonal engagement that usually are not considered as rising to the level of politics, and for precisely this reason, it provides a way into exploring structures of feeling that do not initially appear related to sovereignty but that may provide ways of framing and negotiating it other than the bureaucratic terms of self-determination under U.S. policy.[49] The choice of *erotics* over *sexuality* maintains a link to the phenomena covered by the latter while opening up to additional kinds of sensation and creating the potential for distance from the ideologies normalized within Euramerican discourses of sexuality.[50] Gould suggests that in the process of settler colonization, Native peoples "lost much of our culture, our ways of being in the world, our ways of apprehending reality" (32), indicating that raising the issue of American Indian erotics bears directly on what gets to count as reality in the context of ongoing settlement. The act of writing about such issues, then, takes part in a struggle over the real—the relations among what is, what was, and what could be. In this vein Beth Brant observes, "Our writing is, and always has been, an attempt to beat back colonization and the stereotyping of our Nations. But the writing is *not* a reaction to colonialism, it is an active and new way to tell the stories we have always told" (39–40). Yet are such stories unaffected by the pressures and violence of colonization? Might the articulation of Indigenous erotics register heretofore unrecognized modes of continuity, either not documented or not readily documentable (kinds

of memory, emotion, sensation), while also telling stories of the legacies of colonization, of its effects on the everyday shape, texture, and
apprehension of reality? Might such writing offer ways of narrating
dynamics of shame, trauma, and wounding as intimate parts of the experience of indigeneity, simultaneously making pleasures *and* vulner-
abilities into means of calling and coaxing forms of Indigenous being
out of the realities of settler occupation—forms that are not reducible to the state's literalized narratives of peoplehood?[51] Contrasting
queer Native activism with "a hegemonic gay and lesbian movement,"
Brant insists that movement cannot "give us tools to heal our broken
Nations. But our strength as a family not only gives tools, it helps
make tools" (45). Through their focus on the full range of embodied
and emotional experiences, refusing to bracket sexuality or demonize
nonstraight desires, the texts in this study make tools to transform the
residual and potential into the emergent, a process of healing that
takes feeling as a basis for further materializing possibilities other
than those sanctioned by the state.

Thus, attending to the Sovereign Erotic can open toward an erotics
of sovereignty, reimagining peoplehood and placemaking in ways that
register the complex entwinement of unacknowledged survivals, unofficial aspirations, and the persistence of pain. At one point in "Stolen
from Our Bodies," Driskill observes, "Our erotic lives and identities
have been colonized along with our homelands" (52), and Akiwenzie-
Damm closes her piece by asserting, "We'll free our bodies, our spirits,
our whole selves. We'll live without reservation" (151). These moments
implicitly raise the question of how to understand the relation between
bodies—and their sensory and affective capacities—and "homelands."
The latter term connotatively braids together the sense of connection
to particular lands and participation in the sociopolitical entity whose
lands they are. Similarly, "reservation" serves as a shorthand for signifying territory and polity, the space legally recognized as belonging
to a particular tribe whose juridical existence lies in its extension of
jurisdiction (albeit quite unevenly) over that space. To be "without
reservation," then, seems like a call to eliminate the kinds of Native
national existence topologically signified by that administratively acknowledged space over which sovereignty is extended. Rather than
seeking to end the acknowledgment of distinct Native peoples and

territories, however, Akiwenzie-Damm's statement suggests that the freeing of Indigenous individual and collective selfhood may require exceeding the social logics and practices of Indian policy as instantiated through the reservation system. Historically, it has served less as a means of recognizing Indigenous modes of placemaking than as a vehicle of dislocation and discipline—resettling peoples elsewhere, punishing them for failing to remain on lands designated by the government as Indian, and casting movement from or the absence of such lands as the loss of indigeneity (processes addressed in each of the chapters).[52] Thus, imagining being "without" this system casts *as Native* kinds of occupancy, association, and mobility rendered dangerous or inauthentic within it. A focus on erotics, on forms of quotidian sensation that do not count as conceptions or practices of sovereignty from a policy perspective, can point to ways of experiencing place and its complex enmeshment with peoplehood that are not delimited in advance by U.S.-regulated modes of self-determination.

Reciprocally, while Driskill's statement above implies a parallel colonization of "bodies" and "homelands" ("along with"), it can be read as gesturing toward the ways the implementation of settlement as a set of geopolitical imperatives extends to everyday experience. If settler governance is realized through the construction of reservations, starting at least in the 1870s but arguably earlier as well, it has also powerfully influenced the shape of governance on reservation—including imposing aspects of federal civil and criminal law; needing to authorize tribal constitutions; generating censuses of tribal citizens with blood quantum designations; exerting plenary power over all aspects of Indian affairs; and sustaining the checkerboarding, privatizing effects, and inheritance law of allotment.[53] This management of Indian space, to some extent necessarily extended by Native nations as a condition of being recognized as legitimate governments by the United States, affects the texture of daily life—the kinds of membership, landholding, household formation, collective practices, and kinship relations that are privileged or even legally possible. The colonization of Native homelands contours possibilities for action, association, and inhabitance by Native bodies (as well as affecting which bodies will be intelligible as Native). Attending to erotics potentially opens a way of registering such quotidian effects of settler-managed forms of sovereignty, in that traces of their imposition and of the formations they seek to suppress, displace, or erase may be borne (inchoately) in bodily and emotional sensation. As Mishuana Goeman argues in "Disrupting a Settler Grammar of Place in the Visual Memoir of Hulleah Tsinhnahjinnie," "Government pressure to define ourselves by state definitions of purity ... leads not only to externally imposed colonial logics, but also an internal closing of physical and cultural borders."[54] She adds, "The recovery and maintenance of the land itself is necessary to decolonization, but so too is a careful attention to the social that determines everyday experiences. An examination of embodied spatiality ... is necessary if we are to avoid replication of colonial systems of power at work in the nation-state." Such an examination of "embodied spatiality," following the logic of Akiwenzie-Damm and Driskill's formulations, involves looking to everyday sensation and affect as indexing both the force exerted (re)producing state-authorized sovereignty and the presence of alternative ways of envisioning social cohesion and spatial relation.[55]

In this way, the effort to articulate such an erotics also gives rise to what might be termed an *ethics of sovereignty,* a set of normative principles that can inform discussions about what can and should count as a claim to indigeneity and how to negotiate among competing accounts. All of the authors I address highlight the affective imprint of thwarted relations to place, the generational inheritance of such sensations and the formation of new ones, the ways seemingly individual feelings express ongoing collective histories, the animating desire for contact and engagement with other Native people, and the potential of intimacy and pleasure as means for (re)imagining and (re)connecting to place. Their accounts of how indigeneity inheres in everyday emotions and embodiment constellate around forms of vulnerability, rather than the sense of impervious insulation that tends to characterize juridical sovereignty. If self-determination is the goal, how is it shaped by the particular notions of selfhood that it seeks to materialize? How might articulations of other ways of being, of personhood and peoplehood, suggest guiding principles for determining Native identity and promoting survivance? Discussing the work of Iris Marion Young, Jessica Cattelino observes, "Young criticized prevailing theories that took self-determination to be sovereign autonomy characterized by 'noninterference,' arguing that such theories both neglected to account for the interdependency that pervades relations among peoples and also failed to offer a normatively adequate interpretation of self-determination." Instead, Young proposed "rethinking self-determination as relational autonomy, with freedom based not on independence but on nondomination," a principle Cattelino adopts in analyzing complex networks of reciprocal relation between the government of the Seminole Tribe and municipal, state, and federal governments (163).[56] This perspective might be extended in considering the internal dynamics of peoplehood, approaching interdependency and relationality as crucial as opposed to de facto casting belonging as an abstract aggregation of autonomous, self-enclosed citizen-subjects.[57] As Sara Ahmed notes in *The Cultural Politics of Emotion,* "the everyday language of emotion is based on the presumption of interiority" (8), taking the self-possessed enclosure of individuality as given. That vision of sovereign personhood can be understood as a corollary to the logic of state sovereignty Young and Cattelino critique and as a social dynamic that liberal projects of privatization seek to realize (a relation discussed more extensively in chapters 1 and 2). Accounts that refuse to presume such affective interiority, tracing patterns of feeling and association that generate everyday experiences of collectivity, open the potential for formulations of Native identity less predicated on notions of endangered essence. Inasmuch as the narration and realization of sovereignty depends on a vision of exclusionary enclosure, it casts difference from available standards of Indianness as a threatening incursion and engages space as a quantum of territory over which tribal control can be extended as jurisdiction. To acknowledge the damage done by settlement is to court disaster, as it suggests a possibly fatal rupture in the schema of the body politic (a danger greatly heightened within the process of pursuing federal recognition, as addressed in chapters 2 and 3).

However, starting from an erotics, embodied sensations and sensitivities, yields a different perspective on—a new *metaphor* for—practices and histories of peoplehood. As Ahmed suggests, skin can be considered less as "that which appears to contain us" than "as where others *impress* upon us" (25), and similarly, "bringing pain into politics" entails recognizing how "the past lives in the very wounds that remain open in the present" (33), such that pain is "part of the histories of injustice . . . understood as *the bodily life of such histories*" (58). Rather than privileging an image of insulated continuity (such as Indian blood) or cultural sameness (verging on stereotype) as the basis for Native identity, the texts discussed in this study highlight networks of impression, the implicit and explicit forms of force exerted on Native peoples and how they live on as structures of feeling. Doing so points toward less an adjudication of authenticity—an ability to match set criteria for realness—than a reparative mapping of processes of wounding through which people(s) have been subjected to the institutionalization of settler logics and geographies. Foregrounding such histories of injustice allows for consideration of how outlawed and erased ties to one's people and to their homeland(s) might live on as affect, as reserves of sensation unrealizable as a documentary or legal claim.[58] Efforts to articulate such feeling—as haunting (chapter 1), an internal landscape (chapter 2), a generational transmission and retelling of stories (chapter 3), or remembering as an act of labor (chapter 4)—direct the discussion of Indigenous being toward phenomena and possibilities that emphasize affectability and the impressions of history rather than the apparently self-contained solidity of sovereign autonomy.

Reciprocally, by making erotics a way of exploring the contours and dynamics of indigeneity, the authors I address foreground interdependence and vulnerability as positive principles of peoplehood. Through what kinds of relations does peoplehood gain meaning and cohesion in an everyday way? Ahmed observes, "The intensification of the surface has a very different effect in experiences of pleasure: the enjoyment of the other's touch opens my body, opens me up" (164), and she adds, "Pleasures are about the contact between bodies that are already shaped by past histories of contact" (165). Quotidian interactions offer kinds of routine contact that accrete, generating forms of collective being-in-the-world that do not necessarily coincide with state-sanctioned modes of determining belonging but that produce experiences of enmeshment with others. In addition to one's relation to other bodies, histories of contact might include an engagement with the land. The possibility of pleasure, and the attendant potential for loss, can emanate from a sensuous connection to place, an intimacy that may be accessed and rejuvenated through erotic contact with other people. Further, to understand oneself as open, especially to being touched by history, can involve feeling ancestral presence, sensing and acknowledging how the past spectrally inhabits the current moment—a kind of immediate relation different from the lineal unfolding and inheritance usually posited within racial and familial genealogy. Within the work of these queer Native writers, those various modes of contact interweave, forming a dense matrix in which daily intimacies with others, affection for place, and the felt proximity of ancestors cross-reference and work in and through each other. Though the texture of such sensations is inadmissible as official evidence of Indianness or tribal identity, these texts suggest that they are indispensable as a way of registering and imagining Indigenous being.[59]

None of these authors posit an unchanging essence of indigeneity, the total merger of individual consciousness into collectivity, or the possibility of simply ignoring tools and processes of institutionalization. If they seek to capture administratively unrecognized kinds of Native experience, implicitly making ontological claims about contemporary Indigenous being (what can and should be understood as real), they situate such claims within a sustained engagement with the changing dynamics of settler governance and Native responses to it. In other words, while these writers explore kinds of residual formations and emergent potentials that are irreducible to the existing bureaucratic structures of self-determination, they offer what might be termed *historical ontologies*,[60] fully acknowledging the ways the patterns they trace cannot be lifted out of ongoing conditions and legacies of settler occupation as a template for transhistorically authentic indigeneity. In fact, as I have been suggesting, one of the principal virtues of these authors' strategies is to insist on the ways the effects of settler imperialism need to be reckoned with as intimately part of Indigenous experience rather than as a purely external force against which to define a (racially/culturally pure?) Native real. The emphasis on the circulation of affect, shared forms of sensation, and the collective character of experience—particularly as against models of liberal privatization and possessive individualism—can threaten, though, to fall back into the primitivizing notion of a distinction between Western individuation and non-Western communalism, a tenacious discourse that has a long and infamous history.[61] To present affectability and relationality as conditions of personhood and of peoplehood is not equivalent to rejecting entirely a notion of individuation. Rather, in Ahmed's terms, individuality emerges out of the particular networks of impression, forms of wounding, histories of contact, and pleasurable openings to which a given body is exposed, through which it is formed and which give texture to that person's experience of being. From this perspective individual experience is never entirely separable from ongoing engagement with others (as against a notion of sovereign autonomy or a relation to oneself as property). Such formative connections, however, may be more or less normatively weighted in a given society in ways that affect how they are realized—the feelings, perceptions, and material possibilities they engender. The authors I address each in their own way explore the consequences of institutionalizing bourgeois individualism, along with its underlying privileging of nuclear family homemaking, as the basis of social life, and they suggest that attending to actually existing and potential forms of interdependence (with other people, with place, with the past) can provide less destructive and more healing ways of imagining indigeneity and living as Native people(s).[62]

Perhaps most important, these authors do not eschew legal and political discourses of sovereignty. All of them in some fashion address the violence and trauma generated by the failures of the United States to acknowledge Native polities' existence as such—as geopolitical entities whose status cannot be reduced to domestic policy within the settler-state. In fact, at the time of the writings addressed here, both Sarris and Miranda were members of groups seeking federal acknowledgment as tribes, and Sarris's novel *Watermelon Nights* explicitly addresses that process and its stakes. Yet as I discuss in chapter 3, such an awareness of the potential benefits of U.S. recognition as a Native nation does not erase a sense of not only what cannot be registered under Indian policy but the costs of utilizing settler-formulated categories and processes as means of realizing peoplehood. At one point one of the characters in the novel wonders if the United States ceased to recognize them once, such that they need to pursue acknowledgment now, what's to stop the United States from doing so again? All of the texts in some way take up this problematic: the apparently beneficent recognition of Native peoples as polities, and the consequent legal endowment of self-determination, functions as the flip side of the potential for a campaign of eradication, especially given the persistence for over a century of the legal claim that Congress has plenary power to do whatever it will in Indian affairs. If law and policy are indispensable for Native peoples' continued survival as peoples, are they sufficient? What kinds of relations—in Ahmed's terms, "past histories of contact" and "histories of injustice"—need to be effaced in taking up the mechanisms of state literalization? What embodied memories are derealized, made virtual, through that process, and what possibilities are thereby lost or deferred?

In excavating queer experiences of peoplehood, those that deviate both from normative straightness and the kinds of unbroken continuity (racial, cultural, territorial, governmental) posited by Indian policy,[63] though, these texts do not take up the queer studies penchant for privileging mobility, diaspora, and deterritorialization over place-based forms of political collectivity.[64] Such work presents any kind of political cohesion that might be cast as national or nationalist as a mechanism for imposing normative ideals of familial and sexual order, and consequently, the power of *queer* lies in leveraging the normalizing dynamics of nationalism, contesting their enclosures in ways that open up possibilities for modes of desire, embodiment, pleasure, association, and identification not constrained by the need to construct, legitimize, and manage a territorial and political entity. This scholarship has done excellent work in tracing the ways political regimes and projects stabilize and validate themselves through heteronormative discourses and policies. Further, it has offered necessary and compelling critiques of both the ways marginalized populations have claimed sexual normativity as a way of gaining access to national resources and the ways some sexual minorities have sought to achieve privilege within the state by remaking themselves as otherwise model neoliberal citizens (homonormativity).[65] However, not all nationalisms are equivalent; not all movements that might be termed nationalist seek to achieve statist modes of governance; and not all efforts to achieve relative political autonomy through the adoption of state-like governance can be understood as oppressive purely on that basis. If the political project of defending the weave between collectivity, territoriality, and self-governance—and seeking state and/or international recognition for that matrix of peoplehood—is seen as inherently oppressive or reactionary, what room is there for thinking indigeneity? As against a dismissal of the geopolitics of Indigenous self-determination, the texts I address adopt a perspective of committed skepticism toward the forms of tribal identity available under the current conditions of settler governance.[66]

Thus, rather than suggesting the irrelevance of what might be termed nationalist aims or simply refusing any engagement with the terms of settler recognition, which as I have suggested profoundly affect Native realities and experiences and thus cannot simply be dismissed as exterior to contemporary Indigenous identity, these texts mediate the claim on reality exerted by settler institutions. Attending to erotics—sensations of pleasure, desire, memory, wounding, and interrelation with others, the land, and ancestors—allows for a commitment to Indigenous collectivity and placemaking, an acknowledgment of the ways peoplehood takes shape within and through structures of feeling not officially deemed political, and the imagination of alternative kinds of Indigenous being to those literalized/normalized through Indian policy and the bureaucratic apparatus of self-determination. These texts suggest that the engagement with Native erotics expresses past, present, and future possibilities that can provide principles for defining, envisioning, and living indigeneity less predicated on codes of authenticity and modes of sovereign selfhood privileged in and realized through settler discourses and institutions.

Each chapter focuses on the work of a single author, and I show how these texts connect intimate emotional and physical responses, which might easily be dismissed as merely personal or idiosyncratic, to collective histories and connections to place. The first two chapters address forms of historical continuity, including the effects of trauma, erased within Indian policy and attendant forms of tribal politics. Qwo-Li Driskill (Cherokee) explores how the individual Native body is haunted by continuing legacies of dispossession and diaspora, and ze explores how desire can provide a means for reclaiming abjected aspects of a people's tradition, including connection to one's homeland. Deborah Miranda (Esselen) shows how a people declared extinct can be preserved melancholically within the psychic life of the current generation, further suggesting how fantasy can provide possibilities for retaining what has been officially forgotten and rejuvenating peoplehood in the present. The third and fourth chapters highlight the possibilities for Native self-understanding given the gaps and occlusions in current settler ways of defining Indianness. Greg Sarris (Graton Rancheria) illustrates how stories that cannot administratively serve as genealogical proof of tribal existence generate forms of social cohesion among a people, and he explores how those persons who do not reproduce authentic Indianness, due to their improper intimacies, offer crucial insight into the actual dynamics of contemporary Native community formation. Chrystos (Menominee) investigates the ways the lives of those who reside in urban spaces demonstrate the survival of indigeneity in the city, and she connects the labor of supporting oneself away from one's people and homeland to the labor of reimagining Indianness, queering stereotypes of Natives in nature by turning them into imaginative sites of pleasure. In these ways contemporary queer Native writing mobilizes representations of sensation to illustrate how connections with land, tradition, and one's people are lived as intimate parts of selfhood. Reciprocally, the texts show how states of feeling index collective experiences of place and displacement for which there is no official mode of expression.

What does it mean to be Cherokee at the present moment? Over the past ten years, the Cherokee Nation of Oklahoma has outlawed same-sex marriage and denied people of African descent status as citizens. These seemingly discrepant issues pivot around a notion of reproductive couplehood in terms of marital union and the genetic transmission of racial being (usually expressed as "blood"). From this perspective Cherokee tradition appears as a conjugally centered inheritance in which some essential thing (Indianness of a Cherokee sort) is passed from generation to generation and in which the means of that transmission—heteropairing—must be safeguarded as the privileged, even exclusive, vehicle for connecting the past to the future. This heterosexual imaginary presents Native identity as a characteristic carried in the body, but one cast as insulated from political challenge and history. In hir collection of poetry *Walking with Ghosts* (2005), Driskill develops an alternative archaeology of Indigenous peoplehood and structures of feeling through reference to sensuous bodily experience. Reshaping the contours of what can count as sovereignty, the text articulates a queer kind of self-determination, registering the primacy of lived connections to land and one's people as mediated by the continuing history of settler violence in contrast to a view of Native identity based on the procreative inheritance of Indian substance. Rather than bracketing the trauma of removal and forced assimilation in a conception of tradition as an endangered (reproductive) purity, *Walking with Ghosts* develops a hauntology in which bodily memories of violation and pleasure together register the interwoven strands of Native histories. Driskill's work returns to scenes and legacies of settlement in which the aim of imperial violence is to produce forms of privatization that fracture indigeneity by disavowing and disciplining quotidian modes of feeling and association that are crucial to the maintenance of Native sociality, spatiality, and history. The states of feeling ze chronicles gesture toward the ways the past remains available as possibility in the present, inhabiting forms of everyday corporeality and eroticism as collective memory, although not necessarily recognized or valued as such. In this way, the text seeks to index and make available forms of personal and communal reanimation that privilege interdependence, vulnerability, and love over a vision of insulated autonomy that can collude in the pathologizing, abstracting, and isolating erasures performed by settler narratives of selfhood and of proper Native subjectivity.

In 1978, the Bureau of Indian Affairs adopted a set of procedures to recognize federally unacknowledged Native groups as tribes for the purposes of inclusion within the regulations and protections of U.S. Indian law. The narrative of unbroken continuity built into the recognition requirements, however, privileges government records and accounts by nonnatives in ways that elide the damage wrought by state actions, as well as their traumatic effects. Staged as a positive performance of presence in which a tribe must document various kinds of continuity over time, the procedures of acknowledgment remain shadowed by aspects of shared Indigenous experience for which there is no administratively valorized category, as well as by state-sanctioned (and often state-orchestrated) violence through which Native continuities have been shattered. In her work, particularly *The Zen of La Llorona* (2005), Deborah Miranda explores the disavowed space of mourning—or, more precisely, of melancholy—to illustrate forms of Indigenous subjectivity that evade or exceed the parameters of federal recognition. The text suggests that forms of collective Indigenous identity survive in/as the seemingly individual experiences of Native people. Miranda represents this undocumentable connection to indigeneity, its transmission and retention within states of feeling, through the representation of her emotional life as an internal landscape. Territoriality is not simply a figure through which to designate individual feelings; rather, as a set of tropes, it marks the melancholic retention of prior relations to place—and their disruption and erasure by the settler regime—as a constitutive feature of Native personhood, even (and in some ways especially) when that identification as Native is not officially recognized. Moreover, Miranda addresses how settler logics of property are instantiated and naturalized in everyday ways through heteronormative structures of marriage and conjugal homemaking. In her depiction of her relationships with her Native female lovers, she explores how an Indigenous erotics can provide avenues for feelings that have been denied the status of the real—rejected as an inauthentic basis for proving indigeneity.

Versions of the question, what is an Indian? extend far beyond federal acknowledgment, bedeviling all levels of Indian policy. To be Indian is to belong to or have ancestors that were members of a tribe, and to be a tribe is to have members who are Indians, a characteristic conceived in reproductive terms. If Indianness is deeply, perhaps inextricably, woven into administrative and popular understandings of what a tribe is, Indigenous peoples are left to grapple with racial reckonings of indigeneity as a central, ongoing feature of both their engagements with settler publics and their shifting self-conceptions of their own peoplehood. In *Watermelon Nights* Greg Sarris explores how state regimes of (in)visibility shape Native (specifically Pomo) narratives of family identity and history. These narratives respond to endemic, state-sanctioned forms of assault and erasure by producing Native authenticity—Indianness—as an endangered characteristic that needs to be preserved through proper forms of maritally centered and procreatively directed family formation. The investment in that ideal translates ongoing structural constraints on the performance of sovereignty as a tribe into charges against other Pomos whose lapses into perversity, including cross-racial intimacy, can be blamed for their ongoing poverty and dispossession. Individuals' personal inability to regulate their desires and conduct produces collective declension, a falling away from tribal ideals—or the ideal of a tribe—that threatens to dissolve Pomo identity entirely. The text's attention to the place of homosexuality, prostitution, illegitimate births, and intimacy with non-Indians in the community over three generations reveals the role of fallen persons in the (re)constitution of collectivity, though in ways that do not fit a dominant model of tribal identification. By tracking these impure figures and the social relations in which they are enmeshed, the novel explores ongoing processes of community formation that sustain peoplehood as a dynamic network, even as those very persons are cast by others as having failed to perform Pomoness properly. The novel illustrates how, alongside narratives of tribal declension, Pomos generate their own genealogical analyses, creating an overlapping web of stories through which they can reconceptualize and reorder their lived relations to each other. As against the accusatory narrative of a fall into perversity lies the possibility of a more generous story of continued communal survival that recognizes ongoing legacies of structural violence while positioning being together as an occasion for joy and hope.

During the 1950s and 1960s, as part of the termination policy superseded by self-determination, the U.S. government ceased to recognize a number of tribes, including the Menominee. Indian policy at the time also promoted urbanization, the abandonment of reservation lands in favor of the greater opportunities supposedly available in the cities. Although the Menominee were reacknowledged by Congressional statute and the official promotion of Native diaspora ended, the effects of these patterns of dislocation persist. In her poetry Chrystos explores the relation between the material circumstances of living in nonnative-dominated space away from her people and the affective dynamics of forging a sense of Native identity, highlighting the multivectored forms of labor she performs. Her writing repeatedly returns to the conditions of her wage work, particularly as a maid for whites, illustrating both the relative disparity in access to resources between whites and people of color and the displacement of activity considered unpleasant or degrading onto the bodies of the latter.

Within this broader framework, she foregrounds the ways white wealth indexes the ongoing dynamics of settlement, in which Native lands and people function as a means of extending white interests. In this vein she contrasts the demeaning status she occupies in white households and the poor pay she receives with the symbolic elevation of Native peoples as genericized symbols of uncommodified spirituality and ecological wisdom. Although indicating how the latter functions as an imperial fantasy—effacing her and others' labor to survive, the conditions that produce their presence in urban space, and their impoverishment while also creating an image with which Native people(s) must struggle in gaining public recognition for their specific histories and present circumstances—Chrystos also takes up stereotype as a tool for manifesting indigeneity. The image of Indians inhabiting a pristine natural elsewhere serves as a means for her to represent her own fantasy and erotic life. As against the difficulties of providing for herself as a Native lesbian, the floral, animal, and forest imagery used to discuss her relationships with other women offer a sense of lush respite from such hardship. Seizing upon cliché in this way reveals the limits of nonnative conceptions of Native people, introducing desire into a vision of stoic containment (lesbian desire in particular) while also marking the gap between this state of feeling and her everyday experiences of trying to make a living. Through this disjunction, she investigates how settler codes for Native authenticity erase the labor of survival under settler rule, how such an imaginary becomes part of the psychic life and emotional resources available to Native people, and how they can occupy the imposed terms of Indian identity in ways that queer them—opening them out to new sensations, emotional trajectories, and possibilities for pleasure.

< I >

The Somatics of Haunting

Embodied Peoplehood in Qwo-Li Driskill's
Walking with Ghosts

W HAT DOES IT MEAN TO BE CHEROKEE AT THE PRESENT
moment? If one takes the recent decisions by the government
of the Cherokee Nation as a guide, it minimally entails presumptive
straightness and a denial of blackness.[1] In May 2004, Kathy Reynolds
and Dawn McKinley, both Cherokee citizens, took advantage of an
ambiguity in Cherokee law to secure a marriage license. The next day,
the chief judge of the Cherokee Judicial Appeals Tribunal issued a
thirty-day moratorium on further licenses, and on June 14, 2004, the
tribal council unanimously passed a statute defining marriage as between one man and one woman.[2] Though this act brought the Cherokee Nation in line with the policy of the U.S. federal government as
codified in the Defense of Marriage Act (1996), it was justified not
on that basis but as an effort to preserve tradition. Todd Hembree, the
general counsel for the nation, argued that "throughout history there's
never been recognition of same-sex marriage" among the Cherokees
and that doing so "would fly in the face of the traditional definition
and understanding of marriage of the Cherokee people."[3] Citing Indian blood as the basis for Cherokee citizenship, leaders also sought to
reverse a March 2006 decision by the Cherokee Nation's highest court
that those known as the Cherokee Freedmen were citizens under the
constitution of 1975. This category comprised the descendants of those
who had been held as slaves in the Cherokee Nation prior to the treaty
with the United States in 1866 and the Cherokee constitution in
1867 that made them citizens, but it also included all those people of

< 45 >

Cherokee as well as African descent who due to U.S. officials' perceptions of their blackness were listed as having no Indian blood quantum, despite their actual Cherokee ancestry.[4] To disenfranchise them,
the tribal council passed a constitutional amendment in June of that
year to restrict citizenship to the lineal descendants of people listed
on the Dawes Rolls (completed in 1906) as Cherokee, Shawnee, or
Delaware (the last two having lived in the Cherokee Nation at the
time as citizens), a change ratified by voters in a special election held
on March 3, 2007.[5]

These two measures indicate the institutionalization of a heteronormative vision of Cherokee identity while narrating that frame as
a conservation of foundational principles of peoplehood. Though not
the same issue and leading to different consequences and statuses
for the people concerned, they both pivot on a normalizing vision of
Cherokeeness in which reproductive couplehood insures the unbroken continuity of national identity, including the genetic transmission of racial being (in the form of blood). This legal fortification of
heteroconjugal union as central to Cherokee identity naturalizes the
latter by implicitly envisioning it as a kind of substance that inheres
immutably in individual bodies and that can be conveyed directly and
securely to future generations.[6] The Euramerican history of presenting the nuclear family form as an inevitable corollary of human reproduction itself allows that social formation and anything associated
with it to be cast as self-evident and outside the bounds of political
struggle, as a kind of ontological given,[7] and in this case Cherokee
national policy takes up that discursive ensemble, using it as a means
of projecting the givenness and obviousness of Cherokee survival as
a people—as against the history of U.S. efforts to challenge and di-
minish Indigenous sovereignty, when not trying to outright eliminate
it. That process of linking normative family formation to the history
and futurity of Cherokee nationality is suggested by the invocation of
tradition to legitimize both the denial of same-sex marriage and the
alien(-)ation of the Freedmen. The rhetoric of tradition mobilized in
these instances stages a particular kind of temporality—namely, that
of declension. The past is cast as an origin from which contemporary
Cherokees increasingly are distanced, threatening an attenuation that
eventually could result in the loss of Cherokeeness entirely if people

do not act now to rededicate themselves to that which remains in danger of dissipation. This particular reproductive imaginary envisions continuity across time as a projection of self-sameness via procreation, insulated from the danger of disappearance by its embedding as an unchangeable (if potentially generationally diminishing) element in the very bodies of Cherokee people. Rather than mounting a historical investigation into the accuracy of the government's representation of Cherokee tradition or questioning its legal authority to pass these measures, I am interested in exploring what's at stake in this way of narrating indigeneity.[8] More specifically, how can it be understood as responsive to particular kinds of historical pressures placed on Native peoples? Further, how does the account of Cherokee embodiment offered or the way Cherokee bodies are cast as reproductively inheriting and passing their Cherokeeness close off other possibilities for conceptualizing what peoplehood is and how the present bears the past within it?

Notably, the points in the past that Cherokee officials choose against which to measure (the potential lapses and losses in) the present lie in the allotment era. The period in which Native polities were under greatest assault by the U.S. government due to its overwhelming commitment to the policy of detribalization serves here as a, somewhat paradoxical, site of surety that provides a bulwark against contemporary challenges.[9] Chief Chad Smith has defended the denaturalization of the Freedmen by citing the census of the Cherokee Nation completed by the Dawes Commission as the ultimate authority on who should count as Cherokee. Arguing that the Cherokee Nation is "an Indian government made up of Indian citizens," he insists, "Cherokee Nation citizens must prove that they had an ancestor on the Final Rolls of the Cherokee Nation in 1906, which included categories for Cherokee, Delaware and Shawnee Indians, as well as white citizens and freedmen," observing that direct descendants of those listed in the first three categories "are citizens of the Cherokee Nation and are accepted and are part of the Cherokee family."[10] Speaking about the invocation of the Dawes Rolls in contemporary Cherokee politics, S. Alan Ray has condemned this turn to the past as a "legal fetishism . . . which alienates Cherokees from their sovereign power of self-determination" (445).[11] From this perspective, filtered through

Marx's notion of commodity fetishism, one can read Smith as giving form to self-determination through a thingification of Cherokee identity—as inherited Indian substance—as opposed to investigating the broader social and historical processes involved in generating the apparent givenness of Indian as a category.[12] Ray adds, "When, as now, the Cherokee Nation turns to the Dawes Rolls as its exclusive authority for citizenship, it is perpetuating those categorizations [employed in the rolls] and their race-value significations by embedding them in the very body of the Nation" (462). The Cherokee government can be said to be trying to produce security for the Nation by casting it as a kind of embodiment, equating the polity with (the possession of) a particular sort of blood and creating a sense of permanence for it by aligning the exercise of sovereignty with biological reproduction. In denouncing Reynolds and McKinley's union, Hembree naturalizes the means for that reproductive futurity, declaring, "Same-sex marriages were not part of the Cherokee history or tradition. Cherokee society in 1892 [when the marriage statute initially was passed] did not allow nor contemplate same-sex marriage."[13]

These assertions of the absolute self-evidence of Cherokee identity, bolstered by the allusion to normative ideologies of family, seem more than a little odd given the actual threat to Cherokee tribal existence present in the period to which officials turn for authoritative examples. The mechanism for breaking up Native nations in the allotment period was through the imposition of the nuclear family form, supposedly civilizing Indians by teaching them how to have privatized propertyholding in the place of tribal association, governance, and land tenure.[14] To the extent that allotment and its legacies enact heteronormativity, including the narration of Native identity as calculable quanta of Indian blood, strategies of reading and critique from queer studies can help in gaining conceptual traction on how responses to that system bear traces of its ongoing operation. In *Feeling Backward,* Heather Love addresses contemporary expressions of pride by sexual and gender minorities in ways that suggest an alternative frame through which to read Cherokee officials' accounts of peoplehood. She argues, "Turning away from past degradation to a present or future affirmation means ignoring the past as past; it also makes it harder to see the persistence of the past in the present" (19), later adding, "By including queer figures from the past in a positive genealogy of gay identity, we make good on their suffering, transforming their shame into pride after the fact" (32). This dynamic can be understood as a response to the particular kinds of abjection faced by queer people: "One must insist on the modernity of the queer. . . . For queers, having been branded as nonmodern or as a drag on the progress of civilization, the desire to be recognized as part of the modern social order is strong" (7). For Native peoples, perhaps the supreme figure of the nonmodern within U.S. cultural imaginaries, the issue is less a move from shame to pride than an effort to counter the notion that Indians are vanishing or that their descendants have lost what makes them uniquely and identifiably Indian. Their relation to the past, then, is less one of abandonment, leaving behind degradation, than one of recuperation, the preservation of that which is declared lost. Love observes, "Pride and visibility offer antidotes to shame and the legacy of the closet; they are made in the image of specific forms of denigration" (2).[15] The kinds of shame Love tracks also haunt Native peoples in that a failure to be properly reproductively coupled repeatedly has been taken as a sign of Indian backwardness, and that charge has been turned over into the assertion by the Cherokee government of the corporeal continuity of Indianness in conjugal pairing, transmitted in the *family* of the nation—an image that seems to reflect the terms of allotment even as it refuses the logic of inevitable disappearance.

The fear that current practices will mark a radical and final break with tradition, itself conceived in terms of the transmission of blood, echoes in an inverted way the late nineteenth-century U.S. commitment to breaking up tribes, understood as racial enclaves, and the emphasis on marital reproduction parallels the allotment-era emphasis on training Native peoples in bourgeois domesticity. The Cherokee government's invocations of the allotment period disregard the extreme stress on the Cherokee Nation and the very real threat of its legal eradication at that historical moment, as well as failing to note the ways heteroconjugal homemaking and the calculation of racial identity through the measurement of Indian substance were imposed on the Cherokee people as central features of U.S. policy. Moreover, this vision of Native identity as an internal quality transmitted through reproduction adopts the very ideology of possessive individualism that allotment efforts sought to inculcate as the indisputable basis of belonging to the Cherokee people. The apparent insulation of Indianness as an internal property of discrete bodies serves as an imaginative bulwark against the loss of Cherokee identity due to further seizure of lands: if Indians possess Indianness as a bodily characteristic from which they cannot be alienated, then their individual ownership over it cannot be challenged, producing an aggregate Indian entity that theoretically can survive the total expropriation of the nation's territory. Ed Cohen argues that the figure of bodily immunity "metaphorically affirms the organism as a literal kingdom within a kingdom: the juridical force it ascribes to, and inscribes in, the natural laws of biology seems to offer the organism sovereignty over its own (natural) existence" (61), but he further observes that such a vision of bodily enclosure "remains a reaction to sovereign violence [geopolitical conflict in early modern Europe at the time of its emergence] and as such unwittingly recontains this same violence within itself" (81).[16] Similarly, conceptualizing Cherokee nationality through figures of bodily self-possession, the immutable ownership of reproductively transmitted Indian blood substance, reacts to the "sovereign violence" of U.S. projects of detribalization while "unwittingly" constituting Native sovereignty through their terms. Indigenous collectivity comes to be narrated in a defensive mode organized around the logics of propertied personhood used to legitimize the all-out assault on Native nations that was allotment.[17] In this way, current official articulations of Cherokee identity seem to mirror "specific forms of denigration" dating from at least the allotment period and do so in ways that do not acknowledge the connections between such ideals and this history of settler violence.[18] As Ann Cvetkovich suggests, "The desire for 'natural' reproduction can be understood as a way of refusing the trauma of collective dislocation through a fantasy of uninterrupted lineage" (122).

In "Stolen from Our Bodies," Cherokee scholar and poet Qwo-Li Driskill offers the notion of a "Sovereign Erotic" as a way of connecting Native bodies, individual and collective self-representations, and ongoing histories of invasion, detribalization, and removal. Ze suggests that the project of "healing our sexualities as First Nations people is braided with the legacy of historical trauma and the ongoing process of decolonization,"[19] and from this perspective, "A Sovereign Erotic relates our bodies to our nations, traditions, and histories" (51–52). Driskill offers this concept as a way of marking and contesting how Native people(s) have accepted "the manifestations of an oppressive overculture on . . . erotic life" (51), internalizing "the sexual values of [the] dominant culture" (54). As discussed in the Introduction, such a challenge to settler norms entails a changed understanding of the relation between sexuality and sovereignty. Attending to the former provides a way of developing "process[es] of decolonization" that can fully engage with the persistent "legacy of historical trauma" (as opposed to ordering collective self-representation and the citation of "tradition" around the very terms of that trauma). Driskill suggests a nexus of body, tradition, and history predicated on continuing and changing forms of relation rather than the kinds of enclosure through which the Cherokee government envisions Native identity—either in the body as a kind of "blood" or in the privatized scene of its transmission through heteroconjugal reproduction. Such a shift potentially offers an alternative vision of Native politics and an attendant account of the intimate effects of settler imperialism, foregrounding an understanding of selfhood in which embodiment operates as part of a relational matrix (spatially and temporally) as opposed to an insulated guarantee of lineal self-sameness.

How might such an erotics offer a way of addressing contemporary modes of peoplehood and placemaking—in Love's terms, developing "a vision of political agency that incorporates the damage that [one] hope[s] to repair" (151)? Driskill's essay gestures toward such questions but backs way from their implications. In a footnote ze observes, "My use of the term 'sovereign' is in no way an attempt to challenge or replace the legal definitions of sovereignty," instead pointing "to tribally specific and traditional understandings of our bodies, sexualities, genders, erotic *senses of self*" and "the formation of identities" in "non-legal contexts" (61–62). Bracketing "legal contexts" in this way undercuts the extent to which Driskill's representation of the erotic can highlight the dynamics and effects of U.S. efforts to regulate Native polities, as well as those formations of sovereignty (of Indigenous self-representation, spatiality, sociality, and memory) disavowed within U.S. governmental frameworks. Ze more fully moves in this direction, however, in hir collection of poetry *Walking with Ghosts*. In it, ze develops an archaeology of Indigenous peoplehood and structures of feeling through reference to sensuous bodily experience. Reshaping the contours of what can count as sovereignty, the text articulates a queer kind of self-determination, registering the primacy of lived connections to land and one's people as mediated by the continuing history of settler violence in contrast to a view of Native identity based on the procreative inheritance of Indian substance. Driskill highlights the ways Native, specifically Cherokee, identity and tribal belonging in the present are disjointed by forms of imperial trauma that themselves carry traces of "traditional understandings," the past erupting into contemporary life in transformative and potentially decolonizing ways through structures of feeling.[20]

Living Cherokee Pasts

As the title of hir collection suggests, Driskill seeks to address the ways that contemporary life is permeated by the presence of what might otherwise be described as lost. Carla Freccero argues in *Queer/Early/Modern* that "doing a queer kind of history means . . . an openness to the possibility of being haunted," which involves "a deconstruction of the implicit heteronormativity of historical continuity, the ways historical succession is tied . . . to heterosexual reproduction" (80–81).[21] While quite evocative as a way of talking about how the past is not in fact past, how that which is sealed away as history can emerge in unexpected and unpredictable ways to remake the current moment, the figure of haunting runs the risk of reaffirming the tropes of disappearance and extinction that continue to circulate in both administrative and popular representations of Native peoples.[22] Haunting, however, also can suggest the reappearance of that which otherwise has been thought long gone, indicating the somewhat uncanny entry of the (presumed) dead back into life and paradoxically highlighting the gap between then and now across which the specter must travel. By contrast narratives of unbroken historical succession (including the conceptualization of Native nationalities around the notion of blood-borne self-sameness) leave little room for engaging with the ruptures in Indigenous geopolitics and governance engineered by the settler-state, the profound effects of such intervention on Native peoples' socialities and self-conceptions, the unevenness and perils of cultural transmission in such circumstances of imperial dislocation and disavowal, and the attendant complex intertwining of trauma and tradition in experiences of Indigenous collectivity. The notion of haunting provides a way of indexing these dynamics, and Driskill ties that nonlinear temporality, the ways the present is punctured and remade by the material return of histories that disrupt its terms, to an exploration of the role of physical sensation and affective relation in the survival of indigeneity—the social formations of feeling that bear legacies of violence as well as Native survivance.

Rather than indicating the difference between then and now or their linkage via a smooth continuity, Driskill uses the figure of haunting to index the ways the past splits open the present, undoing what appears as evident, revealing how things taken as given are the effect of ongoing processes (including the normalized legacy of state violence), and giving rise to possibilities that (officially) were foreclosed and forgotten. In this way, the text draws on something like Jacques Derrida's notion of "hauntology," an effort to think "the disjuncture in the very presence of the present; . . . [the] non-contemporaneity of the present time with itself" (25). Derrida's argument highlights how temporality functions as a relation, and a fairly unpredictable one at that, as opposed to a succession. He argues, "Inheritance is never a *given*, it is always a task," and he adds, "All the questions on the subject of being or of what is to be (or not to be) are questions of inheritance." Yet the fact "that we *are* heirs does not mean that we *have* or that we *receive* this or that, . . . but that the *being* of what we are *is* first of all inheritance, whether we like it or know it or not" (54). Unlike a concept of identity in which some thing (such as Indian blood) gets transmitted generationally, this view rests less on the possession of a determinate substance than on a kind of fundamental indebtedness to what has come before, a connection to the past that actively makes it present in ways that (potentially) disjoint the present. In Derrida's account the specter marks a point of transition in which the givenness of the distinction between the incorporeal and the corporeal, between the evanescent and the empirical, is crossed and thwarted. What previously had no material form becomes embodied, as opposed to the idea of inheritance as the passage of an existing, verifiable, determinate entity—whether heirlooms, land, or blood. While addressing the ways the specter returns and, thus, the ways the ghostly past ruptures the present, Derrida emphasizes that haunting undoes the self-sameness of the present in ways that break an imagined teleology between now and what is to come. In other words, the return of the ghostly past makes possible the unpredictability of the future, the potential for change, rather than the staging of a continuity between now and then.[23] In Driskill's case what I am suggesting is that hauntology promises an actualization of a durable relation with the past that does not so much blast it out of the continuum of history, in Walter Benjamin's oft-cited messianic image, as make material an abiding that structures of settlement have sought to foreclose.[24] Acknowledging the often unrecognized work of manifesting the past as the present—the task or labor of inheritance—can allow for a thinking of the current moment as occupied by numerous histories, only some of which are given form as (what counts as) the real.

Put another way, the character of contemporary individual and collective identity appears quite different depending on which histories are actualized as the basis for defining what it means to be Native or, more specifically, to be Cherokee. Haunting points to the other histories that are present but unrealized or, at least, are given less widespread, perhaps less institutionalized, credence as the fact of peoplehood in the present. This "disjointure . . . of the present" can be described through the idea of, in Raymond Williams's terms, a "residual formation."[25] The figure of haunting can indicate the copresence and interweaving of multiple kinds of pasts that abide and intersect in ways that might trouble the present—the coexistence of residualities awaiting (re)emergence.[26] In this way, Derrida's caution that "haunting is not an empirical hypothesis" opens into a different rhetorical/conceptual register (161)—namely, that of the distinction between the literal and the figurative. Put more precisely, the notion of an inheritance awaiting (re)materialization points to institutionalized and normative processes of literalization through which certain histories and social relations are endowed with status as empirically given, such as blood, whereas others are consigned to figurativity, cast as insubstantial and unreal.[27]

Driskill's work traces how other histories—of endurance in diaspora, dislocation, and silence—inhabit and animate Native bodies as states of feeling, producing something like a hauntology of Cherokee sensation. In "Tal'-s-go Gal'-quo-gi Di-Del'-qua-s-do-di Tsa-la-gai Di-go-whe-li/ Beginning Cherokee," Driskill explores how such possibilities are transmitted and activated, tracing the ways trauma and tradition are braided with each other and how they are borne in bodily experience.[28] The central conceit of the poem is the narrator's effort to learn the Cherokee language, the title replicating the name of an actual contemporary primer.[29] In one sense this process indicates a break in the transmission of a significant aspect of Cherokee identity, but the text presents this gap as something other than mere emptiness, the disappearance of a particular sociocultural content. The narrator observes, "I am haunted by loss" (4), suggesting a presence that can only be named as/through negation. It presses upon the current moment, indicating both the return of something thought gone and the ways that which has supposedly been lost persists within the modes of its erasure. The dimensions of this absence appear in a felt sense of lack:

> My cracked earth lips
> drip words not sung
> as lullabies to my infant ears
> not laughed over dinner
> or choked on in despair
>   (1)

This haunting permeates daily life. More than simply noting that the Cherokee language was not present, this litany testifies to how those experiences themselves were shaped by its nonpresence, how an everyday experience of Cherokeeness coalesces around the language's continuing influence in its ongoing effacement. Part of the "First Cherokee Lesson" commands, "Learn to translate the words you miss most"; "Learn to say *home*" (1). The idea of missing Cherokee words implies not so much the acquisition of something that was merely alien before, marking the vast distance between the then of Cherokee fluency and the now of the lesson, as the return of something already familiar. Yet the speaker has never known the words, intimating that the knowledge and identification at play here cannot be captured in the literal possession of linguistic competency or, rather, that the ability to translate, to move between languages in the present, gains meaning within another already existing process of translation that cannot be easily articulated as a distinct cultural practice—the (re)making of home amid the legacy of systematic settler dispossession. This process suffuses current life and is registered in the sensation of a longing for a means of representing that (dis)continuity, of fully registering the complex terms of survival as Cherokee people.[30]

The image of "cracked earth" and the elliptical allusion to "despair" gesture to this matrix of displacement and persistence, intimating how the speaking of Cherokee gives material form to it. The poem personifies the words of the Cherokee language as themselves survivors of the atrocities of removal.[31]

> They played dead until
> the soldiers passed
> covered the fields like corpses
> But we were already gone
> before sunrise
>   (1)

The apparent death of the language appears here as a pretense to avoid relocation, portraying it as a (set of) survivor(s) in hiding separated from the main body of the people and awaiting reunion when it's safe. The image of abandonment, of leaving the language behind, indicates less an attenuation of inheritance, a loss of Cherokeeness, than the results of the exertion of imperial power. Giving a physical presence to the language in this way reframes its relation to contemporary Cherokee identity. The fleeing words resemble those whose descendants would come to be federally recognized in the latter half of the nineteenth century as the Eastern Band of Cherokees; the phrase "escaped into the mountains" is often used to describe those Cherokees, particularly living in the Overhill towns of southwestern North Carolina, who were able to evade the soldiers and remain on or near traditional Cherokee lands.[32] This allusion casts the language as a part of the people that can return rather than as a trait whose possession bespeaks an endangered authenticity, and from this perspective, the narrator's sensation of being haunted suggests the feeling of an unrealized possibility in the present, the potential for a reunion.[33] Furthermore, in figuring Cherokee words as embodied, the text presents them as marked by U.S. Indian policy, as participants in the trauma who bear that legacy instead of simply existing in a state before or beyond it. This apparent act of personification, though, also troubles the self-evidence of the distinction between the corporeal and the incorporeal. Put another way, it raises questions about what constitutes a Cherokee body or, rather, what it means to invest Cherokee identity with bodiliness and by what processes that investiture comes to stand as the literal facticity of Cherokeeness. What histories of flight, trauma, and survival are thereby rendered merely figural (or vanished or fake)? In *Wisdom Sits in Places,* Keith Basso observes that in the language of the Western Apaches, "place-names might be heard by those who use them as repeating verbatim—actually quoting—the speech of their early ancestors" (10), and Driskill's somatization of the language positions it as ancestral, as carrying within it the experience of invasion that has been passed as a generational inheritance.[34]

The loss of the language merges with that of the land, showing the embeddedness of the former within a legacy of settler violence to which it inevitably points. As Veena Das argues with respect to the period of the Partition in India, "Everyday life as a site of the ordinary buried in itself the violence that provided a certain force within which relationships moved" (11): "Potentiality[, specifically for further violence,] here does not have the sense of something that is waiting at the door of reality to make an appearance as it were, but rather as that which is already present" (9). The quotidian recognition of the lack of the Cherokee language indexes the persistent influence of those forces that led to its absence, registering the continuing force of settler presence in the lives of Native people but also the potentiality for the emergence of the very kinds of Indigenous sociality targeted for destruction and abjection.

As Driskill illustrates, everyday relationships are saturated with this tension. The narrator recounts hir mother's story of a childhood encounter with hir grandmother:

> *I knew some Cherokee*
> *when I was little*
> *My cousins taught me*
> . . . .
> *When I came home speaking*
> *your grandmother told me*
> I forbid you to speak that language
> in my house
> Learn something useful
>   (3–4)

The rejection of the language might be described as an internalization of the violence directed against the Cherokees, an incorporation of the possibility of further assault into the grandmother's sense of selfhood. However, in trying to create a place freed from the danger of dislocation, to cleanse the "house" of traces of the indigeneity that seem to call forth imperial force, her disavowal itself reproduces Cherokee identity, not as a positive inheritance but as a legacy of terrified silence. More than a psychological disposition, this repudiation shapes the sociality of the home and the relationships in it, giving them a specificity that takes form around that silence. As Bonita Lawrence says of urban Natives in Canada, "Their struggle to build a base for their families in urban settings may have involved apparent acquiescence to the ways of the white society in some ways, combined with cover or open resistance in others. Their experiences, however, must be understood to be Native experiences" (133). She later adds, "Given the genocidal nature of the experiences of forced urbanization and assimilation that so many Native families come from, these diasporic experiences . . . must be seen as part of their nations' history, rather than the individual 'accidents' they usually are assumed to be" (203–4). Though denied realization as an active connection to the past and derided as useless, the language remains as a disowned presence, almost palpable in the way it marks the lives of the mother and grandmother—and by extension the narrator in the retelling of the story.

The nonuse of the Cherokee language seems to index an inability to name the structures of feeling that arise out of processes of removal and assimilation.[35] In *Manifest Manners* Gerald Vizenor asserts that "what has been published and seen is not what is heard or re-membered in oral stories" (70), adding that "shadows tease and loosen the bonds of representation in stories" and that "the shadows are the silence in heard stories, the silence that bears a referent of tribal memories and experience" (72). The silence here is not the absence of language but the implicit surround of peoplehood in which individual stories/events/experiences gain meaning. While acknowledging Vizenor's caution that "the stories that turn tribes tragic are not their own stories" (16), I want to suggest that Driskill extends this sense of the fullness of silence to include tribal memories of the everyday life of displacement, allowing experiences of settler violence and its legacies to count as experiences of peoplehood that provide a context for understanding contemporary Cherokee identity.[36] One could suggest a fundamental disjunction between the narrator's mother in the poem and her cousins: they have the language and, therefore, Cherokee culture and identity, and she does not. However, the text refuses that easy dichotomy of presence and absence, of possession versus loss. Instead, it suggests a kind of abiding in which the retention of the actual language by some can allow the experience of being haunted—the felt presence of a past that has been rendered silent in the "literature of dominance"[37]—to be narrated as itself part of the inheritance of being Cherokee, an identification that emerges in scenes of relation rather than as a reproductively insulated, internal property (like blood).

This kind of exchange, the work of (re)narration, occurs in the speaker's relation with hir mother. After she recounts her interaction with her own mother, the narrator notes:

> We sit at the kitchen table
> As she drinks iced tea
> . . . .
> I teach her to say *u-ga-lo-ga-go-tlv-tv-nv/* tea
> . . . .
> Try to teach her something useful
>   (4)

Echoing while reorienting the grandmother's dismissal, the insistence on the usefulness of the language suggests that its function in some way intersects with the circumstances in which it was repudiated. More than merely an inversion or negation, the repetition of "useful" gestures toward a kind of redoubling in which the language makes possible an elucidation of the particularity of Indigenous experience produced by the abjection of indigeneity (including Native languages) in dominant discourses and practices.

The language marks the silence and shadows generated in the wake of removal. Braiding hir mother's hair "into three strands / thick as our history" (5), the narrator observes, "This is what it means to be Indian / Begging for stories in a living room," adding, "She passes stories down to me / I pass words up to her / Braid her hair":

> She remembers
> > Great Grandmother Nancy Harmon
> > who heard white women
> > call her uppity Indian during
> > a quilting bee
> > and climbed down their chimney with
> > a knife between her teeth
>
> She remembers
> > flour sack dresses
> > tar paper shacks
> > dust storms   blood   escape
> (6)

In these everyday encounters, occurring in the kitchen and the living room, the kind of "house" the grandmother sought to secure against the past is shown as permeated by the struggles and longings Driskill describes elsewhere in the poem as a search for a sense of home. Through the image of the braid, the Cherokee language and the mother's narratives are woven together, indicating the seemingly separate—and separated—strands that intertwine as "our history." Notably, the "stories" for which the narrator is "begging," the ones that define "what it means to be Indian," are not traditional, in the sense of indexing a period or beliefs prior to Euro-contact or even to removal in the 1830s. Instead, they are about the racism, impoverishment, and fear that have marked Native lives as a result of the normalization of white supremacy and ongoing settler projects of displacement and expropriation.[38] The mention of "blood" and "escape" recalls the scene of removal earlier in the poem, linking these later events and dynamics to that moment of wrenching dislocation from the land and those who went into hiding. The "words" passed up to the mother appear less as direct translations of particular elements in the stories than as a means of naming these events and feelings as part of Cherokee history, providing a way of reconnecting the quotidian experiences and effects of diaspora to the recognizably Cherokee event of removal and thereby intimating how that past and the sense of peoplehood to which it attests continues to be borne amid its apparent erasure.

Driskill suggests that the body itself carries this history of identity and loss and the potential for reunion and regeneration. Thus, the haunting occurs not as the appearance of a disruption outside oneself but as the embedding within the self of unrealized collective presence and possibility. Individual Cherokee subjectivity, physical and psychic, emerges out of the social scenes in which peoplehood and its past(s) are enacted as silence. The narrator notes that the "stories" ze desires are "caught in my mother's hair" (5), implying they are knotted in a tangle and can be freed through the act of braiding—the renarration of everyday indigeneity as such through the connection to Cherokee words. This image also implies, though, that the hair itself is composed of stories, that they suffuse its very substance. Driskill conveys that sense most explicitly in the directions in the opening to this section of the poem:

Gather stories like harvest
and sing honor songs

Save the seeds
to carry you through the winter

Bury them deep in your flesh

Weep into your palms
until stories take root

in your bones
split skin
blossom
   (5)

The text envisions stories, such as those told by the narrator's mother, as like "seeds," with similar properties and arising out of a sustained relationship with the land. While Cherokee words are earlier described as "not sung as lullabies" to the narrator (1), the gathering of stories of Cherokee life, including those of dislocation and diaspora, are connected here to "songs" that further tie them to the land and "honor" them as providing sustenance ("to carry you through the winter"). Rather than being placed in the ground, these seeds are nurtured in the "flesh" and watered through tears, and the resulting "blossom" shows that the stories and the loss they convey have presence and substance, indicating more than mere lack or absence—of language, culture, identity.

The body surrogates for (traditional) land(s), and though the one cannot replace the other, the body is cast as a space of nurturance that facilitates persistence amid devastation. Das's discussion of the aftermath of the Partition of India seems quite apt: "Even when it appears that some women were relatively lucky because they escaped direct bodily harm, the bodily memory of being-with-others makes the past encircle the present as atmosphere" (76), and later in describing a boy who had witnessed the murder of his family in the riots following the assassination of Indira Gandhi, she observes, "It seemed to me that his body was the repository of knowledge not quite his to possess" (201). As she argues, the kind of massive violence usually understood as having a political and historical character gives rise to forms of everyday corporealization that are not publicly, archivally visible but coalesce past collective trauma as part of the operative texture of the present. Embodiment materializes, in Vizenor's terms, the "shadows" cast by "tribal memories." Native disappearance is therefore only apparent; instead, the stories gestate until they "split skin."

Refusing a sustained distinction between inside and outside, the poem refigures generationality less as the heteroreproductive transmission of Indianness than as the passage of forms of knowledge and experience that are lived as an intimate part of individual selfhood awaiting the possibility of expression. Yet this inheritance is not a positive content, a set of traits (biological or cultural) that could readily serve as a referent for Cherokee identity. What emerges as crucial is the capacity for a kind of speaking that could testify to continuity across the catastrophe of removal and associated forms of ongoing assault and assimilation.[39] Again, Driskill emphasizes that the "stories" are not traditional in any conventional sense, although such tales are woven into the poem and nurtured by tears (a relation of care intensified by its connection to figures of "milk," which I address further below).[40] Individual bodies serve as the repository for these narratives of forms of collective Native history not necessarily acknowledged as such, incorporating explicit and implicit scenes of instruction as feeling and sensation. However, such histories also must be spoken in order for hidden pasts to serve as the basis for building a future for the Cherokee people. These pasts that grow within the flesh can be thought of as, in Ann Cvetkovich's phrase, an "archive of feelings," "felt experiences that can be mobilized in a range of directions, including the [re]construction of cultures and publics" (47), but such experiences must be voiced for that mobilization to occur. Speaking of hir mother, the narrator notes, "It's what she doesn't say / that could destroy me / what she can't say / She weeps milk" (6). As in the earlier conversion of the mother's memories into something "useful," the unsaid stories await translation, a renaming of them as/in Cherokee that allows them to be actively connected to the history of enforced diaspora. Without the act of telling, the revelation of "heard stories" that would indicate the presence of tribal experience, the feelings remain trapped, internalized as an individual pathology that can "destroy" both its bearer and those who inherit it in the generational reenactment of toxic shame.[41] Further, given the prior personification of the Cherokee language, its enfleshment, the need to voice stories also indicates the potential for the materialization of something, giving concrete form to what had been thought to be evanescent and disappeared.

The text condenses this nexus of latency, embodiment, and haunting in the figure of the tongue.[42] In the narrator's first Cherokee lesson, ze "crawl[s] through a field of / twisted bodies to find them" (the words that "escaped into the mountains"):

> I do everything Beginning Cherokee
> tells me
> Train my tongue
> to lie still
> Keep teeth tight
> against lips
> Listen to instruction tapes
> Study flash cards
>   (2)

In one sense, the effort to speak the Cherokee language entails a re-molding of the body in what one does with the tongue, teeth, and lips, but in another sense this alteration is a return, an attempt to reclaim that which appears to have been lost. The process of making the mouth suitable to be inhabited by Cherokee simultaneously is a restaging of the potential for reunion in the aftermath of removal, a continuation of the search for home that Driskill presents as animating the shadows of Cherokee life in diaspora. While in a conventional sense "tongue" serves as a metonym for language, it also operates in reverse as a way of linking language acquisition and retention to the ways histories of trauma and tradition overlap in lived sensation.

As suggested earlier, the language is both a significant aspect of Cherokee identity and a means of naming other memories as collective. The poem positions the tongue at the intersection of possibility and danger, as a figure for the ways contemporary Cherokees bear legacies of both indigeneity and settlement that are not themselves necessarily visible as such:

> Your ancestors will surround you as you sleep
> keep away ghost of generals presidents priests
> who hunger for your
> rare and tender tongue
> They will keep away ghosts
> so you have the strength
> to battle the living
>   (3)

The "battle" indicated by the "soldiers" mentioned earlier in the poem has not ended, instead taking a different form, but one that is not merely internal. As a threshold space, the mouth renders ambiguous the distinction between the inside and the outside of the body, and as the vehicle of both speech and digestion, the tongue emphasizes the sense of dynamic relation across that boundary. The image of hungry agents of civilization casts settlement as a cannibalistic consumption of Cherokee bodies, foregrounding how macrological imperial projects and policy take shape in intimately invasive ways. The passage also presents Cherokee identity as a complex negotiation in which it is less innate than remade. The body serves as a site of continuing struggle, as opposed to self-evident Indian substance. The incorporeal past animates the experience of the current moment.[43] The need to "battle the living" further suggests the ongoing threat that the stories will be enclosed within the body, in a wounded, destructive isolation.

As opposed to a secure inheritance transmitted over generations, the relation with "ancestors" needs to be (re)forged in the present. In the first section the narrator asks, "How can I greet my ancestors in a language they don't / understand" (2), and the poem closes with the following:

> We are together at sunrise
> from dust we sprout love and poetry
> We are home
> Greeting our ancestors
> with rare and tender tongues
> (8)

The loss that haunts the narrator appears here less as temporal distance, an attachment to that which is irretrievably gone, than as a felt need to engage with ancestors who remain proximate but with whom there is no ready means of articulating such connection (an inability to greet them). The absence of the Cherokee language at the outset becomes over the course of the poem a meditation on how legacies of dislocation, the search for home, gives shape to the struggles of everyday experience, where history is worked through and made present "in the flesh."

The tongue as an interface between the body and the world—between selfhood and the sociality(/ies) on which it depends—echoes the corporeality attributed to Cherokee words, which makes them not just a cultural trait but themselves ancestors who remember, survive, and are marked by the traumas of settlement. To relearn the language itself, then, is to reunite with ancestors, to materialize the putatively past in/ as the present.[44] Doing so suggests continued possibility in the wake of imperial violence ("sunrise") while acknowledging such violence's continued presence as part of Cherokee identity (the repetition of "rare and tender tongues" implying an awareness of the perspective of settler "ghosts" who continue to "hunger"). As opposed to emphasizing the heteroreproductive transmission of racial substance, occurring within a carefully choreographed genealogical structure, the poem presents ancestry as an active relation. Yet the past does not so much return to rupture the present as one reunites with ancestors (who are, in fact, present) as a way of enabling survivance. That persistence is not the unchanging same (such as in the imaginary of blood quantum) but the maintenance of a connection awaiting real(-)ization.

Earlier in that same section, Driskill repeats hir personification of the Cherokee language; the ancestral, however, becomes descendant in a queer reproductivity that more pointedly contests the dominant vision of heterolineage endorsed in Cherokee national policy.[45] The narrator's body serves as a site of (re)birth—casting inheritance less as intergenerational transmission than as reanimation—in an incredibly rich passage worth quoting in full:

Born without a womb
I wait for the crown of fire
the point where further stretching is impossible
This birth could split me
I nudge each syllable into movement
Memorize their smells
Listen to their strange sleepy sounds
They shriek with hunger and loss
I hold them to my chest and weep milk
My breasts are filled with tears
(7)

Beginning by indicating a male bodiedness that forecloses physical pregnancy, the stanza envisions the work of learning the language as childbirth, the terms of labor ("This birth could split me") reminding readers of the prior description of how "stories" emerge from "flesh" in ways that "split skin" (5).[46] The terms used before to convey dislocation and settlement—"hunger" and "loss"—reappear, refigured as the vulnerability of new life. The sorrow of prior separation has not vanished, instead providing sustenance in the form of "tears" that take the place of mother's "milk" (with the reciprocal image, also used earlier in the text, of milk flowing from one's eyes in ways that further signal a kind of generativity to sorrow). Moreover, the transgendering that occurs here, as well as in the subtler mention of "seeds" earlier given that planting and tending fields traditionally was Cherokee women's work,[47] implicitly recalls the role of Cherokee women within the matrilineal clan system, in which membership did not depend on the conjugal logic of procreative union—passing through the mother alone—and in which adoption—an act of (re)naming that functions as a kind of birth—was a viable vector of belonging. Having a male-bodied person occupy women's role/place does not indicate, though, a disjunction in the present or a loss of tradition so much as the Cherokee possibility of moving away from the conjugally centered procreative imaginary that literalizes a dimorphic sex/gender system, opening up possibilities for gender other than the heterosexual imaginary of racial bloodedness.[48]

Driskill here suggests perhaps most forcefully that the possibility of a future for the Cherokee people, one predicated on a continued relation with the past, is dependent not so much on the unbroken possession of a given set of traits (genetic or cultural) as a capacious kind of collective memory that registers *as Cherokee experiences* the structures of feeling produced by/in diaspora. "Tears" and "milk" remain necessarily intermixed even in the moment of reunion, when possibilities thought lost are reclaimed and given voice. Testifying to the ways peoplehood remains haunted by settlement, this image of regeneration suggests how acknowledging legacies of both tradition and trauma enables a conception of Cherokee identity not tethered to heteronormative understandings of property, intimacy, and purity. In this vision the reproduction of the people can rest on bodies that bear stories and silences that await a language that can articulate them as "our history."

Perverse Indigeneity

"Beginning Cherokee" explores a kind of queer temporality in which inheritance is less a reproductive given than a kind of labor, working from and on the sensations and dynamics of everyday life not necessarily recognized as political or collective. The poem suggests that removal and, more broadly, settler intervention and assault give rise to new forms of subjectivity that remain haunted simultaneously by prior modes of Indigenous sociospatiality and the effects of U.S. policy. Driskill presents Native bodies less as the containers of generationally transmitted blood Indianness than as sites at which these histories intersect and manifest in/as the present, creating a kind of continuity-in-catastrophe that enables current experience to be articulated to and through prior practices, principles, and knowledges. Forging such connections, naming postremoval structures of feeling as Cherokee tribal memories, can be thought of as a contemporary performance of peoplehood, and rather than simply illustrating the persistence of a residual formation, this process transforms the inhabiting of the present by Cherokee pasts into an emergent formation, a kind of subjectivity and sociality that is neither a clean break from what was nor merely a perpetuation of it. However, can the kinds of sensations and translations I have been addressing be understood as sovereignty?

The term usually refers to questions of governance and the geopolitics of jurisdiction, and the very quotidian, intimate quality of the scenes featured in "Beginning Cherokee"—in houses, among family members—would conventionally lead them to be categorized as private, separate from issues germane to the functioning of a polity. As Raymond Williams argues, what dominant formations "exclude may often be seen as the personal or the private, or as the natural or even the metaphysical . . . , since what the dominant has effectively seized is indeed the ruling definition of the social" (125). The ostensibly personal, therefore, can mark forms of collectivity denied the status of politics within dominant discourses and institutions. In this

way, Driskill utilizes bodily experience to mark aspects of peoplehood refused official recognition as such while simultaneously raising
questions about the political effects of certain presumptions about
the character of personhood naturalized/literalized in settler institutions. To explore possibilities for and experiences of embodiment not
intelligible within the ideologies of U.S. Indian policy is to inquire
about the potential for Cherokee collective being beyond a settler-
regulated matrix of what constitutes "the social." Whereas "Beginning
Cherokee" charts the persistence of Cherokee identity in the shadows
of settler occupation, other texts in *Walking with Ghosts* more directly
focus on the mechanics of U.S. policy and its effort to regulate and
reorder the lives of Indigenous people(s), drawing on representations
of sensual pleasure to highlight the relation between the attempts to
normalize private life and manage/erase expressions of indigeneity. In
"Love Poems: 1838–1839" and "Back to the Blanket," Driskill explores
how recasting modes of feeling as perversion works as a key part of the
technology of settlement, positioning felt connections to the land and
to other Native people as retentions from a primitive past that need to
be renounced as the price for entry into American modernity. These
poems' insistence on reclaiming the putatively personal for the project
of envisioning peoplehood transposes the trope of haunting into a
different register, suggesting the ways Indigenous social formations
portrayed as anachronistic in state-sanctioned narratives of progress
and development live on as imperially abjected states of feeling. Such
sensations not only can be inherited, transmitted across generations,
but also can index modes of peoplehood awaiting (re)materialization.

In "Love Poems: 1838–1839," Driskill uses embodiment and desire
as a way of portraying Cherokee territoriality while highlighting the
violence of U.S. projects of dispossession and the jurisdictional logics
that animate them. Driskill creates a parallel structure in which comments by "Tennessee" and "Indian Territory" are laid out in adjacent
columns on the page, creating the effect of an overlapping conversation. The names of the interlocutors and the poem itself make clear
that the context for these articulations is the forced removal of the
Cherokees from their traditional homelands to what eventually would
become the state of Oklahoma in what has come to be known as
the Trail of Tears.[49] In response to the Cherokee development of a

written legal code and bicameral legislature over the course of the late 1810s and 1820s, including the adoption in 1827 of a constitution largely modeled on that of the United States, Georgia passed a series of laws annexing Cherokee territory to state counties, allocating the land to white settlers through lottery, and outlawing the operation of the Cherokee national government. This assertion by the state of sovereignty over Native peoples brought to a head a legal crisis that had been brewing since the 1790s—namely, whether the federal government or the states had authority over Native peoples residing within the boundaries of a given state. To resolve this conflict over the division of powers in U.S. federalism, Congress in 1830 passed the Indian Removal Act, allocating $500,000 to purchase the territory of peoples east of the Mississippi in order to relocate them to an equivalent landbase in the west, in an area that would come to be designated Indian Territory. Although the law did not give the president any additional powers, it indicated a loose consensus that the time had come to resolve the "Indian problem" in the east by engaging in a coherent, sustained campaign of dislocation, moving Indigenous nations out of the potential jurisdiction of existing states and into areas designated as territories and thus under federal control.[50] The act contained a clause specifying that removal was to be accomplished via treaties, suggesting that the systemic exile of the Cherokees and others from their homelands was to be legitimized as having been predicated entirely on Native consent rather than on imperial coercion.[51] As one might suspect, the enormous pressure put on peoples to volunteer indicated that the choice to remove was made under conditions that, in a Herculean gesture of euphemization, could be characterized as duress. In the case of the Cherokees, they repeatedly refused to sign a removal treaty, and over the course of 1835, the National Council officially rejected it on two separate occasions. Despite the clarity and consistency of the Cherokee government's repudiation of this policy, U.S. agents called a council at the former capital of the Cherokee Nation—New Echota—in December of that year, and they secured the signatures of fewer than one hundred Cherokees, none of them duly authorized as representatives of the constitutional government, to a removal treaty that was ratified by the U.S. Senate the next spring. After two years of unstinting protest, the Cherokees were rounded up by the U.S. army and forced to march from 1838 to 1839 to what eventually would become Oklahoma.[52]

"Love Poems" explores the kinds of collective subjectivity rendered unintelligible within the terms of U.S. law and the imperatives of Indian policy. Notably, while the land from and to which the Cherokees were removed are given voice here in parallel columns on opposite sides of the page, the Cherokees themselves are silent, occupying the seeming emptiness between the two. This mute absence and the visual elision of the horrors of the Trail of Tears itself in the apparently neutral blankness of the middle of the page, however, is brought into stark relief by the story told of lacerating excision and wounded arrival. The text begins by asking, "What was left behind?" From the outset absence, or lack, is depicted in terms of unfulfilled longing, the residue of a largely unacknowledged and powerfully unresolved history of brutal dislocation. The impression is heightened by Indian Territory's first line, "I know you were driven away, / taken from everything that / taught you love." If the address for the initial question is somewhat amorphous, posed to the reader as much as anyone, the introduction of "I" and "you" in the parallel statement by Indian Territory indicates a conversation in which one of the participants—the Cherokee people—is mute, depicting the absence of speech not as implied assent but as a kind of yearning and terror that defies easy representation, particularly in the language used by those who drove them away. The seeming silence of the Cherokees points to the shadows of removal, to stories and feelings that haunt official accounts. The official imperative to conceal the evidence of violation, to articulate a subjectivity ostensibly unmarked by imperial force, is reflected in Indian Territory's caveat, "I don't expect you to forget, / only to love me as well," and Tennessee amplifies this intimation of state-mandated amnesia in asking, "(Did you know they tried to / erase you, forbade me to / speak your name?)." In this way, the poem positions itself as an effort to trace the contours of the collective experience sanitized, and thereby falsified, in dominant narratives of removal.

In personifying place and the Cherokee Nation, Driskill uses the tactile sensations of embodiment and the emotional vocabulary of intimacy to explore dimensions of peoplehood that do not register in the archive of settler governance. As suggested earlier, such personification raises questions about what constitutes personhood, pushing the bounds of the literal in order to reveal how existing categories, distinctions, and relations are invested with an exclusive realness through processes of literalization—in which other possibilities for being and becoming are cast as figurative and thus without substance. To speak of polities and territory as having bodies, then, is an attempt to capture modes of being derealized in settler policy. The logic of removal and, more broadly, of acquiring territory through treaties rely on envisioning land as a thing to be exchanged either for an equivalent quantity elsewhere or for its "value" in money and/ or goods. There is no intrinsic relation to place. Put another way, the Cherokee Nation can be conceptualized as separable from any particular place. Within U.S. policy the collective Indigenous subject that consents to the expropriation of land or to wholesale dislocation is not constituted through an embeddedness in a lived geography that provides the condition of possibility for peoplehood. Rather, the voice of the polity can be treated as distinct from any specific spatiality, enacting a kind of disembodiment that is registered in the apparent absence of the Cherokees from the poem. By contrast, Driskill presents the relation between the Cherokees and their land in terms of erotic connection, refusing the homogenizing, commodifying, and literalizing legal narratives of land as fungible object.

The initial juxtaposition of the perspectives of Tennessee and Indian Territory index this nexus of affection and desire. As Indian Territory observes that removal denied the Cherokees "everything that / taught you love" Tennessee answers the question "What was left behind?": "Love formulas / written in dark syllables, / whose incantations / undulated / like our tongues." Implicit in this pairing is that "love" is what the Cherokees learned from their traditional homeland, what bound them to that place. This relation is precisely what the new home calls for, imploring the Cherokees "to love me as well" and then repeating this request as a demand in the next line—"Love me." In this context, speech is not the contractually mediated expression of the arm's length transactor but "dark syllables" laden with spiritual import that are tied to the "undulat[ion]" of "tongues," as in a kiss. As in "Beginning Cherokee," the tongue serves as a border space indicating the centrality of relation to collective Cherokee subjectivity. Voice is here physicalized as a pleasurable entwining with a lover, a connection of sensual sociality to which corporeality is crucial, but not as an innate, internalized (racial) trait.

Moreover, the phrase "our tongues" indicates that Tennessee also possesses one, representing the land as sensate and desiring. "Love" for the land appears as more than an abstract feeling, a broad appreciation for a given locale; "love" indicates a dynamic mutuality in which they are the land's as much as the land is theirs. Both Tennessee and Indian Territory are depicted as bodies, in ways that fairly explicitly sexualize Cherokee inhabitance:

My arms, muscled rivers Love the winding trails to my
you came to   belly,
each morning.   the valleys at my sternum,
         the way I slope towards you like
          promise.

Beyond merely indicating residence, these lines suggest a seduction. However, these images are not similes: the rivers are not *like* arms; the valleys are not *like* a sternum. Driskill here refuses the easy distinction of tenor and vehicle. Instead, ze invokes attraction, arousal, and gratification as a means of conveying what Native territoriality *is*. As Daniel Justice suggests in his discussion of the work of Marilou Awiakta, "This is not mere symbol or metaphor; these relationships are real and tangible."[53] In order to understand peoplehood, the poem suggests, one needs to grasp the physical immediacy and yearning that characterizes the reciprocity of place. The land is both desired and desiring, is not a thing that can be priced and traded, is a feeling entity.

Through this erotics Driskill refigures sovereignty, shifting from the idea of an exertion of juridical control over a dead quantum of space to the emotional interdependence and physical joining of lovers. The Cherokees are not the same as the land, simply an extension of it, but as envisioned here, neither is Native nationhood reducible to administrative processes, jurisdictional claims, and legal personae/ speech acts. The poem's account of the body of the people differs markedly from the conventional personifications through which the state and the corporation are given form. Emerging out of the legacy of the two bodies of the King, in which the vulnerable specificity of the monarch's flesh can be severed from the unified totality of the kingdom as represented by the ostensibly integrated wholeness of his royal form, the political sovereignty of the state is cast as a singular, unbroken entity, naturalizing national boundaries through the fiction of a self-sufficient, enclosed organic system.[54] Similarly, dating from the Supreme Court decision in *Dartmouth College v. Woodward* (1819), corporations in the United States were endowed with personhood,[55] each functioning as an autonomous agent rather than as an aggregation of interdependent persons, limiting liability but also emphasizing the emergence of modes of contractual subjectivity in which institutionally meaningful voice and volition is severed from physicality and place and in which these are understood as epiphenomenal to the grid of intelligibility of legal selfhood.

As against this vision of identities and autonomy predicated on reified insulation, Driskill presents the Cherokee people as a somos whose capacity for erotic, sensuous engagement also makes it vulnerable. As Tennessee asks at different moments, "Who comforted you / as you hugged knees to your / bruised body?"; "Who held you as you convulsed, 'My body is an open-mouthed / moan!'" This image suggests a scream of both rage and wounding, repudiating the supposed voice of consent in the Treaty of New Echota, and when combined with the image of the Cherokee people as huddled knees to chest, it strongly intimates removal as rape, especially in light of its juxtaposition with the pleasurable, sustaining sensuality of place lost with Tennessee and yet to be with Indian Territory. While further specifying the horror of exile at gunpoint, these tropes of corporeal frailty and physical trauma also provide the negative image for a kind of sovereignty for which embodiment is not merely an empty figure of territorial contiguity and the determinate boundaries of government authority. The "open-mouthed moan" is the obverse of undulating "tongues," the possibility of a kind of polity whose presence in space is predicated not on reified enclosure but instead on a dynamic openness signified by sensation. Rather than serving as an inert setting over which political agency/will is extended, the land engages with the body of the people in dynamic ways that are central to their existence as such. Indian Territory asks, "Who gave your body / back to you?" suggesting that the "body" of the people—or the body that *is* peoplehood—does not exist in isolation from a connection to place but instead is (re)constituted through it. Without that symbiotic relation, Cherokee collective selfhood remains wounded and broken, "shriek[ing]" in its very "bones." In contrast to the abstracting, decontextualized voice of the (fraudulent) treaty and the numb, rigid outline of (settler-)state jurisdiction, Native nationhood appears in the poem as affective, dynamic, interdependent, and energized with the excitement of erotic promise.

In addition to refusing the privatizing ideologies by which sexuality is severed from sovereignty, Driskill's intertwining of the two casts Indigenous relations to land as a kind of perverse, criminalized desire, implicitly expanding the critique of heteronormativity to include the imperial process by which U.S. law divorces Native collectivity from place and translates Native territory as an inert, saleable thing. Within the normalizing parameters of bourgeois domesticity, sensual pleasure and enduring emotional bonds are contained inside the boundaries of the conjugally defined household, defining intimacy through isolation. The expansive attraction and gratification between people and place that Driskill envisions transects this distinction between public and private domains, between the governmental and the familial. In addition to proliferating the spaces and functions of desire, the poem suggests that a collective Cherokee sense of space itself is predicated on a sensuous engagement with the specificity of the land they occupy. Tennessee observes what the Cherokees have left behind:

> Rows of corn
> ears swaying slighting on
> their stalks;
> pumpkins thick with flesh;
> tomatoes swollen with juice,
> so acidic
> they could blister your lips.

The "flesh[liness]" of the pumpkins and the tomatoes fairly tumescent with "juice," ready to burst on waiting "lips," further concretizes the "love" articulated at the outset, casting agricultural labor as foreplay building toward climax with the land offering itself to the people in joyous abandon. As in "Beginning Cherokee," a (trans)gendering occurs here through the reference to the work of cultivation, possibly offering the often feminized sense of (erotic) vulnerability as an alternative to the often masculinist vision of sovereignty as self-enclosed. In this context Indian Territory's insistence at the end of the poem that "This is home now," "You are home. / You are home" reads as something other than the interiorizing topos of the single-family household. "Home" here marks a collective connection to territory usually encompassed by the term *sovereignty*, but without the sense of ownership or the implicit invocation of a nuclear imaginary in which the supposed biological imperative behind this formation of kinship and residency helps naturalize the shape of (settler-)statehood.

Desire infuses landholding, suggesting that the seizure of Cherokee space functions as part of a broader effort to insert Native peoples into dominant Euramerican modes of homemaking. The poem plays with the linkage between these two forms of domestication—to bring under the authority of the U.S. government (as in domestic policy) and to incorporate into (the model of) the bourgeois household. Driskill indicates the relay between these two kinds of regulation in Tennessee's comment "(After they seized you / they told me not to touch / anyone again.)" Through this image of prohibited "touch," the poem depicts removal as not simply a struggle over space, a quantity of land, but one over how land tenure will be conceptualized and lived. Portraying the expropriation of territory as part of a management of Indigenous erotics helps highlight the ways the expansion of U.S. jurisdiction relies on other, seemingly nonpolitical discourses to translate Native sociality and spatiality into terms consistent with U.S. governance. More than analogizing settler processes of legalized dispossession to the pathologizing discipline exercised on attractions deemed aberrant, Driskill's fusion of the two narrates the Trail of Tears and other state-orchestrated projects of settlement as predicated on a disavowal of Indigenous modes of "love"—Native geographies in which neither the people nor the land can be understood as disembodied juridical abstractions and in which affect, sensation, and intimacy cannot be insulated/isolated within privatized modular units in ways consistent with liberal political economy and the logics of the United States.[56]

What emerges, then, is a queer critique of removal in which the erotic provides a matrix through which to manifest Native placemaking as feeling in ways purposively rendered unintelligible within U.S. administrative discourses. After Indian Territory's assertion that the Cherokees are "home," the poem ends with Tennessee's final response to the repeated question "What was left behind?": "your body's / silhouette / scratched forever into me." Refusing the objectifying implications of "what" (as opposed to *who*), the poem's last lines point to the memory of the body as a trace of that which has been lost through removal, as a fleshly kind of haunting that signals what remains unspoken and unspeakable within the jurisdictional imaginary of settlement. The tactile and emotional dynamics of embodiment provide a resource for trying to capture the violence and violation of collective exile, while they also provide a means for articulating the experience of indigeneity that the U.S. government seeks to foreclose—an experience neither forgotten nor erased but etched into the body of the land.

If "Love Poems: 1838–1839" seeks to envision sovereignty as a collective erotics of place, "Back to the Blanket" highlights how Native individuals' sense of their bodies is shaped by histories of settler invasion, and it highlights how a reanimation of practices deemed primitive within U.S. government ideologies makes possible the recuperation of forms of collective Indigenous self-understanding targeted for erasure.[57] The title is the denigrating phrase officials used to describe Native students returning from government-run boarding schools in the late nineteenth and early twentieth centuries who failed to keep up the practices and principles of "civilization" taught them, instead choosing to return to the extant ways of their peoples.[58] It referred to men who ceased to wear "citizen's clothes," depicting Native dress as essentially nothing more than a "blanket." The text, then, is framed as an extension of the struggle over what will and should constitute contemporary Native identities, their relation to the past, and the role of the state in trying to manage and reorder Indigenous subjectivities. It begins by observing, "I am learning to take each body part back," presenting the poem's project as a kind of reverse dissection. Its aim is to reintegrate that which has been severed and mutilated due to settler interests and imperatives. This visceral image of corporeal rending casts the dispossession of, and effort to detribalize, Indigenous peoples as a process of tearing apart Native bodies.

In contrast to the image of covering a perverse nakedness implied by the poem's title phrase, Driskill presents the work of enlightenment as a brutalizing, maiming assault on vulnerable flesh. The narrator notes, "They locked us in, away, cut our hair, / burned / our tongues until they were covered with landscapes of stars." These examples are drawn from the boarding school experience and speak to the ways ostensible training for U.S. citizenship was envisioned as a license to batter Native children into terrorized submission. The reference to punishment administered in such institutions to students who continued to speak Native languages ("burned / our tongues") also echoes the representation in "Beginning Cherokee" of the kinds of silence that arise in the absence of a way of naming experiences as Native or of words through which to realize them as tribal memories. The image further portrays U.S. policy as seeking to produce a wounded internality (the tongue as the vehicle of communication and connection—as in a kiss) in which Native individuals are denied a sense of indigeneity by being isolated from each other even while copresent in the same place. Driskill here explores the implications of the dictum by Colonel Richard Henry Pratt, the architect of the boarding school program and founder of the Carlisle Institute, that education should be used to "kill the Indian" and "save the man." The violence unleashed in this murderous intent is justified through appeal to a disembodied deity:

> We were forced to kneel before men who were not God, told to
> work
> that we might be saved from a cursed destiny made manifest
> with each breath.
> They prayed for the starvation of songs created between our
> skins.

"Men" set themselves up as "God" (or "vengeful gods," as in an earlier line) so as to validate as destiny the wounding discipline they enforce. The line structure emphasizes the toll this program takes on Native people, the words "work," "breath," and "skins" pointing to the ways the expansionist ideology of manifest destiny is realized through its mobilization of and inscription on Indian bodies. "Scars" are borne as traces of larger settler designs on Indigenous "landscapes."

The first half of the poem portrays how the body is made an object of torture—cruelty done up as a pedagogy of progress. The individual body and its modes of experience and sensation function as a metonym for Native nationality—images of the violated body standing in for violations of Native sovereignty. Yet even while gesturing toward this connection, Driskill refuses a too easy substitution of the one for the other. Treating the relation this way would seem to leave the concept of Native collectivity unaffected by its conjunction with physicality—replicating the logics of Euramerican jurisdiction, whose power of abstraction appears in Driskill's work as a tool to inflict and erase Native trauma rather than as a means of healing Native nations. What is entailed, then, in the body/sovereignty nexus here? How does Driskill use the depiction of campaigns of expropriation and assimilation in terms of the wounding of bodies to (re)think the contours and content of Native identities and self-representation?

The second line announces that "tak[ing] each body part back" involves "rebeautify[ing] the space between our skin," simultaneously suggesting an internal geography within the body, the shared embodiment of peoplehood ("our"), and the distance between persons/lovers. The poem's account of subjectivity lies in the intersection of these positions. The "I" emerges out of and exists within this matrix, and rather than merely providing a figure for a political entity, the experience of somatically enmeshed selfhood is itself partially constituted through the dialectical interplay of personhood and peoplehood, the ways the former is embedded in the collectivity of the latter and the ways political collectivity is formed out of the shared perceptions/sensations of tribal members. Thus, detribalization works through the assault on Indigenous bodies, the effort to tear Indianness from them, and the larger project of detribalization registers as a (collection of) bodily event(s) for Indigenous people. More than a discourse of institutional recognition, over which the settler-state exerts metapolitical authority, sovereignty appears in the poem as an interwoven network of modes of embodiment through which indigeneity is given form.

In the second half of the poem, the "skin" on and through which imperial regulation is enacted shifts from a wounded surface to a vehicle of self-determination. However, rather than staging self-determination as insulation—as a move from tortured object to isolated, autonomous subject (either the kind of Euramerican body politic "Love Poems" refuses or the individual bearer of blood substance envisioned as the Cherokee national body)—Driskill roots individual and tribal subjectivity and the relay between them in affectability, a capacity for engagement. "Tak[ing] each body part back" is not an individual project but one that occurs in the context of a "we" that has suffered imperial assault. This process of reclamation neither makes the "I" into a metonym for the "we" nor portrays the "we" in terms of an impenetrable bounded coherence, often associated with normative Euramerican selfhood. Instead, the collectivity of "we" is (re)formed through pleasure: "Come here. Let me kiss your wounds away"; "Your body does not smell like candles or scrubbing powder / or centuries of terror we could not lock out." While still distinguishing between inside and outside, these lines highlight the ways the permeability of the body, its capacity for sensation, is in fact crucial to the formation of a decolonized subjectivity. If "wounds" indicates systemic assault, the healing power of "kiss" comes not from sealing off the body but from opening it to erotic possibility, to a kind of contact different from "scar[ring]" violence. The body's boundaries are porous, invaded by settler "terror" but also available to others as scent. Although subjection to the settler regime may leave permanent traces, the Indigenous body Driskill describes remains capable of a different relationship to the world, its "smell" inciting desire rather than discipline, in which the skin is the marker of life-sustaining and life-affirming contact rather than a surface to be lacerated/branded. Subjectivity arises from a recognition of interdependence in which the borders of selfhood are envisioned as a transfer point within necessary sensual flows of touch, taste, and smell. Thus, self-determination inheres less in isolation than in an ongoing negotiation of the dimensions of embodied experience in which identity is predicated on a simultaneous acknowledgment of autonomy, the distinctness and integrity of "I" and "you," and of necessary relation, a "we" (re)created through the potential for vulnerability and penetration by others' impact on the senses.

Driskill connects this potentially existential portrait of the conditions of personhood back to the specific histories and territorialities of Native people in the United States in refunctioning the phrase used to dismiss them as naked savages. The poem observes, "We go back to the blanket. You grasp my hips, handfulls of earth, / my heart softened by the rub of your hands." The "blanket" imagined here is laid out on the ground, designating a place for sexual pleasure, and this shift profoundly alters the meaning of "back," from historical regression to reorientation in space. Driskill refigures the absence of citizens' clothes not as a lack of civilization, a return to a more primitive state, but as a nakedness that leaves them open to each other and to a contemporary "we" (re)constituted through felt connection to other people and the earth. The erotics of touch slides seamlessly into an erotics of occupancy where taking the body back through passionate sensation is part and parcel of reconnecting oneself to one's homeland. As against an understanding of sovereignty as possession and a view of tradition as either distinct from the properly privatized intimacy of the domestic sphere or locked within it, the poem presents the experience of peoplehood as necessarily embodied and sensuous, suggesting that it neither functions like an atomized individual nor can be taken simply as an aggregation of such individuals.

Peoplehood inheres in the circulation of people's shared experiences of intimacy with each other and with the space they occupy. This connection is lived not as a formal political identification, as a thing distinct from romantic or familial attachment, but as an erotics, as inseparable from the feeling of selfhood through the senses.

> Let me wrap you in ceremony, a giveaway of straining muscle,
>   the soft whispered
> stories of our flesh. Let me suck the sickness out with this old-
>   time medicine.

> Make love to me until I forget their stale language.
> From your feet on up you are beautiful. You weave splendor with
>   simple tools.

Troping on the justification of detribalization as introducing Indians to progress, Driskill's depiction of lovemaking as "simple tools" highlights the ways the remembrance and maintenance of peoplehood in the face of the ongoing interventions of settler governance requires returning to and nurturing available knowledges. The "stories of our flesh" are such a place to start, locating the "flesh" as a site in which "stories" are indelibly enmeshed in at least three complementary ways: the skin provides a tactile pneumonic—a touchstone—through which to activate memory; histories are registered not just in an abstract cognition but in the muscles themselves; and erotic play, the straining and sucking to which the lines flirtatiously point, produces its own stories, an embodied relation to other persons and place that can serve as ground for feeling toward a version of peoplehood not superintended by settler norms. Notably, the "flesh" here is "our[s]," generating a sense of collectivity, of conjoined but not necessarily conjugal union, through the "ceremony" of sex or, in Beth Brant's terms, "physical prayer" (61).

Unlike in the narrative of state policy, in which this nakedness is a return to a precultural state of nature, this act of "love" to "rebeautify the space between our skin" occurs in the context, and signals an awareness, of the assault on Native nations. The naming of the joyful surrender to physical sensation as "go[ing] back to the blanket" signifies on and through the legacy of U.S. imperialism, embracing abjection while refusing to experience it as defilement. Rather than trying to rework Native subjectivity into a recognizably respectable form, Driskill claims the very bodiliness supposed to be transcended, individualized, covered, civilized, and privatized as the condition of entry into citizenship as the vehicle for reconnecting with indigeneity. The last line teases, seduces, and commands: "Feed me the traditions your body would not forget." The scarred body remains haunted by legacies of sensation awaiting reactivation. "Traditions" are borne in the body, including its pleasures; sex is cast as an expression of tradition; and an eroticized corporeality serves as sustenance, marking the necessary permeability and vulnerability of the body, as well as its connection with others, and indicating these as principles that Native people must not "forget."

Given that Driskill is male bodied and that this last line offers a fellatio image, the poem could be read as providing a rather queer view of tradition. Read slightly differently, however, the poem seeks to queer peoplehood by focalizing the transection of the skin through which empire is imprinted on Indigenous persons as also the means of reclaiming a sense of collective selfhood. As against the effort to separate sovereignty from sexuality in order to normalize Native nationality, to cast it as a close-enough approximation of U.S. legal forms, the poem takes sensuality as a starting place for reclaiming peoplehood, for reconnecting to older knowledges, to place, and to each other while using this life-renewing process to heal the wounds inflicted in the name of civilization. Instead of offering a disembodied notion of belonging that could parallel that of the state's, a bureaucratized account of citizenship as the holding of an administrative status, Driskill presents connection among the people as forged in and through the flesh, a kind of shared corporeality that is pleasurable rather than scarring and that emphasizes mutuality and persistent relation over indelible properties, such as blood quantum. Or put another way, tradition is woven into bodily experience as a vehicle for satisfying human need and realizing interdependence (as "stories," food, and lovemaking), a means of connecting with others in sustained and sustaining ways, as opposed to segregating such erotics into the space of the bedroom as part of a purely reproductive teleology. Driskill suggests that the performance of peoplehood in the present, particularly given the lacerating wounding and introjection of terror and self-hatred that has characterized state projects for managing the continuing presence of Indians, requires a means of re(-)membering community capable of crossing the boundaries imposed by U.S. policy—between the past and the present and the people and the land and among the people themselves.

The Space of History

In developing the notion of a Sovereign Erotic, Driskill explores how Native people's experience of their own bodies is shaped in fundamental ways by the continuing legacies of settler colonialism, further suggesting that these sensations index the persistence of Native identifications effaced in dominant discourses. Such contemporary states of feeling provide means for conceptualizing how formations of peoplehood persist. Erotic contact can serve as a way of marking modes of indigeneity—knowledges, relations to place, and forms of collectivity—that defy state narratives and survive despite being targeted for eradication. The scene of romantic intimacy, however, also can be haunted by the shadows of settlement, recalling historical trauma in addition to providing possibilities for healing, but Driskill suggests that such recollection actually is crucial in "the ongoing process of decolonization."[59] As against the effort to declare an end to the history of imperial displacement, suggesting it has been superseded by the redemptive recognition of Native self-determination, unofficial kinds of memory continue to understand the present as continuous with past violence, that feeling of relation itself testifying to both a sense of Indigenous belonging and its ongoing endangerment. As in the emphasis in "Beginning Cherokee" on the need to find a way of naming the quotidian sensations and silences of displacement as Native experiences, "Map of the Americas" foregrounds how contemporary sexuality is inhabited by settler–Indigenous conflict, the body bearing impressions of peoplehood that exceed the apparent insularity of erotic encounter and that recast the meaning of that event. In contrast to seeing the meeting of lovers in terms of privatized domesticity or the heteroconjugal reproduction of Indianness, the poem positions the space of intimacy as a site in which residues of the past give rise to a new political cartography of the present moment. Linking the most private of moments to the ongoing dynamics of conquest provides a dialectic through which to indicate how geopolitical struggle becomes encoded and remembered as feeling while also using such feeling as a way of leveraging the logics and narratives through which the assault on Native peoples is naturalized, euphemized, erased, and displaced. Such embodied inheritance opens the possibility for realizing alternatives to settler structures, for making the residual into the emergent in ways that engage and incorporate the legacy of settler violence.

The opening of the poem gestures toward a profound desire that desire itself could be the vehicle for escaping the past. The narrator insists: "I wish when we touch / we could transcend history in / double helixes of dark and light / on wings we build ourselves" (9). The pairing of "touch" and "transcend" connects the tactile to the possibility of a kind of experience that could break the participants free from their immanence in geographies of the everyday, pushing them toward a state more closely approximating the divine (as further suggested by the angelic picture of people with "wings"). Referencing DNA in the image of "double helixes" suggests conception, and the fact that these twining strands are "dark and light" intimates racial difference. The interweaving of this miscegenation imagery with the fantasy of transcendence implicitly locates this race/reproduction matrix within the contemporary push toward postracial promise in which the horrors of the past supposedly can be abandoned in an embrace (here, literally) of the ideal of a color-blind society. Notably, the achievement of this goal is correlated with death—becoming angels. A procreative erotics appears here somewhat ironically as a movement toward a future that simultaneously is the end of "history." The intimate event of "touch" erases difference in the creation of an (impossible) sameness, a perfect equivalence that provides the eschatological aim for a liberal sort of national amnesia.[60]

Both identifying with and mocking this notion of romantic couplehood as an avenue to freedom from history, the text quickly shifts away from the internal life—the wishes—of the couple to focus on the ground that supports them. Whipping back from the imagined heights achieved on the "wings" of love, Driskill directs the reader to the territory beneath their feet: "But this land grows volcanic / with the smoldering hum of bones" (9). The land itself seems to revolt against this intimate union or, at least, to respond by bringing forth the remains of those killed in the invasion of Native space.[61] In contrast to the futurity projected by the DNA imagery, the "bones" will not stay buried, making present a past steeped in violence.

> All that's left
> of men who watched beloveds
> torn apart by rifles
> Grandmothers singing back
> lost families
> Children who didn't live
> long enough to cradle a lover
> arms around waist
> lips gently skimming nape
> legs twined together
> like a river cane basket (9)

The mention of "beloveds," "grandmothers," and "children" refracts the genetic figure at the heart of the first stanza into a generational narrative, one that pushes against the insulated intimacy of the opening. Doing so highlights the ways the desired transcendence depends on erasing the process by which a future has been denied to these other "families," the history of the decimation of their intimacies. Moreover, this eruption into the present as a tangible presence defies the reproductive temporality of DNA, in which the past remains solely as a material trace contained in/as the substance of bodies to be accessed through procreative union. Unlike the dream of romance as an angelic flight away from the killing fields of settler occupation, the sensual "twin[ing]" of those lost is portrayed as deeply connected to that place—"like a river cane basket." Such baskets are a densely symbolic figure of Cherokee cultural practices, shifting relations to their environment, skills passed across generations, and the potential for weaving together disparate materials into a coherent whole.[62] Here, it signals the enmeshment of erotic life within a sense of shared history, daily practice, community, and deep knowledge of the space of dwelling, as against the vision of intimacy as total separation from everyone and everything else.

Although the poem juxtaposes the ephemerality of the "wish" for escape with the brutal materiality of corpses and a land made molten in their "volcanic" reemergence, Driskill suggests that the awareness of this history, the rending of networks of love and care as well as of the bodies that it encompasses, is already woven into the speaker's sense of selfhood. Ze lives this past as part of hir physical and emotional life, engagement with hir lover calling forth what might be called a somatic memory: "Sometimes I look at you / and choke back sobs knowing / you are here / because so many of my people are not" (9).[63] Hir body involuntarily recalls the dead, the "chok[ing]" and spasmming making corporeal their continued presence. They do not remain buried, safely sealed into a then fully sequestered from now. Instead, murdered "families" erupt into the present as bodily shocks. To be part of the "people" is to have one's personal identity routed through a sensory experience of a collective past that is shot through with horror. As Veena Das suggests, "The simultaneity of events at the level of phenomenal time that are far apart in physical time make the whole of the past simultaneously available" (97). A communal "know-ing" of violence is lived as individual trauma, a haunting that seizes someone and breaks the rhythm of breath itself, and this response is triggered by the ways the legacy of settlement suddenly coalesces around the space occupied by the speaker's lover.[64] The juxtaposition of "here" and "not" suggests less a simple opposition than a palimpsest in which the lover's body simultaneously signifies in two dialectically entwined ways: as a synecdoche for the process of conquest that has made and continues to make possible the "you's" occupation of (once) Indigenous space; and as a metonym for the lives and futures lost in securing settler dwelling. This moment echoes the role of silence in "Beginning Cherokee," in that those "families" not present serve as the shadows surrounding settlement and the lover's presence while, recip-rocally, the bodily response of the narrator indicates that ze remains haunted by them in ways that suggest how the past (re)animates in-digeneity in/as the present. Thus, "touch" cannot "transcend" the past, because the Native narrator's senses root hir in the place of hir people and continue to resonate with the force of their planned erasure, while the lover bears (and in many ways is) the legacy of displacement.

Through this embedding of history in the flesh, Driskill suggests that Indigenous feeling—the mesh of emotive and sensory experience I have described as *erotics*—can push against the boundaries inscribed by settlement. Or perhaps more to the point, indigeneity itself can refer to the ways certain bodies in the present bear the impression of—are haunted by—histories of collective occupancy (peoplehood) and the objectifications and dislocations within settler imperialism. Those histories are lived as an affective nexus that helps give shape to Native bodies and consciousness, becoming realized as sensation in ways that challenge the literalization of settlement. Integrating the poem's title phrase, ze declares to hir lover, "Look: my body curled and asleep / becomes a map of the Americas" (9), and the next page typographically approximates that shape, with the speaker compar-ing parts of hirself to various features of the landscape ("My chest the plains / and hills of this land My spine / the continental divide" [10]). Portraying the narrator's body as a map creates an ambiguous relation between hir physical form and the hemisphere. The appear-ance of "a map of the Americas" within the poem indexes the history of conquest that helped produce the very conventions of spatial representation that Driskill both invokes and confounds.[65] To make a Native body a map contrasts a located specificity/subjectivity with the ostensibly objective, encompassing perspective from high above that tends to characterize post-Enlightenment cartographic imaginaries (a maneuver that repeats in a different register the move from "wings" to "land" discussed earlier), and this juxtaposition also implicitly puts into relief the kinds of abstraction, homogenization, and totalization that the imagined view from the heavens can enable—an orientation that potentially effaces the sensations, relations, and knowledges that arise from and constitute an embedded/embodied connection to place. The issue of how the gaze of the nonnative will be directed and framed explicitly is at stake in this moment in the poem; the imperative "Look" is spoken to the "you." The command suggests that the conjunction of the speaker's body with the Americas "becomes" a way of apprehending both differently, opening possibilities for taking the broad and potentially genericizing icon of "the Americas" and endowing it with a new set of meanings by filtering it through the erotics of memory.

Driskill refigures the existing relay between Indian bodies and lands in settler ideologies, using it to stage an alternative way of looking at both.[66] Having already traced the ways the speaker's sense of himself in the present is shaped by persistent feelings of collective belonging (including trauma) and the ways the lover's body occupies the space of those murdered and displaced to secure its presence, the text positions the intimate event of their "touch" as an example of a broader pattern. The body of the "I" emerges out of and bears the impressions of the history of Indigenous occupancy and dispossession, and this feeling of peoplehood frames the text's jump to a hemispheric scale. Instead of approaching Indigenous personhood through a settler imaginary (as a point on the map—a localized example of its objectifying logic of jurisdiction), it takes an Indigenous experience of subjectivity as the basis for extrapolation. The body of the "I" is already immersed within a mapping of peoplehood, or put another way, the Native speaker's sensation of selfhood (emotional and physical) arises out of an already present sociopolitical field and collective memory of its (ongoing) violation, erasure, and dislocation. The overview provided by the map, then, offers less a unified totality than an accumulation of geographies of communal inhabitance, loss, and survival, opening the possibility for solidarity by positing a resonance between experiences in/of "this land" and in/of other territories—all of which "grow volcanic / with the smoldering hum of bones."

By undoing the series of complexly interlocking dichotomies that help efface ongoing histories of Native occupancy and settler invasion (intimacy versus violence, local versus international, past versus present, personal versus political, individual versus collective), the text seeks to refigure the real, opening the potential for knowing differently by rooting that process in an erotics that crosses the boundaries/identities generated by these binaries.

> When your hands travel
> across my hemispheres
> know these lands
> have been invaded before
> and though I may quiver
> from your touch
> there is still a war.
>
> (11)

Bodies and continents appear inextricable here. The confusion/conflation of apparently disparate phenomena operating at discrepant scales works to alter the "you's" (lover's/reader's) understanding of both. Seeing the sensual touch between the narrator and hir lover as a moment in the continuing conquest of the Americas changes the meaning of a seemingly personal event, amplifying and making explicit the political and historical dynamics already contained within it. Simultaneously, characterizing the seizure of territory and the extension of nonnative jurisdiction over it as invasion/violation of Native bodies—as rape—highlights the ways the abstraction of the map is realized through assault, which is experienced and remembered as communal trauma.[67]

Although Driskill does not deny the possibility of pleasure amid this persistent pain ("I may quiver"), ze emphasizes that such moments of what may appear as transcendence are embedded in an ongoing

"war," despite settler efforts to declare the violence as merely history—
the past of conquest supposedly having given way to the peaceful
wholeness represented by the map. The narrator observes:

> It is not without fear
> and memories awash in blood
> that I allow you to slip between
> my borders
> rest in the warm valleys
> of my sovereign body.
> (11)

The lover's "touch" recalls collective "memories" that can only be
understood through the kinds of political and territorial identification associated with narratives of invasion and conquest but usually
absented from depictions of intimacy. Moreover, the significance of
such "borders" and of sovereignty itself shifts through their association with the body. Unlike in legal geographies of the state—in which
land is a thing, national citizenship overrides tribal belonging, and
desire must be privatized—peoplehood is here made somatic, lived as
a structure of feeling in which sensation and affect are not separable
from self-determination, and vice versa.

The text pushes the nonnative "you" toward engaging with forms
of Native experience in which sovereignty does not occupy a space
separate from that of intimacy and embodiment, in which it is lived
viscerally as part of individual selfhood. References to Native lands
indicate the ways felt connection to them persists despite the apparent distance of time and geographies of state-orchestrated dislocation.
The final line reenacts the text's critical juxtaposition between scales
and spheres, which has characterized its effort to disjoint both the
privatizing insulation of intimacy and the imperial abstraction of state
jurisdiction and knowledge: "I walk out of genocide to touch you"
(11). As opposed to the image of transcendent interracial union with
which the poem opens, it closes by forcefully resituating the "you"
and the moment of physical contact within a topography of death,
implicitly making present the "families" whose decimation shapes the
"here" in which these lovers meet. Rather than offering a reproductive

futurity that enables a break from the past, this ending indicates that for the narrator the erotics of pleasure cannot be divorced from the unfinished project of conquest and ongoing war in which hir people and other Indigenous peoples of the Americas continue to be seen as expendable.

Driskill's poetry consistently refuses the notion that Native identity can be understood as an unbroken succession that subsists in the inheritance of insulated bodily substance. As against the idea of a heteroreproductive transmission of authentic Indianness, ze explores the ways Indigenous bodies bear a complicated history in which trauma and tradition are inextricably intertwined. The intimate stories and sensations of ongoing life under settler rule provide an invaluable archive that neither conforms to dominant notions of normality and civilization nor provides a respectable Native nationality fit for liberal expectations—one protected/legitimated through a heteronormative framework. Driskill's work returns to scenes and legacies of settlement in which the aim of imperial violence is to produce forms of privatization that fracture indigeneity by disavowing and disciplining quotidian modes of feeling and association that are crucial to the maintenance of Native sociality, spatiality, and memory. The states of feeling ze chronicles gesture toward the ways the past remains available as possibility in the present, inhabiting forms of everyday corporeality and eroticism as collective memory even if not necessarily recognized or valued as such. Rather than bracketing the trauma of removal and forced assimilation in a conception of tradition as an endangered (reproductive) purity, *Walking with Ghosts* develops a hauntology in which bodily experiences of violation and pleasure together register the interwoven strands of Native histories. In this way, the text seeks to index and make available forms of personal and communal reanimation that privilege interdependence, vulnerability, and love over a vision of insulated autonomy that can collude in the pathologizing, abstracting, and isolating erasures performed by settler narratives of selfhood and of proper Native subjectivity.

<

2

>

Landscapes of Desire

Melancholy, Memory, and Fantasy in
Deborah Miranda's *The Zen of La Llorona*

H OW DOES ONE TESTIFY TO THE EXISTENCE OF A PEOPLE
that has been disappeared?[1] How does one negotiate a melancholic relation with that which is not actually gone but is still foreclosed? In many ways these questions are the same, just framed in
different idioms, and at their intersection or overlap lies the dynamics
of Native survivance made invisible in the process of pursuing federal recognition. Chapter 1 addresses how the lives of contemporary
Native people and the self-representations of Native peoples remain
haunted by ongoing forms of settler-induced trauma and the related
attempt to disavow modes of Indigenous collectivity and experience.
In a similar vein, Indian policy can be said to be haunted by those
peoples whose continued existence it has denied by declaring them
extinct. The attempt by such groups to achieve federal acknowledgment partakes a bit of the uncanny, the return of those presumed dead.
The movement to be recognized as a people by the United States
draws on and exceeds the possibilities of juridically intelligible testimony. Staged as a positive performance of presence in which a "tribe"
must document various kinds of continuity over time, the procedures
of acknowledgment remain shadowed by aspects of shared Indigenous
experience for which there is no administratively valorized category,
as well as by state-sanctioned (and often state-orchestrated) violence
through which Native continuities have been shattered. In what ways
are grief and loss (in)admissible, and what sort of evidence do such
states of feeling provide? What kind of account could capture them?

< 93 >

To what mode(s) of collective being might they point, and what relation could they bear to the structure and adjudication of the acknowledgment process?

In 1978, the Bureau of Indian Affairs (BIA) adopted a set of procedures to recognize Native peoples as tribes for the purposes of inclusion within the regulations and protections of federal Indian law.[2]
As Mark Edwin Miller has argued, this administrative development
resulted from the BIA's seeking to reinsert itself into the acknowledgment process that had largely passed to the courts and to Congress,
with federally unrecognized peoples (such as the Penobscot and Passamaquoddy Indians of Maine) suing over late eighteenth- and early
nineteenth-century takings of land and winning and other peoples
who had been "terminated" in the 1950s and 1960s—or had been
mysteriously dropped from federal roles over the previous century—
successfully petitioning Congress for reacknowledgment.[3] The BIA
put in place a series of criteria that groups needed to demonstrate
before federal recognition could be extended to them. As amended
in 1994, these requirements include that petitioners prove the following: "a group has been identified as an American Indian entity on a
substantially continuous basis since 1900"; "a predominant portion . . .
comprises a distinct community and has existed as a community from
historical times until the present"; "maintenance of their political influence and authority over its members."[4] The attendant picture of
collective Native identity is that of a coherent, integrated political
unit whose existence as such has at no time since Euro-contact (or at
least since 1900) been disrupted in any significant way by the vicissitudes of nonnative territorial encroachment, institutionalized and
popular racisms, economic exigency, or government-initiated projects
of displacement/detribalization. This portrait has, as one might suspect, more to do with the ideologies and bureaucratic needs of the
BIA than with the actual circumstances, socialities, and histories of
petitioning peoples. "BAR's [Bureau of Acknowledgment and Recognition] function depends on its authority to categorize, classify, legitimate, and exclude as an arm of the policy-making machinery of U.S.
Indian policy," and "a group seeking recognition must render itself
visible to the BIA."[5] That effort to construct an administratively intelligible model of Indianness mandates that a people recast themselves

in the image of "a mythic Indian," a vision itself generated within settler discourses, so that they favorably can be measured against this fictitious ideal.[6] As Dan Gunter suggests, "We may—and should—assume that a group of Indian persons who identify themselves as belonging to a tribe have some authentic sense of tribal identity; but to obtain tribal status, they must demonstrate instead that they have a European sense of tribal identity" (108). That "technology of tribalism," in Gunter's terms, refashions indigeneity in ways that not only dislocate it from Native peoples' narrations and understandings of themselves but also seek to create a more manageable homogeneity in which Indigenous selfhood takes on a predictable, positivist shape—one that can be recognized without either challenging liberal notions of what constitutes a polity or engaging with the continuing legacy and force of settler imperialism.

Having a way to acknowledge peoples as tribes promises redemption from the bad, monocultural past while also constructing those who fail to achieve that status as wannabees whose claims can now be displaced in righteous indignation at their pretensions.[7] Yet the narrative of unbroken continuity built into the recognition requirements privileges government records and accounts by nonnatives in ways that elide the damage wrought by state actions, as well as their traumatic effects.[8] In implementing the guidelines, "the government makes no allowance for its past culpability," "not account[ing] for 230 years of state-sponsored violence."[9] More than rendering irrelevant evidence of the destructive effects of settler policy, the process demands the effacement of resulting disruptions in Native life, since any perceived break in the performance and transmission of tribal identity will be construed as a fatal failure to meet the criteria for recognition. Rather than interpreting gaps in the archival record of tribal presence as incompetency on the part of government agents, a temporary response to particular political and economic pressures, or a strategy of concealment by (a) Native people to protect themselves from nonnative discrimination and violence, the Federal Acknowledgment Process (FAP) presumes an Indian will-to-disappearance, a voluntary cessation of tribal relations.

Within the logic of this administratively invented and imposed subjectivity, silence equals a desire to abandon peoplehood, not only putting the burden of proof on petitioners to demonstrate their historically unflagging identification with a particular (stereotypically formulated) model of Indianness but also actively denying public representation of the devastating impact of ongoing settler occupation on Indigenous sociospatiality. To mourn is to court the possibility of a ruling that the entity for which acknowledgment is sought is, in fact, gone. In this way, the recognition process does more than set the terms and dimensions of the particular legal status of "Indian tribe"; it regulates acceptable forms of collective affect and ways of narrating the relation between the past and the present, foreclosing the possibility of working through trauma by demanding as a condition of politically meaningful voice that a people speak as if there has been no systemic program of invasion and cultural genocide, as if pride in an unbroken, unchanging continuity were the only mode of contemporary Indigenous subjectivity.[10] As Marc Nichanian suggests of the Armenian catastrophe, "What disintegrates forever, for generations, is having been at one time . . . the target of a will to annihilation. . . . What disintegrates is the interdiction of mourning. When justice redoubles the crime, it does nothing other than to announce this interdiction" (116). In similar ways to the Cherokee statutes discussed in chapter 1, these regulations demand an identification with the terms of settler governance that have produced the very wounding to which these official forms of recognition/belonging appear as a response.

These limits do not mean, though, that a people can simply choose to forego the acknowledgment process. Recognition allows a "federal tribe the power to exercise sovereignty and participate in federal Indian programs, emanating from the BIA and the Indian Health Service[,] . . . affect[ing] issues as diverse as Indian self-government, health care, Native American cultural repatriation, Indian gaming, and public lands held by the National Park Service and other federal agencies."[11] In this way, it is something that in Gayatri Spivak's terms, one "cannot not want," since in many senses it provides the condition for a people's possible continuing existence given the legal and property structures of the United States.[12] To testify to grief, then, is to risk administrative consignment to oblivion as inauthentic pretenders to tribal identity, with the very present danger of being denied access to political and economic resources due to a negative judgment on recognition—a bureaucratic assessment that translates rather directly to increased loss and deprivation.[13]

In her work, particularly *The Zen of La Llorona*, Deborah Miranda explores the disavowed space of mourning, or more precisely of melancholy, to illustrate forms of Indigenous subjectivity that evade or exceed the parameters of federal recognition. Rather than seeking to challenge the terms or dynamics of that process, the text maps the boundaries of the tribal ontology that FAP helps institute and enforce. More specifically, the text suggests that forms of collective Indigenous identity survive in/as the seemingly individual experiences of Native people. Miranda represents this undocumentable connection to indigeneity, its transmission and retention within states of feeling, through the representation of her emotional life as an internal landscape. The kinds of connection to place registered and required in federal acknowledgment appear here as a collection of emotional responses conveyed through tropes associated with spatiality and territory (such as "container," "soil," and maps, as later discussed). Like in Driskill's work, Miranda suggests a kind of haunting, one that puts into question the relation between the figurative and the literal and thereby foregrounds the politics of what gets to function as real and what is consigned to metaphor. Yet Miranda's text offers a more elliptical sense of her relation to forms of sociality, spatiality, and subjectivity that precede/exceed the violence of settlement. Here, haunting is an unshakeable feeling that one's quotidian sensations are shaped by ongoing legacies of struggles over history, place, and peoplehood for which there are no apparent referents. In this vein, Miranda's poetry uses figures of absence and landscape to represent both the reality effects of discourses of Native disappearance and the ways seemingly individual states of feeling index a collective history of survival-in-erasure.

Apparently ephemeral sentiments and sensations are presented as kinds of Native memory—of peoplehood, as well as imperial assaults on it—that cannot officially serve as evidence for enduring tribal belonging and claims. In "Felt Theory," Dian Million underscores the need for Native women to "creat[e] new language for communities to address the real multilayered facets of their histories and concerns by insisting on the inclusion of our lived experience, rich with emotional knowledges" in ways that "underline again the importance of felt experiences as community knowledges" (54), further noting that the forms taken by such language do "not always 'translate' into any direct political statement" (64).[14] The internal landscape envisioned in Miranda's poetry functions as an effort to articulate such "community knowledges" while also indicating how Native peoplehood inhabits and shapes individual experience, such that the latter cannot be understood as ontologically separate from or logically prior to belonging to Indigenous community. The text suggests that the kinds of individual sensations/experiences Miranda charts can be indicative of forms of collective identity, history, and placemaking disavowed in accounts by government agents and nonnative experts, and in this way, its vision of internality also differs from the heteronormative notion of an enclosed, innate, racial Indianness that Driskill's work critiques. The image of a topography contained within her but out of which her sense of self is constituted serves as a rejoinder to the declaration that a people has become extinct, an assertion that has had particular force with respect to Native peoples in central California, including the Esselen Nation to which Miranda belongs.[15] Depicting her emotional life as landscape becomes a way of implicitly revising the demand for continuity in federal regulations, suggesting the presence of modes of Indigenous persistence illegible as such within the documentary paradigm of Indian policy. More than using images of land and spatiality to capture emotional states, Miranda's poetry seeks to forge a language for indicating a direct relationship between how Native selfhood is lived and the kinds of enduring connection to place that serve as a crucial aspect of Native peoplehood. The text, then, raises questions about the capacity of settler policy and logics to literalize their mappings and their criteria for defining Native identity—to install them as the basis for determining what is real as opposed to imagined, invented, or fake. The depiction of feelings as space in Miranda's poetry works to reveal how Indigenous identity persists within and despite the dislocations and elisions of settlement.

Her emphasis on the significance of states of feeling as a medium for survivance, even though they do not seem "direct[ly] political," further allows her to position fantasy and pleasure as means for preserving and rejuvenating peoplehood. In "Dildos, Hummingbirds, and Driving Her Crazy," she argues, "We cannot be allowed to *see* indigenous women in all their erotic glory without also *seeing* and acknowledging all that has been done to make those women—their bodies and cultures—extinct" (145).[16] Reciprocally, to "*see* indigenous women in all their erotic glory" involves understanding how eroticism also works as a vehicle for sustaining and realizing the forms of indigeneity declared extinct. Fantasy can serve as a way of naming the relation between emotional life and engagement in the world, the effort to reconnect the internal landscape of Indigenous selfhood to the still-existing external landscape that has been remapped through settler ideology and policy. As against an understanding of the real in which settler frameworks form the grid of intelligibility (literal versus figurative, documentable versus invented), fantasy and desire provide a way for Miranda to address the connection between feeling, embodiment, and action, the dialectic through which the ephemeral becomes material and vice versa, thereby opening up alternative possibilities for what may count as real. Moreover, Miranda addresses how settler logics of property are instantiated and naturalized in everyday ways through heteronormative structures of marriage and conjugal homemaking. In her depiction of her relationships with her Native female lovers, she explores how an Indigenous erotics can provide avenues for feelings that have been denied the status of the real, thereby enacting survivance. These structures of feeling do not substitute for that which is made possible by federal acknowledgment but instead generate new modes of Indigenous subjectivity, sociality, and spatiality in the wake of the supposed literality of extinction—a process of creating newness from existing materials, seemingly out of nowhere, that Miranda marks through the figure of birth.

Melancholic Mappings

Miranda's work highlights the ways loss structures her and her people's sense of identity as Native. "After Colonization," a piece from her first collection, *Indian Cartography*, captures this ongoing history of erasure:[17]

the land divided her loyalties between native
and foreigner, then and now. We fell
between the cracks like a laugh cut short,
or a sob
. . . .
. . . Whether by rape
or love, violence or choice, we are survival
made flesh. We walk through life unshielded

and find boundaries, treaties, reservations
that don't speak our names.
. . . .
. . . We look
for our own land to claim . . .
   (82)

This passage helps illustrate the kinds of memory that constitute indigeneity, a relation developed more fully in *The Zen of La Llorona*.
From a conventional psychoanalytic perspective, it conveys a melancholic sensibility in its retention of that which is gone. Unlike mourning, which involves a gradual transfer of affect away from an object
that is no longer present, melancholy continues to invest libidinal
energy in the object, thereby denying its absence and absorbing it
into the psyche.[18] This passage presents "land" as that object, alienated due to colonization but never fully mourned (the arrested "sob")
and internalized as an animating force in the present ("survival made
flesh"). Within this dichotomized understanding of grief, melancholy
expresses an unhealthy attachment that blocks personal progress by
denying the reality of loss, directing one's emotional life inward and
thus cutting oneself off from engagement with the world as it actually
is. Such an account seems to shape the procedures for tribal acknowledgment, enjoining groups who cannot document their continuous
presence as a collectivity to give up their pretentions to an indigeneity that is gone and the maintenance of which is, in the face of the
documentary actuality of its disappearance, at best a failure to adapt
to the facts of contemporary life and at worst a pernicious invention
that undermines the claims of real tribes.

As against this pathologizing narrative, scholars have turned to melancholy as a way of conceptualizing the formation of subjectivity itself. Perhaps the most influential version of this argument appears in Judith Butler's *The Psychic Life of Power*. There, she suggests that the internalization that supposedly marks the distinction between melancholia and mourning depends on the image of the self as a kind of space that in fact only emerges in the wake of melancholic attachment. "According to the narrative of melancholia that Freud provides, the ego is said to 'turn back upon itself' once love fails to find its object and instead takes itself as not only an object of love, but of aggression and hate as well." Yet "it is unclear that this ego can exist prior to its melancholia," such that "only by turning back on itself does the ego acquire the status of a perceptual object." Through that turn "the ego itself is produced as a *psychic object*," and "the very articulation of this psychic space, sometimes figured as 'internal,' depends on this melancholic turn" (168). There is no ego that precedes melancholia, but rather, loss is the condition of possibility for giving form to the ego, the lost object shaping the contours of what will be experienced as psychic interiority. In this sense, individual subjectivity functions less as a self-confident, fully self-present entity that can then participate in social life than as a metalepsis—not the cause of consciousness but an effect of an ongoing process of attempting to approximate a lost/impossible object.

Such a model offers a particularly useful way of approaching modes of racialization and the dynamics of interpellation into racial identity. As Anne Cheng argues, melancholy provides a framework for tracing how racial types neither are exterior to consciousness and the experience of self nor simply can be falsified, to be replaced by a more authentic account of selfhood and social life: "The melancholic activities of racialization imply that assimilation may not only be a consequence of the dominant demand for sameness but also intimately related to identity itself. In melancholia, assimilation (acting like an internalized other) is a *fait accompli*, integral to ego formation for the dominant and the minority, except that with the latter such doubling is seen as something false (acting like someone you're *not*)" (125).[19] Assimilation operates less as a call to the minority to perform properly the identity of the dominant than through the production of an image/ideal of identity that all inhabitants of the state have always-already lost, in the sense of having to internalize it as an object that shapes ego formation as national subjects. Those persons typed as nonwhite are cast as occupying a more vexed relation to that ideal, suspended as they are between the call to be generic citizens and the demand that they embody the nation's own melancholic investments. "Racialization in America may be said to operate through the institutional process of producing a dominant, standard, white national ideal, which is sustained by the exclusion-yet-retention of racialized others ... retroactively positing the racial others as always Other and lost to the heart of the nation" (10). Such objectification occurs through "the figuring of the injured/injurious 'minority' through either denigration or fetishistic attachment" (99–100). For people of color the approximation of racial typology provides the measure of authentic selfhood (what one really is) even as the imperative toward assimilation regenerates those types as the truth of nonwhite subjectivity while still insisting that they be abandoned.[20]

Looking back to the passage from Miranda's "After Colonization," one can see the aforementioned dynamics thematized in ways that contest the logics of authentication that would translate ongoing Indigenous grief as a sign of an unhealthy, or simply false, attachment to a Native identity that is gone. To have fallen "between the cracks" is to lack the state-generated markers of tribal identity that can stand as proof of it. To be without "boundaries, treaties, reservations" is to fail to approximate a particular administratively conjured ideal/fiction of Indianness and, thus, to be left "unshielded," insecure, vulnerable. The absence of such evidence generates a desire for that status, for a kind of "claim" that can underwrite the bureaucratic recognition of a collective "name." In measuring themselves against the ideal produced in Indian policy, the object called a "tribe," the "we" suggests the role played by that objectification within U.S. Indian policy. The existence of "treaties" and "reservations" indicates a form of official acknowledgment whereby indigeneity is excluded yet retained, narrating Euramerican occupation as if it were an equitable division of land while localizing Native claims to carefully bounded plots that can then provide an alibi for nonnative claims to everywhere else. Miranda has a melancholic relation to the ideal of the tribe as a demonstrable set of traits that will authenticate Native-ness, but that ideal itself is constituted through the melancholic dynamics of federal policy, which preserves a (stereotyped) image of "tribe" in order to disavow the ongoing violence of settlement. Miranda's self-identification as Native, then, is routed through the impossibility of conforming to an ideal that works to render unspeakable the very histories of imperial erasure ("the cracks") that make that status unachievable for many Native people(s).

From this perspective tribal identity operates as the object of a melancholic relation in which the (ever-present potential) loss of it shapes the contours of contemporary Native being. However, this formulation overlooks a kind of fundamental attachment and mode of grief that exceeds the terms of Cheng's analysis. The phrase "we are survival / made flesh" points toward a process of internalization in which the state participates but that exceeds its logics. The bodies of the "we" are composed out of the "survival" of something that precedes the point when "the land divided." "After Colonization" casts the dislocation caused by settler occupation not as the disappearance of the "we" but its transposition into another form, their very bodies taking shape around a collective connection to place that persists as a constitutive feature of Indigenous personhood.[21] If in one sense the "we" searches for "land to claim" in order to make it properly a tribe, having internalized the state-generated ideal of Indianness, in another sense that process of searching is animated by a residual impression of place-based peoplehood that is lived as a formative feature of daily experience in the flesh even in the absence of state-authorized identification.[22]

This envisioning of selfhood as an internal(ized) landscape is articulated even more explicitly in *The Zen of La Llorona*. In "After San Quentin," a piece that traces her father's life and situates it within the broader history of imperial violence in California, Miranda closes by turning to the comfort he receives from tending his garden. She observes,

This piece of earth is the one place
you don't fight with walls;
the only peace handed down to you.

> All this time, I thought we had nothing
> —no land, no prayers, no language.
> I was wrong.
> We are the containers
> that hold our colonized history.
> I turn and stir the past
> for my hungry soil.
> (17)

Land, prayers, and language would stand as proof of indigeneity, and their absence seems to signify its disappearance. Miranda, however, refutes this apparent dissolve into "nothing[ness]," instead asserting a kind of contemporary presence that bespeaks an "our" who has survived. The passage envisions the forms of sociality and spatiality that are "thought" to index Native identity as having been converted into the shape of embodiment itself, depicting corporeality as a preservative enclosure for what otherwise would be narrated as merely having vanished. The dimensionality of a "piece of earth" morphs into a structure of feeling—"peace"—that stands in for the generational transmission of land ("handed down"). The enforced severing of Esselen and Chumash connections to their traditional territories, and the kinds of collectivity practiced there and engendered by that relation to place, produce a melancholic incorporation in which that loss provides the contours of individual selfhood—each person operating as a seemingly distinct "container" for a shared past of occupancy and dispossession. Moreover, the phrase "colonized history" implies both a history of being colonized and a colonization of history. This double sense suggests that the feeling of being "nothing" is the result of a program of imperial elision that works to (re)define what can count as an Indigenous mode of being. That erasure narrates the relation between the present and the past either as a (stereotyped) continuity, generating an endless process of "*measurement and approximation*," which "*renders impossible the experience of being secure within such a fiction*" or as a complete break, an unrecuperable loss.[23] The "past" that Miranda "stir[s]" is one within her, the figure of "soil" intimating that the "my" comes to exist in this form only as an aftereffect of the ongoing legacy of settler displacement.[24]

The history of dispossession and erasure to which Miranda points, represented as shaping her interiority, extends beyond a generic narrative of Native dislocation, gesturing toward specific forms of imperial elision for Indigenous peoples in California.[25] European jurisdiction first was extended in what is now California starting in 1769, with the onset of Spanish settlement. Over a little more than fifty years, Spanish forces constructed twenty-one missions extending largely up the coast. They became central to the imperial occupation of the territory, providing a site to which to send Native insurgents, a vehicle for training Native people (particularly children) in the ways of "civilization," a carceral space of detention through which to compel the acquiescence of Native men to work by holding their families, and, most important, a source of cheap labor for producing goods used by missionaries, soldiers, and settlers as well as commodities traded abroad. Though Spanish authority never extended far inland, despite escalating efforts to tame the "wild" tribes to the east and vast expansions in the land claimed by the missions themselves, the presence of these institutions severely disrupted the lifeways of peoples near them, especially due to the taking of territory and the massive population loss resulting from exposure to European disease (as much as a 95 percent decline on the coast), as well as the horrifically unhealthy living conditions for Native people at the missions themselves. The process of secularizing the missions began in 1834 and continued unevenly for approximately a decade, and though it was justified as the return of territory to the Indians, the lands claimed by the missions were distributed to Californios (nonnative Mexican citizens), many of whom were able to amass significant holdings. Often living in Native towns called *rancherías*, not uncommonly on their traditional lands, peoples formerly associated with the missions quite rarely received title to them, instead inhabiting areas officially held by nonnatives. There were some legal protections for such rancherías under Mexican law, but for the most part, residents depended on the largesse of rancho owners, for whom they worked. Service as cheap, substantively enslaved labor at the missions shifted into similar activity on ranchos.

The annexation of California by the United States in 1846 did not improve this situation. The Treaty of Guadalupe-Hidalgo (1848), which ended the Mexican-American War and placed what had been Alta

California under U.S. jurisdiction, promised American citizenship to former Mexican nationals and a recognition of the property they held under Mexico. With respect to Indian policy, however, the federal government took the absence of treaties with Native peoples in California under Spain and Mexico to mean that they had no legal status as distinct geopolitical entities, unlike those groups to the east who functioned as "domestic dependent nations."[26] Due to a legislative error in which Congress allocated funding for treaty commissioners rather than for Indian agents, three men were sent out to negotiate treaties with peoples throughout the state (in practice this did not include the "wild" tribes in the interior). Eighteen treaties were signed at the end of 1851 and the beginning of 1852, notable for their failure to specify lands that were being ceded and instead simply quit-claiming all land rights in exchange for reservations (often with other peoples and not in their traditional territories), but California representatives lobbied against adoption, leaving the treaties unratified and hidden until accidentally discovered in the early twentieth century. Moreover, the California Land Act, passed by Congress in 1851, subjected all prewar land titles to inspection, and while it included protection for Native rancherías, that provision was not heeded, leaving Native villages to be lost due to the failure of rancho owners to prove their claims or to withstand the financial burden of defending their claims against squatters. Reservations were created periodically, usually by executive order, from the 1850s onward. However, they often were underprovisioned, located in unsustainable areas, and later abandoned by residents (often due to lack of supplies) or officially dissolved due to settler pressure—a pattern that did not abate until the early twentieth century (although many peoples recognized and allocated land during that period would then be "terminated" by the federal government in the 1950s, California being one of the primary sites for enacting this defunding and detribalizing policy).

This broader dynamic of dislocation, exploitation, and erasure was intensified for peoples in the Monterey area. Not only was Monterey the military capital of the province, but San Carlos, the nearest mission, was the central headquarters for the mission system in California. Although some former inhabitants of San Carlos (the mission with which Esselen people were most closely associated) did receive land grants as part of secularization, they do not appear to have been included in the process of treaty making, suggesting even less federal cognizance of their presence, and those grants appear to have also been overlooked in the Land Law adjudication process, which the U.S. Supreme Court in *Botiller v. Dominguez* (1889) found to be mandatory in recognizing prewar Native land claims in California. At least one communal grant, known as La Ranchería, remained occupied until at least 1883, when it was noted and described as endangered in Helen Hunt Jackson and Abbot Kinney's report on the situation of "the Mission Indians of California." The report and its aftereffects are telling, however, inasmuch as public interest tended to focus on Native peoples in the south (near Los Angeles and San Diego), to whom the phrase "mission Indians" most regularly referred, and when resources were made available to Indians in the state, such as executive order reservations, they usually were directed to this group, leaving peoples like the Esselen with little support for maintaining their already meager and precarious landbase.

The most egregious and directly damaging example of this neglect and erasure came in 1927 due to the actions of Lafayette A. Dorrington, the superintendent of the Sacramento Indian Agency. Congress had ordered the Bureau of Indian Affairs to report on the needs and potential for purchasing additional land for Indians in California, a directive communicated to Dorrington by E. B. Meritt, the assistant commissioner of Indian affairs. In his report Dorrington concludes that numerous "tribes and bands" of Indians (including the Esselen), which he acknowledges as lacking legally recognized territory, do not in fact need to have land purchased for them. This conclusion was reached without actual site visits to these communities by anyone in his office, and the effect of his determination was the de facto official detribalization of about 135 Native groups in the state. Both before and after this ruling that denied the possibility for them (including the coastal groups near Monterey) to make collective claims to place, individual Esselens were registered with the BIA as "Carmel Mission Indians" or "Costanoans," including from 1928 to 1932, 1948 to 1955, and 1968 to 1972. Those registered as such officially were recognized as descendants of a people who had possessed valid land claims, since they (along with other government-registered Indians in California) received per capita cash awards from the Indian Claims Commission due to the failure of the government to honor the promises of the unratified treaties of 1851–52. Such an acceptance of documentable individual lineal inheritance and of a federal debt to those persons' ancestors is not equivalent to recognition that those persons continue to exist as distinct political collectivities—peoples—like the Esselen Nation.[27] Such acknowledgment has been further hindered by the anthropologist Alfred Kroeber's infamous declaration in 1925 that Esselen and Coastanoan peoples, if they ever existed as distinct entities, are "extinct so far as all practical purposes are concerned."[28] Academic knowledge production, therefore, has colluded with federal malfeasance to generate a seemingly authoritative archive of Esselen disappearance, in which individual inheritance of Indian blood substance appears as the only modality of indigeneity cognizable within U.S. policy.

In presenting individual subjectivity as coalescing out of Native experiences made unintelligible as such within administrative discourses, Miranda clearly responds to this history, and her figuration of her psychological and emotional life as an internal landscape also challenges some of the political and ontological presuppositions that provide the frame for psychoanalytic accounts of melancholy. The critics I have noted take the ego less as a pregiven entity than as itself the result of a melancholic process that can be described only in retrospect as internalization, a process that actually provides the contours for the very entity into which the lost object supposedly is incorporated, but they continue to locate this dynamic within a generic narrative of personal maturation that preserves the individual as the site/subject of melancholy. While seeking to depathologize melancholia and to expand what can be conceived of as being lost, they do not present it as itself a historically and sociopolitically located phenomenon that helps inaugurate a particular kind of (liberal) subject. In other words, rather than implicitly understanding melancholia and the affects and forms of identification it engenders as occurring in all times and places, just with different contents, can it be rethought as produced by a particular kind of social structure? What is the political ecology/ geography that gives rise to the processes Cheng, for example, describes, and how might those processes be predicated on prior modes of loss, such as the imposition of settler jurisdictional logics and their ways of narrating/authenticating/effacing indigeneity?

Cheng's account foregrounds how people of color are denied full inclusion within the nation. The forms of "racial grief" she chronicles emerge out of the ways "the economic, material, and philosophical advances of the nation [specifically the United States] are built on a series of legalized exclusions" (10), and she situates the possibility for acknowledging such grief within "the hypothetical space of citizenship" (192), which provides the potential for identification and interdependencies not founded on the (re)production of racial types. In some sense the ultimate wounding here is the inability to participate in U.S. nationhood as a full subject; the imperative to perform/approximate nonwhite racial identity generates the fundamental insecurity of being caught between authenticity and assimilation—each impossible ideals that are always-already lost.

What makes U.S. citizenship the normative horizon? Put another way, how does presuming citizenship as that horizon lead to the foreclosure of modes of collectivity that could provide another model of subjectivity? In exploring how people of color are called on to be representatives of the racial group to which they ostensibly belong, and critiquing the "documentary impulse" that this demand enacts, Cheng posits an "inherent gap between individual and collectivity" (155). Extrapolating beyond racialization per se, she explains a sense of belonging to a collective in the following terms: "The individual fantasmatically invests in a representation of him/herself through communal relations, and it is that fantasy that confirms, retroactively, those relations" (157). Even as her account repeatedly suggests that the sensation of identity arrives after the fact as an effect of forms of melancholic identification, the individual appears as the ontological predicate for thinking communal relations; they are a psychic projection/pathway that the individual precedes and into which she enters. The analytical distinction "between individual and collectivity" seems to replicate the terms of liberal citizenship, in which belonging to the nation trumps any other kind of communal enfolding while simultaneously being characterized as a status occupied by persons rather than groups.[29] In other words, recognition as a subject of the state provides the context in which individuality can signify as such, as against other kinds of social relations. Although Cheng challenges the logic of possessive individualism and its positing of the cohesion, insularity, and boundaries of a selfhood structured as a kind of property, her account individualizes melancholia as an internal dynamic of the psyche in ways that smuggle back in the very sort of a priori enclosure that she elsewhere disputes.[30]

In the absence of liberal citizenship as a framing mode of belonging, what other accounts of selfhood become possible? Flipping that question over, how does the imposition of citizenship on Indigenous peoples work to generate an image of isolated individuality—a "container" in Miranda's terms—in ways that seek both to fracture communal relations that compete with the political geography of the settler-state and to repudiate that loss?[31] At one point in *The Psychic Life of Power*, Butler notes that "the state cultivates melancholia" (191), and though she is addressing the rerouting of officially sanctioned norms into consciousness "as the ideality of conscience," the kinds of individuality posited by Cheng (and Butler, as well) might be understood as the mark of ideologies of citizenship, an aftereffect constituted through the ongoing assault on competing modes of collectivity. If as Butler suggests, "forms of social power emerge that regulate what losses will and will not be grieved" (183), we can think of the positing of a foundational opposition between individual and collectivity within the frame of settler citizenship as a way of regulating Native grief, as a trace of an Indigenous melancholy produced by the attempt to elide forms of place-based peoplehood that precede and exceed the terms of state belonging.[32] Thus, while contesting "the assumption of a pure sovereign subject" (15), Cheng's argument and those premised on a model of individuality whose contours are shaped by the juridical category of citizen implicitly reinstitute the sovereignty of the settler-state as the precondition for conceptualizing subjectivity.[33]

Without assuming the primacy of the individual as the one who has a melancholic identification, melancholy can name the affective and experiential effects of a process of individualization that seeks to dismantle and erase collective Native relations to their homelands. As Mishuana Goeman asks in "Notes toward a Native Feminism's Spatial Practice," "How do we uproot settler maps that drive our everyday materiality and realities?" (169). Miranda's attribution of dimensionality to her emotional life (including its figuration as a landscape—a "soil" she can "stir"), as well as her representation of her body as the corporealization of her people's history ("survival made flesh," "a container"), articulates a Native kind of melancholic internalization. The image of land serves less as a way of figuring individual psychic dispositions than as a means of indicating how a contemporary structure of feeling marks the persistence of modes of indigeneity that do not fit the (documentary) ideal of state-endorsed tribalism.[34]

In "The Place Where Grief and Rage Live," she explores how her own emotional dynamics bespeak less a personal(ized) sense of loss than her embeddedness in a history of expropriation. While the poem's name suggests a figurative locale in which negative affect resides, its initial lines indicate that this "place" emerges out of a legacy of imperial assault:

> It's big, that space.
> Measure it in years
> instead of inches—
> four decades high,
> one memory wide,
> five centuries deep.
> Multiply by
> time lost to find
> the total area.
> Grief and Rage
> live down there
> as punishment
>   (48)

"Five centuries" serves as a familiar trope of the initiation of Euroconquest, especially when read in light of the earlier depiction of Indigenous peoples as "containers" for a "colonized history" and the text's linkage of its title figure—La Llorona—to the Spanish invasion of Mexico (which I will address in the next section). Here, the reference is both allusive and elusive, signaling something less like a fully conscious awareness of the connection than like the most inchoate of intimations, an unnamed impression that adheres to the notion that "according to the melancholic, 'I have lost nothing.'"[35] The "space" in which "Grief and Rage / live" is formed out of the "deep" inheritance of settler presence and dislocation. Yet that "space" appears as if it simply functions as background for the violent and disruptive emotions that inhabit it, implying that part of what has been "lost" is the role of "time"—of history—in creating the "area" of individual(ized) consciousness that is treated as self-evident.

Even as Grief and Rage are brought to the fore as the central problem with which the narrator must grapple, the poem insinuates the metalepsis on which that effort depends. Managing these destructive feelings by locking them "down there" within the narrator treats them as the cause of interpersonal damage, rather than as an effect of centuries of settler occupation and the various modes of alienation that generate the "space" of the speaker's subjectivity. The construction of the psyche as a "place" draws attention to the fact, in Butler's terms, "that melancholy is precisely what interiorizes the psyche through such topographical tropes." The spatiality attributed to the psyche is an "effect of melancholia," emphasizing an apparent "loss of the social world"—"the substitution of psychic parts and antagonisms for external relations among social actors." If the representation of individual consciousness as a topography marks a "lost or withdrawn sociality" in which "the ego thus becomes a 'polity,'" what happens when that sociality is itself a polity's relation to the land?[36] In this vein, Miranda's account of psychic "place" suggests less a way of concretizing individual emotion than an exploration of how her grief and rage function as the trace of the foreclosure of Indigenous geopolitics. Individual interiority appears here not opposed to Native collectivity but rather composed out of its disavowed elements that have been "lost" under settler rule ("five centuries deep").

Topographical tropes in Miranda's work, then, function less as generic figures for states of feeling than as ways of situating such affect within an Indigenous ontology of loss, in which a blocked relation to place comes to serve as the predicate for seemingly individual experiences of emotion and embodiment. For example, the poem portrays Grief and Rage as independent entities who keep threatening to escape the internal enclosure of the psyche and to run rampant in the external world. Miranda asks,

How do we tell
our loved ones,
warn of the violence
Rage might commit
when laughed at?
What if there's no room

for Grief's wails of anguish,
the painful, slow stories?
   (49)

This personification of them as agents driven by inexplicable forms
of shame and "anguish" parallels the personification of political and
historical processes as a clearly demarcated "space" of selfhood. That
vision cordons off feeling as a kind of individual property instead
of examining how a conception of Native subjectivity as resolutely
atomized relies on closing off "room" in which to acknowledge "painful, slow stories" of dispossession and detribalization. Put another way,
the history of displacement is collective (indicated in the passage by
"we" and "our"), but its effects are narrated and thus end up being experienced, as individual, creating a kind of isolated/isolating personhood through the denial of "room" for the expression and transmission
of prior forms of Native sociality.

Saying the poem personifies Grief and Rage implies that it metaphorically endows them with characteristics that properly belong to
persons. I am suggesting, however, that Miranda's text undoes the
distinction between the figurative and the literal by investigating how
mappings of the real, such as the self-evident enclosure of individual consciousness, depend on the elision—or treatment as merely
figurative—of other structures of being that contest the obviousness
of the geopolitics of settlement. What conception of personhood un-
derwrites the personification of Grief and Rage? And what makes
that conception the real against which to register the metaphoricity of
personification?[37] In what ways is the individuality of subjectivity, the
"space" of the psyche, itself an effect of a personification that has been
ideologically and institutionally installed as the real, the ground, the
literal? In their influential retheorization of psychoanalytic principles,

Nicholas Abraham and Maria Torok also characterize melancholy in topographical terms. They describe it, however, as an effort to block a particular "topographical shift" in the psyche, to freeze it in place, by creating an intrapsychic "crypt" through which the lost object is incorporated into the psyche yet preserved in a "separate and concealed existence"—"a whole world of unconscious fantasy" that "has its own topography" (125–30). Risking the danger of treating the figures of territory too literally, I want to investigate what happens if we understand Miranda's melancholy as the creation of an internal topography in response to the Esselen people's violent dislocation from their traditional topography, as well as the erasure of that ongoing violence in the declaration by officials and experts that they have gone extinct. According to Abraham and Torok, melancholy's pathological character is revealed by the fact that it "implement[s] literally something that has only figurative meaning" (126), blocking mourning by denying that the lost object remains *only* as metaphor. The preservation of the lost object as "its own topography" within the psyche constitutes a relation of "*antimetaphor*"—"the active destruction of representation" (132). From this perspective Miranda's representation of herself as a "container" that holds the "soil" of her people's homeland is a denial of reality, a failure to fully acknowledge the undeniable fact of its loss. To truly grieve would be to recognize and accept the absence of indigeneity in the present, of a collectivity organized around a relation to place.[38] If one starts by treating Miranda's depiction of the "place" of her emotional life as "five centuries deep" as descriptive fact, that seemingly inappropriate literalization, the supposed failure to understand that the retention of Indigenous topography in the psyche is *really* figurative, opens the possibility for addressing how sociospatial formations are preserved in and through fantasy. The experience of individuality as its own discrete "space" can itself mark the effects of imposing a logic of possessive individualism—the reality of social life under liberal settler rule—while the structures of feeling designated as internal within this frame might be interpreted as the trace of Indigenous occupancies and ontologies that have been assaulted and effaced.

The text develops the idea of an interior psychic landscape that registers a felt sense of connection to territory, a connection that has been made unreal due to the repeated disavowal of its existence by government agents and settler experts. Lynda Hart notes that for many historians "memories are either 'fact' or 'fiction,' and the space between the two borders on the psychotic." She cautions, "It is imperative to remember Lacan's famous formula that 'reality is a fantasy-construction which enables us to mask the Real,'" adding that the "feeling of 'unreality' . . . [is] an artful reconstruction of the survivor's *present,* a set of coping mechanisms or survival strategies however 'psychotic' they may appear" that provide "a way to function with the 'reality' of the dominant order" (177). Through the incorporation of the geography of (prior) Indigenous landedness and the history of settler displacement into individual subjectivity, Miranda illustrates how indigeneity survives as a structure of feeling despite its potential failure to meet state criteria for determining *tribal* facts.

In this way, the persistent emergence of "we" and "our" in Miranda's text at moments when she seems to be addressing the particularity of her own emotions and psychological dispositions indicates less an aggregation of individuals' experiences than that the ontological privileging of the individual within liberal political economy remains haunted by prior modes of Indigenous collectivity that function differently. In *Talkin' Up to the White Woman,* Aileen Moreton-Robinson suggests that Australian Aboriginal writing evidences "how bodies are enacted and experienced in very different ways depending on the cultural and historical position of different subjects," adding that "in Indigenous cultural domains relationality means that one experiences the self as part of others and that others are part of the self" (15–16). Miranda's poetry suggests that a sensation of "we"-ness is transmitted from one generation to the next. In "After San Quentin," the "peace" her father gets from the "piece of earth" he tends is "handed down," a trace of belonging to a once-landed "we" who appear now to have/be "nothing" (17), and in "The Place Where Grief and Rage Live," the "space" they inhabit is presented in terms of inheritance:

Grief and Rage live in the lining
of your womb,
clotted walls

of your artery,
unleashed cells growing
into your children's lungs
  (49)

Fusing reproductive imagery with that of cancer ("unleashed cells growing"), the passage envisions the children's interiority as composed of the legacy of the "five centuries deep" history of colonization, a melancholic despair that appears here as formative of personhood itself (resonating with the earlier imagery of the "container"). As opposed to a notion of the reproductive passage of Indian substance—of blood quantum—the text emphasizes the construction of individual internality out of a past and set of sociospatial relations that have been disavowed, derealized—made into "nothing"—as a result of settler narratives and policy. What initially may appear as individual fantasy, a delusional (and thus also fake) literalization of a disappeared past, instead comes to mark a residual formation in which the "we" of a people inhabits the "I" of liberal personhood, distending its contours by preserving the topography of indigeneity despite the ways nonnative accounts and mappings have sought to delegitimize that retention as merely figurative.

For Butler the construction of selfhood through the melancholic internalization of a "lost or withdrawn sociality" means that the ego functions as a kind of "polity," but Miranda's text literalizes that proposition, exploring how the Esselen polity in particular persists within her experience of her own subjectivity. The "we" is not composed of a collection of I's, each of whom, in Cheng's terms, "fantasmatically invest" in an imagined set of "communal relations" (157). Rather, a prior "we," dislocated, repudiated, and erased within settler formulations of the real, provides the substance of the Native I. We see, then, the retention of prior modes of collective place-based *being* lost within settler regimes of the real but preserved within forms of Indigenous experience characterized as metaphor or fantasy because they institutionally are denied the status of literal claims to land. In *Frames of War,* Butler argues, "The state both produces and presupposes certain operations of power that work primarily through establishing a set of 'ontological givens'" (149), among which can be included "specific ontologies of the subject" based on "the idea of personhood as individualism" (3, 5).[39] To understand the figurations of landscape as an internal topography in Miranda's text requires marking the "ontological givens" that structure existing accounts of melancholy, which echo those of settler citizenship in their assumption of a primary individualism. Within that perspective, indigeneity appears as a readily documentable exception rather than as a distinct (set of) ontology(/ies) rendered unintelligible—made *lost*—within the categories of U.S. law and officially sanctioned histories.

The (Dis)location of Home

How are such "ontologies of the subject" realized in daily life, and precisely how do such quotidian relations enact the larger dynamics of settlement? The answers can be found in Miranda's representation of the ways heteropatriarchal household formation is ordered around the logics of possession animating the broader project of imperial occupation. *The Zen of La Llorona* begins with an origin narrative that provides the conceptual template for the text's movement between seemingly incommensurate scales—the geopolitics of conquest and the sphere of domestic intimacy. The preface, "The Legend(s) of the Weeping Woman," starts with the following: "*For Indians, mestizos, and Chicanos of the Conquest, she is La Llorona, an Indian woman claimed by a Spaniard as part of his reward for furthering the colonization of North America*" (1). From the outset Miranda merges the Euro-effort to control Native peoples and places with the patriarchal claiming of women, presenting the latter as a crucial vector in the broader project of colonization.[40] More than offering a generic story of the interdependence of territorial and sexual forms of possession, women's bodies both symbolizing and extending a property right in the land, the text quickly indicates the mythic status of this particular tale.[41] It notes that the Indian woman's "real name may have been Maria, Marina, or even Malinche" (1), thus invoking La Malinche, Hernán Cortés's translator and a central figure of the Spanish invasion of what would become Mexico who throughout the twentieth century came to serve in various political incarnations within Mexican and Chicano nationalism as a symbol for both the betrayal of Native peoples by one of their own and the birth of New World *mestizaje.*[42] This reference clearly extends beyond the scope of Esselen history, or even the Euro-occupation of California, and it seems to situate the text within the tradition of Chicana efforts to grapple with the conventions surrounding the portrayal of La Malinche so as to highlight forms of masculinism and heterosexism within Chicano communities and politics while also opening room for writing women in as historical agents.

Yet Miranda's version of the story brackets Malinche's supposed treason and her putative role as mother to the Mexican "race." Rather, this emplotment focuses on Cortés's betrayal of her for unknown reasons, her retaliatory murder of the children she had with him, and her subsequent existence as "*a ghost who haunts river banks and lonely places after dark,*" wailing for her lost children. Their murder is "*the Spaniard's true victory,*" having "*transformed her into a destroyer like himself*" (1), and it functions as an allegory of "the violence and domination" that characterize the nexus of "colonization and patriarchy" and the fate of "anyone seeking power in a patriarchal system" (3).[43] As against a genealogical imagination predicated on blood (the Hispano-Indio mestizo body giving rise to cultural/national *mestizaje*), Miranda re-makes this mythic tale as paradigmatic of the ways dominant Euro-modes of family and homemaking not only replicate in miniature the dynamics of colonialism writ large but serve as the crucible for generating unliveable kinds of subjectivity that further the decimation and disappearance of Indigenous peoples—"passing on that twisted religion of devastation to her children and every dwindling generation that follows" (3). To observe that "these poems exist because my ancestors survived" (4), therefore, suggests less the procreative transmission of Indian blood substance than an inherited capacity to maintain other ways of being that thwart the imperial project, which itself is partially realized through the isolating effects of the nuclear family form as it divorces persons from peoples and molds them into destroyers.

Why, though, would the text locate La Malinche as origin? Doesn't doing so further obscure the past and continuing presence of the Esselen people, folding it into a Chicano/a mytho-history that threatens to reinforce rather than contest the charge of having invented a connection to indigeneity that cannot possibly qualify as worthy of political recognition? Miranda seems to compound this problem by fusing the historical person of Maria/Marina with the folk figure of La Llorona.[44] The preface gives these maneuvers an additional twist by noting, "My grandmother, Marquesa, told my father and his brothers the story of La Llorona in a walnut orchard late one night, as they huddled in their tent after picking all day, and heard a weird, horrific wail out among the trees," and she adds that "La Llorona is not a legend I can tell my own children, and then put back on the shelf, encased within paper and binding" (2). Although combining the story of the weeping woman with that of Cortés's mistress serves as a way of integrating Miranda's (white) mother (who accidentally let her daughter drown prior to Miranda's birth) into the frame of colonization, understanding the patterns of Miranda's family life in terms of the legacy of ongoing imperial occupation, here I want to highlight how the text foregrounds the ways its contextualizing title narrative is a "legend." It is a story passed down that cannot function as history in the sense of a documentable set of events and relations that can be "encased within paper and binding" but that also cannot function as (a claim to) property, a kind of inheritance for which there is legal title. The scene of its transmission bespeaks the very absence of such status as an owning subject—it's told after a day of picking in a walnut orchard. That activity could indicate either subsistence activity not officially cognizable as a right to occupancy or service as cheap labor to the *real* owners. In this vein, the choice of a Mexican/Mexican American narrative as the title for the text can imply the long-standing refusal of the United States to acknowledge Native land rights in California, its translation of the territory as simply and straightforwardly Mexican prior to annexation,[45] and/or it can signify the ways Native people have been proletarianized as part of a nonwhite workforce in which Indians are largely understood as generically Mexican/mestizo.[46] The invocation of La Malinche as La Llorona, then, mobilizes "legend" as a way of further problematizing what gets to count as history, gesturing toward processes of derealization that render Native presence, identity, and territoriality as merely figurative. The framing of the text as "legend"—and as this legend in particular—helps highlight the ways

Miranda is not and cannot be a proper Native subject, inasmuch as state-sponsored and state-endorsed systems of property and propriety work to fracture, discipline, and disappear indigeneity.

From this perspective conjugal homemaking both enacts and effaces the broader dynamics of colonization, naturalizing certain practices and geographies of possession by helping regulate what kinds of claims to inheritance, land, and belonging will count as legitimate. The text elaborates this colonial/patriarchal nexus, toward which the preface gestures, in Miranda's portrayal of her father in "After San Quentin." In the previous section I address the poem's ending, which figures Miranda as part of a "we" whose bodies serve as "containers" holding a "colonized history." The poem builds to that image of internalization (or of an internality composed out of officially disavowed history/territoriality) by tracing the ways her father's perpetration of domestic violence operates as an extension of the ongoing dynamics of federal occupation. His terrorizing of his wife and children reiterates in a different register his own experience as a Native man of being the object of state terror. The poem begins by depicting her father's way of exerting authority in their home:

> We are his inmates, the trailer
> our prison.
> It's all here: riots, accusation,
> the leather strap of justice rising and falling.
> On his belt my father carries
> keys to the front door, his truck,
> our hearts swinging
> like scalps.
>   (14)

The metaphors clearly point to his treatment of his wife and children as criminals in a "prison," maintaining discipline through the threat of assault where the power to inflict damage is the sole measure of "justice." Presenting home as a space of incarceration in one sense indicts her father for violating the proper dynamics of private life, turning the place of intimacy into one of surveillance, control, and abuse. Yet the stanza also intimates that the constrictive dimensions of the household, of domestic insularity, are precisely what facilitate and even encourage such exaction of patriarchal discipline. Describing the trailer's inhabitants as "inmates" suggests the kind of regime operative within it but also the lack of an appeal to some external authority that could ameliorate such conditions. The privatized sphere of homemaking provides the condition of possibility for such practices of domination.

Characterizing these relations as like those in prison also implies that the space of home becomes a conduit within a wider network of violence, a social formation in which these seemingly disparate sites are linked. Miranda's father's life marks this continuity: "so long in a place / where each movement he made is chronicled, my father became like them" (14). Here, the poem indicates that her father's actions result from his own incarceration, repeating against others what was done to him. While "them" most directly references guards and prison officials, the ambiguity of this term implies a wider field of meaning, a more entrenched structural distinction between her father and those who exert authority over him. If Miranda's father has internalized a system of violence, that process appears less as merely the transfer of prison roles to the qualitatively different sphere of the home than as incorporation into a kind of carceral logic/sociality that encompasses both. The poem gestures toward such a larger framework of force and containment in its representation of her father's abuse as his having "our hearts swinging / like scalps." The image of several "hearts" hung like property on "his belt" viscerally captures a rending of bodies, a dissection in which the stereotypical metaphor of romantic and familial affection—losing one's heart—is literalized in ways that provide a corporeal corollary for the violence made possible by the isolation that is conjugal homemaking.

This figuration of patriarchal aggression as licensed by ideologies of possessive individualism is given a further turn by its fusion with the taking of "scalps," connecting bourgeois homemaking to the Indian wars. The image suggests that the assault within Miranda's home results from a kind of bloodlust innate to her father as an Indian, but the very hyperbolic quality of this particular way of figuring Natives— as bloodthirsty savages—implies an ironizing of that logic. The next stanza explains that his actions are a function of having become "like them," and if her father's domestic violence marks his interpellation into a brutalizing regime, his performance of stereotypical Indianness appears as an extension of that process. Returning to the discussion of melancholy in the previous section, his subjectivity is formed through the interplay of two different impossible ideals: proper patriarch ruling over his household and vicious Indian killer. Miranda presents her father's abusive relation to his wife and children as a result of training in prison, a pedagogy in which his violence marks his successful internalization of dominant norms, but in which the discrepancy between this realization of the possibilities latent in conjugal privatization and the sentimental image of the household as a space of blissful comfort can be attributed to his failure as an Indian to understand intimacy. Similarly, the imprisonment of her father can be portrayed by the state as simply an effort to protect the public by managing the inborn Indian tendency toward destruction.[47] In other words, for her father to be "like them" is to be called on to assimilate to a social structure that dissimulates its own systemic modes of violence while he simultaneously has to embody a racialized figure that serves as an overdetermined symbol for that very violence.

The mention of "scalps" suggests how the effects of state-orchestrated dynamics of regulation and coercion are presented as if they simply result from the (racial) propensities of a few bad individuals, but this reference also implicitly situates the social spaces the poem addresses, and the relations among them, in a history of imperial displacement. Miranda locates the household and the prison within a settler geography of property that disciplines and erases Indigenous presence. The third section of the poem contextualizes her father's movement among spaces and institutions in the present within the legacy of Euro-invasion dating back to the Spanish colonization of Alta California:

My father sleeps inside the bone walls
of mission and mythology
condemned to hell slammed, bolted—
confined at night, listening,
while women and girls choke
in airless *monjeras*

suffer violations by *soldados y padres,*
like the names they force
on us, patronymics of shame.
San Quentin was not his first prison.
   (16)

The mention of missions, *monjeras* (the cramped and ill-vented dormitories in which missionized Indians, particularly women, were forced to sleep), and *soldados y padres* (soldiers and fathers, referring to the twin imperial institutions of the mission and the presidio that shaped Spanish rule in California) collapses her father's life into those of his ancestors.[48] Doing so suggests that the "violations" of the past continue to be felt in the present. His sensation of *confinement,* then, cannot be traced to his time in prison, instead casting the experience of that literal incarceration as an extension and concrete, contemporary realization of a long-standing pattern of remapping. Native peoples are deterritorialized, dispossessed of their lands through Spanish settlement, and reterritorialized as cheap, expendable labor occupying rigidly demarcated sites that are heavily monitored. The stanza further points to the ways the rape of Native women and girls served as a crucial feature of colonization in California, providing a central provocation for armed conflict between Native men and Spanish soldiers. This collective memory reveals how the history of Euroconquest makes moot the apparent distinction between home and prison, the civilizing process of Christian conversion—including the promise to domesticate properly "women and girls"—functioning as a vehicle of brutalizing, regulatory assault. The patriarchal enclosure of familial homemaking, therefore, arises as an effect of imperial imposition. *Patronyms,* with their implication of clear conjugal pairings that preserve indisputable lines of inheritance, are "names" that bear the "shame" of an inability to protect noncombatants from sexual violence as well as to prevent the expropriation of Native territory. In this way, the nuclear family home appears less as a place of refuge than as a reminder of the ongoing *enforced* incorporation of Indigenous peoples into a privatizing, policed social topography that divorces them from each other and the land.

The continuity between domesticity and imperial abjection, though, is not readily available to her father as a way of conceptualizing and narrating his own life. Instead, this past appears as "mythology"—a kind of dream that emerges "at night" during "sleep." The relation between the history of settler invasion and her father's circumstances actively is obscured by the translation of Indigenous peoples into European "patronymics," an isolating and racializing process that effaces persistent Native presence: "We don't know our name: / generations answer to *Miranda*" (16). Though borne by "generations," this marker of Spanish force does not become "our name," but simply an imperial call to which they must "answer." That Hispanicizing discourse of familial identity further marks them as nonwhite within an Anglo-dominated system, thus making her father a target of state containment.

> Here, Miranda means *you have the right*
> *to remain silent . . .*
> it means
> our own words can and will
> be used against us; it means
> a court of law is not surprised
> to find my father, again and again, within its gates:
> and his son after him.
>   (16)

Patriarchal inheritance means being subjected to racist surveillance and juridical violence, and from this perspective her father's actions within Miranda's childhood home appear as an effort to claim some kind of authority through occupying a subject position that is itself inextricably enmeshed within networks of racialization, property, and state management that seek to discipline him as a Native man while denying his connection to legally meaningful indigeneity. Playing the social role of father in the space of domestic privacy cannot provide insulation from the continuing legacy of dispossession and violation, since that very structure of naming and possession is the vehicle of settler force.

Moreover, if "Miranda" remains a technology of imperial interpellation, the insistence that there is another, unknown "name" through which the "we" could understand themselves suggests a kind of collective belonging irreducible to conjugal homemaking but that survives within and despite it. However, this negotiation—"we don't know"—suggests less an alternative regime of possession, a true name that could replace "Miranda" and thereby found a legally cognizable set of claims, than that the "we" is predicated on a sustained, somewhat inchoate sensation that available systems of knowledge and claiming—of property and propriety—themselves turn history into "mythology," (re)mapping the past and present so as to nullify the possibility of naming indigeneity ("I thought we had nothing" [17]). That feeling of an impossible presence made unreal is captured in the portrayal of the "we" as "containers / that hold our colonized history" (17), a trace of Indigenous spatiality whose lack of a place in settler legal geographies distinguishes it from both the household and the prison, as well as the subjectivities they produce.

The text further develops this disjunction between marital homemaking and the internal landscape of indigeneity in its depiction of Miranda's relationship with her husband. She differentiates between a sexuality formed in the weave between colonization and patriarchy and the "indigenous erotic" she explores in her connections with Native women (which I discuss in the next section). In "Driving Past Suicide for Three Novembers," Miranda explores her decision not to kill herself, the choice not to surrender to "this beast called bereftness" (54)—the sense of grief she has inherited.[49] The poem is driven by its opening question, "Who will explain it to my children," which is followed immediately by the reference to the "beast" (the memory of loss and the collective loss of memory), suggesting that her children also will have to bear this legacy of melancholy and will need to be taught how to live with/through it. However, while invested in a vision of generational futurity as a way of validating her own survival, she depicts the conjugal union from which her children emerge as providing less comfort than it does confinement, animating desperation rather than allaying it. The poem observes:

When I arrive home tonight
my husband will reach for me in the dark—
his need, his comfort, his right.

> Who will tell my children
> marriage is more
> than a glistening soul
> served up on a silver platter?

The sense of warmth and care associated with the term "home" gives way to a logic of possession. Marriage appears as a sexual exchange in which her husband can claim a kind of ownership—a "right" of property that allows him to satisfy "his need" within *his home*. Miranda experiences herself as an object available for her husband's consumption, presenting the space of domestic intimacy as one that leaves her further "bereft" of a liveable subjectivity. Although the poem does not address imperialism or indigeneity per se, its description of how her body is mapped within a patriarchal and privatizing economy (especially the implication of state-sanctioned identities and claims conveyed by the idea of a "right") is continuous with her earlier portrayal of her father. In this way, the poem implies that her white husband occupies that social status even more "comfort[ably]" than her father, even as her feelings of incarceration parallel his—notably, though, in ways that seem less readily narrated as carrying the kind of political and historical significance apparent in "After San Quentin."

If "Driving Past Suicide" highlights how marriage and bourgeois household formation function as a relation of property, "Sleeping Beauty, 1978" more fully investigates the kinds of subjectivity such homemaking effaces and forecloses, including how it contributes to her sensation of unreality as a Native person. In a reversal of the fairy tale of its title, the poem begins by observing, "He kisses me and I fall asleep for twenty years / transported to a happier world" (45).[50] The achievement of marital bliss is a kind of waking dream, one produced through the circulation of narratives of its salvational promise. Such stories seem to overwrite Miranda's self-understandings, promising "a happier world" through identifying with a heteronormative ideal. The cost of this trade, though, is her own disappearance: "I walk the Riverway as a ghost, / believe in heroes and damsels in distress, hope / without disappointment[.]" The image of her "ghost[liness]" reiterates in a different register the text's running depiction of how Native history is experienced as "myth" due to its denigration and erasure within popular and official accounts, and situating her *invisibility* within the frame of an inversion of the story of Sleeping Beauty ("I fall asleep") suggests that her sense of her own immateriality arises out of the superimposition of a dominant cultural fantasy. Again, as Lynda Hart notes, the "feeling of 'unreality'... [is] an artful reconstruction of the survivor's *present*," which provides "a way to function with the 'reality' of the dominant order" (177). Moreover, the figure of the "ghost" suggests the vestigial presence of something that properly should be gone, not only a powerful trope for Native persistence in the wake of discourses of the vanishing Indian (as discussed in chapter 1) but also one that speaks to the text's portrayal of how forms of Indigenous presence disavowed by the state are preserved melancholically within/ as individual structures of feeling. In such moments, the text accretes meaning rather than displaying it, illustrating a process whereby the larger dynamics of settlement ("one memory wide, / five centuries deep" [48]) occupy everyday experience in ways that prove quite difficult to narrate, and this rhetorical strategy can be read as an effort to track the fraught process by which Miranda comes to consciousness, waking up to the role of ongoing settler imperialism in shaping her own life.

In the gradual unfolding of that realization, the notion of "home," with its connotation of insulated domesticity and located occupancy, serves as an ideological pressure point for investigating the relation between normative modes of personal identity and the elision of indigeneity. Describing her time in Boston with her husband, Miranda notes,

> . . . I am three thousand
> miles from where October means rain, gray sky: home.
> I am three thousand miles from where home means
> the fury of fathers beating children with belts,
> mothers who leave, little brothers whose dear hearts
> are twisted into something unspeakable and rank.

The poem does not simply substitute a positive sense of home for what she lacks with her husband, instead suggesting how the territory with which Miranda identifies is transected by excruciatingly painful memories from which she fled into the fairy tale of marital happily-ever-after. The actual spaces of both her husband's and her father's households are experienced as carceral, in which Miranda feels like an object of patriarchal ownership—a dynamic itself repeatedly linked in the text to the ongoing legacies of colonization.

From this perspective, the yearning for a place utterly unencumbered by these twined legacies, for a "home" that is "without disappointment," appears as its own dream from which she needs to awaken. In its stead the text offers readers an alternative in which embracing emotional and erotic possibilities denied in the hetero-conjugal household becomes a means of realizing forms of indigeneity for which there is no place in existing geographies of property. What brings Miranda out of her "dream" is "the tender mouth of a woman's lips on mine" that "seeps like a spring into old crevices, leads moisture / to the dormant seed of my own honest heart." Recalling the representation of her affective life as "soil" in "After San Quentin," this moment returns to the figure of the internal landscape as an avenue for the reemergence of collective sensations, histories, and memories for which she serves as a "container." While here the direction is inward ("seeps … into"), the image of a "spring" watering a "seed" highlights the imminence of growth that will burst the confines that have made it "dormant."

Land does not function in the text merely as an evocative figure for affective dynamics, but rather, as I have argued, Miranda uses that relation as a way of illustrating how indigeneity persists in individual subjectivity despite its official disavowal. The "seed," then, suggests more than a coming to consciousness about the limits of the fairy-tale promise of marriage; it implies that the rejection of the inevitability, and even the desirability, of that norm makes room for acknowledging other kinds of constrained affect, including those associated with forms of Native identity unrecognized by the state. The text consistently links processes of family and household formation to settler cartographies and displacements (for example, the slippage among home, prison, and mission), and within this frame Miranda's challenge to the obviousness of heterohomemaking contests the ways settler occupation is rendered self-evident and the violence of its imposition is effaced. The critique of marriage as an institution becomes a way to avoid being *"transformed . . . into a destroyer,"* to trace the system of *patronymics* through which logics of property are naturalized and thereby to access a collective past registered and retained melancholically as states of feeling. If the ideal of "home" remains fraught in the weave between "colonialism and patriarchy," intimacy with other women offers less a way to transcend or escape that matrix of possession than an avenue for making ongoing patterns of displacement legible and liveable. Creating relationships shaped by an improper relation to genealogy and property enables a kind of remapping, bringing Indigenous geographies of loss into focus by eroticizing them and making nonnormative desire a vehicle for reconnecting memory to the lived landscape of the present.

The Territoriality of Fantasy

The Esselen people were declared "extinct" by both government officials and nonnative experts, casting persons of Esselen descent as a vestigial remainder who bear a reproductively transmitted substance (blood) divorced from *tribal* identity. Taking up this individualizing narrative, Miranda revisions inheritance as the passage of a sense of place-based peoplehood that is experienced as internal due to the persistent assault on Native peoples in California and the insistence on their disappearance. The topography of mental and emotional processes here suggests less the particularity of individual psychic life than it does the melancholic preservation of Esselen collectivity amid efforts to eradicate and erase it. In this way, Miranda's text portrays indigeneity as occupying the space of fantasy, although not in the sense of that which is not real (invented, inauthentic, false) but that which is denied the status of the real. As Lynda Hart suggests in her discussion of incest narratives, "The 'experience' itself surpasses the lexicon of 'reality'" (188), a lexicon that in the case of federal recognition for "tribes" requires proof of continuity that edits out intentional efforts to displace and destroy those very peoples. Since "the survivor is *not meant to survive,"* she must create "her own symbolic if you will, that is necessarily discordant with the dominant order's symbolic" (178). What Hart suggests here seems particularly pressing for unacknowledged peoples in light of the effort to legitimize settlement: they "become witnesses not to private acts secret-ed by personal shame and guilt, but to an entire symbolic system that erects itself on the foundation of the negation of their experience" (203). In *The Zen of La Llorona,* feeling that one has/is "nothing" slowly gives way to the sense that personal shame at the loss of land, prayers, language marks a "colonized history" and that seemingly private structures of feeling index the survival of an Indigenous symbolic—an experience of indigeneity negated by U.S. law.

Notably, Hart is addressing how incest is made unspeakable by the dominant image of domestic space as a site of care and compassion, the privatized territory of intimacy from which violence definitionally is excluded, and as discussed in the previous section, Miranda depicts nuclear homemaking as a technology of possession that is continuous with the colonization of Native peoples and places, helping to normalize the political economy and legal geography of the settler regime. To desire otherwise, then, can denaturalize that "symbolic system," opening up other possible forms of sociality and spatiality. By fusing articulations of her attraction for and relationships with other Native women to figurations of land, Miranda forges a connection between eroticism and indigeneity, drawing on fantasy as a way of reconnecting her internal life to the external landscape. However, that process neither is mourning, the surrender of the object (in this case Native identity and territory) as utterly irretrievable, nor is it a simple restoration of what has been taken. Rather, it is a kind of working out.[51] By this I mean that the text presents Miranda's sexual and emotional connection with women as teaching her how to recognize the role of systemic forms of settler assault and elision in shaping her shamed subjectivity (her status as a "container") and to shift her relation to these forces and histories by creating a new, nonpossessive relation with the land itself, which has not disappeared even if Indigenous people's connections to it and to each other remain legally effaced and unintelligible. Miranda's "depiction of a sexuality that is formed through and fantasized within the traumatic memories" (178–79), drawing on Hart's terms, becomes a way of engaging with the ongoing violence of imperial displacement and the state-enforced amnesia that denies Indigenous memory the status of tribal history.

If in *Indian Cartography,* Miranda "look[s] for our own land to

claim" (82), *The Zen of La Llorona* diffuses this search into a less jurisdictional image, suggesting how her desires are permeated by a relation to the land. It provides the means for representing not only her
attraction to other women but what she is drawn to in them. In "From
a Dream, I Wake to Tender Music," she describes her butch lover's
flute playing as a kind of foreplay:

> Our kiss makes no sound, but outside
> the river leaps, a long wild note.
> I find a cry like all the rivers we've lost:
> waters captured, dammed, living still.
> (64)

The external landscape appears to reflect, and even to be animated
by, their passion, suggesting a fusion of the two. Yet the depiction
of the water's "leap" as itself a "wild note" reciprocally implies that
the music that seduces Miranda is actually an expression of the nonhuman force of the river, presenting the overwhelming connection
between she and her lover as indicative of a kind of ambient power
that also drives the river. The simile of "like"-ness, then, does not so
much compare her erotic fulfillment to something "outside"—of her
body, her intimacy with her lover, the space she occupies—as portray
it as expressive of how "the rivers we've lost" actually move inside her.
The "cry" illustrates a feeling of connection to both the "rivers" and
their "lost"-ness, in which her surrender to her passion opens up an
experience of selfhood as fundamentally shaped by loss (of Indigenous lands) and as simultaneously an absence of control that cannot
be equated with being "nothing"—the "thought" that she inherits as
part of "our colonized history" (17). Though the "waters" may be "captured" and "dammed," they persist, and Miranda's sensation of a kind
of self-shattering, a "cry" of pleasure in which she is neither possessing nor possessed but instead is held in the "wild" rush of feeling,
seems to open the potential for seeing herself as integrated into a
"living" landscape that endures even as it remains owned and managed. Her relation to her lover provides an emotional and sensual
framework ("like") through which to renarrate her place in a land
made alien by settlement, bridging the apparent gap between inside

and outside without fully remediating the ongoing effects of that alienation ("lost").[52]

The "our" of their lovemaking morphs into the "we" of imperial dispossession, indicating both that her lover also is Native and that the intensity of their sexual connection arises from its capacity to provide a meaningful response (although not a solution) to that legacy of displacement. In the text, sexual fantasies about and experiences with Native women offer a symbolic space in which to experiment with forms of subjectivity, providing a way for Miranda to acknowledge and address unrecognized forms of grief generated by the ongoing trauma of settler occupation while integrating the melancholic topography of her psychic life into her interactions with others. If life with her father and husband involves seeking to control and forget this internalized formation, living with "patronymics of shame" that leave her feeling "invisible as a ghost" (16, 45), a woman-centered erotics thematizes the logics, histories, and geographies of possession rather than naturalizing them, making them (and attendant erasures of indigeneity) into a subject of shared emotional work as opposed to an elided past enclosed within individual consciousness. That engagement with disavowed structures of feeling facilitates an experience of indigeneity, although one that is not equivalent to the reclamation of Native homelands. Instead, landedness emerges as a central feature of fantasy itself, pointing to the process by which peoplehood is disappeared and how it lives on as a force in quotidian forms of affect. In "Home," Miranda describes Margo, the last of her lovers in the text, highlighting her connection to nonhuman aspects of place: "skinner of bear and moose, multiplier of mosses"; "walker of clay and smooth granite paths, / digger of red ochre earth, guardian of the cedar grove" (93).[53] Margo's engagement with animal and plant life and her familiarity with and care for the land mark her as "traditional," as retaining an awareness of the environment conventionally understood as endemic to Native knowledges. This portrait suggests that she has created a kind of "home" quite distinct from one ordered around a father's belt or a husband's "right," and she appears to have found the kind of sustained "peace" on a "piece of earth" that eluded Miranda's father (17). In many ways, the first half of the poem positions Margo as having achieved what Miranda craves—"the act of living as a balanced being in a balanced world" (3)—due to her ability to (re)connect with the land as a Native person, and in this way she seems to serve as the paradigmatic figure for how one resolves the melancholy of Native identity, how one moves beyond the lack of recognition by the state to realize a sense of indigeneity in the world.

In a fascinating insistence on the irresolution produced by legacies of settlement, however, the second half of the poem seems to assert the irrelevance of land. In its stead, attraction to women functions as "home":

> . . . Ah, sweetheart, this pillaged continent's not
> what I've lost, not the sanctuary searched for since birth.
> All lusts ever harbored, each stolen deed of desire—
> these fantasies aren't native land. What's home?
> I can't draw a map, but I've wandered each curve and hollow.
> The place that knows me is a woman.

At first glance, these lines exchange Native for lesbian identification, disqualifying the former by suggesting that the latter is the real referent of her "desire." Yet even in its apparent negation, a sense of territoriality suffuses this declaration as its principal metaphoric vehicle— "harbor," "deed," "map." Land provides the condition of possibility and intelligibility for what ostensibly replaces it, animating her erotics as that which endows it with meaning. Moreover, desire arises out of the conditions of dispossession, as a "stolen deed," pointing back to the very "pillag[ing]" from which she appears to distance herself. An Indigenous sensibility drives this declaration even as the obvious object of such sentiment—an enduring relation to place—appears to pass from view. That very dynamic of a structuring retention of what otherwise would be declared gone is the essence of melancholy, and Miranda's description of her "fantasies" reiterates a kind of belatedness in which they emerge in the wake, and in the space, of a dislocation treated as so obvious as to need no further comment. The phrase "these fantasies aren't native land" suggests that "land" is not the object of her "fantasies," of her desire, but to what extent does that nonequivalence point to the fact that such land already is "lost"? To what degree do the "fantasies" respond to that absence, to the inability to locate Esselen territory on a "map" that she cannot draw? How might her desire index the way that absence remains present as a formative aspect of her subjectivity, as a relation without a proper object, as an affective force whose reach and effects extend beyond the claiming of ownership over a piece of territory?

In discussing the process of living through profound violence, Veena Das highlights the process of "reoccupying the very signs of injury that have been marked to forge continuity in that space of devastation" (74). This effort to occupy an impossible subjectivity as a condition of survival illustrates how trauma can become not simply assaultive but constitutive, giving rise to ways of being that incorporate without simply reproducing the terms of suffering. The ending of "Home" condenses this dynamic, replaying and reworking Indigenous loss. The last line, "The place that knows me is a woman," creates a productive confusion between the tenor and the vehicle that suggests they animate each other. The concrete finality of "woman" presents that term as the proper referent of the poem's sentiments, as the horizon for Miranda's desire. However, the placement of the terms—"place" "is" "a woman"—conventionally would indicate that the former is the tenor, with the latter as the metaphoric substitute. Both of these options are at play simultaneously and work in and through each other. The absence of a "place" that "knows" her is woven into her homoerotic "fantasies," and reciprocally, she desires "place" in the way that she would desire "a woman," as other than a privatized possession. These inflections converge in the depiction of her desire for Margo, the careful maker and tender of Native place, in the first half of the poem. Her articulation of her "fantasies" conveys how her desire for women is suffused at every point by the longing for (and dislocation from) "native land," and the mapping of "place," of "sanctuary," as erotic connection to the bodies of other Native women reiterates in a different register the text's running trope of psychic life as an internal(ized) landscape, suggesting the emergence of an intersubjective way of *realizing* the desire for place—of externalizing Indigenous structures of feeling—without presenting that sensation as fully commensurate with a legacy of loss or a transcendence of it. If "these fantasies aren't native land," they cannot substitute for (dispossession from) Indigenous homelands, do not merely represent or stand in for such territory (as a symbol whose meaning can be reduced to the aim of a legally recognized right of occupancy), and also do not signify outside of the "signs of injury"—the "pillag[ing of the] continent"—that serve as the broader context in which such desire is situated. Her fantasies bear her desire as a sign of an encompassing sense of indigeneity that colors all her experiences.

As noted earlier, the text repeatedly observes that the land itself remains, and in this vein Miranda casts her desire as a way of learning to inhabit it differently, to see her feelings as a mode of mapping that can reveal possibilities for melancholic survivance as against the official call to accept the fact of extinction. That process, though, can be difficult and painful, if necessary for her to move toward a kind of subjectivity with possibilities richer than those of grief and rage. "Old Territory, New Maps" charts the movement through desire to a changed sense of place. The poem chronicles a road trip with her lover (the same one as in "From a Dream"), and it weaves together the changing dynamics of their relationship with their experience of the terrain through which they pass. In addition to noting that they "are two Indian women alone," Miranda subtly draws attention to the fact of Native presence in the spaces through which they move, remarking that a mountain they pass is located in "Ute country" and observing, "Like those people whose land we cross, / we don't live by lines drawn on paper" (75). These moments create the sense of a shared Indigenous understanding of land and placemaking, specifically as occupied by Native peoples and as a kind of occupancy at odds with the political mappings of officials and experts. Simultaneously, though, the land they traverse is not theirs, reminding readers of both the fact that peoples have particular homelands (as opposed to a generic, stereotypical connection to nature) and that Miranda does not know precisely the land to which her people belong. In this way, the poem implies a potential sense of Indigenous landedness while also gesturing toward its absence; Miranda's ability to recognize indigeneity speaks to her simultaneous retention and loss of it, another melancholic ambiguation of the difference between the real and the imagined.

The mention of a mode of life other than one shaped "by lines drawn on paper" suggests a kind of sensuous engagement at odds with bureaucratic or academic abstractions and their ability to render persons and communities invisible (such as in the repeated declarations of the disappearance of the Esselen people). Such an emphasis on the concrete materiality of place itself is complicated by the depiction of the land as mutable and haunted: "We drive hundreds of miles / across deserts sculpted by wind and story"; "Ghosts are everywhere" (75). That which appears to be immaterial also intimately is bound up with, and makes impressions on, the landscape. "Story" has the power to alter the terrain, and those thought dead and gone abide, won over through her lover's music—"the cries of your flute pleasuring old spirits" (75). Though usually cast as intangible, feelings and memory have substance and force here, a perspective or ontology accepted by the "people[s] whose land we cross."

Rather than being ephemeral when compared with the enduring thereness of the landscape, Miranda's desire appears as potentially an active relation to, and element of, such placemaking, even as it also highlights the ways that this place is not one she could understand as hers. Her efforts to orient herself in the territory through which they pass extends to her relation to her lover. "I learn the distance from my hand to your thigh / your mouth to my mouth," but this erotic mapping is figured as in the service of a kind of mutual ownership that can "bring you through the barrier of your skin / into my blood so that I can possess you and yet be entirely possessed" (75). That longing for possession echoes her depiction of her husband's claim to a "right" over her body, recalling the geographies and dynamics of (patriarchal) propertyholding that the text elsewhere portrays as the quotidian realization of colonial logics of regulation, alienation, and dispossession. Here, though, the impulse is less toward a conjugal bounding that demarcates the insulated (and also terrorizing) space of privacy than toward a crossing, a transection of the "barrier" of "skin" that makes possible a greater intimacy. Yet the idiom for that fantasy is that of the very system from which her desire appears to be posited as a break; her attraction to women violates the proper rules of homemaking and leads her to feel the legacies of indigeneity previously dammed within her. At the same time, to remember the suppression and erasure of Indigenous presence due to a liberal regime of propertyholding (with its demands of documentary proof for Native land tenure) also is to experience the ongoing legacies of settlement on one's subjectivity— its formation in relation to dominant ideologies of possession.[54]

As in "Home," Miranda's fantasies here do not transcend the history in which she is enmeshed but rather help highlight its imperial dimensions and elisions. In this vein, she envisions her desire as its own topography, one toward which she has a semicolonial orientation:

After twelve hundred miles together
we enter green forest thick along a fearless river
. . . .
There at last you clasp my hand, guide it
to a place beyond maps,
no universe I have ever known.
It is a raw landscape; we are the sojourners
overcome by the perilous shock of arrival.
    (76)

The sense of moving through other peoples' land, a belonging registered in ways other than "lines drawn on paper," morphs into a feeling of "place" in which they are explorers surveying a new "landscape." This arrival in an emotional/erotic space "beyond maps" replicates the colonial tropes of discovery—an empty space awaiting occupancy by those newly arrived. "The Territory of Love," from *Indian Cartography,* makes that connection even more explicit: "There is no end to the territory of love . . . There may be natives sauntering along naked . . . This is their land. You are the stranger"; "Beware. The territory of love does not take kindly to being colonized. To live there, you must give up what you think you have learned, take back what you fear is forsaken . . . , you can only win by losing" (48). In this piece Miranda lays out what might be taken as the moral of "Old Territory, New Maps," foregrounding the nexus of romance and ownership and its replay of an imperial mentality that itself must be unlearned in an embrace of other principles (themselves thought to be gone— "forsaken"). The latter poem, though, dwells less on the lesson to be learned than on the process by which she gets there. It emphasizes the excruciating emotional negotiation by which Miranda comes to recognize the ways her own psychic topography—even in the experience of pleasure—remains shaped by the very forces that have caused her grief and rage ("these are the maps we made together, / territories we foolishly vowed to own" [76]). To accept ownership as the form of her desire is to accept the very terms of alienation that cut her off from "the rivers we've lost," which are "captured, dammed, living still" (64), but reciprocally, to imagine fantasy as a kind of transcendence that marks a total break with the dynamics of ongoing settler occupation is once again to position fantasy in opposition to reality rather than as a means of denaturalizing what passes for the real—making legible, in Lynda Hart's terms, "the dominant order's symbolic" while opening ways of feeling and remembering otherwise. In other words, "Old Territory, New Maps" implicitly asks, under a settler regime how can love not be experienced, at least initially, within its logics of possession? Given that unavoidable inheritance, how can desire become an avenue toward another sense of place?

The answer offered by the poem seems to be embracing loss, not as the absence of a once owned thing but as a way of renarrating Miranda's relation to the world around her, in which longing cannot be requited by possession. The imagination of emotional and erotic gratification as occurring on some new terrain sealed off from a painful elsewhere rehearses the ideology of conjugal homemaking in which ownership of space, sex, and affection seem guaranteed within the enclosure of privatized domesticity. Miranda's desire leads her out of that "dream" toward a place in which the "dormant seed" within her can grow (45), and the mobility that tends to characterize her poems about her female lovers (they are travelling or united in temporary ways rather than sharing a household) suggests that her queer attractions do not and cannot serve as the basis for "home"(-)making, especially given the text's connection of that process to patriarchal authority, state-sanctioned modes of property, and the construction of legally legible lineage. In this vein, to come to understand loss through desire involves surrendering the dream of an unencumbered space generated within imperialist and heteronormative mappings, and giving up the dominant fantasy of a secure ownership of people and place, of possession as the means of materializing one's emotional life, makes possible an engagement with the landscape that can acknowledge the stories and ghosts that abide in it, the histories and structures of feeling that cannot be registered in property lines "drawn on paper." The poem closes with Miranda's appeal to her lover, "Help me / translate loss the way this land does— / flood, earthquake, landslide— / terrible and alive" (76–77). The most immediate loss is of the relationship with her lover ("I don't know how to survive awakening / in a woman's body with a child's / broken heart" [76]). However, these lines return the reader to the sense of place offered in the first half of the poem, which is presented as Native, and they suggest that the kinds of impermanence that characterize Miranda's time with her lover—as opposed to the promise until death of marriage—can enable her to recognize a way of being predicated less on an absolute distinction between presence and absence (the realness of legalized claims versus the immateriality of memory) than on a kind of accretion in which change is "terrible" while itself marking that one is "alive." The landscape survives such destructive alteration, and more than providing an image to capture Miranda's movement beyond this particular relationship, the trajectory of this relationship (re)connects her emotional life to the land, experiencing nonownership as the condition of possibility for a sense of Indigenous persistence. The poem suggests the potential for externalizing the subjectivity formed by her people's "colonized history" in ways that facilitate the *translation* of the melancholic traces of collective loss into the possibility of a new sense of place and belonging, albeit one of a different sort than the "boundaries, treaties, reservations" of settler law.[55]

Creation as the Limits of Testimony

Reconnecting the internal landscape of selfhood to the external landscape, engaging with other Native people and the still living land, involves taking seriously fantasized forms of subjectivity that bear the traces of collective histories and that offer forms of relation other than (hetero)patriarchal ownership. How, then, can we conceptualize what is produced by the work of fantasy? What is generated in the refusal to conflate Native melancholy with tribal disappearance or to experience loss as simply the objective absence of Native identity? The most obvious answer is that this process materializes the book itself. *The Zen of La Llorona* is the concretization of the dynamics it seeks to chart, providing a counterpoint to existing narratives both of conjugal inevitability (like Sleeping Beauty) and of Native vanishing (like those by officials and experts writing about the Esselen people). In this vein, the text could be thought of as a kind of testimony, as bearing witness to past and present formations that cannot be manifested within the evidentiary protocols of the official acknowledgment process.

Miranda's work, however, cautions against this move to align Native states of feeling with state procedures and knowledges through the deployment of juridical metaphors. In "I Am Not a Witness," from *Indian Cartography*, she observes of her Native ancestors, in this case Chumash:

> Some of our bones rest in 4000 graves
> out back behind the Mission.
> . . . .
> Some of our bones washed down the river
> whose name I do not know
> past islands I cannot name
> to the sea where
> I have never sailed.

She adds:

> I am not a witness. I am left behind, child
> of children who were locked in the Mission
> and raped. I did not see this:
> I was not there—but I am here.
> (73)

The piece emphasizes the lack of knowledge, the inability to fill in gaps in the documentary and historical record. To be a "witness" requires that one have a kind of experience that can count as empirical, verifiable, grounded in facts, and the refusal of that status here suggests the inapplicability of such criteria to Miranda's understanding of her own connection to indigeneity. The absence of testimony, though, does not correlate to being/having nothing. As discussed previously, her repeated use of "our" insists on her belonging to a collectivity that itself survives, and it persists in the feeling of being "left behind," an uncanny sensation of a relation to the land that does not have a proper referent (she asks, "Where is the place that knows me?" [73]), as well as an inheritance of past imperial violence and erasure. These legacies are transmitted generationally ("child of children"), and in this vein, the figure of birth provides an alternative framework for understanding what emerges out of fantasy—one that reorients creation from heteronormative reproduction (and its property logics) to the realization of the potential for living amid ongoing loss.

The text of *Zen*, including its generic form as a collection of poetry rather than as a history, therefore functions less as testimony than as a way of giving form to a structure of feeling—a means of realizing aspects of contemporary indigeneity that remain unintelligible as a legal claim and that are more evanescent and simultaneously more enduring than state recognition. Discussing the idea of "an indigenous erotic" in the book's preface, Miranda observes, "Life began when I gave birth to my own children. I tasted creation: discovered an ability to love and appreciate that I'd never experienced," and in referencing the devastating legacies of colonization and its instantiation through patriarchal rights, she asserts, "We must know those stories as starting places, not endings" (3–4). Although it links sexual pleasure to reproduction, the text avoids the presentation of the latter as the aim of the former, instead depicting procreation as part of a broader process of learning "to love and appreciate" that she casts as the essence of eroticism. That expanded conception of birth as emotional, embodied engagement and connection enables a transformation of histories of dispossession into "starting places." They provide the basis for "maintain[ing] a thread of memory" that connects her to her people while retooling inheritance as hope—"joy"—an opening to what is yet to be, as opposed to even the simple retention unchanged of what was (4).[56] Or perhaps more precisely, the figure of birth indexes a yoking of the past to the future, in which the present cannot be defined by what supposedly is gone (as a series of "endings") and in which what seemed contained within the (privatized) space of intimacy gains its own distinct public presence. Miranda presents the collection as the most tangible result of this rejuvenating experience of an "indigenous state of creativity," noting, "These poems exist because my ancestors survived" (4), and in addition to serving as an example of what emerges from such creativity, the text works to coalesce and convey how love can transform the bare fact of survival into possibility and growth.

Highlighting the crossing of the threshold between inside and outside, the figure of birth endows desire with a materiality and presence that challenges the (heteronormative) effort to isolate it within individual subjectivity or the domestic sphere. In "Husband," Miranda describes the end of her marriage through the image of reproduction:[57]

> remember this ruptured moment when something
> unbidden and passionate emerged from my body
> as if we gave birth one last time together.
> Can we heal, is this strange labor a cure?
> My desire demands a life of its own, sucks air,
>
> gives tongue to words you swear you can't hear.
>   (51)

Even as she positions her "desire" as like her children, another "birth," these lines suggest that it exceeds a procreative paradigm. Her passion "rupture[s]" the relation with her husband and the order of their home by introducing something alien to it. If children are a kind of creation that seems to follow from the structure of marriage and conjugal homemaking, to fit easily within its contours, the attraction to other women does not. It brings into being something that violates the fairy-tale promise of marital bliss and enclosure (as depicted in "Sleeping Beauty, 1978," addressed earlier), revealing Miranda's participation in that narrative of the natural as itself unreal ("I'll try to live your lie"). The poem further concretizes its central conceit, characterizing her feelings as having a "birth-cry," as a "creature" that "shares our house," and as sucking "hungry at my breast." Doing so conveys a sense of desire as less an emotional state contained within the psyche than a force that enters into the world, possessing a vitality and set of relations all its own. It occupies and reorganizes space, particularly that of heterohomemaking, but that transformation arises out of what initially appears to be merely internal.

Whereas Driskill's work displaces the reproductive inheritance of Indian substance as the basis for Native (and specifically Cherokee) identity, Miranda's emphasis on birth does not simply reinstitute that logic as a means of marking Native presence in the absence of federal recognition. Instead, she refigures creation as more than simply the biological transmission of Indianness. While not explicitly addressing indigeneity, this depiction of erotic longing recalls the image of Miranda as a "container" holding a "colonized history," invoking that sense of bodily enclosure only to recast it as generative. Given that the text consistently presents her love for other women as complexly enmeshed with her (re)connection to the land and Native histories, as discussed in the previous section (and as alluded to in the poem's reference to her husband's belief that her homoerotic inclinations are "brought on by warm spring rain"—echoing the figures of dammed rivers in other poems), the vision of birth here suggests that desire functions less as a reclamation of what has seemed gone than as a process of gestation in which something new arises out of the hidden remains of the past carried within her. Melancholy does more than preserve what has been lost; via the work of fantasy, what has been lost is reconstituted and returned to the world in an unforeseen shape, one that upsets normative geographies of possession and selfhood. The poem reflexively links this process to that of writing by describing desire as "giv[ing] tongue to words," presenting the text of *Zen* as no less a birth than literal children would be while also suggesting that the potential realized through the expression of an Indigenous erotic far exceeds the domain of the (vision of) home into which it enters.

If intimations of indigeneity appear within the emergence of an apparently alien desire, the figure of birth/creation dwells within the more explicit articulations of Miranda's relation to Native history and the landscape, even if not explicitly named as such. "Steele Street" tells the story of her last contact with the lover from "Old Territory, New Maps," as her husband and children look on. Their attraction for each other is a "raw, half-crazy hunger," echoing the terms of "Husband." Here, desire gives rise to interactions with other women that violate the implicit terms of the patriarchal "right" exerted over her within marriage, and that seismic shift in "the geography of [her] life" not only generates new potentials but reveals buried ones: ". . . Under our feet, cracked / asphalt and old brick, dirt and sewers, / layers of civilization's debris. / The city's archaeology, muffled histories / of a relocated tribe" (70). Linking her newly found "hunger" with the residue of "muffled histories" of dispossession and erasure casts the former as a means of revealing the latter. Cracking open the heteronormative "geography" of daily life opens avenues to a changed consciousness, in which the contours of Euro-imposed "civilization" cease to be taken for granted and the "archaeology" of the everyday turns up unexpected traces of indigeneity. What comes out of such discovery, though, is not the recovery of what is gone—the "tribe" has been "relocated" to some other space. Moreover, the movement of the relationship in the poem is toward an ending ("You did not come back. / You were not going to come back." [70]). Is anything born out of this experience? Can loss yield creation?

The experience of losing her lover, acknowledging the dangers of pursuing desire beyond the seeming guarantees of marital property/propriety, opens her to the potential for reconceptualizing selfhood as porous and changing in ways that refuse to treat loss as disappearance. Describing her response to her lover's leaving, Miranda observes, "... I broke / for hours, for days, / for years—flailing, snatching / at fragments and shards / sure that healing mean[t] setting / each break, believing / what shattered / should be made whole" (71). Mourning here is a process of trying to regather "fragments," to piece back together a cohesive totality that serves as the a priori model of normative, liveable subjectivity. To fully grieve involves reknitting the parts into an integrated, insulated "whole," like the skeletal image suggested by "setting each break." Unlike in "Husband," where "rupture" appears as a condition of possibility for the birth of desire that demands life, these lines portray such yearning as destructive of the fragile architecture of personal identity, a vision in which "healing" entails (re)containment and to be "shattered" is to be utterly lost to oneself. However, speaking in the past tense signals to readers that this notion has been revised, that Miranda has moved on from the idea that subjectivity must be safeguarded from intrusion. Instead, the poem's ending offers an alternative perspective on loss: "I wish I'd known then: / we must break the casting / to reveal what's been fired within" (71). These lines are indented, emphasizing the disjunction between the sentiment they capture and what has come before while also privileging disjunction itself—breaking—as a mode of creation. Shaped around the image of firing pottery, they cast grieving for lost love as a process in which what emerges is not what had been before—a "whole" in need of restoration—and to which the violence of rupture is necessary. As against the sense of a self in "shards," this final stanza suggests that the potential for loss that attends the disorienting experience of desire, a reaching beyond the existing boundaries of subjectivity, catalyzes an ongoing transformation within selfhood that refigures her relation to the world. Such a remapping of "the geography of [her] life" requires fracturing existing connections in order to forge new ones.

More than conveying a generic sense of the inevitability of change, though, the poem indicates that the appearance of absence—a lost lover, a "shattered" self—dissimulates the preservation of something that serves as the kernel for a kind of growth that is neither merely a retention of the past nor a transcendence of it. In this way, the figure of the "casting" reiterates in a different register the topos of birth, of an internal gestation whose trajectory is toward emergence, and the poem links this process of becoming visible, of externalization, to the engagement with the erased history of Native presence and imperial dispossession. The image of her breaking echoes the earlier one of tearing open the city streets to reveal traces "of a relocated tribe." If in one sense this reference indicates what is gone, it also implies something encased and hidden awaiting an expanded sphere of possibility—voices "muffled" rather than silent. As a breach in her life with her husband, Miranda's "hunger" opens an avenue to other forms of rupture, including within the geography of settlement in which her life is embedded. Like the recognition of ongoing Native identification that comes in the wake of her sensation of being/having "nothing" (17), apparent absence here is transmuted through desire into a process of becoming that connects her back to the landscape to which she has no proper title. She notes that she "broke like the sheer face / of a cliff" (70), and as in the request in "Old Territory, New Maps" that her lover "Help [her] translate loss the way this land does" (76), this reference suggests that the sensation of loss links her to the territory, which survives periodic fracturings that are both natural and inevitable. Shattering appears as part of an unstoppable process of change, less alienating her from herself than enabling a way of being in the world more closely aligned with a nonpossessive sense of place—one not concerned with maintaining the territory's "whole[ness]" as a commodified thing. In connecting those seemingly disparate breakings, the poem subtly indicates that the fragmentation Miranda experiences, as well as the sense of pregnant subjectivity that arises out of it, not only resonates with a putatively vanished indigeneity but actually enables her to hear "muffled histories" in ways that combine with the "colonized history" contained within her to gestate new possibilities for Indigenous being within and through loss.

Though generated through "break" and "rupture," the kind of Native subjectivity arising out of Miranda's experience of desire is neither quite continuous nor discontinuous with the past. The depiction of the workings of an Indigenous erotic as birth renders ambiguous the distinction between old and new, insisting on a way of envisioning survival that evades such binaries—seeing the past as either fully present or totally gone. As against a mourning for lost indigeneity that understands it as shattered fragments in need of reassembling into a prefabricated whole (like the ideal of the "tribe"), ostensibly individual structures of feeling contain collective Native histories that can reenter social life, in this case through sensations and relationships that deviate from the property logics of settler occupation. In this way, the text frustrates the ontological presuppositions of federal acknowledgment by implicitly rejecting the dichotomy of preservation versus loss, instead casting peoplehood as mutable in its persistence despite state-sanctioned catastrophe and planned disappearance.

For that reason, the work that Miranda's text performs is not that of testimony. Although it certainly registers the ongoing legacy of state ideologies and practices, its employment of the trope/topos of birth suggests that its aim lies less in intervening within or deconstructing the system of Indian policy than in creating (and documenting the creation of) forms of sociality, subjectivity, and spatiality that operate differently from those institutionalized as real Indian/tribal identity. In discussing women's participation in the postapartheid hearings in South Africa, Fiona C. Ross argues, "As practice, testifying threatens culture's limits, remaking the everyday by uncovering silenced domains of experience that underpin habitual ways of being," highlighting the "need [for] ways of hearing the effects of the dissolution of the everyday" (48).[58] This process, though, involves inhabiting state terms and processes in order to distend them, opening them to "domains of experience" that cannot be accommodated easily within existing administrative frameworks. Yet while *The Zen of La Llorona* can be understood as attending to "ways of being" that take shape around state-sanctioned displacement and erasure, does such sustained reflection on, and critique of, the dynamics and effects of settler violence constitute testimony? What does it mean to write as if one were testifying, and what is the horizon of such activity? Such questions have clustered around readings of *testimonios*—nonfictional texts often in a semiautobiographical mode generated by oppressed groups (examined most extensively in the context of Latin America) that speak to state policies of systemic domination, exploitation, and disappearance of those who dissent.[59] In *Testimonio,* John Beverley, perhaps the most consistent commentator on the genre over the past twenty years, suggests that this kind of writing indexes forms of "ungovernability" within contemporary political life, which he defines as "the incommensurability between the 'radical heterogeneity' of the subaltern and the reason of state," which "designates the failure of formal politics and of the nation—that is, of hegemony" (18).[60] The nation-state has failed to integrate such groups in a meaningful way into the circuit of citizenship and/or to adjust law and policy in ways that would generate room for substantively recognizing and legitimizing alternative sociopolitical formations. More than merely indicating the presence of domination, though, testimonios "trac[e] the frontiers of the authority of the state," "expanding the compass of what counts as expression in civil society" (19), and in this way they position the subaltern "as agent of a transformative project that aspires to become hegemonic in its own right" (75).

Does Miranda's text fit this frame? Although in many ways indexing the multivectored effects of "the authority of the state" and pointing to the ways experiences of indigeneity have been rendered subaltern by histories of official erasure, the text neither makes a bid for hegemony nor presents its account as representative. *Zen*'s figuration of birth suggests a collective self-creation that seeks less to gain "expression in civil society" than to acknowledge how the *I* already is a *we,* bearing within itself links to an Indigenous past, connection to the land, and the potential for rejuvenating both in the present if one can accept loss as its condition of possibility. Even as it traces processes by which Native people come to experience themselves as having/being "nothing," the text resists the notion that such structures of feeling could themselves become the basis for public policy, or at least the text does not appear to call for state recognition of what previously had been disavowed. Miranda's declaration that she "is not a witness" marks how official accounts and actions have denied to her and other Esselen and Chumash people a knowledge of their history and lands while also indicating her distance in time from their appearance in official records, but that statement also inflects the meaning of her insistence that "I am here," implying that her existence as a Native person is not dependent on or articulated to the kind of official acknowledgment suggested by the image of testimony. Thus, while in some sense seeking to index and document subaltern knowledges and modes of identification through its attention to affective formations, the text's portrayal of the Indigenous erotic as a process of creation envisions a mode of peoplehood that cannot be captured through a conception of sovereignty or self-determination defined primarily by reference to the juridical apparatus. Mishuana Goeman argues that "conceiv[ing] of space as not bounded by geo-politics, but storied and continuous, is necessary in developing a discourse that allows Native nation building its fullest potential and members of nations its fullest protection."[61] As suggested earlier, Miranda's exploration of Native melancholy does not so much present an alternative to federal acknowledgment as highlight aspects of contemporary indigeneity that cannot be accommodated within it, that do not obey its logic of archivally visible, tribal continuity. Such attention to forms of subjectivity that coalesce around attributes other than the official criteria for determining Indianness foregrounds the ways Indigenous experience is powerfully affected by state discourses but cannot be encapsulated within them.[62]

This dynamic coalesces in the closing piece, "dia de las muertas." The proem begins, "It's your own heart, your old heart, buried under the dry brown earth," but rather than taking this apparent scene of mourning as an occasion for sorrow, the "you" should "Buy yourself a handful of sugar skulls, crunch them between your back teeth, make sweet juice of saliva and sugar cane" (106).[63] A celebration emerges out of burial, loss becoming a site of joy. That potential for transformation seems to depend on a kind of self-splitting between the "heart" capable of such happiness and the "old heart" given over to the "earth." Although the heart's internment suggests a connection to the land, the chiasmus of "own" and "old" (emphasized by the terms' alliteration and length) implies that what is being buried is a kind of possessiveness—a conception of oneself and one's relation to place in terms of ownership. As I have argued, the text casts such an imaginative and emotional investment in property both as an endemic feature of the settler landscape, and thus an inescapable element of contemporary life for Indigenous people, and as a structure of feeling that produces Native shame and invisibility, from which indigeneity can and must be differentiated. Here, though, rather than Indigenous identity serving as the object of mourning, implying its disappearance, the funeral seems to be for settler notions of reality. In describing the Day of the Dead festival, Miranda enjoins,

> Let the songs work their seduction; sing yourself hoarse, fake the Spanish words you don't know, will never know. You don't care! One colonizer's tongue is the same as the next. It's yours now—you've earned it, untied it, flayed it, learned how to ride it. Let's dance on this grave, then, in any language so long as they all say goodbye, farewell . . . so long as they all say so long, thanks for all the tears.[64]

Using the Spanish language does not entail the eradication of a sense of indigeneity; to inhabit the language of the "colonizer," even in ways that (re)shape the body itself (suggested by the image of the "tongue"), cannot be equated with simple surrender to the program of colonization itself. While "any language" will do, "they all" speak of loss and "tears." Burial seems to indicate less an ending than a transmutation, whereby that which is supposedly gone becomes something else.[65]

Moreover, the invocation of the Day of the Dead provides an improper context for discussion of the survival of Indigenous peoples in California. Linked to Mexican identity, it cannot authenticate a claim to indigeneity—ties to a specific people and homeland. It does not signify as Native within the "technology of tribalism" utilized by nonnative officials and some experts,[66] within which the extinction of the Esselen people is a fact disprovable only through appeal to documentary evidence of demonstrably Indian continuity. As with the figure of La Llorona, the weeping woman referred to earlier in the text as a "legend" rather than (official) history (2), the Day of the Dead is from the wrong tradition to index identification as Esselen or Chumash. In this way, like the earlier allusion to the missions, it expresses the enduring legacy of Spanish imperial presence in California, but as in that earlier moment in the text, it also speaks of survival through loss. Unlike in the story of La Llorona (cast in the text as La Malinche), whose pursuit of retribution results in "*her power to create*" being "*stolen*," "*transform[ing] her into a destroyer*" (1), the celebration of La Dia de las Muertas engenders a very different result: "Ah, this is the only true revenge: picnicking in the cold November air on the fresh grave of your own worn-out heart." Implicitly directed against the "colonizer," this "revenge" leads not to destruction but to possibility. Rather than becoming "like them" (as Miranda describes her father in "After San Quentin"), the transformation here involves accessing the potential for a sustaining sense of connection to other people and to place amid continuing loss.[67]

Returning to the trope of birth/creation, Miranda closes the piece, and the collection, with the following: "At midnight, your lover plants a new seed in you, a flower only she knows how to coax into bloom. At dawn, she calls down the rain." This image echoes the moment in "Love Poem to a Butch Woman," addressed to the same lover as "From a Dream, I Wake to Tender Music," in which Miranda declares:

> I want to mother your child made only
> of us, of me, you; no borrowed seed
> from any man. I want to re-fashion
> the matrix of creation, making a human being
> from the human love that passes between
> our bodies . . .
>   (65)

This reference to "seed" draws on the term's use as a synonym for "sperm," indicating a wish to merge the creative potential of her desire for women with the literal conception of a child. By choosing this term, Miranda implicitly draws on its meaning as the basis for germinating plant life, as well as its connotation of immersion in the land. Those associations, though, are somewhat attenuated, providing a vague impression of a relation to territory without developing it. By contrast, "dia de las muertas" makes that connection explicit, presenting Margo's care for Miranda as an extension of her careful tending of the land. Rather than replacing the other sense of planting seed as having sex, this final piece redeploys it in ways that weave it through the figure of sowing, intertwining the two in ways that indicate the generativity of their desire and its connection to an immersion in place that itself enacts "revenge" against the "colonizer's" effort to destroy and erase indigeneity. Notably, the "seed" is planted "in" Miranda, instead of the ground, recalling her description of her emotional life as "hungry soil," as well as her observation that "The place that knows me is a woman" (17, 93). As in Driskill's description of "stories" as having the capacity to "split skin," Miranda's depiction of her relation with her lover as a seed planted within her emphasizes the movement from the internal to the external, the process of growing, developing, and changing in ways not initially visible and not intelligible within administrative grids of acknowledgment and sovereignty. The figure of the seed suggests that something is retained from the past in order to germinate new possibilities that are composed out of yet not equivalent to what came before.

Unlike the notion of testimony, the figure of the seed suggests that something is retained from the past in order to germinate new possibilities. In depicting her erotic life—and its representation in the text—as a "seed," Miranda highlights the simultaneity of preservation and transformation, positioning desire as a crucial source of both commemoration and vitality in which loss actually can engender creation. This final image coalesces the movement from the internal to the external landscape that the text charts, reaffirming that a sense of landedness persists within/as Native subjectivity in the wake of dispossession and erasure. As opposed to understanding this survival in grief as a blocked form of mourning, a refusal to let go of what is literally gone, it appears as an act of melancholic (re)birth, Native modes of sociality and spatiality arising out of what appeared to be "nothing." Fantasy, a refusal to take official declarations and mappings of reality as given, provides a way of turning, in Dian Million's phrase, "emotional knowledges" embedded within seemingly individual structures of feeling into the basis for giving expression to collective reimaginings of indigeneity in the contemporary moment.

Settler ideologies of possession and personhood can be characterized, returning to Lynda Hart's formulation quoted earlier, as "an entire symbolic system that erects itself on the foundation of the negation" of Indigenous peoples, whose experience must be erased, since it disjoints the governing categories of the social order of settlement. From one angle Miranda's poetry seeks to trace that negation. As Hart also suggests, however, survival entails creating "her own symbolic," one that is "discordant with the dominant order's symbolic" (178), and *The Zen of La Llorona* suggests such a process of invention through its representation of desire as reconnecting psychic life and collective memory to the still-living landscape. That process is not one in which land provides a figure for dynamics that fundamentally are internal to individual consciousness. Rather, the text repeatedly works to indicate how such consciousness is formed out of a disavowed history of settler violence, tracking the ways it bears the impress of legacies of Native occupancy and imperial displacement, and Miranda illustrates how serving as a "container" for "our colonized history" opens the potential for reuniting selfhood and place in ways not defined by possession. Yet in warning against the pursuit of a "whole[ness]" or a "land without scars" that somehow escapes or transcends the inheritance of loss, the text also insists on situating the possibilities it explores within an entrenched geography of settler presence. In seeking to investigate how the symbolic system of settlement is realized in quotidian ways, such as through the property logics of marriage, Miranda offers a kind of counterlegend to that of La Llorona, one that gestures toward and itself performs the potential for alternative Indigenous ways of living within the system formed by colonization and patriarchy. However, in emphasizing the contingency of that sense of possibility and the material difficulties it faces, Miranda avoids suggesting that it can substitute for legal recognition, even as the text implicitly raises questions about the version of peoplehood acknowledged and awarded self-determination by the state and the elisions enacted by that endowment of *tribal* status.

< 3 >

Genealogies of Indianness

The Errancies of Peoplehood in Greg Sarris's
Watermelon Nights

THE REGULATIONS THAT STRUCTURE THE FEDERAL ACKNOWL-
edgment process specify that petitioners must demonstrate that
they comprise an "American Indian entity." Doing so can involve proof
of "identification as an Indian entity by Federal authorities," "relationships with State governments based on identification of the group
as Indian," and "dealings with . . . local government in a relationship
based on the group's Indian identity."[1] However, what does "Indian"
mean? What entities count as Indian, and perhaps more pointedly,
how does characterizing such entities as Indian work to contain the
challenge they pose to the self-evidence of U.S. jurisdiction over Indigenous peoples and lands? The search for a definition of "Indian"
in the regulations leads one into tautology: "Indian group or groups
means any Indian or Alaska Native aggregation"; "Indian tribe . . .
means any Indian or Alaska Native tribe, band, pueblo, village, or
community that the Secretary of the Interior acknowledges to exist
as an Indian tribe."[2] "Indian" delimits what kinds of "aggregation[s]"
can apply for recognition as a "tribe," but what makes a given "aggregation" *Indian*? Genealogy appears crucial in answering this question.
Substantive evidence that "the petitioning group comprises a distinct
community" includes "significant rates of marriage within the group"
and that "at least 50 percent of the marriages in the group are between
members of the group," and one of the crucial criteria for acknowledgment is that "the petitioner's membership consists of individuals who
descend from a historical Indian tribe."[3] Representing Indianness as

< 153 >

a function of marriage and descent, a quality transmitted as an inborn generational inheritance, positions it within extant U.S. notions of racial identity.

Versions of the question, what is an Indian? extend far beyond federal acknowledgment, bedeviling all levels of Indian policy, and scholars have explored how U.S. legal and administrative discourses utilize racial and political criteria in engaging with Native peoples, inconsistently employing logics and rhetorics that are both contradictory and at odds with principles at play in other aspects of U.S. governance.[4] The concept of an "American Indian entity," though, suggests that these two approaches—race and politics—are not so easily differentiated, instead providing the condition of intelligibility for the other. To be *Indian* is to belong to or have ancestors that were members of a *tribe,* and to be a *tribe* is to have members who are *Indians,* a characteristic conceived in reproductive terms distinct from the dynamics of governance.[5] Concepts that one could categorize either as racial or as political intersect in crucial ways, fundamentally cross-referencing each other and thereby frustrating any effort to tease these two modes apart. If Indianness is deeply, perhaps inextricably, woven into administrative and popular understandings of what a tribe is, Indigenous peoples are left to grapple with racial reckonings of indigeneity as a central, ongoing feature of both their engagements with settler publics and their shifting self-conceptions of their own peoplehood.[6]

While race requires a logic of genealogy—the passage of something via reproduction and the sense that one can locate one's personal identity/social position by tracing backward one's family line through procreative unions—does genealogical reckoning necessarily indicate an at least implicit notion of race? Increasingly, scholars have turned to kinship as a concept that can index forms of genealogical continuity and regularity within Native social formations that are not reducible to the inheritance of Indian blood substance.[7] Yet this line of analysis runs headlong into a long-standing anthropological critique of the notion of kinship, given its emergence from nineteenth-century Euro-American ethnology, as simply taking the nuclear family model as a neutral basis for cross-cultural comparison.[8] From this perspective, invoking kinship can naturalize the heteronormative paradigm of reproductive couplehood that also subtends notions of racial inheritance, less producing an alternative frame than complexly supplementing existing discourses of Indianness. In *Watermelon Nights* Greg Sarris explores how state regimes of (in)visibility shape Native narratives of family identity and history, illustrating how certain kinds of genealogical emplotments are privileged over other accounts of peoplehood.[9] These narratives respond to endemic, state-sanctioned forms of assault and erasure by producing Native authenticity as an endangered characteristic that needs to be preserved through proper forms of maritally centered and procreatively directed family formation. As with Driskill's poetry discussed in chapter 1, Sarris reveals how the effort to pool and protect Indian bloodedness reenacts state-induced trauma as a condition of collective identity, and through the story of three generations of a single Pomo family living in the vicinity of Santa Rosa in Northern California over the course of the twentieth century, the novel investigates how demands for purity and charges of perversity shape relations among a people while also defining the terms of debate over belonging.[10] As Renya K. Ramirez argues in *Native Hubs*, scholars need to consider not only official definitions of tribal identity/membership but "Native *vernacular* notions of citizenship and belonging" (15). Such notions may include those that have been circulated as part of U.S. policy regimes, and Sarris's novel situates everyday Pomo identification as *Indian* within broader efforts to regulate eroticism, intimacy, and morality, presenting racialization as of a piece with other attempts to evaluate Pomo behavior and association by measuring it against a normative genealogical grid. Rather than casting that attempt by Pomos to manage each other as antithetical to the exertion of sovereignty as a polity, the text portrays how such policing of seemingly private associations is conceptualized as integral to maintaining tribal coherence, whether in the pursuit of federal recognition in the present or in responding to displacement from traditional lands in the past. Sarris illustrates how a tight genealogical structure comes to be treated as a metonym for Pomo peoplehood, and in this way, the novel explores how peoplehood becomes literalized as the possession of (genealogically regulated) Indianness.

The investment in that ideal translates ongoing structural constraints on the performance of sovereignty as a tribe into charges against other Pomos whose lapses into perversity can be blamed for their ongoing poverty and dispossession. The focus on interpersonal relations within a given Native community and their imbrications in the politics of tribal identity differs from Miranda's representation discussed in chapter 2. If *The Zen of La Llorona* substitutes an inherited (if somewhat inchoate) sense of loss for blood Indianness as the index of the persistence of indigeneity, *Watermelon Nights* investigates how claims to bloodedness, as well as associated narratives of genealogical order, shape negotiations in the present among members of the community over the contours and meaning of indigeneity amid persistent settler violence. The issue in the novel is less the state-imposed demand for a kind of documentable continuity, which effaces histories of assault and rupture, than the circulation of discourses of Indianness (themselves a residue of U.S. policy frameworks) among a people in ways that naturalize the dynamics of settler political economy by treating peoplehood as a function of relative conformity to a heteronormative model of reproductive couplehood.[11] In this vein, the text demonstrates how communal experiences of "sadness" due to the legacy of expropriation of Pomo land and labor are (re)narrated as a result of individuals' failures to uphold kinds of familial/racial/sexual purity, pegging survival as a *tribe* to the continued maintenance of the genealogical boundaries of Indianness. This process gives rise to forms of "hatefulness"—cycles of blame in which everyone understands shared destitution as the result of other individuals' moral errancy. Individuals' personal inability to regulate their desires and conduct produces collective declension, a falling away from tribal ideals—or the ideal of a *tribe*—that threatens to dissolve Pomo identity entirely.

As against this vision of a pure past that must be reclaimed through the performance of proper Indianness in the present, the novel redirects attention to the contexts informing, and relations among Pomos generated by, that investment in normative genealogy.[12] Broken into three sections arranged nonchronologically and told in the first person (one focused on Johnny, a young adult in the 1990s; the next on his grandmother Elba in the 1930s; and the last on his mother, Iris, primarily in the 1950s yet continuing up to Johnny's story), the text explores the dynamics of Pomo community in each period. Sarris attends less to what is passed within the family than to how the narrators violate (heteronormative) standards of propriety. In this way, the novel tracks how charges and countercharges of perversity—*hatefulness*—function as a way of negotiating conditions created by the ongoing exertion of settler power while also illustrating how such animosity actually bespeaks the presence of a malleable, durable social network that testifies to the existence of a kind of peoplehood neither reducible to reproductively conveyed Indianness nor readily captured in the policy construct of *tribe*.

The text's reorientation from the attempt to preserve unbroken lineage to exploration of the historical and social formations out of which that project of purification emerges resonates with Foucault's notion of genealogical method. In "Nietzsche, Genealogy, History," he offers a conception of genealogy that challenges its commonsensical associations, "oppos[ing] itself to the search for origins" (77). It "does not pretend to go back in time to restore an unbroken continuity" (81), and in this way, it refuses the narration of the relation between the past and the present as the preservation of an (endangered) essence—the "purest possibilities" of "carefully protected identities" (78). In noting that "the origin always precedes a fall," that it "lies at the place of inevitable loss" (78), Foucault's critique connects the positing of an origin to the threat of loss in ways that describe well the conditions of settler policy and displacement that produce and circulate the sense of tribal purity in need of protection. In other words, charges of perversity work to secure the impression of an effort to safeguard an original Pomo identity, but the novel suggests that particular perspective on Pomoness only emerges in the wake of settler-instituted losses and that it indexes kinds of community dynamics—*sadness*—that result from such losses. In a sense, then, the novel offers a critical genealogy of Pomo deployments of normative genealogy. However, unlike Foucault's emphasis on "maintain[ing] passing events in their proper dispersion" (81), "fragment[ing] what was thought unified" in order to reveal the appearance of unity as the work of an interested "will to knowledge" (82, 95), Sarris tracks how an experience of peoplehood persists in and through the violence of displacement and exploitation.[13] Rather than demonstrating the fragility of Pomo identity, its contingency on the conjunction of a set of historically quite circumscribed factors, the novel highlights the density and durability of Pomo peoplehood, the ways shifting modes

of communal cohesion are irreducible to the will to Indianization—
or will to tribalization—animating U.S. policy. The text's refusal of a
frame based on lineage-based reprosexuality opens the potential for
exploring how peoplehood exceeds that logic and how the adoption of
that logic by Pomos themselves intensifies their alienation from each
other without addressing or redressing the structural conditions that
produce collective sadness.[14]

Conversely, Sarris's genealogical method highlights key features
and figures in Waterplace Pomo life that are pathologized when measured against a racializing, heteronormative standard, and he explores
the forms of communal solidarity, affective bonds, and cultural knowledge elided through that abjection. The text's attention to the place
of homosexuality, prostitution, illegitimate births, and intimacy with
non-Indians in the community over three generations reveals the role
of fallen persons in the (re)constitution of collectivity, though in ways
that do not fit a dominant model of tribal identification. By tracking these impure figures, and the social relations in which they are
enmeshed, the novel explores ongoing processes of community formation that sustain peoplehood as a dynamic network, even as those
very persons are cast by others as having failed to perform Pomoness
properly. In this way, Pomo identity appears less as an entity based on
an unfolding from a pristine origin than as continually in flux, made
and remade amid the changing conditions of settler occupation—as a
mesh of multiple (potentially incommensurate) *vernaculars*. What
gives it coherence, then, is not the transmission of Indian blood substance or the regularity of heteroconjugal inheritance. If as Foucault
suggests, there needs to be an "affirmation of knowledge as perspective" (90), the novel investigates a Pomo will to peoplehood that draws
from shared histories and stories, recirculating them with a difference in the present. The act of storytelling about collective experiences
(re)produces intense emotional bonds that reflect existing interdependencies while offering the potential to redirect sadness and hatefulness
toward support and understanding. Such stories figure other ways of
being Pomo—other modes of Pomo *being*—than those that conserve
bloodedness, taken as the literalized marker of belonging. The novel
illustrates how Pomos generate, alongside narratives of tribal declension, their own genealogical analyses, creating an overlapping web of

stories through which they can reconceptualize and reorder their lived relations to each other. Laura Furlan Szanto suggests that in the novel "stories become a means to entitlement in an age of dispossession" (81). The novel suggests that as opposed to the accusatory narrative of a fall into perversity lies the possibility of a more generous story of continued communal survival that recognizes ongoing legacies of structural violence while positioning being together as an occasion for joy and hope.

Authenticating Hatefulness

As discussed in chapter 2, the pursuit of federal acknowledgment requires that a people narrate themselves in ways that fit the *tribal* mold of U.S. administrative discourses. Part of this process involves proving descent from persons whose Indianness is archivally verifiable.[15] To make claims for official recognition entails tracing lines of lineage that can establish the group's existence as an "American Indian entity." What aspects of Native sociality and history are occluded in that effort to legitimize *Indian* collective selfhood? Or put another way, how does the need to stage collective identity in these terms affect intratribal relations—the narratives the people tell of themselves to themselves and the kinds of community dynamics those discourses engender and propel? In *"Real" Indians and Others,* Bonita Lawrence argues that "understandings of Native identity have been couched in terms of *primordiality,*" in which tradition is imagined as "transmitted in relatively unbroken lines from a distant past, and generally [it is] combined with 'racial' purity" as a means of "defin[ing] membership in a specific tribal group" (1). For this reason, "to theorize Native identity not as an authentic essence but as something negotiated and continuously evolving can have dangerous repercussions for Native people in terms of asserting Aboriginal rights" (3), and "these bodies of legislation have had powerful effects on how Indianness is seen in common-sense ways" (16).

In the first section of *Watermelon Nights,* set in the 1990s and centered on a young adult named Johnny Severe, the Waterplace Pomos are pursuing federal acknowledgment, and the text addresses how the genealogies he and others collect intersect with and help shape

commonsense understandings of Pomo identity, transforming pervasive "sadness" into a "hatefulness" that often takes the form of charges
of perversity and sexual license—including against Johnny for being
queer.[16] Sarris juxtaposes this portrait of how heteronormative kinds
of state intelligibility circulate among Pomos with his account of earlier revivalist projects of purification. Set primarily in the 1930s and
narrated by Johnny's grandmother Elba, the second section fills out
readers' sense of the historical and structural context that produces the
sadness of the first section. Reciprocally, this section implicitly compares the call for greater racial/sexual order in the Bole Maru movement of the late nineteenth and early twentieth centuries with the
pursuit of acknowledgment, presenting the former less as the transmission of untrammeled Pomo tradition than as itself a reaction to
settler violence that replicates dominant genealogical norms and uses
them in ways that exacerbate tensions among the people.[17]

As part of the bid for official recognition, the Waterplace Pomos
gather "genealogy charts" that trace their individual ancestry back to
a set of nineteenth-century figures (the two Rosas), a job that largely
falls on Johnny, but as he performs this required task, he offers commentary on both the limits of such recognition and the ways the
modes for securing it aggravate insecurities in the Pomo community.
The first description of this project emphasizes how it remains inextricably interwoven with several modes of distinction that seem to
vitiate the kinds of integration and affirmation recognition promises:

> He [Raymond Pen—the illegitimate son of Steven Pen, the
> tribal chairman] pulled out his genealogy chart and placed
> it on the table so I could see the work he'd done. Which was
> another thing to lord over me. Each one of us was supposed
> to complete our charts. It was one of a list of things we had to
> do to prove to the government that we was real Indians. Our
> tribe was trying to get what is called 'federally acknowledged'
> so we could have a reservation and gossip and fight each other
> there instead of in town on Grand Avenue, where most of
> us live. That's what the upcoming meeting was about, these
> charts each of us was supposed to fill out and turn in, which,
> if you ask me, look no different from dog pedigrees. (5)

Though acknowledgment could lead to the acquisition of a "reservation," federally protected land over which the tribe could exert sovereignty as a coherent polity, that vision of unification depends on bracketing the current conditions of community life. Not only does it seem to invalidate the kinds of networks and placemaking already present "in town on Grand Avenue," in some sense cordoning off Indianness into a "there" separated from "where most of us live," but the granting of semisovereign space will fail to ameliorate the causes of "gossip" and "fight[ing]."[18] In fact, the passage suggests that the effort to "prove ... we was real Indians" can inflame such conflict, as indicated by the ways Johnny experiences Raymond's completed genealogy chart as an effort to "lord" something over him.[19] Comparing the genealogies to "dog pedigrees" indicates that what is at stake in them is proving purity of bloodlines; to be "real" is to have proper "Indian" breeding, illustrating the absence of contamination or mongrelizing mixture in one's family line. This documentation of descent creates a similar impression as the logic of the reservation, in that it seems to wedge apart the ideal and the actual in ways that denigrate the latter as adulterated and in need of cleansing through segregation.

The need to mobilize evidence of Indian "pedigree" contributes to divisions within the community, intensifying feelings of genealogical inadequacy. Johnny notes that he is "light-skinned, hardly a quarter Indian," an observation that comes in the wake of Raymond's assertion that despite the fact that his "mother's from another tribe," he is "full Indian" (5). Being "Indian" clearly appears inadequate for being identified as Pomo, since the former can be inherited from persons not in the "tribe" (thus seeming definitionally distinguishable from tribal identity), but the experience of one's Pomo identity draws on Indianness as a condition of authenticity. It provides a gradient for assessing tribal belonging, serving as a literalized marker of Pomoness. The invocation of "full" bloodedness here functions, though, as a way of deferring the questions raised by Raymond's parentage—that his mother and father never lived together as partners and certainly were not married, making him a bastard. The idea of blood simultaneously operates as part of the state's process of accounting—corroborating the *realness* of petitioners for acknowledgment—and as part of a broader calculus of legitimacy among Pomos based on forms of genealogical reckoning. That very reliance on lineage as an index of relative status within the community seems to have less to do with Pomo beliefs unrelated to the process of recognition than with the legacy of efforts to inculcate certain conceptions of family among Native peoples, of which the genealogy charts are the latest example.[20]

At one point Johnny exclaims, "A tribe, hell, it's a family. One big family" (7), and although that image seems to suggest a capacious, horizontal conception of communal identity, one focused on the complex sets of relations among Pomos in the present moment, it gives way to a vertical understanding organized around the hetero-reproductive structure of the chart itself. Johnny indicates that

> a blank space there [in the line for "father"], or anywheres on the chart, meant one of two things: Either you didn't know who the person was or, if you did know, you was ashamed. Both of which causes embarrassment. Particularly if you're Indian, since lots of us have blank spaces; and now with everybody wanting to be full blood and all, nobody wants to claim relations that ain't Indian. (11)

The chart is organized around a straight line passing from parent to child, so connections with other Pomo people who are not one's direct progenitors appear irrelevant within this frame. Instead, it generates a comparative framework in which relative inherited Indianness serves as the sign of what it means to be properly Pomo, and the *blankness* illustrates an embarrassing failure in one's relation to the community, one that is irremediable. This process suggests "how a classificatory system produces a way of thinking—a grammar—which embeds itself in every attempt to change it."[21] The eruption of negative affect—of *shame*—that comes from implicitly or explicitly comparing charts is a significant feature of how Pomos engage with each other now, but such emotion seems simply an effect of individuals' deficiencies due to the inability of their families to fit the terms of the chart, which itself appears as a neutral framework rather than as an imposed structure predicated on the nuclear family logic of conjugal pairing that also subtends the notion of the biological passage of racial substance. Normalizing this genealogical model effaces the collective conditions that lead to "lots of us hav[ing] blank spaces" (due to having non-Indian relatives or being the result of nonmarital intercourse), and doing so further occludes the ways that similarity points to the pathologizing inadequacy of the chart as a way of apprehending Pomo sociality.

The apparent obviousness of the chart also brackets the role of settler policy in incentivizing certain genealogical "claim[s]" by tying valid tribal identity to bloodedness. The basis of a collective claim to real Pomoness rests on everyone being able to link themselves to each other via these lines such that all intersect in the past at a point that can then be understood as the origin of the tribe—a place of pure Indianness cast as distributed downward generationally. In *Queer Phenomenology* Sara Ahmed argues that a key part of dominant notions of "straightness" (heteronormativity) lies in the projection backward of a genealogical line:

> The normative dimension can be redescribed in terms of
> the straight body, a body that appears "in line." Things seem
> "straight" (on the vertical axis), when they are "in line," which
> means when they are aligned with other lines. Rather than
> presuming the vertical line is simply given, we would see the
> vertical line as an effect of this process of alignment. (66)

The production of a "vertical line" for inheriting Pomo Indianness occurs through a "process of alignment" in which "blank spaces" on the chart indicate threats to tribal identity, intrusions into the pedigree that will secure a government-recognized right to existence as a people. Such deviations need to be hidden, kept silent, but they are also the subject of community policing, given that their accretion endangers the possibility of maintaining the integrity of the "tribe." Ahmed suggests that "straightness gets attached to other values including decent, conventional, direct, and honest" and that "any non-alignment produces a queer effect" (70, 83), and in this case concern for the well-being of the tribe means affirming its racialized/racializing straightness, maintaining the coherence of its genealogies by managing and abjecting relations that produce *blankness*—itself a "queer" disruption of Pomo identity (at least as envisioned through the prism of state documentation).

This kind of self-policing, as well as the embarrassment and shame it generates, seems to be counterproductive to everyone unifying around acknowledgment and its promise of a reservation for the tribe. Yet even as some characters make versions of that argument, the novel illustrates how engagement with the process of acknowledgment, as well as the naturalization of its codes of authenticity, actually incites the kinds of instability, accusation, and recrimination that recognition is supposed to transcend. In the middle of a regular tribal meeting in response to the outbreak of conflict, examined below, Steven Pen, the chairman, exclaims, "Listen, no use hashing over the past," "We've got to look at the ways we've hung together, not split apart," and he adds, "We're a tribe. One people. One blood" (59). The call to leave behind "the past" is an effort to bracket ongoing antagonisms in the community, but the pursuit of acknowledgment requires reliving it, if only to prove the forms of descent and continuity the federal government demands. However, the very need to mount this effort recalls the circumstances that have produced Pomo landlessness, and the fight Steven interrupts is precisely over allocating responsibility for that loss. Whereas this battle between the Bill sisters (Mona and Lena) and the families of Zelda Toms and Nellie Copaz over how to narrate that history lays the blame at the feet of particular individuals, Johnny's assessment of the situation takes a different tack: "It's a crazy thing, having to prove to the United States that we're Indians when they seen us as Indians once before . . . I say, what's to keep them from changing their minds again, even if we do prove ourselves Indians to their satisfaction" (58). Rather than understanding specific Pomos as guilty for their displacement, Johnny suggests that this insecurity is due to U.S. officials "changing their minds" in ways that Pomo people can neither predict nor control. *Proving* "we're Indians," as well as the genealogical architecture on which that claim rests, appears as bound up in the capriciousness of settler-state policy. Recalling Steven's attempt at pacification, one can see how the administrative logic of Indianness shapes his vision of what being "together" entails—"we're a tribe," "one blood." To be a "tribe" involves measuring oneself through the genealogical codes enshrined in the acknowledgment regulations, and the call to let go of "the past" disables analysis of how certain inherited terms and strategies through which to articulate peoplehood bear within them histories of settler efforts to regulate and erase indigeneity and the anxieties such efforts generate.

Johnny's discussion of the fickleness of the U.S. government with respect to recognizing Pomo presence suggests a pervasive insecurity that can be seen as generating collective structures of feeling,[22] but instead of taking the form of a critique of the *craziness* of settler superintendence of their identity, they achieve expression as charges of deviance against other Pomos, including while exceeding the issue of blood quantum. In response to Steven's assertion that "each of us is related," the Bills, who are the primary instigators of hatefulness in this scene, publicly name two of his illegitimate children, overlooking Raymond. Steven's reaction to their effort to humiliate him by highlighting his failure to respect wedlock as the valid site of procreation is to remind the Bills that they have not submitted their genealogy charts, so "at this point you're not on our tribal rolls. Which means at this point you're not a member of this tribe." They explode, "Me and my sister here is the only ones got Waterplace Pomo full on both sides," and then they turn to Raymond, offering a stream of invective worth quoting in full:

> "Him, that boy of yours there. His mother ain't from this tribe. Was a drug addict, wasn't she? Explains why he's got AIDS. He ain't that sick and skinny for nothing." . . .
>
> "Speaking of AIDS," she said, and pointed to Edward [Nellie Copaz's grandson]. "Look at that." Then she turned back and pointed at Frances [Zelda Toms's daughter and a member of the tribal council].
>
> "Shut your mouth. Don't be saying I'm gay, you fat bitch!" Frances said with nothing less than a barroom challenge now. (60)

While indicating entrenched tensions, especially given that this attack is on members of the Toms and Copaz families (who are blamed for the land loss noted earlier),[23] this exchange frames them in terms of sexual indiscretion and perversity, as charges of adultery, bastardy, and homosexuality (AIDS functioning as a similar kind of sign given its long-standing association with stigmatized sexual desires and practices—as indicated in its use as a way of transitioning to the verbal assault on Edward). The failure to submit the proper genealogical documentation—the chart—puts into play a series of charges about what constitutes membership in the tribe. Claiming to be full-blood Waterplace Pomo as a mark of authentic belonging leans on the image of conjugally joined "sides," of heterocouplehood as the imaginary through which to derive blood purity. Calling out others based on their failure to approximate this ideal, then, seems less a diversion from the real purpose of recognition than, in many ways, an extension of its internal logic. As Ahmed suggests, "The queer orientation might not simply be directed toward the 'same sex,' but would be seen as not following the straight line" (7).

Frances's reaction, revulsion at the prospect of being labeled "gay," further suggests that the deployment of such heteronormative standards by Pomos against each other is certainly not new—that the paradigm of Indianness guiding recognition criteria plays on existing principles in the community. Linking this conflict so closely with the process and terms of acknowledgment, though, presents them as interwoven, bespeaking an ongoing legacy of settler intervention that has affected Pomo modes of self-representation. In discussing the vicissitudes of government recognition, Johnny notes his own doubts about Steven's optimism, who says, "We can control our fates, be as one as a people again, have a home that is ours and truly ours. Sounds good, I think. What does it mean?" (58). The question highlights how the criteria the Pomo need to meet for acknowledgment seem to confirm an existing entity, the apparent obviousness of "people[hood]" and "home," while actually ambiguating those very concepts, implying a longer struggle over how to conceptualize collective identity in which settler discourses have generated confusion and acrimony—another version of "changing their minds again."

The dynamic of ostracism and pathologization displayed in the tribal meeting is turned on Johnny himself when his own homosexuality comes to light, and through this episode, the novel more tightly ties the denigration of sexual nonnormativity to the broader histories of shame and uncertainty coalesced and reactivated through the genealogy chart. After a sexual encounter with Felix (who is staying with Mollie Toms, Zelda Toms's grandniece and Johnny's second cousin once removed)[24] and a conversation with Edward in which Johnny obliquely alludes to his desire for Felix, Johnny is asked to come to a meeting of Pomo young people by Felix. Once there, Felix makes clear that Edward has claimed that "you me and him was faggots," and in response to this assertion, Felix knocks Johnny to the ground and kicks him in the face so hard it actually punctures his cheek. In response, Johnny leaps up, chokes Edward, and then runs out (109–10). Notably, Felix had persuaded Johnny to attend by saying that the meeting is "about what we could do to help the tribe" (107), and he prefaces his assault on Johnny by asserting, "We have to deal with lying, people putting down tribal members" (109). While the claim to aid "the tribe" can be thought of as merely a ruse to fool Johnny, it also can be conceptualized as expressing extant understandings of the relationship between homosexuality and tribal belonging. To punish people for their perversity in some sense is *helping* the tribe, inasmuch as the latter is organized around a notion of heteroreproductive lineage to which homosexuality is considered a threat. Moreover, as seen in Frances's response at the tribal meeting, to insinuate that another Pomo is gay can be nothing but "putting [them] down," suggesting that the support and uplift of the tribe itself depends on avoiding contact with such contamination while also reinforcing the idea that "faggot" and "tribal member" should remain mutually exclusive categories. As Johnny suggests when contemplating the fallout from the stories about him that would circulate as a result of the meeting/beating, "No matter how kind or gentle, no matter what folks wanted to think, whether or not they'd be friendly with me, I'd see it. It would be in their eyes. Something that called me a stranger" (113). To be gay is to be a "stranger," which itself seems to gain its meaning through distinction from the kind of familial imaginary guiding tribal identification—Steven's earlier remarks that "we're a tribe . . . one blood," "each of us is related." Homosexuality positions one as outside that field of *relation*.

The novel illustrates how that process of alienation extends beyond homoeroticism to other deviations from normative straightness. Both before and after the assault, Johnny expresses no regret for his desire for and sexual experience with Felix, saying that it "felt good to me" and later adding that "I wasn't ashamed of what I had done . . .

because in a time like that I knowed I would do it again" (102, 123).[25] However, he observes how the stories circulated about him as a "faggot" would take their place among a series of similar narratives about other disgrace-inducing elements of Pomos' lives:

> How it works with them thing stories folks pin on one another and then talk about endlessly. Thing stories like drunk parents dying in the cold on lower Fourth, fathers that don't up front claim you, white blood, being a queer. Thing stories that make folks bow their heads in shame only to look up a day, a week, a year later with suspicion and hate at all the world and everybody they know. And then, so they won't be alone, singled out in their shame, they take to the business of collecting and spreading things stories about everybody else. (123)

Conjoining "being a queer" with other failures to live up to a social imaginary ordered around racially preservative conjugal couplehood, the passage suggests, turning back to Ahmed's terms, that Johnny's "queer orientation" cannot readily be distinguished in its effects on the community from other departures from the "vertical line" of Indian genealogy. Despite the ubiquity of such lapses (everyone "collecting and spreading thing stories about everybody else"), each person experiences his or her fall from grace as being "singled out." Although the ideal against which they are measuring themselves clearly has little relationship to the actual circumstances of community life, they continue to mobilize it in ways that demean and distance them from each other. The mention of "white blood" in the above passage hearkens back to the earlier discussion of the role of blood quantum calculations in the acknowledgment process (even implicitly in the demand to document *Indian* descent), and the text makes that connection explicit in Johnny's meditation on what it means for him now to be "something to talk about." That fact is like "the blank spots on folks' genealogy charts. The story nobody wanted told about themselves, the one they tried to forget or change into something other than what it was. I'd be wearing a story now like a shirt I couldn't get off" (118). This comparison to the genealogy charts implies that the sentiments that

turn him into a "stranger" based on his nonstraight desire are themselves part of a history of settler impositions/imperatives that have
played a prominent role in affecting Pomo self-conception, individually and collectively. The "blank spots" are expressions of the "thing
stories" that people seek to hide, but reciprocally, that linkage implies
that the narration of certain behaviors, associations, and pleasures as
"thing stories" can be traced, at least in part, to efforts to approximate
settler standards that promise to make them intelligible/acceptable as
an "Indian tribe."[26]

Thus, the novel situates homophobic denigration within a mapping
of contemporary collective patterns of affect and accusation that cannot simply be bracketed in the embrace of a state-sponsored vision of
unity predicated on shared origin. When talking with Johnny, Edward
insists, "We can't do anything, not a single thing together, nothing will
work until we deal with the hatefulness . . . the insecurities," citing
as an example "the way we talk to one another. The way they talked
to me!" (98; ellipses in original). Positioning the tribal meeting as a
paradigmatic instance, particularly the pathologization of Edward's
gayness, the novel here indicates that the actual dynamics of being
"together" are irreducible to the image of shared (lineage-based) tribal
identity, and the kinds of communal cohesion seemingly projected by
the notion of a tribe will remain impossible absent an engagement
with the existing relations among community members. The mention
of "insecurities" suggests a multiplicity of fault lines within Pomo
sociality—the absence of a crisp, clear line between normality and deviancy—while also alluding back to Johnny's earlier contextualization
of acknowledgment within a longer history of cycles of elision and
abandonment in U.S. Indian policy. In the wake of the tribal meeting,
but prior to the attack on Johnny, Felix offers his own commentary
on intratribal relations: "Every time anybody else starts to move, they
got to stop them, knock them down. We're at the bottom of the barrel, man, and nobody wants nobody to get out. It'll make everybody
confused because if we're all not at the bottom of the barrel then who
are we?"; "All Indians is like that. . . . Last hundred years—the entire
century—what've we done? This tribe. Lost. Lost. Lost. Lost. A hundred years of doom" (68–69). Here, hatefulness appears as a kind of
mutually assured destruction in which everyone seeks to disable the

possibility of movement or change for everyone else, maintaining the semblance of a "we" through elaborate rituals of disparagement and shaming. This somewhat apocalyptic perspective, itself bespeaking an almost sociopathic disdain for the feelings and welfare of others, is characteristic of Felix, further suggesting the community-destroying character of the attack on Johnny even as it is framed as for the good of the tribe. Yet amid the sense of impending "doom," the passage also presents these seemingly ingrained and immutable webs of spite as a function of an ongoing oppressive history—one that has put Indians "at the bottom of the barrel" for at least the "last hundred years."

Even as this story is rendered in terms of an aggregation of individual failures ("what've we done?"), reiterating the logic of interpersonal blame, it opens the potential for another kind of narrative. Expressions of hatefulness can be reread as indicative of both the ways Pomo people's lives are tied to each other in enduring ways and the structural conditions that help turn such interdependence into acrimony and that fuel charges of aberrance. Conveying his grandmother's sentiments, Johnny observes, "Indians is a mean, unhappy bunch. . . . She says Indians can't help it on account of Rosa and that Mexican general. Meanness. It's a song, she says, that keeps getting told over and over, passed from one generation to the next. The words might change, the melody don't" (6). "Rosa" refers to the mother of the woman seen as the nineteenth-century progenitrix of the tribe, whose people had died of a smallpox epidemic and who was taken as a wife by a Mexican general ("she was his wife in name only: She wasn't treated any better than a whore, a slave" [6]). The "meanness" that circulates in the present moment appears here as a legacy of histories of mass death, rape, and enslavement, transposing the normative genealogy of lineage (needed to prove that one is an "American Indian entity") into a critical genealogy of settler violence and its role in shaping relations among contemporary Pomos. Additionally, Johnny repeats Felix's barrel image just prior to his discussion of "thing stories," adding as a concluding thought, "A poisonous basket weaved together with their fear and hatred. My Indian community. And Felix knew it well, well enough to see the weave" (123). Implicitly invoking Felix's earlier reference to an "entire century" of "lost[ness]," Johnny's anatomy of "thing stories" (including "white blood," illegitimacy, "being a queer"), as well as the communal affect surrounding and circulating them, appears as part of the history of violence that unfolds in the wake of the virtual enslavement of the first Rosa in marriage to the Mexican general, itself an act of impressment into an alien genealogical order.

The description of meanness, fear, and hatred as a "song" transmitted across generations or as a "basket" somewhat ironically presents such apparently corrosive and destructive emotions as the very substance of the people's tradition, aligning them with two of the most well-known elements of Pomo culture. Songs have power within them, often appear to a person in dreams, serve as a key feature of Pomo knowledge production and engagement with the human and nonhuman worlds, and are owned and passed within families. Similarly, baskets historically have been one of the most prominent and significant features of Pomo material culture, also can be associated with spirits and dreams, play an important role in spiritual life, and involve skills that largely are learned through one's family.[27] In one sense, these moments somewhat sardonically cast hatefulness as just as much a crucial feature of Pomo collective identity as songs and baskets, but taken from another angle, they suggest that expressions and dynamics of hatefulness contain, albeit in a potentially "poisonous" way, elements of the history of the community that actually are vital to its survival.[28]

Moreover, attempts to preserve Pomo identity, to maintain the existence of the people in the face of nonnative aggression and dispossession, may rely on the deployment of hatefulness in ways that make it into a mode of tradition. When the novel in its second section turns from Johnny's story in the 1990s back to his grandmother Elba's childhood and young adulthood earlier in the century, it offers something of a history of hatefulness, illustrating how the kind of "thing stories" Johnny notes are ritualized as a way of trying to guard against pollution by whites. Big Sarah, the spiritual leader of the Waterplace Pomos, serves as the principal figure in this defense of tribal purity. Every night, she preaches for hours in the roundhouse—the building at the center of the village that functions as a sacred space.[29] Warning "about the evils of the white people" (149), she decries education in white-run schools and participation in Catholic or Pentecostal churches. These associations with nonnatives are described as *masan*—"the word she used, which means white, or white person," but which she also links to "traitor" (150–51). To interact with whites entails the risk not simply of inviting additional attention, surveillance, intervention but of betraying one's people through that very relation. Having sustained connections with whites and white-controlled institutions constitutes a violation of Pomo identity, an act of treason that would result in one being wiped away when others were saved: "There would be a flood, she said, cleaning the earth of white people. The faithful Indians would be planted back here with all the animals and plants the way it was before the white devil come; the unfaithful would drown, their souls left wandering . . . caught between this world and the next" (150). Maintaining tribal cohesion in the present depends on disavowing all things "white," an orientation that looks toward the wholeness of the past ("the way it was before") and the promise of future restoration of it ("would be planted back here").

This vision of redemption from the violence of "the white devil" is part of the Bole Maru religion, which began in the late nineteenth century. Like the later, more well-known Ghost Dance of the eastern Rockies and the Plains, its emergence responded to the increasingly invasive presence of settlers and their escalating disruption of Native lifeways.[30] As Sarris observes in his discussion of the Bole Maru in *Keeping Slug Woman Alive*, it "is not ancient. Rather it is a revivalistic religion, a religious, and ultimately political, response to European and Euro-American domination and ideology": "The Dreamers were predominantly women, and while they were not called chiefs, they assumed the role of tribal leaders, organizing their respective tribe's social and political activities around the doctrine of their Dreams" (65–66). Emerging out of Paiute communities in Nevada in 1870, a movement that promised the eradication of whites and the return of the Native dead through the practice of new ritual, especially dancing, moved quickly into Northern California. There, it was reformulated in terms of local traditions, mixing with existing Hesi and Kuksu ritual formations before spreading farther north up the Pacific coast. In this process of transmission and transformation, the Bole Maru— or in other places Bole Hesi—emerged, marked by the prominence of dreamers, mass participation in rituals that previously had been restricted to a select few, and the increased role of women in public spiritual life.

The novel presents Big Sarah as such a dreamer, and her rhetoric and leadership can be understood, in this way, as aiming to "inculcat[e] an impassioned Indian nationalism in the homes and roundhouses."[31] Yet while Sarris's account of such activity in his scholarship emphasizes its role in supporting tribal autonomy against ongoing settler incursion, exploitation, and erasure, the portrait offered in *Watermelon Nights* tends to highlight the ways the discourses and activities centered on the roundhouse seek to produce tribal unity through a pathologizing narrative of degeneration. Big Sarah warns "if you mingled unnecessarily with a white person—in particular if you married a white person—you wouldn't get to see [the promised afterlife]; neither would your children if they was mixed blood" (151). In this vein, one of the principal targets of her ire is Elba's aunt Chum, whose children were born out of wedlock, who had a child with a white man whom she had abandoned, and who was in the midst of a love affair with a white man and pregnant by him—Westin Benedict, the son of the owner of the ranch on which they reside. The text presents Chum as a person with good humor, good sense, and compassion, positioning her as the subject of reader identification (certainly of Elba's). Similarly, Big Sarah and those associated with her decry a mysterious figure known only as "Old Uncle," who arrives to care for Elba's guardian, Clementine (who had been selected to care for Elba after her mother's death and whose own children, save one, all had died), when she is dying. Not only does Old Uncle clearly possess extensive knowledge of Pomo medicinal practices and their traditional lands (as discussed in the next section), but he treats Elba with kindness, providing a point of reference to her in instructing her daughter and grandson in Pomo principles. However, Big Sarah suggests, "If he'd taken up with anybody down there [to the 'south' from which he had arrived], it sure wasn't an Indian, not the way he was dressed. 'Only a *masan* can put clothes like that on a man'" (191). A little later, some of the men, including Elmer Bill, who had been appointed tribal chief by Big Sarah, surmise, "Ain't no women taking care of him. . . . It's a man. . . . He's that kind of guy, you know. The kind that likes men" (202), a possibility that also marks Old Uncle as a *stranger* given that "according to Big Sarah" being "a homosexual" "was a white-man sin like drinking whiskey" (261). Forms of sexual impropriety are marked by their connection to whiteness, and such linkage indexes that person's treason to Pomo peoplehood, a falling away from "the way it was before."

The boundaries of tribal identity are secured through the policing of the distinction between white and Indian, and although the putative purpose of that effort lies in preserving the continuity of Pomo identity and lifeways, it relies on a reactive stance that takes up settler sexual logics. "The Pomo Indians donned Victorian clothing and lived seemingly Christian lives."[32] The charge of "treason" associated with things *masan* implies a rejection of the nation, a nationalism that is then constituted through a repudiation of whiteness. *Masan* simultaneously describes a turn away from the people and an infection by a kind of alien substance. This orientation/contamination is understood not only as a problematic engagement or extended copresence with certain kinds of bodies (whites) but as kinds of embodiment that bear the imprint of whiteness (like homosexuality). The integrity of Native nationality, therefore, depends on a normalization of bodily practice in which certain Pomo bodies are conceptualized as inhabited by treasonous tendencies,[33] treating the disruptions and dislocations of everyday life due to settler violence as a quality that inhabits certain (kinds) of Pomo persons. Particular forms of sexual practice come to symptomatize a disposition toward whiteness or away from properly national/tribal modes of embodiment.[34] To protect Pomo identity against loss due to white incursion, then, entails, in Ahmed's terms, a process of alignment in which "any nonalignment produces a queer effect" (83).

Although this guarding of community morals works to defend tribal independence, it takes up white Christian standards of sexual rectitude—and racial insularity—in ways that license violence by Pomos against each other while also creating an image of collective identity that is fairly disconnected from the lives of community members and that helps generate shame and alienation among them.[35] In ways that resemble the discussion of the "blanks" in the genealogical charts, the novel's depiction of Big Sarah's preaching and community response to it suggests the gaps between the ideal she projects and the everyday lives of Pomo people. Elba notes, "Big Sarah always said it was no good for us to go there and stand around like beggars. Gives the white people the wrong idea, she said. 'Ha!' Mama said. 'What does she think we are?' And Chum said the same thing" (167). A little later, she observes, "Like everybody else, if I felt anything while sitting in the roundhouse, listening to Big Sarah go on about our duties to the tribe, it was hunger" (182). Anxiety over white ideas about Native people seems to supplant concern for the latter's welfare, in the sense that the activity decried is a result of desperation and deprivation that cannot be remediated through the preservation of an image of propriety. Additionally, in her speeches "the tribe" appears to exist as an entity over and against the needs of its members, as a kind of abstraction disconnected from their experience of their own situation—even at the level of bodily sensation.

More than raising doubts about the relevance of Big Sarah's injunctions, the disparity between her vision of normative Pomo conduct and extant community practices serves as an indictment of the latter, creating the impression that the conditions that produce "hunger" result from Pomos' inability to live up to the moral standards she articulates. After a visit by the Moki—a spiritual leader invited from another village to help purify the community "and bring back the old-time harvest ceremony" (152)—in which he ends up throwing coals from the fire into the crowd at the roundhouse in condemnation of their state of pollution, Big Sarah holds out the possibility of redemption:

> We still had a chance, she said, if we mended our evil ways.
> The *Moki* would come back, she didn't know when, maybe
> not until the spring, and he would test us again. Not until
> everybody in the roundhouse was clean would he perform his
> ceremony. Which meant that not until everybody was clean
> would Creation pay attention to us. Which meant that not
> until everybody was clean would we have enough food and
> luck. (154)

These comments suggest the limits of her appeal and the consequences of it for communal self-understanding. Having failed the "test," they must assign blame for their starvation and immiseration to themselves as a function of their *uncleanliness*. The idea of being "clean" conjoins the spiritual and the physical, suggesting that impure modes of sensation (like interracial intimacy or homoeroticism) are expressive of an indwelling corruption that provides the explanation for their abject situation. What vanishes from view here is the ways their destitution can be traced to the failure of the federal government to "pay attention to" them, in the sense that at this point they have no legally recognized landbase (living on Benedict's land at his suffer-ance, although it is their "ancestral lands" [146]) and have little access to prior modes of subsistence—leaving them with no way to support themselves except through scant manual labor and domestic work for Benedict and in the surrounding areas.[36] Historically, this neglect of Indigenous geopolitical claims in California allowed for the wholesale seizure of Native lands and the extension of systems of enslavement, indenture, and peonage over Native populations.[37] The possibility to "bring back" a prior closeness to "Creation," as Big Sarah frames it,[38] rests on the restoration of a kind of moral rectitude cast as lost, or in decline, but the terms of that norm themselves are a response to current circumstances, bear little relation to earlier modes of Pomo sociality,[39] and efface the role of settler policy and political economy in shaping current exigencies (even as whiteness is repudiated).

While locating the potential for change in Pomos themselves, thus acknowledging their agency rather than presenting them merely as buffeted by uncontrollable forces around them, the perspective Big Sarah offers demands forms of community self-surveillance and inspection that exacerbate existing tensions and incite accusations, attacks, and alienation from "the tribe." At times the drive toward purification results in outright violence. During the visit of the Moki, before he starts throwing the coals, he takes a stick of wood, sharp and burning at its end, and stabs it "into Chum's bare throat, all but nail-ing her to the wall" (154). She survives the incident but is permanently scarred. Though less directly assaultive but no less wounding, Elba's Auntie Maria sells her into "marriage" to a Native man named Harold Tatum, with Big Sarah's blessing, proclaiming, "Maybe this'll help so you don't turn out like your mother" (205), who had been classed with her sister Chum for her sexual looseness, including relation-ships with whites.[40] Elba is placed in de facto sexual slavery for five years, until she runs away with the aid of Tatum's other wife (a Native woman named Annie). After she returns to the reservation, she joins her cousins Ida and Zelda (Maria's children) in prostitution with local men, and she becomes pregnant with the child of one of her johns, a Filipino immigrant named Del.[41] While she is pregnant, she begins doing domestic work for a white woman who lives nearby, and after the baby—Charlie—is born, he is cared for by Zelda, who has oscillated between prostitution and redemptive returns to her mother's home and the roundhouse. Herself pregnant from a white man she met while doing migrant labor in the area, Zelda sets a fire that burns down the shack in which they had lived, intentionally killing Charlie. Elba discovers this fact when listening in to Zelda's conversation with Auntie Maria and Big Sarah in the latter's cabin in which Zelda confesses, "If some sinner's baby was going to get sacrificed like you said, I wanted it be hers, not mine" (285), responding directly to Big Sarah's preaching on the consequences of violating the community's sexual norms. As these examples suggest, the novel presents the pursuit of this vision of Pomo authenticity and respectability as requiring brutal acts of purification, recalling the assault against Johnny earlier in the novel (although later in time) in the name of "help[ing] the tribe."

Elba does forgive Zelda, however, suggesting a way of understanding Pomo social relations other than their assessment against an inverted version of the racializing, heteronormative standard used against the Pomos themselves. "I seen in her . . . a pitiful representative of all of us, Zelda just being more obvious about the fear and related wretchedness in each of our lives. . . . Wasn't we all burning some baby or other so that we'd be safe in that home?" (286). As against the localization of blame in the bodies of individual Pomos, as a sign of their internal moral failing, Elba here interprets Zelda's horrific actions as indicative of the structural conditions facing them all. Seeing that state of "wretchedness" as a shared condition provides a stark contrast to Big Sarah's condemnation of personal deviancy and the attendant effort to shame and exile community members. She is not wrong to warn of the dangers of Indian–white unions, since they are not accepted among whites and lead to ferocious retribution against Native communities. The principal example of this is the fact that Mr. Benedict exiles the Waterplace Pomos from his property due to Chum's affair with his son Westin (170).[42] The difference, however,

lies in making settler discourses of sexuality into the matrix of intelligibility for Pomo subjectivity, turning those structures, imperatives,
and injunctions into animating principles of Pomo self-conception
and sociality while they are cast as an effort to preserve an *Indian*
essence—to "bring back" a prior state of cleanliness. At one point Elba
describes Zelda's attempted returns to godliness in terms of the latter's need to repudiate those with whom she had been living: "Twenty
years old and following her fat-as-ever mother [Auntie Maria] back
and forth to the well and to listen to Big Sarah still preaching in the
roundhouse every night about the evils of white people and Indians
like me" (232). Earlier, Elba notes that she "believed" this vision of
her as "lost, a sinner" (227), and that condemnation of her and others
engaged in dissipated ways of living leads to their virtual invisibility within the community. While out walking the reservation with
Charlie, Elba notes, "More than once we passed people on the road,
probably on their way to or from the roundhouse, but they said nothing, took no notice . . . as if to them we was spirits they couldn't see"
(269). As compared with Elba's acknowledgment of mutual desperation
("wasn't we all . . ."), Big Sarah's inveighing against sinners fragments
the community, producing an inability to recognize each other or at
least to do so in ways that acknowledge forms of sustained relation
among them instead of transforming those who fail to fit the heteroconjugal ideal into *strangers*.

In this way, the second section of the novel provides a genealogy
for the anxiety over the "blanks" in people's charts and the fear of
homosexual contamination seen in the first section, casting them as a
legacy of a history of struggling to define Pomo identity in the context
of settler denigration. Speaking of the Bole Maru, specifically under
the leadership of Annie Jarvis at the Kashaya Reservation, Sarris suggests that "a subjugated people may not see the ways their resistance
may further their alienation from the dominant culture and so weaken
their resistance to it and even hasten their demise as a result,"[43] but
in *Watermelon Nights* the issue appears less to be "their alienation
from the dominant culture" than *their alienation from each other* due
to the adoption of Euramerican conceptions of sin and racial taint
in which nonnormative sexual practices appear as a kind of treason
to the Pomo people. As against this license for *hatefulness*, the novel

proposes *sadness* as a less pathologizing way of naming and conceptualizing the circumstances created by ongoing settler occupation, an understanding that can engender solidarity.

As a structure of feeling, sadness marks the patterns of violence, exploitation, and "wretchedness" that form the structural matrix in which Pomo shame takes shape while refusing to present that affect as localizable to individual persons' supposed inability to remain pure—to maintain the *straightness* of the genealogical line leading back to the tribal origin. Discussing the disquiet in the shack she occupied with her cousins, Elba explains, "We wasn't peaceful because there was more than the simple stories, more than we talked about. There was other memories"; "I'd start walking up and down the road, happy with the stars and crickets singing . . . but, before long, the heaviness would overtake me, all these thoughts and memories, the sadness, and I'd hurry back to the house and close the door tight behind me" (270). As in Miranda's internal landscape discussed in chapter 2, Sarris here suggests how present forms of individual affect register communal histories. "Sadness" is a collective feeling that emerges out of shared "memories," if not always of the same events than of similar kinds of difficulties emanating from the conditions in which they live. In the first section Johnny recalls a conversation with his grandmother in which he observes, "This neighborhood, everybody's trapped. The same old crap over and over again—sadness" (119), later adding when considering Felix's genealogy chart, "I seen the name I knowed, where our histories come together in a woman called Juana Maria and run back to the first Rosa. Lots of sad stories, the same stories sung over and over through the generations like a song" (141). If from one angle sadness indicates a kind of communal paralysis, a wounded and unconscious repetition,[44] from another it appears as history, as a sort of generational inheritance—"like a song."[45] To be "trapped" is also to be bound together, to be "one big family" (7), but when considered from the perspective of something like a community ontology of sadness, that sentiment is sundered from the sort of racial/sexual inspection implied by Steven Pen's invocation of the tribe as of "one blood" (59). Instead, sadness provides an affective index of the ways Pomos' individual lives are interwoven as part of an entity and story that exceeds the terms of the normative genealogical grid through which Pomos have become accustomed to mapping it. As Elba at one point says to Johnny, "'That's why you help the tribe,' she said, 'Sadness'" (31).

Perversions of Descent

The novel critiques the ways Indianness comes to serve as the condition of intelligibility for Pomo identity, including among Pomos themselves, suggesting how Pomo modes of self-identification respond to conditions under settler governance. As I have argued elsewhere, Native peoples have been translated into U.S. administrative and legal discourses as a population, ordered around the reproduction of a particular kind of racial subject.[46] In this way, biopolitics supplants geopolitics as a way of framing indigeneity.[47] Moreover, what I previously have described as the "bribe of straightness" calls on Native peoples to identify with heteronormativity (for example, by disowning long-standing patterns of homoeroticism and social roles that exceed a dimorphic model of sex/gender) as a way of gaining limited settler acknowledgment of Native cultural and political difference, a condition of recognition that even affects efforts to resist incursion and erasure.[48] To be recognized as an Indigenous political subject (individually or collectively) requires the maintenance of a distinctness defined in terms of a racially insulating reprosexuality, itself fused to conjugal union as its condition of legitimacy/respectability. Though often cast as a preservation of Native identity, that image of the tribe bears little relation to Native life in California prior to Euro-presence, nor does it account for the contemporary circumstances of settler assault and erasure that make that ideal virtually impossible to achieve even as it serves as the basis for authenticity. How can one address social networks of *sadness*? What kinds of community relations and histories are occluded by the process in which deviations from a racializing heterosexual imaginary are cast as forms of queerness in need of excision? The novel suggests that those stigmatized and ostracized within a genealogical reckoning of proper Indianness possess knowledges that serve an important role in sustaining the community and that can provide a less normalizing model of Pomo identity, one that is more capacious and more capable of engaging with the actually existing conditions of settler occupation.

Old Uncle serves as a central example of this potential. As noted earlier, he arrives, seemingly from nowhere, in order to care for Elba's guardian Clementine, and he is resented and derided by Big Sarah and those associated with her. Suspected of consorting with whites and of having sexual relationships with other men, his presence challenges the social order organized around the nightly preaching at the roundhouse, particularly the purity/*masan* binary promoted by Big Sarah as necessary to the salvation/redemption of the Pomo people. Before Old Uncle's appearance in person in the narrative, Johnny references him in a conversation with Elba. In response to the question, "What's love?" she invokes the first Rosa, who was married/enslaved to the Mexican general, to which Johnny responds, "Can't it be like good things? . . . Like what you say about Old Uncle. Like flowers and stuff" (104–5). This moment suggests not only that Old Uncle serves as a staple in Elba's stories but that he represents what she considers to be "good" in Pomo tradition. Unlike "the second Rosa"—whom Johnny also mentions and about whom Elba observes, "She had problems too" (105)—Old Uncle does not seem to be the bearer of "problems" in Elba's memory. Though knowing virtually nothing about him at this point, readers are called on to identify with him, positioning him as an uncontested figure of possibilities for happiness that exceed the genealogical imaginary in which the Rosas serve as origin. Such an initial characterization seems particularly notable given his later association with homosexuality, indicating Elba's refusal to abject or even critique him on this basis, and her feelings about him and experiences with him revealed in her section of the novel also retrospectively demonstrates a refusal on her part to accept Johnny's estrangement from the community due to his homoerotic desires.

Old Uncle seems to provide an alternative to the hatefulness that produces "thing stories," emerging as it does out of the pursuit of sexual/racial purity as the condition of possibility for sustaining Pomo collectivity. Though he practices medicine, indicated by his singing of ceremonial songs and information on the healing potential and spiritual power in various plants and animals, his knowledge follows from principles and practices other than those of the Bole Maru. Elba recalls, "It wasn't what I expected—ceremonies in the roundhouse" (191), later noting, "I hadn't gone to the roundhouse the night before—in fact, I hadn't gone since Old Uncle come" (197). Whatever power he possesses arises out of another source than that of Big Sarah, one that is not predicated on the maintenance of a lineage-based understanding of belonging that seeks to conserve Indianness. In fact, although called "Old Uncle," he lacks a clear familial connection to anyone in the community. "One person would say how [Clementine] was related to him, and then a half dozen others would refute what she said, coming up with their own stories and genealogies. 'My mother told me this,' one person would say. 'Well, my aunt, she told me something different,' another argued" (190). Although he cannot conclusively be placed into the genealogical grid of the tribe, occupying and in some ways embodying the *blankness* that deeply troubles later generations, no one seems to question his belonging to the community. The very inability to assign him a proper place within the Indianizing order of reproduction generates "stories and genealogies" whose proliferation turns history into an active process of community formation in the present, negotiation among competing narratives providing a mode through which people engage each other and reflect on their own embeddedness within a shared set of experiences and stories.

At one point Old Uncle takes Elba up into the hills that overlook Benedict's ranch, the "ancestral lands" of the Waterplace Pomos (146). Elba recalls that he "turned this way and that, in every direction, talking about whatever his eyes found—rocks, trees, snake, moon. When I'd heard stories before, when Mama and Chum told stories . . . , there was a beginning and an end. Here with Old Uncle, it seemed there was lots of stories, or pieces of one story I couldn't fit together" (201). The linearity of others' stories, the clear progression from "beginning" to "end," ruptures into a profusion of stories, distributed over the landscape. Instead of a single narrative unfolding in time, forming a kind of straight line, the dispersion of narratives in space suggests that the territory provides the coherence for this rather queer assemblage of apparently disconnected fragments. Elba's inability to "fit together" the "pieces" can be seen as a function of the fact that Old Uncle's knowledge does not fit within the particular kind of alignment produced by Big Sarah's preaching or Benedict's disallowing of cross-racial intimacy. As against a lineal narrative in which Indianness is transmitted reprosexually from one generation to the next, Old Uncle's bodily experience ties him to Pomo territory. Turning "in every direction," his connection to "ancestral" space spontaneously generates stories, and it emanates not from unbroken genealogical connection to a person positioned as the origin of the tribe but from an immersive relation to place in the present. The roundhouse does not provide the means of authenticating him, because his awareness of the community's language, medicinal practices, and homeland indicates his enduring belonging. In this way, Old Uncle points to the presence of modes of social cohesion that exceed logics of sexual/racial puri-fication, and through this character the novel highlights the kinds of stories and social bonds endangered and potentially lost through the abjection of those deemed perverse within a heteronormative frame.

Rather than repudiating the Bole Maru, however, the text implies it contains possibilities for collective sustenance and regeneration if they could be disentangled from the imperative to save the people by straightening them. When describing where he has been, Old Uncle says simply that he had "gone south" (191, 199). This elliptical refer-ence, especially when coupled with his fine clothing and possession of a car, can be taken to mean that he had moved to an urban center with more access to commodity culture, such as San Francisco, which given his homosexuality would be a particularly prominent possibil-ity for contemporary readers. However, the invocation of the south in this context also speaks to associations with that direction in Pomo cosmology. It is not only the land of the dead but also where creator and hero figures reside, making it both dangerous and generative in ways that cannot be extricated from each other. Moreover, although the Bole Maru reorders older spiritual beliefs and practices and thus should not be read merely as continuing what came before, round-houses among many Pomo groups were built to face south, intimating the persistence of this older spatial orientation amid a new social con-figuration.[49] In this way, the association of Old Uncle with the south, when combined with the text's emphasis on the medicinal power and knowledge he possesses, casts him as in some sense embodying the very forces of regeneration invoked by Bole Maru dreamers (particu-larly given the prophecy of a return of the dead who in Pomo tradition would be coming from the south).

Similarly, the text insinuates that the practices of the ritual can be separated from the kinds of condemnation preached by Big Sarah.

While noting the difficulty of "last[ing] through the long speeches without falling asleep," Elba declares that she "liked to watch the dances," which were "beautiful" (152). Coming after hours of speeches that decry the descent into perversity and away from the straight line of tribal continuity, the dances inspire a different kind of feeling, one that seems to actualize the kinds of communal bonds alluded to in the nightly harangue but not produced by it. Although her aunt Chum is reviled for her promiscuity and affairs with white men, she participates in the dances. After having been assaulted by the Moki, she "come back to the roundhouse too," and "when it was time to dance, she joined the circle of ladies in their ribbon dresses and danced" (154). Even once she knows she is pregnant by Westin Benedict, "she stood straight in the roundhouse. Stood there, and even danced" (166). Chum's willingness to continue to participate in activities in the roundhouse suggests that something about the activity there calls to her in ways that exceed the propositions and injunctions offered by Big Sarah, that the process of engaging with other Pomos in a way that celebrates their presence with each other—the joy of dancing—provides a kind of experience that does not so much supplement as supplant the normative logic of the dreamer's discourse.[50]

If the project of purification depends on a genealogical model in which Pomo identity is transmitted generationally through blood, the figure of Old Uncle also provides a model of inheritance sundered from such reprosexual continuity. After discovering that Zelda had been responsible for the death of her first child, Elba starts walking toward Santa Rosa, the town adjacent to Benedict's ranch—their "ancestral lands." When trying to sleep in Chum's old shack, one of the few remaining structures from when she lived there, she discovers a baby cradle that she had left upside down years before when they were exiled by Benedict in the wake of Chum's suicide (171). She remarks, "I knowed what a downturned basket meant—it was how to poison someone's baby—and you wasn't to look at it, let alone touch it," and "I done this: turned the basket upright" (287). Carrying the basket out with her, she begins to hear words spoken by Old Uncle, and as she picks up her speed, his speech turns into "singing." On her way back to the reservation in Sebastopol, she comes to the realization that she is pregnant, due to a gang rape by white men at a local bar: "I'm pregnant,

I thought. What am I going to do?"; "I lifted the cradle up and called her to me" (288). This moment closes the second section, providing the transition to the final section, which focuses on Elba's daughter Iris. The act of redeeming the overturned basket through Old Uncle's medicine, contained in his song, also offers the possibility of reclaiming her mixed-race daughter as Pomo, in some sense also transforming Chum's legacy from one of shame and destruction to the potential for survival. In fact, Chum is the one who taught Elba to make baby cradles (165)—a skill we see her using in the first section of the novel (15). The novel employs Old Uncle, then, as a means of reconnecting Elba to Chum while also positioning him as the frame through which Elba will engage with her own daughter, whose introduction to Pomo beliefs and practices is through Old Uncle stories (292).

While Iris resists this call to see herself as part of the community, in ways addressed in the next section, her son Johnny's own connection to Pomo people is presented in similar terms. She observes that "he saw Old Uncle in things" (295), and Sarris intimates that this nonreproductive transmission of Old Uncle's perspective/song helps explain the abilities attributed to Johnny earlier in the novel. He notes, "Grandma said one day I could heal people" (22). The powers he possesses emerge after visitation in four consecutive summers by a particular "frog with a missing toe," which according to Elba, "Means you got that spirit—you're gonna see things" (21), and although his abilities precede Felix's appearance, their intensification and abatement correlate with his presence in Johnny's life. "Things like that, diseases and pains, I seen more regular, maybe a couple of times a week, before Felix. Now that I was thinking about it, I seen that my special abilities had faded away gradually without me taking much notice" (102). In the wake of their separation after having had sex in the creek, "vision wasn't kicking in no more" (101), suggesting a connection between realizing his queer desire and the loss of his "special abilities." Such a causal relation would confirm the logic of those for whom his sexuality makes him a "stranger," someone whose alienation "help[s] the tribe" (107). The novel refuses this reasoning, however, actually inverting it. In a moment that seems fairly conclusive, Johnny declares, "No, Creation wasn't punishing me for what I done with Felix. That felt good to me. The way vision did. Parts of you is alive that's bigger than the life you normally know. It's after, after it's gone that feels bad. Felix was gone and vision tiptoed out behind him" (102).[51] His feelings for and with Felix resemble those of his "vision," further presenting that attention as a catalyst for Johnny's abilities. The absence of that force in his life leads to the waning of his powers, previously having heightened rather than diminished his potential.

This moment provides a prism through which to refract Big Sarah's claim later in the novel that only sociosexual normalization could induce Creation to remember the community, an assertion ironized by Elba in ways already discussed. Here, the excitation of Johnny's queer desire amplifies the kind of spiritual power on which Big Sarah draws as a Bole Maru dreamer, abilities that should make one "bigger" and presumably less embroiled in quotidian dynamics of hatefulness. The pursuit of pleasure, as opposed to purity, provides the conditions in which vision can flourish. In contrast to the "sad stories . . . sung over and over through the generations," Johnny reminds readers of the existence of "other songs": "Not-hitting-back songs. Old Uncle songs" (142). Beyond being tied to Old Uncle by their shared homoeroticism, Johnny inherits the former's "songs," which seem of a piece with his vision. As against the proliferation of sadness, assuaged by neither the pursuit of federally intelligible identity nor intraracial cleanliness, these songs offer the possibility of a "bigger way" that "sees the whole story" (142). That story includes the transmission of forms of knowledge that can aid in sustaining the people, errant modes of inheritance and vision that do not fit the generational formula of heteroconjugal lineage.

"Whore" Histories

Although seeking to redress entrenched patterns of sadness, the novel suspends the attempt to transcend it, the notion that the legacies and conditions producing such collective affect could be readily left behind. Whether tribal chairman Steven Pen's advice to be "positive" by not "hashing over the past" or Big Sarah's promise of a return to "the way it was before" (59, 150), the call for a clean break with a degraded past proves unable to grapple with the ongoing effects of the history of "blank spaces" that trouble Pomos individually and communally. If homoeroticism appears as a deviation from the normative structure of official genealogy that does not need to be excised from Pomo people-hood, the novel also addresses other kinds of "thing stories" that can-not be recuperated into something that "felt good" or made one more "alive." In particular, Sarris explores the patterns of prostitution and rape that produce many of the gaps in the charts.[52] The novel's most sustained consideration of the meaning and dynamics of such *blank-ness* occurs in the third section, the one devoted to Johnny's mother and Elba's daughter, Iris.

Whereas at the end of the second section of the text Elba symboli-cally reclaims her for the Pomo people through the singing of Old Uncle's song, Iris does not see herself as Pomo. Or more precisely, she seeks to distance herself from identification as Native, a tie she conceptualizes in terms of visible racial markers of Indianness. She notes, "I was lighter than Mother. At night, while taking a bath, I'd hold her white, enamel-backed hand mirror over my stomach and on my thighs, where the sun hadn't touched my skin, and imagine my entire body the fair color reflected in the round glass" (302). In ad-dition to trying to dream herself white, she repeatedly expresses her revulsion at her mother's appearance, describing her as having a "hard, sun-blackened face and fat, hanging arm" (302), as "a brown sack of rags" (335), as "a scene out of *National Geographic*" (360), and at one point she screams at Elba, "You're nothing but a fat, ugly Indian" (321). Her mother's darkness correlates for her with a kind of excessiveness. She views Elba as a formless "sack" lacking an orderly shape, both savage and debased in her poverty and lack of bodily discipline. Iris's mixedness, the "blank" in her own genealogy due to her conception as a result of her mother's rape by whites, becomes both a space through which to fantasize an escape from Indianness and a prism through which her mother can be seen as defiled and disposable flesh. Indige-neity appears to Iris as the possession of a body that can be violated because it remains extraneous to the familial intimacy and insularity of whiteness (the example provided by the Polks, the wealthy family for whom Elba works as a maid). Iris's perception of Elba suggests a kind of flip side to Big Sarah's prohibitions, in that mixture here emerges from settler violence that seeks to rob Native people of the possibility for dignity, respectability, autonomy. The *blankness* in Pomos' personal histories, then, testifies, at least in part, to a collective vulnerability for which the maintenance of a normative genealogy of Indianness and identification with whiteness are inversely related responses.

In indicating the ways that Native women are subjected to sexual assault and, more broadly, seen as available for sexual gratification by nonnatives, Sarris does not disavow this position of abjection. Rather than seeking to develop or define an Indianness in which sadness-inducing violations and indignities can be bracketed as not authentically Native experiences, the novel treats this relative absence of choice for Pomo women as a potential source of solidarity among them. While acknowledging that some of the characters decide to engage in prostitution due to the absence of other available means of subsistence, the text does not make a clear distinction between the conditions that shape that determination and rape by white men. Instead, they appear on a continuum of coercion, as suggested by the fact that after Elba informs her cousin Ida what had happened to her, Ida (who recently had returned to prostitution) responds, "What, they didn't pay you?" (280). That spectrum is captured in the novel by the term "whore." Implying volitional participation, the word lumps together all nonmarital sexual activity, presenting such acts as forming an intentional pattern of promiscuity that indicates a woman's moral failings. While showing how this heteronormative standard gets applied, by nonnatives and Pomos alike, the text also uses the term "whore" to emphasize the continuities among Pomo women's lives, the ways they are bound to each other by shared circumstances, and the possibility for understanding resulting genealogical "blank spaces" as sites of connection rather than alienation.

In contrast to the emphasis on racial bloodedness earlier in the novel, the distinction between Indian and white in this section turns on whether one is or is the child of a "whore." After Iris attempts to take part in a de facto whites-only beauty pageant, her schoolmates inform her the next day why she can never be "a Rainbow Girl." Mary Beth, the daughter in the household for which Elba serves as a maid, asserts, "Because you're an Indian" and "you don't even know who your father is," adding as an aside, "Her mother is a whore, a prostitute" (319). To be "Indian" means having a kind of genealogical indeterminacy due to Native women's sexual impropriety, but this equation is made by Indians as well as whites. When Iris is confronted on the street by Billyrene, Zelda's daughter, the latter screams at her, "You, squaw," further accusing her, "You think you're so good, don't you squaw?" (353). This address seems forcibly meant to remind Iris of an innate Indianness from which she has sought to distance herself. That suturing of her to her own racial identity occurs by invoking her mother's sexual license: "Don't act like your mother's not a fucking whore, because she is" (354). To "act like" something other than an Indian is to forget "your mother's ... [a] whore," and reciprocally, to remember oneself as a "squaw" is to place oneself outside the proper genealogical order. One could view this association as a viciously racist stereotype, internalized by some Native people, that works to align whiteness with, in Ahmed's terms, the "straight line" that "gets attached to other values including decen[cy]" (70). Yet rather than decrying the inaccuracy of this vision and/or substituting a more "positive" image in its place, Sarris explores how this mode of denigration encodes the lived experiences of a number of Pomo women, while simultaneously refusing to privilege conjugally centered lineage as the proper means of performing and transmitting Native identity.

In this part of the novel, being Indian is thought to entail occupying a "blank space" in normative genealogical reckonings, falling outside the heteronormative family structure due to Native women's lack of sexual discipline. From this perspective the terror of blankness in reproductive reckonings of Indian bloodedness and proper tribal descent emerges as the inverse of the "squaw"/"whore" image. Put another way, understanding Native identity as a function or as expressive of familial/sexual disorder measures indigeneity against a white standard defined by the "intimate event." In *The Empire of Love*, Elizabeth Povinelli defines this concept as indicating the ways "the intimate couple is a key transfer point between, on the one hand, liberal imaginaries of contractual economies, politics, and sociality and, on the other hand, liberal forms of power in the contemporary world" (17). To be outside the framework of conjugally managed couplehood is to be consigned to an aliberal limbo of diminished acknowledgment and protection in which suffering and harm appear as the result of one's own improperly regulated associations. To be "Indian" in a legal sense requires, however, that one demonstrate proper "breeding" (5), the reproductive transmission of racial substance—a criterion of political recognition that can be satisfied by documenting "significant rates of marriage within the group" such as that "at least 50 percent of the marriages in the group are between members of the group."[53] Moreover, as suggested in the discussion of the charts earlier, the absence of such genealogical continuity, as well as the attendant failure to conserve bloodedness, leads to shame, "everybody wanting to be full blood and all" (11), partially due to government demands and partially as a response to nonnative presumptions of the amoral sexual license of Native people.[54] As Povinelli argues, a crucial "aspect of the cunning of recognition is the bracketing of the incoherence of these multiple external demands on the indigenous subject as she traverses the incommensurately coordinated social institutions" (54). From one angle, to be authentically Indian is to be a "whore," and from another, to be authentically Indian is to be pure/full blooded. To be Indian is to fall outside the intimate event of conjugal union, but to prove Indianness, a people must maintain the intimate event of racial reproduction across generations, unfolding from an uncontaminated origin. The disjunctions and complex refractions among popular discourses of Indian dissolution, Native women's experiences of sexual coercion, and governmental requirements for tribal recognition create forms of incoherence that are borne by individual Native persons, felt as the failure to embody an ideal coded either as white (thus marking deviation as Indianness) or as Indian (marking deviation as a threat to the identity of the tribe).

The imperative to conserve bloodedness and respectability through the proper marital channeling of desire and reproduction seeks to undo the equation of indigeneity with licentiousness, but that reversal still pivots around the figure of the "whore," preserving it as a site of defilement—as that which normatively must be disowned in the construction of a viable identity. Without minimizing the violence of white men's demand for sexual access to Native women's bodies, the novel tracks the potential for mutual understanding and aid among Pomos lost in that disavowal. When Zelda and Elba are reunited for the first time since Elba left the reservation, and Zelda meets Iris, the former, after noting Iris's "high-class looks," "all at once . . . blurted out, 'White girl,' and began laughing uncontrollably," and when Elba joins in her laughter, she offers as an explanation, "Don't mind us. . . . Couple of goddamned whores, eh!" (355–56). Zelda captures Iris's attempts to identify with whiteness, reading her demeanor and self-presentation as an (impossible) effort to escape the orbit of Indianness. As a response, Iris in her mind performs the very act of distancing that Zelda mocks: "I saw Mother as I had never seen her before, in her element, with her kind. She was common, low class. . . . Billyrene and Zelda had to do with Mother—Indians" (356). Iris represents the continuity among them as a sign of their inability to perform middle-class respectability, and that lapse provides the substance of their status as "Indians," a "kind" to which she imagines herself as not belonging. By contrast, Zelda and Elba's shared amusement suggests less a burdened, tortured abjection than a camaraderie that emerges from a recognition of shared experience, albeit of a kind cast in dominant terms as degraded. Moreover, the tone of this exchange presents whiteness less as a treasured ideal, as it is for Iris, than as a laughable attempt to evade the linkage of "Indian" with "whore." At this moment, "whore" names the possibility of a mutual acknowledgment among Native women not predicated on routing one's identity and aspiration through a settler-circulated vision of bourgeois sexuality—an image of maritally centered purity that from a settler perspective Native women have always-already failed to embody.

Although this scene turns the presumption of whoredom into a joke, in the sense that humor reorients the meaning of that accusation away from innate debasement and toward affirmative solidarity in the face of ongoing racism, Sarris further investigates the horrific consequences of the persistent dislocation of Native women from normative notions of family, their construction as disposable objects of white desire/aggression. Through the figures of Billyrene and Anna (Ida's daughter), the novel indicates the persistent violence enacted through the denial of Native women's place in the straight line of nuclear genealogy, but it also illustrates the ways such patterns of sexual assault and exploitation can be understood in ways that do not reinstall identification with the ideal of maritally regulated sexuality as the (inverted) response—as occurs in the dialectic of blood and blankness in the recognition petition. When accosting Iris on the street, calling her a "squaw" and insisting her mother is "a fucking whore,"

Billyrene concludes by saying, "Hear me" (354). The phrase demands that Iris notice her. More than simply punctuating her presence, that command seems linked to the prior statement: the possibility of Iris's recognizing Billyrene, of hearing her, is predicated on the former's acknowledging a proximity to whorishness or, more precisely, on ceasing to define herself by repudiating that connection. If Billyrene's insult functions at one level as an attempt at debasement that seeks to close the gap she feels between herself and Iris, at another level "whore" indexes the circumstances in which Pomo women continue to find themselves—the actually existing context of settler occupation—such that to disown one's relation to it is to foreclose the potential for acknowledging mutual enmeshment in those conditions. When Iris's friends Mae-mae and Roberta intervene, beating back Billyrene, Iris notes the look on Billyrene's face, "It wasn't as if she was mad, or even sorry, but rather as if I had somehow betrayed her" (354). The combative and even assaultive posture Billyrene takes, as condensed in the insistence that Elba is "a fucking whore," appears after the fact less as an attack than as a failed gambit for recognition, Iris's distancing of herself from her cousin serving as a *betrayal* of that attempted connection. Seeing herself in the degraded terms of address Billyrene uses—"squaw," "whore"—would require Iris to surrender her effort to align herself with the dominant norm, an identification that makes her, in Zelda's words, into a "white girl."

Such a shift in her self-conception and experience of her relation to others, particularly other Native people, would entail less embracing a version of Indianness sundered from its defiled status in a racist imaginary than reckoning with the forms of degradation Native people live with as Indians, understanding herself as implicated in that process of debasement rather than bracketing it through the attempt to occupy a less soiled subjectivity.[55] After being raped by a white college boy named Mike Bauer, whom they both know, Iris's cousin Anna charges her with refusing to own up to the fact of her own rape:

> The reservation, Iris. . . . Don't stand there and act like you
> don't know. . . . Or maybe he [Mike's friend Patrick Polk,
> whom Iris was dating] didn't take you up there again too. . . .
> [T]he reservation, it's their place to take Indian girls, Saturday

nights, fun times. Don't stand there like you don't know. . . .
Come on, Iris, you said to be honest, so tell what happened.
You're an Indian, you're no different, tell what he did to you.
(395)

Anna does not know that Patrick actually had not assaulted Iris, and
at this point neither Iris nor the readers know what had been done
to Anna. The passage intimates what is made explicit later, and Iris's
inability at the time to know "the horrible thing that happened to
Anna" (395), despite the clear implications of what Anna says, suggests
her need to avoid the equivalence on which Anna insists—"You're
an Indian, you're no different." Iris experiences something like a
will-to-ignorance ("like you don't know") that allows her to distance
herself from the violence occurring on the reservation, a distinction
that plays out in the events immediately following (which I address
momentarily), but even more important, Anna's accusation repeats
in an intensified way the stakes of Iris's earlier exchange with Billyrene, framing the significance of the rapes on the reservation as the
construction of Indianness through sexual defilement and the relative
capacity of Native women to recognize each other's enforced position
within that system of settler subjection/subjectification (to be *Indian*
is to be a *squaw* is to be a *whore*).

In the wake of her conversation with Anna, Iris "went straight to
the reservation": "I was inside out. I had to know. I had to see for myself" (395). Once there, she leaves her car and moves to a position where
she can see into the roundhouse through a missing slat, witnessing
Billyrene being gang-raped by Mike Bauer and five of his friends and
then hiding in a nearby thicket "for more than an hour" before going
in to the roundhouse (397). Soon after she enters and discovers who
the victim is (Billyrene's face had been hidden by her dress during the
rapes), Iris hears her mother calling her, who had been brought there
by Anna, and a newly conscious Billyrene responds to Iris's gaze by
asserting, "Your mother's a whore" (399). Recalling their earlier confrontation, this moment initially seems like an effort by Billyrene to
force Iris to share in her abjection, in ways reminiscent of Felix's earlier
comment about Indians being at "the bottom of the barrel" and no one
wanting anyone else to get out (68). When read in light of Billyrene's

prior sense of betrayal, however, her apparent accusation here serves as something like an indication of shared Indianness, in the sense that Anna implies ("you're no different"). Seeing herself as "no different" from Billyrene in the scene of the latter's violation, though, is not the same as accepting the terms of abjection. To recognize shared deg-radation is not to normalize it but to acknowledge the conditions of violence to which one is subjected as part of a community—the ways the subjectivity of the community is shaped by structures and processes of degradation.

That potential for solidarity, for an identification that acknowl-edges the terms of collective denigration without naturalizing them, is precisely what Iris continually defers or denies. Through her the novel perhaps most acutely poses the problem of how to engage with modes of settler-induced shame and the histories borne by that structure of feeling. When Iris and Elba get home, Elba furiously castigates Iris for her failure to understand fully what happened to Anna, to acknowledge Anna's courage in seeking aid for Iris ("she was scared you gone up there" [401]), and to protect Billyrene. At one point Iris recalls Billyrene's statement and observes, somewhat perfunctorily, "OK. Mother, you were a loose woman. I saw how I was made," and she conceptualizes this gesture at recognition as an effort "to show sympathy." Elba responds in rage, "If you seen that, if you seen that much, why didn't you help her?," adding, "I would've beat the hell out of them, taken a rock, and tried to kill every damn one of them" (402). Notably, Iris conflates sexual "loose[ness]" with assault, implying that promiscuity and/or prostitution explains and in some sense excuses rape, and more significant, Elba does not try to uncouple them, to differentiate between chosen and coerced sexual relations. Such a dis-tinction does not speak to the spectrum of settler control over and access to Native women's bodies in conditions of invasion, occupation, and exploitation, and it could encourage an attempt to separate the innocent (rape victim) from the supposedly guilty (the *true* whore) in ways that would further pathologize and estrange the latter. In-stead, Elba's implicit refusal to disaggregate the two leads her away from a paralyzed shame and toward action. Identifying with Billyrene prompts an effort to end her suffering, and from this perspective Iris's inaction, justified by her as self-preservation ("what could I do? . . .

Risk my life?" [402]), appears as a willful incomprehension of the ways she is tied to other Pomo women, as a turning away from them in order to preserve the integrity of a selfhood that is other than "whore."

Her show of "sympathy" toward her mother makes Elba's supposed looseness into a pitiable fact, confirming Iris's distance from it, from contamination by her mother's Indianness. In *The Cultural Politics of Emotion*, Sara Ahmed suggests that feelings of disgust erupt at sites of boundary confusion. "The subject feels an object to be disgusting (a perception that relies on a history that comes before the encounter) and then expels the object and, through expelling the object, finds it to be disgusting" (87), and objects, including other bodies, incite disgust due to the ways they accrue meanings, become stuck to them: "feelings of disgust stick more to some bodies than others" and such "stick[iness]" "relates to the historicity of signification," "to the attachments that implicitly govern ways in which signs work with other signs" (92–95). Iris's sympathy marks a boundary, one constituted through disgust at her mother's "loose[ness]," at the possibilities of herself being stuck to the sign "whore," which itself is stuck to Indianness. The maintenance of a body removed from such disgust involves avoiding associations that could make it sticky, trying to insulate oneself in ways similar to those addressed in chapter 1, and appreciating the historicity of the attachment of signs of sexual availability/deviance to Native women's bodies entails the risk of oneself becoming vulnerable to white violence ("You're an Indian, you're no different"), making oneself vulnerable to other Native people (as in Driskill's work).

Such knowledge involves putting one's body on the line ("I would've beat the hell out of them"). The alternative, the novel suggests, involves containing the shame-inducing effects of the exertion of settler power—the construction/imposition of shamed/soiled subjectivities—by locating them as a quality that inheres in certain disgust-inducing bodies, the "whores" whose "loose[ness]" produces "blank spaces" in family genealogies. During Elba's attempt to confront her daughter, she asserts, "See? You don't see nothing," "Maybe I should've let you feel what it's like to be hungry. Maybe I should've let you starve like the rest of us" (402). Understanding what it means to be part of an "us," of the Pomo community, requires that one "starve," experience the shared circumstances of deprivation as a form of bodily sensation. To do so would provide a material context through which to "see" what happened to Anna and Billyrene and for Iris to recognize their suffering as part of her own. In this way, the novel positions Billyrene's exclamation, "Your mother's a whore," as less simply the circulation of another *thing story* than as a condensation of, in Foucault's terms, a form of "subjugated knowledge." Also described by him as "local" and "illegitimate," such knowledge runs against the grain of dominant means of constituting subjectivity, individually and collectively, making possible "a genealogy" that enables "a painstaking rediscovery of struggles."[56] The figure of the "whore" opens onto the historicity of the struggle for survival as (a) Pomo people, and Iris's inability to "see" results from her personalization/personification/thingification of whoredom as a quality borne by/in her mother rather than as a settler-managed system in which Native women's bodies are interpellated as perverse, as out of alignment with civilized norms, in order to validate violence and displacement.

Setting the rapes on the reservation further allows the novel to explore the ways the pursuit of Indigenous sovereignty can itself codify the erasure of such knowledges. The desire for a reservation in many ways drives the pursuit of federal tribal recognition, and the image of a place cordoned off from settler intervention—at play in the first section of the novel and present in Big Sarah's preaching, as well—is vitiated by the rapes. Earlier efforts at purification/segregation are shown to have failed in the face of intimate assertions of white dominance, and the space to be reclaimed as the site of Pomo wholeness is haunted by the work of ruination that abides there. In both periods the pursuit of sovereign space is linked inextricably to the defense of the tribe as a collection of authentically Indian bodies, and as I argue, the text illustrates how that process of purification relies on measuring Pomo practices and identity through a (hetero)normative genealogical frame. The literalization of Native space as *reservation* is enmeshed in the literalization of Native bodies as *Indian*.[57] That dynamic does not speak to the existing circumstances of Pomo life (such as the sheer number of people who are subjects of assorted "thing stories") and, thus, does not account for the conditions that produce sadness, while also alienating those with important knowledge and "abilities" in the name of "help[ing] the tribe."

Iris's section suggests that the fantasy of a place insulated from settler assault is a response to, and simultaneous disavowal of, violence that already has occurred and its ongoing legacies. Her shifting narration of her own relation to the reservation indexes this (effaced) history. When Patrick Polk initially takes her there, as part of a double date with Anna and Mike Bauer (foreshadowing Anna's rape), Iris declares, "I'm an Indian. I'm from this place" (367), but later in the same scene, she revises her initial statement: "'I'm not from this place, not exactly,' I confessed, and then it went on from there, my whole life story, the *i*'s dotted and the *t*'s crossed with my fear and shame, each sentence punctuated with a brown and round woman named Elba" (369). She both is and isn't "from" the reservation, suggesting a complex legacy of diaspora due to the effects of dispossession and exploitation—and associated patterns of sadness and hatefulness. The metonymic soldering of "Indian" with "reservation"—their mutually reinforcing self-evidence—opens onto a more complicated story. That narrative, however, along with its attendant affect ("fear and shame"), coalesces around and in some sense becomes the excessive body of her mother. Her mother provides a way of giving concrete form to the history that makes Iris *from* and *not from* the reservation, but in doing so, that history potentially can be contained and dismissed as the effect of pathologized persons, whose deviant corporeality and sexuality stand in for the effects of nonnative intrusion and assault. This dynamic appears in the Bills' explanation of Pomo territorial loss in the twentieth century as a result of choices by the "whores that stole our land" (60). Whereas Iris disowns her Indianness, seeking to avoid becoming soiled by its connection to "whore[ness]" and all that entails, others construct a notion of the Indian as always-already separated from contamination by whiteness. If Old Uncle represents one kind of blankness, due to homosexuality's status as "a white man sin" (261), Anna and Billyrene's rapes represent another, evidence of the extreme difficulty of securing a place of Native occupancy and autonomy not perforated by the potential for settler violation.

As in Driskill's work discussed in chapter 1, particularly "Map of the Americas," neither the body nor the land serves as a metaphor for the other but instead each gains meaning through their coimplication. The practice of raping Indian girls on the former reservation is a project of settlement, of claiming control over (once) Native territory,[58] and reciprocally, the figure of the genealogically coherent Indian body serves as an index of a sociospatiality protected from white invasion. The "blank spaces" indicate threats to that coherence, not simply in terms of racial mixture but with respect to the conditions of settler occupation that continue to threaten to destroy Pomo peoplehood. The condensation of such threats as the aberrant actions/tendencies of certain individual Pomos brackets the ongoing effects of settler political economy. Although the Bills refer to the ranchería on Benedict's land as a "reservation," it was not, in the sense of a place federally recognized as part of Indian country, and at one point Johnny tells Iris that the reservation in Sebastopol was lost as a result of federal termination (422). Blaming the displacement on "whores" elides the history of (non)acknowledgment of Native land tenure in California and the vicissitudes of changing U.S. policy formations. In this way, the potential to enclose Pomo experience in ways that can stave off white domination is given form through the intertwined topoi of the full blood and the reservation, and these literalizations work to hold at bay the kinds of subjection that turn Indians into objects of settler disgust.

Reciprocally, aspiring to an Indianness purged of queers and whores, Pomos reveal themselves to be worthy of land of their own.[59] The implementation of normative genealogy reduces deviations to an amorphous, anxious *blankness,* denuded of any historical or social dynamics that do not fit the straight line of heteroconjugal inheritance, but it does so in ways that align Pomo self-representation with settler expectations. If to be Indian presumptively is to be degraded and degradable, Native people must prove themselves to be proper genealogical subjects, capable of familial self-governance, in order to be allowed to govern themselves as a polity. One mode of Indianization—as reproductively transmitted racial being—remains ever poised to flip over into another mode—as tendency toward perversion and dissolution. The latter is less the opposite of the former than its disavowed condition of possibility, the structures of abjection out of which the ideal of purity emerges in ways that also efface the historicity of that ideal and displace attendant knowledges as markers of shame. What Iris cannot *see* becomes no more visible through the prism of the genealogy chart.

Only after tracing the ways "whore" (mis)names a legacy of settler violation, as opposed to a deviant personal predilection, does the novel substantively turn to the subject of Iris's own errant desires. She chooses to have a one-time sexual encounter with a horse trainer named John Severino, and afterward, she cannot return to her comfortable middle-class life with her white husband.

> I didn't know there was a problem. I didn't know until I bit
> the fruit. But it wasn't just the fruit, not just the affair, but also
> the garden, the not-home place, I found myself in even before
> I saw the serpent and the tree. Unlike Eve, who left a garden,
> I felt as if I had walked into one, and I had no desire to return
> to where I had been before. (410)

As in the biblical tale, committing sin correlates with the acquisition of knowledge, yet here, rather than becoming ashamed of desire (needing to cover one's nakedness), the knowledge is of the power of pleasure, of bodily experience that does not fit the protocols of bourgeois domesticity. Iris contrasts her awakening to her previous aims:

> I wanted a good husband. I wanted a family.... I wanted
> a split-level home with a view, in Montecito Heights.... I
> began to see things I'd never seen before, though they had
> been before my eyes all along.... Order was what Harold
> [her husband] loved, and he loved things in the way, and to
> the degree, they fit into that order. A perfect house. A perfect
> wife. A perfect family. (411)

This vision provides the model toward which the genealogy chart moves, made *perfect* in the absence of blankness and thing stories. Harold and Iris's house appears as the kind of secure spatial enclosure promised by heteroconjugal order, one insulated from violence, invasion, degradation, but it is a "not-home place," an awareness that arrives only in the wake of improper desire.

Earlier, the novel links Iris's actions to Johnny's queerness in her response to hearing the thing story circulating about him. She says to him, "It's OK to love whoever," offering her own experience as instructive: "'I loved your father and that was wrong—people would say that was wrong. But look . . . ' She lifted both hands for a second, pointing to me. 'Look,' she said again" (126; ellipses in original). While this moment connects her affair to his homosexuality as forms of "love" deemed inappropriate by others, seeming to give counternormative weight to individual pleasure, that impression is recontextualized by the later sections' exploration of the relation between Pomo condemnations of nonnormative desire and intertwined modes of settler violation and dispossession. To create an insulating/isolating vision of *home* involves making *whores* and *queers* of those who threaten that ideal, but it is rendered unhomely by the denigration and denial demanded to bring people in line with its (genealogically conceived) order. Moreover, though "wrong," her affair produces Johnny, whom the novel positions as an inheritor of Old Uncle's abilities—which readers later learn are disowned by Pomos in his tribe and unheeded by Iris until after she becomes pregnant (Elba singing his song "now . . . sounded beautiful" [417]). Violating the terms of respectability taken as the framework for tribal identity makes possible the reclamation of knowledges—of the land and medicine as well as of histories of settler domination—made blank, shameful, and deviant in the construction of a (hetero)normative vision of peoplehood.

Weaving Stories

Discussing translations and transcriptions of Pomo stories in *Keeping Slug Woman Alive,* Sarris notes that nonnative editors tend to make Native speech, both in Pomo languages and in English, seem less verb driven than it likely was (95–98). Such shifts alter the feel and emphasis of Pomo accounts, making them appear less structured by movement and more by nouns—stable entities. This tension arises in a different form in *Watermelon Nights* in the contrast between the action that is storytelling and the vision of Pomo identity as a given racial substance transmitted across generations. As discussed in chapter 1, inheritance can be conceptualized less as the passive acquisition of something via reproduction than as a kind of work in the present, realizing (one or more of) the (possible) past(s). Instead of viewing it as the unfolding of a lineage from a privileged moment of origin, understanding Pomoness as a reiterative process—a doing—foregrounds existing relations among Pomo people as they are (re)made now through acts of narration. As against the literalizations of the Indian body or the tribal reservation, storytelling offers the possibility of realizing alternative accounts of the present through realigning its relation to the past. Such practice functions as a form of knowledge production, incorporating current community dynamics, circumstances, and affects and offering commentary on the legacies that generate these formations. In particular, the story of the two Rosas (cast as the nineteenth-century origin of the tribe) provide a means of (re)defining the terms and horizon of peoplehood, not just what it has been but what it can and should be. Offering multiple and conflicting versions of this story, the novel presents it as less descriptive than performative, as a means of responding to and negotiating existing dynamics of sadness.

The telling and retelling of this narrative foregrounds the ways bodies become invested with meaning, more specifically how they are woven together in processes of community formation in circumstances not entirely of their creation. Diana Taylor has explored the distinction and tension "between the *archive* of supposedly enduring materials (i.e., texts, documents, buildings, bones) and the so-called ephemeral *repertoire* of embodied practice/knowledge (i.e., spoken language, dance, sports, ritual)" (19), and in this vein, we could conceptualize the story of the Rosas as part of a repertoire, the Pomo oral tradition, at odds with the archive of settler governance, such as the official BIA granting of reservation status to certain examples of Native occupancy or the collection of genealogy charts in order to document Pomo existence for the purposes of federal acknowledgment. As I've been arguing, however, the novel illustrates how settler discourses intimately influence the terms and contours of the stories Native people tell about themselves to themselves, suggesting the difficulty in separating oral tradition from official records. Taylor notes the tendency "of thinking of embodied knowledge as that which disappears because it cannot be contained or recuperated through the archive" (193), but as suggested through the prior discussion of queerness, thing stories, and whoredom, the novel indicates that the kinds of dominant formulations that one might name as "the archive" shape Pomo representations and experiences of embodiment—serving as part of, in Renya Ramirez's terms, *"vernacular* notions of . . . belonging" (15). What would it mean to arrive at an awareness of that enmeshment? In what ways might the accessing of subjugated knowledges entail less the recovery of something lost to or distinct from the archive than a recognition of the role of the archive in shaping the possibilities for current self-representation, treating the process of self-narration as a Pomo-specific kind of making, but one, as Taylor suggests, whose "efficacy depends on its ability to provoke recognition and reaction in the here and now rather than rely on past recollection" (188)?[60]

At several points Sarris portrays storytelling as like basket-weaving, and that depiction of Pomo self-narration, an intersplicing of seemingly disparate elements to create a whole, also suggests the novel's way of theorizing what the experience of peoplehood is, a binding together that follows inherited designs but that also continually draws on previously unused materials and patterns.[61] Earlier, I noted the significance of basket-weaving as a Pomo cultural practice, and the novel positions it as both a central vector of traditional knowledge and a way of conceptualizing knowledge production more broadly. At one point when talking about Elba's perspective on Felix, Johnny notes, "There were parts of him she didn't understand. Pieces that didn't match up . . . , she couldn't see how the words fit together to make a whole story" (53), and at the beginning of her section of the novel, Iris observes of her recollection, "I must work from here, from earth, take my language with its inferior fibers and stitch together a tapestry of what Mother sees from above. I must go back, take clues, gather designs from our past. It is the hard way. It is my story" (296). Neither description addresses basketry per se, but both represent a story as a process of construction in which "pieces" must be "fit together," as opposed to an unfolding from a point of origin. The story emerges from individual effort, shaped by "patterns" from a shared "past" that provide guidance while not predetermining the form the story will take. Moreover, that absence of givenness makes the effort "hard," suggesting the labor involved in crafting "whole[ness]" out of disparate elements. While difficult, the effort, the novel suggests, also is necessary.

The idea of making something, realizing inherited patterns by working available materials in and through each other, resonates with the practice of basket-weaving, which itself appears in the text as an index of commitment to remembering Pomo traditions and reconstituting them in/as the present. Early in the novel, readers learn that Johnny's third cousin Alice is learning this skill from Nellie Copaz (she is Johnny's first cousin twice removed and Chum's daughter) (8–9, 90), and Elba tells Johnny that the songs Nellie sings in healing others are "ancient" and that "she couldn't have learned the songs no other way but through the spirits" (57), positioning Nellie's knowledge and, thus, the weaving practices in which she trains Alice as ancestral. Unlike racial blood, such knowledge is not inherently passed through lineage and is not a characteristic embedded as an innate feature of one's body; in this sense it cannot signify as Indianness in the terms of federal recognition or Big Sarah's revivalism. Yet these skills mark an ongoing, dynamic relation between the past and present that carries healing power within it. Alice's mother, Mollie, who previously had been an addict, finds solace and order in them, "joining Alice over at Auntie Nellie's for basket-weaving lessons . . . Auntie Mollie, of all people, settling down to weave baskets. So many rules, sacred songs, and her doing all that?" (130). Notably, Nellie is a person denounced by the Bills as one of the "whores that stole our land" (60) because her mother, Chum, "was fucking that white man" and "she fucked the white man's son" (33). Sarris juxtaposes the Bills' authentication of themselves as full bloods, discussed earlier, with Nellie's performance of Pomo identity, a central feature of which lies in her basket-making abilities and transmission of those skills and related knowledges ("sacred songs" and "all that"). Moreover, conceptualizing storytelling as of a piece with basket-weaving emphasizes the former's materiality— its role as embodied practice rather than as an ideal(ism) to be contrasted with the physicality of *Indianness*. Basket-weaving provides a counterpoint to the discourse of whoredom and the racializing heteronormative standard that produces thing stories, instead offering a model for conceptualizing Pomo sociality that is less estranging and more integrative—"gather[ing] designs from our past" in order to forge connections among people in the present. Neither kind of storytelling is, to borrow Taylor's terms, more a part of the repertoire than the other. They all involve a weaving together of elements, and the text suggests how these various forms of narration all have become part of the ongoing life of the Pomo community. However, certain versions of stories possess a greater resonance with the archive and its structuring principles than do others, and portraying narration as involving something like the knowledge and skills entailed in basketry—as doing rather than as reference to static entities—provides some critical leverage on the kinds of genealogically ordered being posited in some of the stories that circulate among Pomos in the novel.

Through the tale of the two Rosas, Sarris explores the work of storytelling as a mode through which Pomos come to understand themselves as intertwined while also suggesting how that process itself can reinforce a notion of Pomo identity that promotes forms of exclusion, racialization, and pathologization. As noted earlier, the tribe traces its origin to the second Rosa: "We all come down from one woman. Her name was Rosa and she was half Mexican. Her mother was named Rosa, too, and she was the wife of a Mexican general. . . . She wasn't treated any better than a whore, a slave" (6). "The second Rosa" "when she was old enough, she run away[;] . . . when she come back years later, she had her kids with her, and, that way, with her and them kids, this tribe started up again" (30). In these accounts by Johnny and Elba, respectively, the daughter emerges as the beginning of the lineage that will eventuate in the Waterplace Pomos of today; she is the "one woman" from whom they all descend, the one from whom the "tribe started up again." She provides the point toward which all the genealogy charts ascend, producing coherence for them *as a tribe* by serving as the shared basis for their inheritance of Indianness of a Pomo sort.

However, given that documentation exists for her mother, why isn't the first Rosa the origin point? What about the function of the origin story in this instance disqualifies the first Rosa from being the (re)starting point for the people? As Julie Cruikshank argues with respect to the workings of oral tradition among Yurok peoples, "Meaning does not inhere in events but involves weaving those events into stories that are meaningful at the time" (2). The events of the story of the Rosas become "meaningful" in the context of an effort, in multiple periods, to coalesce and defend tribal identity, and the first Rosa provides a poor model for that process. Big Sarah's version of the story makes clear why, or more specifically, it highlights what needs to be disowned in order to produce the kinds of genealogical continuity constitutive of Indian identity. Speaking of the first Rosa, Big Sarah exclaims, "She gave up. She died a slave and a whore. . . . The second Rosa, the daughter, ran away, escaped her Spanish father, reunited with Indian people, and settled this land again. She was a hero" (149). Later, after they are exiled from Benedict's ranch, she insists, "Got to survive so that we can go back one day like the second Rosa" (180). In order for her daughter to be a "hero," the first Rosa must be a "whore"; to fail to make a decisive break from circumstances of settler violence is to *give up*. Within this story frame, *survival* entails an effort/ability to refuse settler presence/influence, since contamination by it threatens enslavement and the disappearance of the people as such. Making the first Rosa the origin would link tribal existence too closely with the horrors of settlement, and in this way the novel suggests how the creation and circulation of an origin story involves more than locating a biological progenitrix. That genealogical project takes shape around imperatives of authentication amid an ongoing crisis in which Native collectivity and territoriality remain under assault and potentially subject to erasure. The starting point must be pure in order to cast the present as a smooth unfolding from it. Telling the story of the Rosas performs cultural work, (re)constituting Pomo identity in ways related to conditions at play in the moment of telling. In this way, the novel reveals the purification of Pomo history through the refusal of the first Rosa to be a strategy for coping with the circumstances of settler rule, an attempt to contain and distance the unimaginable, unspeakable terror and grief condensed in "again": "started up again," trying to hold at bay the genocidal decimation and its legacies suspended in the singular figure of the first Rosa, sole survivor and slave. If she's the "whore" who "gave up," her experience can be discounted, excised from the operative narration of Pomo peoplehood.

Yet the very territory they seek to occupy marks her presence. Elba tells Johnny, "They say them Mexican folks named this town after her: Santa Rosa" (30), and Iris notes, "I knew the story of Rosa, the one surviving member of our tribe who was taken in by the Mexican general, who the priest baptized and named the town after—This town, your living history, Mother always said when she used to tell this story" (346). If the second Rosa "settled this land again," it remains infused with the "living history" of her mother, which disturbs the construction of a sense of tribal being/space separable from the enduring effects of Euramerican violence. In talking of the first Rosa, Elba adds as a coda to the story, "Sadness," and when Iris reminds her, "But her daughter, the second Rosa, got away," she responds, "Away, but not free. . . . Sadness, it followed" (346). *Sadness* dwells in the place and the people, a residue that exceeds and troubles the celebration of *heroic* commitment to the tribe and that helps engender the retelling itself. The story of the second Rosa seems to be about the uninterrupted transmission of Pomo substance intergenerationally, but if that inheritance is so secure, why must the story of genealogical origin be repeated so insistently? Often, the story appears in the mode of a cautionary tale that seeks to distinguish decisively between the Rosas in ways that the circumstances of the telling seem to thwart, the danger of becoming—or being—the first Rosa erupting amid the apparently confident articulation of continuity. Part of the story lies in its effort to suspend sadness even as such feeling remains ubiquitous in the space of enunciation.

The novel raises the questions, what kinds of living are privileged by that telling and at what cost? Moreover, how does the act of telling point toward modes of being in the present at odds with the content/ lesson of the story? Before going to talk with Edward and prior to the meeting at which he is beaten by Felix, Johnny asks, "What can anybody do but tell their story over and over again?" (97), and just before telling the story of the Rosas to Iris's date, Patrick, a scene to which I return shortly, Elba observes, "It's always the same story, just different places—and times" (378). These moments imply an unchanging same, a repetition of narrative that reflects the equivalence of circumstances. That sense of an unbroken line, a continuous self-presence, in many ways is the point of the tale of the second Rosa, demonstrating the (reproductive) persistence of Pomoness, but such consistency also echoes Johnny's lament, "The same old crap over and over—sadness" (119), suggesting that to repeat the story "over and over" testifies to the endurance of "the same old crap," which can be neither remedied by nor recognized explicitly within the terms of the story. The pathologized figure of the first Rosa again and again is made to embody the conditions of displacement and exploitation that cannot be evaded, but that process cannot contain, dispel, or address those circumstances. The denigration of the first Rosa as a "whore" and failure, like other kinds of thing stories, becomes a way of managing the affective traces of the ongoing collective experience of being subjected to, and subjectified by, settlement.

Incorporating other strands of that history, elements and "songs" disowned as impure, though, opens the potential for telling the story differently. At the end of his section of the novel, Johnny notes the presence of "lots of sad stories, the same stories sung over and over through the generations. Rosa and the Mexican general, for instance. But there was other songs, too. Not hitting-back songs. Old Uncle songs" (142). Old Uncle provides a counterpoint to the first Rosa, a different set of songs that have a parallel intergenerational trajectory. Embracing him, even in the face of his disavowal as a stranger/sinner, makes available other kinds of knowledge not contained in the more familiar stories and effaced by their modes of articulation (distinguishing the "hero" from the "whore"). Rather than positioning "Old Uncle songs" as separate from the more well-known stories, however, the novel later weaves them together in ways that actually change the contours of the narrative of the Rosas. In Elba's retelling to Iris and her date, Patrick, the story takes a darker turn. After noting that "Old Rosa, the first Rosa, had managed to pass down the language" to her daughter, Elba insists,

> There was something wrong with it, something wrong with
> the language, because there was something wrong with her,
> the second Rosa. A story left that place with her . . . that old
> Rosa heard, that the animals and trees heard, that the spiritual
> people like Old Uncle, who dreamed the old songs, heard. . . .
> Old Rosa's story mixed with the other stories, sometimes
> killed them like the new animals and grasses that spread over
> the land at the same time killing the old animals and grasses.
> Sadness, anger, hatred: That was the story. (380)

Old Uncle's songs are not merely "other" to those of "sadness" but provide a perspective from which to recognize the latter, especially as it occupies the ostensibly nondegraded site of heroism. Though the story that engenders "hatred and anger" is "Old Rosa's," it manifests itself in the language and disposition of the second Rosa. If she provides a genealogical starting point, she also serves as an origin for the dissemination of "sadness," which cannot be extricated from the story of Pomo history. In Elba's retelling, Old Uncle less stands apart, as a kind of alternative tradition, than is woven into the story as a way of seeing other dimensions to the Pomo past, a repetition with a difference. This version emphasizes change and engagement with it over the reiterative attempt to perform seamless continuity, an effort to deal with the altered social ecology (as much as physical—"new animals and grasses") brought about through settler presence.

As with basket-weaving, which draws on established patterns while making use of materials available in one's environment now, Elba's account of the second Rosa reworks the tale to help account for the dynamics she observes. As William S. Penn suggests in "Tradition and the Individual Imitation," "We are memorizing stories and not remembering them. . . . The membering of identity demands re-membering . . . you may achieve the recognition by the community as a member of its story" (108). Elba provides a situated historical account responsive to current conditions that understands sadness as a relation among people rather than as qualities borne by particular persons who can be excised from the community. Neither the first Rosa nor the second can be renounced in order to reclaim a lost wholeness or transcended on the way to a future free of all traces of settlement. Instead, the very being of the people remains shot through with the legacy of decimation, assimilation, and racialization. Elba's version of the story, the last we hear in the novel, describes the second Rosa's effort to start up the tribe again as a function of "spite," which is what "drove her." The parents of the Mexican boy with whom she is in love do not allow their marriage, despite the social position of Rosa's father, because she is "an Indian," a rejection that prompts her to run away, marry a Native man in Sebastopol, and begin the process of reconstituting the tribe. She returns to try to convince her mother and siblings to come with her, but they do not (380). Her *heroism*, then, emerges out of a process of *Indianization* by which she is denied access to a non-Indian partner, a narrative twist that casts the attempt to preserve Indian blood, seen elsewhere in the novel, as predicated on a resentful inversion of settler racism/racialization.

In this way, Elba's account turns the story of (a search for) origin into a commentary on that desire and the social matrix out of which it emerges, "re-membering" the history of the Pomos. Rather than providing a remedy for sadness, a means of transcending conditions of settler degradation and disgust, the attempt to recapture a primary, pure, insulated Pomoness transmitted in the blood itself emerges from spite and regenerates "sadness, anger, hatred." In *For the Record,* Anjali Arondekar argues that the notion of gaps in the archive that need to be filled partakes of the structuring logics of the archive itself in ways that shape the supposed absence in terms of archival protocols of recording and intelligibility. She calls for "an understanding of the processes of subjectification made possible (and desirable) through the very idiom of the archive," suggesting the importance of "a theory of reading that moves away not from the nature of the object, but from the notion of an object that would somehow lead to a formulation of subjectivity." She condenses this problematic in the idea "that if a body is found then a subject can be recovered" (3). The story of the second Rosa, in earlier tellings in the novel, suggests that in locating an originary Indian body, a Pomo collective subjectivity can be founded, provided with a documentary basis despite the dislocations and erasures of the twentieth century.[62] The repertoire of Pomo storytelling, Sarris suggests, embodies—gives form to—a kind of archival desire, a desire to be recognized in terms intelligible to settlers that reaches its apotheosis in the pursuit of federal acknowledgment and its modes of *tribal* subjectification. Haunting this implicit aim is the issue Johnny raises, discussed earlier, "What's to keep them from changing their minds again, even if we do prove ourselves Indians to their satisfaction?" (58). Elba's version of the story of the Rosas offers the other side of this question, an analysis of how Pomos have sought to "prove [themselves] Indians" to themselves in ways that propel, rather than ameliorate, *spite* and *hatefulness.*

If Pomo identity cannot escape the effects of the ongoing history of settlement, how can it cease to reproduce the terms of settler subjectification? The fact that the second Rosa's brothers and sisters repeatedly refuse to join her suggests that Pomo belonging inheres less in blood per se than in a kind of choice, a commitment to claim relation with other Native persons as part of a people. That recognition of interdependence and decision to act on it occurs amid, and is affected by, sadness but cannot be reduced to it. Making this kind of ethical choice is precisely what Iris fails to do with respect to Billyrene; she has not learned the lesson of Elba's story, that the survival of the people depends on individual persons' understanding themselves not through a distancing disgust—toward the Indian or the whore or the queer—but as woven together through shared experiences. Elba ends her account of the Rosas by observing, "Sadness. See, the same story . . . Sadness . . . It kills people" (381), implying that to live, (the) people must engage directly with the legacies and conditions that produce sadness and their mutual imbrication in it.[63]

In the scene that provides the title for the novel, Johnny, just as he is planning to leave the community the next day after having been assaulted by Felix, sees people out on their porches late into the evening and early morning eating watermelons, which had been taken from an open truck by a couple kids in the neighborhood. He is attempting to answer Elba's question to him about this scene, "What does it mean?" (136), which, significantly, is the same question Johnny asks earlier in wondering about the efficacy of pursuing recognition given the historic fickleness of the U.S. government in its relations with Native peoples (58). What finally triggers his response is Mollie saying, "It's kindness. It's a kindness them kids done," and his own image of "Mollie weaving baskets with Auntie Nellie": "My mind flipped what made no sense before and then let me see as plain as the shirt on my back what I could say to Grandma" (139). The image/activity of basket-making condenses an experience and understanding of what it means to *be* Pomo, a shift in orientation from the pursuit of purity that emerges out of the same history and circumstances as the latter. Making "sense" out of the conditions and relations that surround him entails "weaving" into his story elements that did not appear to fit previously, that could not be incorporated into the privileged narrative of Pomo identity. The invocation of baskets, as well as their association with a range of "sacred" practices, casts storytelling as a doing—a material act of creation—that cannot be dismissed as merely ideal, as opposed to the reality of raced bodies or proper genealogical inheritance.

In Pomo traditions there is a deep and abiding relation between baskets and stories. As Sarris observes in *Keeping Slug Woman Alive*, "So many baskets I have known have stories, songs, and genealogies. They have helped us on our travels and told us who we are as a people. They have healed the sick and forecast momentous events. The weaver's hands move, and the basket takes form so that the story can be known. And the basket keeps talking" (61). Moreover, baskets signal the possibility of altering existing conditions through song/story, as in Elba's reclaiming of the turned-over cradle for Iris (287–88).

That process requires engaging with and opening to the possibility for "kindness," for making oneself vulnerable to others in a gesture of relation. Johnny notes:

> Kindness, which is nothing more than the sweetness of watermelon and the thought that somebody might like a taste. It was always there, even in the hardest places, the sad deaths and the loud, hate-spewing meetings, only we needed to see it, like on a watermelon night. It had become more and more of a secret, something we hid with the tough times, but nothing else ever held us together. (142)

This potentiality overcomes the alienation of thing stories, including the awareness of Johnny's homosexuality that threatens to make him a "stranger" (113), and Johnny links it to "Old Uncle songs" (142), implying it partakes of older modes of knowledge, songs, and stories. The project here lies not in tracing the provenance of "kindness," positing it as originary or transcendent, but in recognizing its presence, its immanence even in the hardest and most acrimonious circumstances. The capacity for generous relation with each other arises out of the fact of "together[ness]" while also making it possible. Realizing that potential in the present is the substance of tradition, since "being a medicine person" means "see[ing] the whole story" (142).

The end of Johnny's section implies that he will stay in Santa Rosa rather than travel to San Francisco to escape the thing story circulating about him, but readers are unsure to what extent the "watermelon night" can overcome the shame of queerness and others' idea that his exile "help[s] the tribe" (107). At the close of Iris's section, the end of the novel, this question is resolved: "He bounces in and tells me he's not moving after all, at least not for a while. He says he has a lot to do for the people first, meaning, I'm sure, the tribe" (424). The text's pause over this synonymy—that "people" equals "tribe"—opens up a distinction between them. Conceptualizing the Pomos as a *tribe* requires a will to official visibility that is organized around generating evidence of seamless *Indianness*. The "charts" testify to unbroken, reproductive lines while pathologizing "blank spaces" as signs of individual deviance. To what extent does "do[ing] for the people" suggest an activity whose orientation differs from *helping the tribe*, including the procedures of authentication that manifesting such identity entails? Might the former open options for acknowledging other Pomos and their complex histories in ways foreclosed by the latter? If in Johnny's watermelon story kindness can appear to run parallel to sadness, in Iris's associations they merge. When he asks her to attend "a tribal meeting," she flashes to Anna and Billyrene: "No doubt they would be there. From Mother, I learned they attended the meetings regularly. What would I say to them? And to the countless others? . . . 'Sure,' I say, and think to myself, What have I got to lose?" (424). As opposed to the Bills' interrogation of others' credentials, and use of sadness as a weapon, here the tribal meeting serves as a potential site of reconciliation, in which legacies of disavowal might be engaged and altered. The flight from spoiled subjectivity—as Indian, as whore, as queer—might be redirected toward those from whom one has turned in disgust, telling a different story in which shame, spite, anger, and hatred are neither ignored nor excised but taken as a condition of mutual recognition, as part of the embodied/affective experience of what it means to live as a *people* under settler occupation.

The novel illustrates how the (re)production of proper Indian genealogy demands far more than simply demonstrating common ancestry. Sarris explores how that image of coherent racial subjectivity helps literalize (hetero)normative structures for regulating and disciplining Native sociosexual life as the condition of intelligibility for indigeneity itself. Maintaining that ideal as the measure of realness requires disowning those whose desires and whose experiences (chosen or not) create "blank spaces." Through its elaboration of Johnny's and Old

Uncle's homosexuality and the charges of being a "whore" that in one way or another are made against almost all of the female characters, the novel explores the costs of that account of purity. In addition to marginalizing and alienating members of the community and driving suspicions and accusations that make them strangers to each other, the pursuit of normative Indianness in order to prove and sustain their existence as a tribe effaces the structural conditions of settler presence, assault, exploitation, and expropriation that threaten the existence of Pomo peoplehood and that give rise to the very modes of authentication they employ against each other. Rather than redoubling the quest for authenticity by positing a true tradition that can provide a counterpoint to the genealogical order falsely propagated as tradition, Sarris provides a critical genealogy of the forms of storytelling that confirm the logic of the "charts." Such narratives of Pomo identity emerge as a response to conditions of immense stress as a means of trying to preserve the integrity of an embattled people, but in doing so, such narratives present Pomoness as a racial/genealogical unfolding from a clear point of origin in ways that cast deviation from that reproductive imaginary as deviant. In Ahmed's terms, the failure to align oneself with that straight line indicates a "queer orientation" that needs to be disowned in order to protect the tribe, and that process casts the conditions of relative impoverishment and displacement Pomos face as due to the failings of wayward individuals.

This kind of explanation, however, cannot grapple with the collective affect of sadness that those conditions engender. Whether Steven Pen's call to avoid "hashing over the past" or Big Sarah's insistence on forms of self-discipline that can return things to the way they were before, the attempt to transcend sadness fails because it does not engage with the circumstances of everyday life and the ways they are shaped by continuing histories of dispossession and degradation. Acknowledging and grappling with sadness entails telling different kinds of stories about what peoplehood was, is, and could be. Such stories less posit heroic forms of overcoming than address the quotidian ways Pomos have patterned their lives for themselves in an effort to survive amid virtually impossible circumstances. Instead of an untroubled genealogy, what arises from these stories and the novel itself is a sense of continuity-in-sadness in which the ability to maintain connection in the context of racism, erasure, poverty, and dislocation generates forms of knowledge and solidarity that also can yield possibilities for *kindness,* for practices of mutual recognition that incorporate the sense of a shared legacy of settler violence without distributing its effects as personal pathologies to be shunned. In this way, the novel rethinks peoplehood less as relative proximity to an ideal Indianness than as a nexus of historically contingent, but stubbornly enduring and continually rewoven, relations among the people themselves—a tradition of impure negotiations whose story needs to be told.

< 4 >

Laboring in the City

Stereotype and Survival in Chrystos's Poetry

L EGALLY, THE PHRASE "INDIAN COUNTRY" EXTENDS TO RES-
ervations, allotments, and "dependent Indian communities."[1]
Notably, it does not refer to space inhabited by Native people per se
but to those areas that fit within particular jurisdictional parameters.
Chapter 3 addresses how Indian identity is constructed around normative racializing genealogies, but given the connection of indigeneity
to place, the discussion of the meaning of "Indian" begs the question
of where Indians are to be found. More specifically, how do narratives
of spatial authenticity help define who can and cannot properly occupy the category of *Indian*? More than half of all Native people in
the United States do not reside on reserved lands, and of those, the
majority live in urban areas.[2] Beyond the period in which the U.S.
government explicitly was committing resources to move Indians off
reservations as part of the broader program of dismantling Indigenous
landholding and governance,[3] the context of Indian policy from the
late 1940s through the 1960s contributed to this pattern by rendering Native land tenure insecure through the continuing threat that
peoples would lose their status as federally recognized tribes,[4] disin-
centivizing economic development that could have provided work to
residents and thus enabled them to remain. Additionally, the actual
termination of numerous peoples, including the Menominee (Chrystos's people), produced land losses and increased conditions of impoverishment that helped generate—or at least exacerbate—Native diasporas.[5] Given its launching as a reversal of the logics and principles
of termination, the policy of self-determination would seem situated

< 215 >

to address the continuing dislocations engendered by the history of U.S. efforts to eliminate Native peoples as such. The American Indian Policy Review Commission, however, found in its 1976 report that "Indian people in substantial numbers came to urban areas because of a lack of employment in addition to other social and economic problems on the reservation" but that "these Indian people . . . have become victims of a Federal policy which denies services, if not thereby their very existence, while at the same time substantially subsidizing and contributing to an increase in the population of the urban multi-racial poor" (2). Although access to federal funds for Native people living in cities has increased in the last thirty-five years,[6] the ongoing effects of the long history of detribalization, including allotment and termination, continue to haunt the putative U.S. commitment to acknowledging Indigenous peoplehood. U.S. policy helps propel an urban/reservation dichotomy in which the former kind of space may provide a site of residence for accretions of Native people, but it, and they, are not part of "Indian country," lying outside the legally recognized jurisdictional field of what can constitute sovereignty.

If the policy of self-determination attempts to expiate national shame for the violent past of settler invasion and dispossession, that performance crucially is supplemented by a vision of Indianness in which indigeneity inheres in the enduring occupation of an officially acknowledged homeland, as if the very shameful dislocations for which the settler-state seeks to atone had not occurred. With respect to gestures of reconciliation in Australia toward Aboriginal peoples, Sara Ahmed argues in *The Cultural Politics of Emotion*, "*By witnessing what is shameful about the past, the nation can 'live up to' the ideals that secure its identity or being in the present.* In other words, our shame *means that we mean well,* and can work to reproduce the nation as an ideal" (109).[7] The enunciation of collective guilt not only can provide a vehicle for unifying the settler nation ("we" have redeemed ourselves for past crimes and can move toward a future unmarked by that legacy) but also can install an image of indigeneity to be rescued/preserved that has little relation to the lives of Indigenous persons/peoples, whose current experience continues to be shaped by forms of state regulation and erasure. In *Fugitive Poses* Gerald Vizenor suggests, "New traditions and cultural distinctions were created to separate the national *indian* from the actual, more elusive native. These modernist simulations of the *indian,* once seen as the fugitive on a course of disappearance, became the new measures of cultural diversity." The figure of the Indian marks a "tease of *mother earth*" while simultaneously serving as "an aesthetic absence in the course of dominance and victimry" (98).[8] In this way, the contours of contemporary policy can be conceptualized as ordered around stereotype, a vision of Native identity that not only is organized through, in Dan Gunter's terms, a "technology of tribalism" (as discussed in chapters 2 and 3) but which imposes a static territorial imaginary that edits out Native movement.

Within this frame urban indigeneity appears as an impossibility. Paul Chaat Smith encapsulates the experience, remarking, "If you are Indian and live in the city you basically are screwed. This is because a large flashing asterisk floats above your head, which turns into a question mark, before again becoming an asterisk. You are in the wrong place and you know it and everyone else knows it too" (163). Urban Natives exceed the terms of *Indianness,* since they do not appear to have a connection, individually or collectively, to a particular tribal landbase. Or more precisely, their complex modes of placemaking cannot be encompassed within a jurisdictional paradigm.[9] In this vein, Vizenor argues that "notions of native sovereignty must embrace more than mere reservation territory. Sovereignty as transmotion is tacit and visionary; these notions and other theories of sovereignty are critical in the consideration of native rights, and the recognition of those rights outside of reservations, and in urban area[s]" (190). He defines "transmotion" as "a natural right of motion" on the continent (181), a sense of persistent presence that cannot be measured through "the metes and bounds of land allotments" (54).[10] When viewed through a reservation-based prism, this "tacit" indigeneity becomes unintelligible, instead appearing as an individual failure to be properly Indian. The circulation of that image, as well as its indirect sanction by the state in the failure to extend anything resembling a notion of sovereignty to urban Native people, creates the "asterisk" to which Smith refers, disowning the possibility of peoplehood in the city. Native urban life signifies, in Vizenor's terms, more as "disappearance" than as "diversity."

Beyond effacing actually existing Native people, the construction of Indianness further can be understood as a form of extraction. Following Vizenor, the *simulation* that is the "Indian" effaces the reality of Native identities, producing a new reality in which Native peoples contend with—and are assessed against—a standard whose stereotypical installation plays a significant role in constructing the sociopolitical formations that they must negotiate.[11] However, is the simulation simply false? Rather than juxtaposing it with an Indigenous truth that it displaces, the figure of the Indian can be seen as generating and managing a surplus within the contemporary political economy of settlement in the United States. While accepting the sovereignty of Native peoples as semimunicipal entities and giving legal acknowledgment as *tribes* to groups previously unrecognized as such, as discussed in previous chapters, the United States also asserts an underlying plenary power in which Congress has the authority to do whatever it will in Indian affairs, without exception or check.[12] This institutionalized potentiality licenses the U.S. government to define legally and administratively cognizable indigeneity in whatever ways it sees fit, allowing for notions of Indianness actually to become formal principles of governance.[13] That stereotype in its various aspects (including enduring occupancy in a single location, an inherently nonexploitative relation to "nature," "primitive" technology and material culture, a lack of wealth and resources, and difference from all things Euramerican) tactically can be activated in any given situation so as to repudiate Native persons, actions, or groups as inauthentic.[14] As Paul Patton observes, drawing on concepts from the work of Gilles Deleuze and Felix Guattari, "The legal imposition of sovereignty effects an instantaneous deterritorialisation of indigenous territories and their reterritorialisation as a uniform space" of state jurisdiction (124), adding, "In strictly legal terms, aboriginal or native title amounts to little more than a limited and relative deterritorialisation of the legal apparatus of capture of indigenous territory" (128).[15] In deterritorializing Native peoples in order to construct the space of U.S. settler sovereignty and reterritorializing them as *Indians* in *Indian country*, U.S. policy does not so much replace the one with the other as make limited exceptions for aspects of indigeneity that can be taken up and circulated as Indianness. As in Marx's analysis of commodification, that process of fetishization enables the operation of systems of value while treating it as simply an innate quality of objects themselves. In particular, recognizing Native peoples as *Indian tribes* within the reterritorialized space of U.S. national boundaries allows for the following: the promotion of an attenuated relation to land and generational drift from it, narrated as Native persons' (inevitable?) loss of Indian identity; the national performance of multicultural awareness and redemption from past violence; and the increase in cheap labor in sites that do not count as *Indian* space. Indigenous diasporas expand due to the ongoing effects of more than a century of state-sanctioned land seizure and structural underdevelopment in Native homelands, and simultaneously, Native people are measured, officially and popularly, against a stereotypical standard that offers a reified vision of peoplehood. Together, these dynamics extract a surplus through the promotion of *Indianness,* in which settlers both celebrate (a rigid and constricted version of) indigeneity and profit from the extrusion of Native persons from it.

Chrystos theorizes how this fetishization produces urban Natives as its exploitable excess, exploring the relation between the taking of Native territory, the conditions of wage work in urban space, and the work of survival as a Native person.[16] As Bonita Lawrence suggests of Indian affairs in Canada, "To a phenomenal extent, urban centers also represent the places that Native people migrated to because they lost their Indian status or never had it in the first place. . . . From this perspective, urban Native communities are to a tremendous extent composed of the fallout from government regulation of Native identity" (208). Chrystos's poetry does not so much focus on issues of tribally specific belonging (in terms of citizenship in Native nations, federal recognition, or interactions among tribal members—as discussed in previous chapters) as on the ways individual Native people are made unintelligible as such through discourses of Indian realness that map indigeneity as coterminous with "tradition" on-reservation. She consistently juxtaposes nonnative investments in things Indian— whether desire to possess ceremonial objects, New Age images, or ecological concern for particular locations—with the simultaneous erasure of Native people, or their displacement as an impure, racialized remainder. Celebration of Indian culture, then, not only does not translate into concern for Native welfare but helps produce and profits from the marginalization of those deemed not Indian enough. Tracing contemporary economies of settlement and their connection to historical patterns of dispossession, Chrystos further explores the labor of enduring amid these conditions, particularly as an Indigenous person in the city. More than naming participation in systems of production and exchange, "labor," as Jackie Grey argues, can be defined "as the expenditure of social and psychic energy deployed in pursuit of concrete purposes and intentions" (3), and she asks, "Is there . . . a certain type of indigenous performance, a certain genre of 'labor,' that non-indigenous recognition labors to provoke in pursuit of a set of desires, some of which may be unspeakable and un-nameable within the rhetoric of jurisprudence and regulation?" (5). Articulating oneself to the figure of the Indian, to the reified portrait of indigeneity circulated through popular and administrative discourses, can be conceptualized as such a "performance," as a taxing draw on Native psychic and emotional resources.[17]

Tracking the operation of this system of extraction and erasure through attending to her own experience, Chrystos chronicles the effects of having to live these dynamics in the flesh and the ways doing so entails hard labor, in the sense of low-paying, menial wage work, as well as exhausting affective *expenditures*. She attends to the ongoing personal cost of policies of detribalization, particularly how legacies of dispossession and actual Native people are rendered invisible through ostensible forms of multicultural recognition, and Chrystos suggests that the work of coping with that structure *is* an index of contemporary urban indigeneity, one that exceeds the congealed and commodified contours of Indianness. While tracking the energy expended in quotidian encounters with settler modes of elision and expropriation, and the ways histories of occupation are registered in everyday forms of bodily sensation, she also explores how desire can reanimate stereotype. In depicting her attraction to and pleasure with other women, Chrystos often draws on natural imagery, which might be read as reiterating the very discursive strategies through which Native people are displaced from contemporary life. However, desire appears as itself a form of labor, an expression of bodily being in the world through which it is (re)produced but also potentially transformed—a capacity through which settler reifications can be made Native in ways that extend the bounds of indigeneity. Chrystos's fusing of nature with explicit descriptions of erotic need, connection, and satisfaction makes figures of Indianness mobile, dislodging them from fetishized traditional objects or locations and proliferating spaces for the expression and reclamation of Native identity while also investing potentially disembodied images with sensuous experience. In this way, her poetry enacts a sovereignty divorced from the terms of state-sanctioned self-determination, insisting on the apprehension of urban experience as authentically Native and thereby marking and refusing the task of managing the relation between interested settler expectations and the geographies and conditions of contemporary Native life.

Putting Frozen Images in Motion

Rather than being understood as a false image, stereotype can be interpreted as indicating the operation of a system of value, one in which the circulation of such images takes part in the production and regulation of access to resources and public visibility. In addressing the "*ethnicization of labor*" in *The Protestant Ethnic,* Rey Chow argues that "the ethnic as such stands in modernity as the site of a foreignness that is produced from within privileged societies and is at once defined by and constitutive of that society's hierarchical divisions of labor," facilitating the "project[ion] onto some imaginary outside elements it deems foreign and inferior" (34–35). The stereotype functions as a mode of interpellation through which ethnic (read nonwhite) subjectivity recasts a group's relative position within existing divisions of labor as an effect of their "foreign" *culture* and in which they need to renounce their *ethnic* identification in order to become generic citizens. "Ethnicity," then, indexes the framework for participation in the political economy of the state, including the process by which subordination takes shape around and through an apparent recognition of collective difference. Moreover, this relation relies on "coercive mimeticism—a process . . . in which those who are marginal to mainstream Western culture are expected, by way of what Albert Memmi calls 'the mark of the plural,' to resemble and replicate the very banal preconceptions that have been appended to them, . . . to authenticate the familiar imagings of them as ethnics" (107). The performance of ethnicity, itself an assemblage of (potentially shifting) stereotypical traits,[18] is the condition of possibility for entry into public discourse for nonwhite subjects, and through that performance, they are measured against an impossible standard of racial authenticity that they cannot enact properly (as Anne Cheng suggests in ways discussed in chapter 2), while these "familiar imaginings" simultaneously cast the marginalized, exploitative conditions that such populations occupy as simply an effect of the transparent reality of ethnic identity.

What happens, though, when the image is not one of foreignness but of Nativeness—or more specifically, of Indianness? If others are called on to replicate their stereotype mimetically in order to become intelligible to Euramericans, their existence as such is not at issue, whereas it is for Indigenous peoples. The problem indigeneity poses for the state is not that of managing racialized groups within an ostensibly democratic public culture but of the fundamental legitimacy of the settler-state's creation and continued existence. The nature of the surplus extracted from them, then, has less to do with the regulation of laboring bodies than with access to Native lands—the biopolitics of population versus the geopolitics of jurisdiction. For this reason, ethnic stereotype localizes Native people on reservations or effaces them entirely, producing the effect of erasure rather than a rendering foreign. In the introductory note to her first collection, *Not Vanishing*, Chrystos foregrounds this dialectic of appropriation and elision and its animation by figures of Indianness.[19] She begins by noting, "Because there are so many myths & misconceptions about Native people, it is important to clarify myself to the reader who does not know me," observing that she "was not born on a reservation, but in San Francisco" and that she is "part of a group called 'Urban Indians' by the government." The act of *clarification* most centrally entails challenging the assumption that she must be from "a reservation," that her presence in the print public sphere must emanate from space legally coded as Native.[20] The role of U.S. policy in helping create, sustain, and disseminate such preconceptions appears in the use of "Urban Indians" as a generic, somewhat dismissive, catchall for those who are not inhabitants on a landbase officially recognized as Native. In addition to refusing to be "representative of Native women in general" or to play the role of "Spiritual Leader," she asserts that "the fury which erupts from my work is a result of seeing the pain that white culture has caused my father," who refuses to speak Menominee to her. Not only do the "myths & misconceptions" circulated about Natives elide the experiences of people like her father, but within their terms Chrystos's absence of *authentic* knowledge, like the language, brands her as not-quite-Native. Rather than providing a valid means of assessing her, though, the equation of Indian with "spiritual" insight marks a broader process of expropriation: "Our rituals, stories & religious practices have been stolen & abused, as has our land." The former can be seen as an extension of the latter, the loss of territory forming the core of a network of governmental interventions in Native life—such as "treaty violations, . . . ridiculous jail terms, denial of civil rights, radiation poisoning, land theft, endless contrived legal battles which drain our wills, corrupt 'tribal' governments, harassment & death at the hands of the BIA & FBI." As Janice Gould notes in "Disobedience (in Language) in Texts by Lesbian Native Americans," "Some of the angriest work in *Not Vanishing* . . . exposes the continuing legacy for Indians of living in a colonized state" (38), and Chrystos articulates the ongoing politics of displacement, detention, and denegation that subtend the narrative of Native people as "Vanishing Americans," suggesting that "the books which still appear" offering that story operate as a vector within a settler system whose ultimate aim is the making impossible of Indigenous persistence.

That imperative to disappearance, though, entails less the utter elision of indigeneity than its translation (or perhaps condensation) into a format that contains it spatially and temporally while making it available for nonnative identification. Indigenous self-expression from within this frame requires inhabiting a version of Native identity sundered from contemporary Native life. In "Looks Like I Have That White Fang #2," Chrystos describes her experience of watching "another pale movie with a pretty / white boy in buckskins / communing with a wolf / & probably saving some Indian folks from themselves."[21] More than *playing Indian*, as suggested by the "buckskins" and ability to engage with animals, the "pretty white boy" out-Indians the Indians, "saving" them from their semi-innate inability to do Indianness in a way that actually would allow them to persist. Moreover, she notes that the Indians in the film "might actually / *be* Indians / instead of Jewish folks in max factor red #10 / & braided wigs / which is how they did it in the good old days." We see a progression in the performance of Indianness, but one toward actual Native people rather than away from them. Instead of marking a time in which Indians were more authentic, having a natural/ primitive connection to place that contemporary Natives progressively have lost, "the good old days" refers to the period in which Indianness properly was embodied by nonnatives. The assumption of the mantle of Indianness by Indians appears as a recent phenomenon, with "some Indian actors" getting to play "supporting roles" and, thereby, gaining some of the capital accrued through the mass-mediated circulation of settler-constructed images. While suggesting how commonsensical notions of Indigenous identity disseminated in popular discourse depend on the construction of a more natural elsewhere to which Native peoples are consigned as their sphere of authenticity, Chrystos reverses the conventional genealogy of Indianness by suggesting that Native people are the latest ones to occupy this subjectivity, not its originators. Thus, what makes "the Indian" attractive, what generates its potential for seemingly infinite iterability in yet "another pale movie," is that it is made to be lived by others. More than producing a kind of embodied concretion for nonwhite populations, as distinguished from the ostensible generality/universality of whiteness, the figure of the Indian functions as a flexible, mobile form that enables settlers simultaneously to enact modes of recognition and appropriation, in which the signification of indigeneity is not in fact separable from its occupation and consumption by nonnatives.[22]

One could present the stereotype as false, as a *simulation* that replaces the *real*, and at times Chrystos does so, emphasizing the disjunction between the settler imaginary and the lives of actual Indians. However, more than seeking to replace the former with the latter, to install a more authentic portrait of indigeneity in the place of the lie propagated through the citation of Indianness, her work tracks the circuit of stereotypical representation, the work it does in shaping the social landscape that Native people must negotiate even as it puts their existence as such into question. The film "is a sincere sweet movie / by laladisney," but her ability to appreciate the "ad on TV" for it is undercut by the fact that she is "scrubbing out a white sink / for mr. white": "since I'm sick of weeping / all I feel like / is throwing up."

The movie does not reflect her experience, but more than that, the image actively annuls it. Put more precisely, the juxtaposition of the "pretty white boy" performing exemplary Indianness on the frontier with the unromantic, not particularly *Indian,* work of cleaning the bathroom of wealthy white people illustrates how the ongoing imaginative banishment of indigeneity to a bygone, rural beyond makes the Indian into an impossible, unliveable subjectivity for Native people. Rather than having to embody the stereotype as a primary facet of her personhood, she experiences the unbridgeable disjunction between her everyday life and the image with which she is confronted as a kind of dissolving, either in tears or in nausea. The "sincer[ity]" and "sweet[ness]" of the depiction does nothing to remedy the ways that she is undone by it, by its well-meaning repudiation of the reality of her existence as a Native person.

What makes the economy of representation in which the movie participates so overwhelming is that it operates as a central feature of the broader structure of settler occupation. More than simply substituting the stereotype for Native people in the present, the figure of the Indian mediates a process through which indigeneity is captured and made consumable by nonnatives. In "The Real Indian Leans Against," Chrystos compares the "real Indian" of the title to "the pink neon lit window" on which he "leans," observing that it reveals a display "full of plaster of paris / & resin Indians in beadwork for days with fur trim / turkey feathers dyed to look like eagles."[23] The image highlights the artificiality of the inanimate figures and the fabrication necessary to transform the more pedestrian "turkey feathers" into a facsimile of the rarified eagle feathers more appropriate for Indian spectacle. Yet even while foregrounding the synthetic deceptiveness of the commercial display, the ways its items substitute for the "real" thing at multiple levels (such as "a headdress from hell / with painted feathers no bird on earth / would be caught dead in"), the poem observes, "The fake Indians, if mechanically activated / would look better at the Pow Wow than the real one in plain jeans." The question arises, of course, to whom would they "look better"? As a site of contemporary Native expression, but one often populated by nonnatives in search of Indianness, powwows are a place where the "real" and the "fake" intersect, but in which, from a nonnative perspective, the jeans-wearing Native exceeds the terms of authenticity, appearing to be fake. In addition, though, these lines intimate that the synthetic spectacle of the Indian with the "headdress from hell" might "look better," more "real," to some Native people present as well.

What constitutes the basis for adjudicating realness? Or more to the point, what are the contours and scope of the network through which *the real* is produced and circulated? In the wake of the powwow image, the poem declaims, "For Sale For Sale / with no price tag." What does it mean for something to be salable but with "no price"? If price indicates value within a capitalist system, its absence would seem to imply that the item is not exchangeable, remaining outside or beyond circuits of commodification. However, here the "fake Indians" are what lack a "price tag," even as they are visible through the storefront window. Perhaps, then, *they* are the marker of value, substituting for "price." Within a Marxist framework, fetishism refers to ways value is incarnated, given material form (particularly as money). In order for disparate objects to be exchanged with each other, they all must be articulated to a single equivalent that can serve as the means of expressing their relative value with respect to each other. As Marx notes in *Capital: Volume 1*, "A particular kind of commodity acquires the form of universal equivalent, because all other commodities make it the material embodiment of their uniform and universal form of value" (160), and that commodity now "serves as money" (162). The object so constructed and invested with meaning stands in for the system in which value is generated and circulated: "It is however precisely this finished form of the world of commodities—the money form—which conceals the social character of private labour and the social relations between the individual workers, by making those relations appear as relations between material objects" (168–69). The social relations that enable and sustain the system of exchange appear as "natural" and "immutable" (168), and since the operation of exchange requires that "the money form" function as if it had inherent value, "relations of production therefore assume a material shape which is independent of [the] control and [the] conscious individual action" of participants in that system (187). Value appears to emanate from the mediating object that bears it as if it were an innate quality of the object rather than the condensation of a larger set of social processes, and the working of those processes endows the object in practical ways with that value, such that the apparent misrecognition of the object as value also can be understood as a recognition of the ways the system coalesces and distributes value through the object and its circulation. We can understand *the Indian* as such a fetish within settler political economy, both serving as the bearer of value and functionally enabling its extraction and dissemination. In this vein, the poem notes:

> There are certainly more fake Indians
> than real ones but this is the u.s.a.
> What else can you expect from the land of sell
> your grandma sell our land sell your ass
> You too could have a fake Indian in your parlor
> who never talks back

Chrystos casts the proliferation of "fake Indians," exceeding the number of "real ones," as axiomatically part of what it means to be in "the u.s.a.," linking it to the commercialization of everything within the nation. Put another way, the "fake Indians" emerge less as a problem due to their failure to adequate Native "real[ness]" than as symptomatic of an enveloping *fakeness*, in the sense that everything is understood as reproducible, purchasable, and exploitable.

More than an indication of the ills of capitalism per se, claiming ownership over a "fake Indian" is an extension and condensation of the fundamental process of seizing "our land" necessary for constructing and sustaining the United States. The production and circulation of Indianness as a kind of fakery indexes and perpetuates the reterritorialization of Native presence within the matrix of settler political economy, facilitating the seizure/absorption/appropriation of indigeneity by making it ubiquitous, possessable, and impotent ("never talks back"). Returning to the land, Chrystos notes at the end of the poem, "I want to bury these Indians dressed like cartoons / of our long dead / I want to live / somewhere / where nobody is sold." The image of interring "these Indians" envisions a (re)embedding in place, reciprocally implying that such a relation is disjointed by the circulation of these images. "These Indians" appear to nonnatives as expressive of indigeneity ("look[ing] better at the Pow Wow than the real one in plain jeans"), but that version of Indianness has no determinate relation to any particular location, unlike the "long dead" these figures resemble as caricature. They simulate the idea of connection to land without connection to any particular territory, except "the u.s.a.," whose jurisdictional pretentions demand the deterritorialization of Indigenous peoples—their translation as *domestic subjects* within its boundaries. From this perspective, the longing for a "somewhere / where nobody is sold" can be seen less as a desire to occupy an elsewhere free from fakery than to inhabit a here of Indigenous space that cannot be "sold."

As Chrystos illustrates, the figure of the Indian—mobile yet deadened and silent—helps make possible a broader economy of expropriation by seeming to recognize Indigenous presence while simultaneously effacing and enacting systems of settler occupation. It makes indigeneity available as a form of value transferrable to nonnatives through the acquisition of Indian objects or the inhabiting of Indian spaces. In this vein, Shari Huhndorf defines "going native" as the "conviction that adopting some vision of Native life in a more permanent way is necessary to regenerate and to maintain European-American national and racial identities" (8), and it "constitutes a series of cultural rituals that express and symbolically resolve [the] anxiety about the nation's violent origins" (14).[24] "Going native" entails dwelling within Indianness, taking the stereotype as empirical—a determinate identity/subjectivity ostensibly correlated with Native peoples but one through which settler desires and geographies can be lived as (if) commensurate with Indigenous persistence. As part of elaborating the broader logic of commodity fetishism and the kinds of condensations and equivalences on which capitalism depends, Marx suggests that "the characters who appear on the economic stage are merely personifications of economic relations" (179). Nonnatives can come to be the bearers of a generically conceived and regenerative indigeneity, participants in the economy of a putatively nonviolent process of settlement, by *personifying* Indianness. Or more to the point, the Indian is already a personification that nonnatives can inhabit as the basis for determining and claiming ownership over authentic Nativeness. As discussed in chapter 2, personification can be thought of less as treating an object or entity as if it were a person than as the ideological, institutional, experiential process by which a certain ideal of personhood (such as the model of the individualist liberal citizen) is realized as the norm, and Chrystos's work explores how circuits of Indianness recast Native identity as a mediating placeholder, both congealing and obscuring the ongoing violence of settler annexations, arrogations, and assumptions.[25]

The pursuit and dissemination of Native spirituality serves as a notable example of how nonnative systems of extraction work through the circulation of the figure of the Indian—bearing the value of indigeneity while remaining fungible. In "Zenith Supplies," Chrystos observes:

> Smashed into the corner of a glued sawdust bookcase
> next to the incense charcoal
> are Sweet Grass braids
> for $3.50 with a blue label saying *Native Scents*
> & a computer code
> I can't catch my breath
> All night I'm angry
> as I dream of selling eucharists on street corners
> This sacred gift is never to be sold
> but hippies don't care as they give themselves new names
> for the same old rip off of everybody to get some kulture
> just like their parents[26]

"Sacred" objects appear as ways of acquiring a piece of "*Native*" identity, of accessing Indian *culture*. Foregrounding the violence of this fetishization, the poem emphasizes that what is at stake here is more than the dislocation of items from their proper spheres of use or modes of dissemination. As the Eucharist gains meaning through the act of transubstantiation, another kind of transformation occurs in the "hippies'" adoption of "new names," a process of *Indianization* in which they can come to occupy a "*Native*" subjectivity. That promise—the reification of indigeneity as a matrix inhabitable by nonnatives—drives the dynamic of sale while effacing the ways it remains a "rip off," part of a long history of imposition and exploitation ("just like your parents"). The text asserts, "We don't want you / anymore than our grandparents wanted yours & their mission schools / Leave us alone / find your kulture & your spirituality in our mutual history / Stop selling out ours." The apparent appreciation of Nativeness cannot be divorced from a "mutual history" in which settler institutions sought to wrench apart Indigenous peoples and to eradicate Native traditions (as suggested by the allusion to systemic campaigns of conversion and the boarding school system), and the very possibility of "get[ting] some kulture" in the present rests, Chrystos suggests, on the forms of intervention and dispossession enacted by those prior policy imperatives.

The act of *naming* performed through the sale and purchase of "*Native*" items and the consequent promise of proximity to indigeneity can be described as a mobilization of "symbolic capital." As Pierre Bourdieu indicates in "Social Space and Symbolic Power," the concept refers to "the power to make groups," which "depends on the social authority acquired in previous struggles" (137).[27] A "symbolic" struggle is over "the production of common sense or, more precisely, for the monopoly over legitimate naming," a conflict that "is nothing other than economic or cultural capital . . . when it is known through the categories of perception that it imposes" and that "tend[s] to reproduce and to reinforce the power relations that constitute the structure of social space" (134–35). The ability to filter, reconstellate, and recirculate indigeneity as the "common sense" of stereotypical Indianness reflects existing forms of authority that emerge out of the settler restructuring of social space, giving rise to a category of perception—the figure of the Indian—that bears "the power relations" of settlement but realizes/reifies the principles at play in them as merely the inherent features of the category itself. Bourdieu adds that one can "see in the state the holder of the monopoly of legitimate symbolic violence. Or, more precisely, the state is the referee, albeit a powerful one, in struggles over this monopoly" (136–37),[28] and as Chrystos indicates, desires by "hippies" and others to claim indigeneity in this form arise within the contours of the legacy of state intervention and invasion ("this world your ancestors made"). Indianness gains value within this nexus—as endangered and thus rare, as available due to earlier forms of dislocation, and as a path to expiation for the sin of settlement. Chrystos notes that the purchase of sweet grass is a bid for redemption, "Still trying to buy your way to innocence," but even as the significance of this incorporation of things Indian depends on the legacy of guilt from which nonnatives would seek absolution, the commodification through which it is purchased effaces that very "mutual history" and its ongoing effects.

Within this frame, Native people bear the burden of symbolizing forms of Indian value that recapitulate legacies of state violence while appearing to evade them. "I Am Not Your Princess" asserts, "I'm not / a means by which you can reach spiritual understanding or even / learn to do beadwork / I'm only willing to tell you how to make fry bread."[29] The search for "spiritual understanding" positions Indians as avenues to a kind of higher awareness, one that putatively exceeds/transcends the binds, struggles, divisions, and trauma of the settler colonial past. The title gives a turn to this wish, alluding to the oft-circulated myth of descent from an Indian princess or of being saved by one (who defies the will of her people in doing so).[30] Similarly, the pursuit of the "spiritual" represents a desire for proximity-as-inheritance, to become the bearer of *Indian* "understanding" in ways that make indigeneity available to nonnatives in the absence of exploitation and coercion. In offering the recipe for "fry bread" as the knowledge/value she will impart, Chrystos draws attention to the imperial dynamics encoded within and animating the hunt for Indianness: "This is Indian food / only if you know that Indian is a government word / which has nothing to do with our names for ourselves." The very authenticity that nonnatives crave, which fetishistically condenses and circulates indigeneity as a form of appropriable value, arises only as an effect of the process of seizing Native lands and consigning Indigenous peoples to the circumscribed space of the reservation. The symbolic categorization of fry bread as "Indian food" points to while occluding the conditions of violence and deprivation that make possible and sustain the reservation system. Made of flour, salt, baking powder, and a liquid (as Chrystos notes, whether "milk or water or beer"), fry bread indicates the absence of viable options for subsistence on the reservation, due to the denial of access to traditional sources of sustenance and efforts to impose Euramerican forms of agriculture on lands usually ill suited to growing the kinds of crops officials and white benefactors thought best.[31] It indexes a reliance on insufficient and poor government rations, an enforced dependency that Chrystos juxtaposes to the desire to distill a "spiritual" essence of Indianness that itself denies the persistence of the kinds of destitution signaled by the fry bread: "Look at me / See my confusion loneliness fear worrying about all our / struggles to keep what little is left for us / Look at my heart not your fantasies"; "I have work to do dishes to wash a house to clean / There is no magic." The yearning for Indian wisdom—"magic"—bespeaks an inability to "see" Native people, not only to acknowledge their coresidence in the space/time of the supposedly sympathetic settler but to comprehend the *fantasy* of the reservation as a denial of both an ongoing history of "struggles" and the materiality of daily Native sociospatiality in the present (of "work," "dishes to wash," and "a house to clean").

Thus, more than seizing upon particular objects or ideas that bear special Indian meaning, the proliferation of invocations of Indianness reaffirms geographies of settlement while actively disavowing the possibility of acknowledging the presence of contemporary Natives in spaces not considered to be *Indian*. Chrystos illustrates how the symbolic reproduction of the category of the Indian in popular culture and commercial life reaffirms earlier, and ongoing, state imperatives even as it disseminates a version of indigeneity for nonnatives to inhabit through consumption. The poem "Crazy Horse" begins by observing, "I'm ironing a shirt with your name / blue 100% cotton the label says made in Macau," "our connection frayed with Mohawk gas stations / Winnebago trucks, Navajo moving & storage / This is not my shirt, or my kin's."[32] These peoples' names become markers of distinctness for various products that have nothing to do with anything specifically Native. The very banal ubiquity of these acts of nomination suggests an almost total disarticulation of relation between signs of Indianness and actual Indigenous persons, even as such branding indicates the exotic frisson generated by stereotypical iteration. "Crazy Horse" endows something ineffably appealing to the cotton shirt that bears its label, even as the value communicated through the utterly fungible figure of the Indian relies on the elision of the laboring body of the Native women whose job entails facilitating the use of this product. The power to designate something as Indian follows from one's position within existing structures of, in Bourdieu's terms, "economic or cultural capital," and thus, in ironing this garment owned by someone else, the speaker may serve as the temporary caretaker of an Indian value that emanates from elsewhere while she cannot *be* the bearer of that value.

Chrystos here traces the symbolic violence through which non-native visions of indigeneity are realized and disseminated via mass production in ways that depend on the sustained political economy of settlement. At several moments the poem directly connects the availability of commodified icons of indigeneity to the long history of invasion and expropriation, the former scaffolded on the latter:

> Our mother moans under the weight of cement
> they want to choke her out of herself
> Crazy Horse don't look
> Our home shrunk to land stabbed with oil rigs
> coal strippers, uranium mines
> . . . .
> Crazy Horse I saw a book yesterday talking
> about the brave
> & daring conquest of the savage wild west
> They're experts at calling murder any other name

Apostrophizing Crazy Horse, the text moves through the shirt that supposedly celebrates his legacy to the continuing struggle over land for which he serves as an icon.[33] Notably, these lines connect the space of the city to that of the reservation, refusing the isolation of Native people onto the latter while marking the history of the reification of proper Native place. The proximity between the depiction of the earth as trapped under "the weight of cement" in urban centers and the description of the territory of recognized Indigenous occupancy being "shrunk" link these two to each other, and the reference to "oil rigs," "coal strippers," and "uranium mines" speaks to the ongoing exploitation of land legally acknowledged as Native.[34] Through the invocation of Crazy Horse, Chrystos suggests that the Indian wars of the nineteenth century persist, although the mode of imposition/extraction has shifted to accommodate new forms of *development*, but reciprocally, the circulation of Crazy Horse as a brand both remembers prior scenes of imperial struggle and remolds the possibilities for capital expansion opened through the displacement and regulation of Native people(s)—engagement with (a fetishistically rendered version of) indigeneity. Paul Patton argues that within settler colonial regimes "the territorial domains of the prior inhabitants become transformed into a uniform space of landed property" (124), but they, along with other "capitalist societies," "simultaneously reterritorialise what they deterritorialise, producing all manner of 'neoterritorialities' which may be 'artificial, residual or archaic' but which have the effect of resuscitating or reintroducing fragments of earlier social codes, or inventing new ones" (97). The poem illustrates how the reservation functions as a neoterritoriality within the broader settler project of reterritorialization, a dynamic that also recycles "fragments" from the history of settler occupation—like the figure of Crazy Horse—in ways that simultaneously celebrate the surpluses generated by the "conquest" of the "savage" *and* proliferate forms of multicultural recognition via consumption.

In condensing while revalorizing the history of settler exploitation, the circulation of reified Indianness surrogates for the presence of contemporary Indians. More precisely, in order for the commodified spectacle of the Indian to retain its value, it must stand in the place of Native persons and peoples. Put another way, the dissemination of stereotypical Indian symbols safeguards the space of settlement from the challenge of persistent Indigenous presence. The fetish not only stands in for and effaces the social process of its production but stands in for and effaces the competing materiality of Native residence in un-"Indian" places.

> Yesterday as we stood watching speakers
> after the Gay Day Parade
> a Black man threw a bottle of beer at us
> screamed *What are you mother-fuckin' Indians*
> *doing here?!*
> Through clenched teeth I wondered
> What is anybody doing here
> but us
> We're surviving

The poem here explores how the branding of Crazy Horse, among other icons of Indianness, generates something other than amnesia—a response more like denegation. Even more than disavowing the possibility of Indians in the city, the assailant actively repudiates their right to be there. The "here" seems to be the issue, the presence of Native people in a place that's not properly Native or occupying place in ways that cannot fetishistically be circulated and appropriated as Indian value. As Mishuana Goeman asks in "Disrupting a Settler Grammar of Place in the Visual Memoir of Hulleah Tsinhnahjinnie," "Why do bodies belong in one place, the rez, and not the other? What bodies belong where and when? What does it mean when these bodies are undisciplined and unreadable"?[35] Those attending the rally may be acknowledged as Indians, but they cannot be both Indian and present in the urban time/space of the parade as generic participants/spectators. They cannot exist *as Indians* alongside the Crazy Horse shirt, the "Mohawk gas stations," and the "Winnebago trucks." The condition of possibility for the latter lies in the consignment of Native people to the "shrunk" space of the reservation as their sphere of authentic occupancy, and that symbolic displacement both generates and preserves the value of Indian items while in Bourdieu's terms quoted above, "reproduc[ing] and . . . reinforc[ing] the power relations that constitute the structure of [the] social space" of settlement.

The poem responds to this derealization of urban Natives with a countersymbolic, one in which Native people possess an underlying, encompassing sovereignty. In "wonder[ing]" about the presence of anyone other than Native people, Chrystos presents indigeneity as a kind of ongoing dwelling rather than a determinate content (like particular practices or "spiritual" knowledge). More than attaching to legally acknowledged sections of territory, referred to as *Indian country,* connection to place arises out of the priorness of Native presence. If reservation lands can be "shrunk," what cannot be undone is the history of relation to the space now claimed by/as the United States, and the poem extrapolates outward from the specificity of given peoples' forms of occupancy and dislocation to address the broader system of seizure and erasure through which Native people have lived. The place of the city remains Native because it is one of the spaces in which "we're surviving"; to *survive* is to enact persistence in ways that cannot be registered within an Indianizing system of value but that take part in the assertion of Native endurance, vitality, and continued self-making that in policy terms is addressed through the rhetoric of sovereignty. In this way, Chrystos's poetry can be seen as tracking the fetishizing effects of putting Indianness in motion for nonnative identification and consumption, as well as charting how that circulation both extends and effaces broader histories of regulation and appropriation, but simultaneously, her work posits largely ignored circuits of Native movement and presence—of, in Vizenor's terms, *transmotion*—irreducible to the extractive itineraries of stereotype.[36]

Embodying Endurance

If Native people can reject reified accounts of *Indian* existence, in which they either are cast as peddlers of tradition or are displaced as inauthentic remnants, that gesture of refusal comes at a price. Chrystos suggests that being Native in ways that do not map easily onto Indianness (itself constructed to be occupied by nonnatives) generates forms of unvalued and unacknowledged labor for Indigenous people. In "I Am Not Your Princess," the greeting of nonnative declarations of the inappropriateness of Indian presence in the city with "clenched teeth" indicates the emotional cost of having one's existence denied. In *Magical Criticism*, Chris Bracken argues, "When we say that one thing belongs to representation and another to reality, we are not 'respecting' them, . . . but gauging how much was spent enriching them. . . . A greater expenditure produces an impression of fact; a lesser expenditure, an impression of fiction" (92). Settler discourses' disavowal of Indigenous experience—particularly when occurring in places other than those that are apparently Indian—creates a "reality"-effect due to the kinds of "expenditure" that propel them, in Bourdieu's terms the other sorts of capital that undergird the wielding of symbolic authority. Being outside the real in this way means that one does not have the resources to secure one's status as something other than fiction, that certain Native people cannot manifest themselves as such because they do not serve as bearers of settler modes of value. Chrystos's poetry occupies and charts this space of nonbeing, illustrating how survival as Indigenous people entails both complicitous participation in the political economy through which one is made unreal and painful affective wrestling with the "fact" of one's own impossibility.

The stereotype gains concretion by not being extended to forms of Native identity that do not fit into the dominant network of signification/commodification. Such nonstereotypical modes of indigeneity are rendered immaterial—irrelevant and lacking in substance. As Chrystos observes in "Night Watch Me Closely," "Being Indian is being a surrealist," noting that nonnatives who "cried & cried / after reading *Bury My Heart at Wounded Knee*" "patrol reality with a stick / beating back our tears."[37] The tearful sympathetic investment in an Indian past, or in Indians as past, guards against the possibility of seeing Native people in the present as inheritors of the legacy of nineteenth-century violence (as chronicled in Dee Brown's book) or as struggling with the continuing force of settlement. Part of that structure of imposition, displacement, and foreclosure operates through "patrol[ling] reality," a quotidian, though also systemic, process of settler adjudication in which Native people's "tears" in the present do not count as authentically Indian.[38] The translation of indigeneity into a fetishized Indianness that can be borne, disseminated, and accumulated by nonnatives is made possible and enacted through the denial of indigeneity to those whose presence disjoints its circulation as a form of settler value—as origin, as connection to the land claimed by the United States, as redemption for the guilt of imperial occupation.

This production of reality generates a supplementary effect in which contemporary Natives are made to experience themselves as a kind of "surreal" trace or shadow. In *Ghostly Matters* Avery Gordon argues that *"making contact with the disappeared means encountering the specter of what the state has tried to repress, means encountering it in the affective mode in which haunting traffics"* (127). Gordon's perspective, however, is that of someone in search of *"the disappeared"* rather than of those who have been made such. If not sequestered or murdered by government agents, Native people living off-reservation have had their existence repressed by the state in that official recognition for forms of indigeneity and sovereignty does not extend to the spaces they occupy. What does it feel like to occupy the impossible subjectivity of *"the specter"*? Put another way, how is "being Indian," particularly in nonreservation space, also being specter, living in a condition in which one's identity as a Native person continually is ghosted within nonnative discourses and institutions? In chapter 1, I discussed the spectral and processes of haunting, addressing how Qwo-Li Driskill's poetry explores the active presence of unrecognized histories and their availability for alternative performances of embodied peoplehood. For Chrystos, though, the issue is less the return of an unacknowledged or blocked inheritance than a kind of dematerialization, less the breaking open of the present to a plurality of residual pasts that can animate emergent futures than the dissolving of selfhood such that affective resources are expended in proving one's own existence. As discussed in chapter 2, Deborah Miranda highlights how indigeneity persists melancholically in Native corporeality and psychic life despite its official erasure, but Chrystos emphasizes the difficulty of enduring the everyday forms of elision through which indigeneity is seized by nonnatives. In response her poetry seeks to recast the sensations of daily life—including emotional crisis, the tedium of wage work, and felt connection to local landscapes—as expressive of a distinctly Native structure of feeling. Her poetry illustrates the necessary labor entailed in reenfleshing the spectral, in seeking to make "real" that which routinely is rendered "surreal."

Native people in the present haunt the accounts of them authored by nonnatives. "Night Watch Me Closely" insists, "You won't find us in anthologies of american poets / We forgot to sign that treaty / Everybody likes to read the whites writing myths of us / Us telling about us is too hard." Native writers do not count as generically "american," but the "american" is constituted through "myths" of Indianness in which "whites" are the proper speakers of stories about Indigenous peoples, stories that can generate tears of compassion while avoiding the really "hard" task of confronting Native proximity in the now. Referring to the absence of acknowledgment for contemporary Native self-representation as the lack of a "treaty" ties entry into the public sphere to the construction of the domestic space of the nation.[39] Gaining the ability to signify within the former entails (re)confirming the legitimacy of U.S. narratives, validating the incorporation of indigeneity into/as "american" identity even if in a somewhat elegiac mode ("volumes of defeat speeches / they call our literature") that chronicles the bygone tragedies of the national past. To have current

Native poets "telling about us" indicates less the apparent resolution, for good or ill, represented by the "treaty" than an ongoing conflict/ negotiation in which Indigenous intellectuals actively take part. In addition, the figure of the "treaty" suggests that the space of Indian presentness necessarily is limited to those sites officially delineated as such. Indians can serve as a feature of the "american" past, an anachronistic remainder contained elsewhere about which citizens can have complex feelings, rather than as a speaking presence with which others need to reckon. Of the specter, Derrida notes, "Let us not forget that, unlike the spirit, for example, or the idea or simply thought, this nothing is a nothing that *takes on a body*" (141), adding that the system of commodification "renders the non-sensuous sensuous" (151), giving form to saleable items. Chrystos depicts the embodied experience of Native identity, however, as the feeling of becoming ephemeral, of having one's sensuous existence rendered nonsensuous through quotidian acts of nonrecognition. She says to those who want her to play the role of remnant in their tales of settler remorse, "*Hey, I'm not screaming since you're not listening.*" The image suggests that a vocal, visceral Native claiming of space would be heard only as the emptiness of silence or, conversely, that any act of speech other than sympathetic reflection would register for nonnatives as a kind of deafening noise, given the inability to hear Native people as contemporary interlocutors.

In contrast to this sensation of being disappeared, of paradoxically being called on to accept having vanished as a condition of reciprocal engagement, Chrystos explores how Native histories are given substance through her flesh. Reciprocally, these pasts are portrayed as endowing her with an Indigenous materiality denied by forms of settler ghosting. She observes in "Night Watch Me Closely," "Millions / of dead / are in my voice," adding, "I'm a ghost dancing with hands on fire." Her speech in the current moment, as opposed to, in the poem's terms, the "defeat speeches" collected "in your local library" in which Native people are "stoic & strong," bears the remains of those killed in the process by which "the west was won," not only disinterring them from their burial in the past but suggesting that their presence within her helps give substance to her "mean angry words" as a Native woman. Her "dancing" appears as a response to efforts to "whitewash" her words, and in describing herself in this way, she invokes the Ghost Dance, most directly alluding to the Native revitalization movement begun in the late 1880s by the Paiute prophet Wovoka that promised the cleansing of Euro-presence from the continent and the return of the Native dead.[40] In this image she shifts from being a "ghost" to a Ghost Dancer, from being outside reality to serving as the agent of regenerative transformation in which the settled history of occupation potentially is undone through the sensuous physicality of contemporary Indigenous people.

The reference to the Ghost Dance also implicitly calls to mind the military campaign through which it was put down among the Teton Sioux in 1890, in what has come to be known as the Wounded Knee massacre.[41] Chrystos's choice to draw on this history in her work plays on the conventional narration of that incident as the end of the "Indian wars" and of significant resistance to U.S. incursion onto Native lands, and she enfleshes this stereotype in ways that alter its meaning and operation. The massacre functions as a crucial symbol in the history of U.S.–Indian relations, providing a dense point of identification for nonnatives to lament the loss of Native autonomy while simultaneously investing in the ostensibly unalterable finality of the triumph of U.S. expansionism.[42] As discussed earlier, the expression of national shame can serve as a way of consolidating national identity by expiating the guilt of a program of settlement cast as already accomplished and irreversible, as in Chrystos's portrayal of the tears shed by nonnatives in reading Dee Brown's *Bury My Heart at Wounded Knee*. In "I Walk in the History of My People," though, she shifts the association of Wounded Knee with the end of Native opposition to an emphasis on the enduring commitment to survival within a legacy of state projects of containment.[43] It begins by observing, "There are women locked in my joints / for refusing to speak to the police," depicting her body as shaped around various forms of imprisonment, whether in jails or constricted reservation spaces where, as noted later in the poem, Native people "are not allowed / to hunt / to move / to be." This corporealization of policy and collective experience counters the ghost-effects generated through the fetishization of Indianness and its attachment to certain sorts of artifacts, styles, places, and (spiritual) knowledges, instead presenting the legacies of settler violence as immanent in the speaker's materiality—her ontological experience of her own embodiment. The historical genealogy of these woundings is intimated most strongly in the poem's closing lines:

My knee is wounded so badly that I limp constantly
Anger is my crutch I hold myself upright with it
> My knee is wounded
> see
> How I Am Still Walking

The insistent connection of the terms "knee" and "wounded" gestures toward Wounded Knee without explicitly naming it as *the* referent, drawing on its iconic visibility while refiguring its significance. Encompassing a vast array of desecrations, detentions, and invasions, the text's allusion to the massacre foregrounds the continuance of Native people(s) despite the multifaceted assaults they have endured—the capability to keep "Walking" despite having been "wounded." Not only can the "anger" be understood as a response to settler violence and violation, it appears as the affective corollary to the erasure of such pained survival by the presentation of Wounded Knee (or other "last" events and persons) as an end to Indian history.[44] The quotidian yet visceral sensations the poem addresses provide a means of concretizing contemporary Indigenous selfhood as against its dematerialization in the symbolic (re)production of Indian value.

Suggesting that indigeneity remains immanent in the inheritance of systemic settler *woundings,* Chrystos does not juxtapose the breadth of the stereotype with the empirical particularity of a given Native nation. She uses the phrase "my people," but inasmuch as intimations of Wounded Knee are crucial to the work of the poem, it most directly points to the Oglalas rather than the Menominee. The text's references to U.S. initiatives that affected numerous peoples suggests, though, that the "my" is not meant to be Oglala *rather than* Menominee. As Victoria Brehm notes, Chrystos refuses to play the role of Native informant on the Menominee (74), and the somewhat generic quality of the policy patterns of which the text speaks, such as "children torn from their families / bludgeoned into government schools," implies less the choice of one people over another than an effort to extend "people" to include an expansive sense of shared Native history and contemporary life. In the place of tribally specific images, she suggests a pan-tribal ethos, one in which similarities among histories of imperial subjection provide a basis for solidarity and for discussion of shared experiences of embodied endurance and persistence. Such generalization can be critiqued, though, as recirculating stereotype, helping disseminate damaging kinds of genericization that undo the claims of particular Native nations to their own delineated spheres of sovereignty. To the contrary, Nancy Marie Mithlo argues, "The rejection of a pan-Indian sensibility indicates that Natives are not able to conceptualize and appropriate the homogeneous identity that has been exercised against them since contact" (147). From this perspective, she insists, "not all stereotypes are bad," in that the forms of "homogeneous identity" generated through settler policy and public discourses "can be put to socially progressive ends" by Native people themselves (102). Yet rather than redeploying the same stereotype to different ends, Chrystos seeks to reframe the conversation by offering what can be described as a countersymbolic. If Indianness makes Indigenous pasts and forms of Native knowledge available for nonnative inheritance/consumption (whether as spirituality or sympathy), thereby ghosting Native people in the present, highlighting the physicality of the continuing pain of settlement provides a way of broadly characterizing indigeneity that differs markedly from the dominant system of value she chronicles.

The use of Wounded Knee as a means of figuring pervasive forms of settler violence also bears the legacy of tying proper Native inhabitance to government-recognized and government-regulated Indian spaces. The massacre emerged out of the campaign to move the Ghost Dancers back to the reservations created the previous year, and the poem signals as much in its emphasis on the constriction of Native people to unliveable places. In this way, the image of walking despite being wounded can be seen as highlighting not only Native survival but, more pointedly, a refusal to be bound to lands legally coded as Indian. Instead, the very means through which Native occupancy is tribally specified—on distinct jurisdictionally circumscribed units over which Native nations can extend a sovereignty continually mediated by the reterritorializing plenary power of the United States—implicitly appears here as an assault on Native movement, as a kind of hobbling. The apparent lack of tribal specificity in the text, then, functions as a critique of how federal policy defines tribal identity in ways that (stereotypically) seek to render it inert and elsewhere. The image of a body in motion, one that bears ongoing legacies of collective *wounding,* opens possibilities for envisioning a kind of Native presence and inhabitance uncoupled from, in Vizenor's terms, "a monotheistic, territorial sovereignty," instead understanding Native "transmotion" as "*sui generis* sovereignty."[45]

Such movement, though, is not equivalent to a lack of place but of a relation to the landscape different from that of ownership. Chrystos illustrates how settler geographies are materialized and made obvious through the coding of land as property, and she leverages the apparent empirical self-evidence of this system by narrating her affective responses to the quotidian, unselfconscious performance of settler possession. In "Gazing out the Kitchen Window," she "watch[es] / 3 young children of the rich whites / playing on the beach" while on a "break" from her work as a maid in their home.[46] Literally framed by the window, her viewpoint suggests she is trapped inside, as if locked within the domestic space to which she will always be both a necessary supplement and an alien intrusion—her labor giving her entry even as her bodily expenditures do not endow her with a right of inhabitance. In contrast, the children appear absolutely at home: "This is Private Property"; "They're raised to know this is their beach / an ownership profoundly lacking in history." They experience this place as an extension of their (white) bodies, as part of them, in an everyday relationship made possible through the legalities of "ownership." That sensation of being and belonging, though, depends on a disavowal of the past. Chrystos notes:

It is a delicate art to enjoy this fragment
of their pleasure
I have to scrape back all the ghosts
of slaughtered Indian children
& silence the Suquamish mothers & fathers

The fullness of their "pleasure," the sensuous immediacy of their connection with this place accomplished through the regime of property, requires clearing away the residual presence of those who were killed and removed in making it available for white ownership. As someone who cannot claim possession in the ways the "rich whites" do, she must "scrape back" and "silence" the traces of "history," suggesting that her relation to this space needs to be vacated—made ghostly—in order to make possible theirs.[47]

Her sensations are mediated by a kind of Indigenous memory; the children's impressions also are mediated, but by a privileged relation to capital that makes the nonsensuous abstraction of property into the basis for sensuous feelings of possession.[48] Indigeneity, then, enters here in two distinct yet related forms of labor: the physical tasks involved in facilitating their domestic life, itself predicated on histories of dislocation (explicitly that of the Suquamish and implicitly those that make Native women available as maids); and the emotional difficulty of grappling with the active erasure of Native presence, the rendering self-evident of settlement in their completely unreflexive "pleasure" in "ownership." These two merge in the poem's closing lines:

> The crash of sun on waves
> draws me back to work
> They'll always have more time than I do
> & do nothing much with it
> They won't be servants
> I can only know their joy
> as a fragile shell
> over my grief

The land provides the key for understanding the materiality of her status as a Native person in non-Indian space. Highlighting the elision of legacies of struggle over this place, the amnesia at play in "their joy" reframes the "work" she performs, endowing the menial physicality of her labor as a "servant" with an affective density ("my grief") invisible beneath the "fragile shell" of ongoing acts of settlement. Her connection to this place, as well as thwarted identification with the children, draws her and the reader's attention to the *work* of sustaining a sense of indigeneity amid the reification of settler occupancy, which derealizes Indigenous presence (both hers and the Suquamish).

Yet her discussion of this ghost-effect suggests that her service in this space itself functions as a material trace of the affective histories that abide within and despite the seeming transparency and fullness of white property claims.[49]

Chrystos's poetry observes the ways the continuing erasure of Native pasts is borne in the present by the labor of a person who experiences her embodied relation to place through that process of effacement, but more than that, it charts what it envisions as Native modes of placemaking that defy the consignment of indigeneity to a stereotypical elsewhere/elsewhen. "Crazy Grandpa Whispers" and "Wings of a Wild Goose" explore how other ways of being are possible in the current spaces of settler occupation/ownership, indicating how they are haunted by that deferred potential.[50] The latter poem begins with a purposeless act of hunting:

A hen, one who could have brought more geese, a female, a wild one
dead   Shot by an excited ignorant young blond boy, his first
His mother threw the wings in the garbage   I rinsed them
brought them home, hung them spread wide on my studio wall
A reminder of so much, saving what I can't bear to be wasted

The wings serve as "reminder" of both the ongoing conquest of that which is considered "wild" and the prospective developments "wasted" in that display of aggression/mastery. The image of the wings hanging in her studio suggests that her poetry marks that evacuated potential, registering an alternative system of value that persists alongside that of the child—who "will always think of the woods / as an exciting place to kill." Like the children of "Gazing out the Kitchen Window," this boy's pleasure in possession of the land emerges from his privileged position within a political economy of private property. He "was recently paid / thousands of dollars to be in a television commercial" and loses in the couch "a passbook" indicating greater savings than the speaker has acquired in thirty-eight years of living and working. Moreover, "[t]his family of three lives / on a five acre farm They raise no crops not even their own / vegetables or animals for slaughter." The "woods" are a playground, a space for miming and/or taming *wildness,* and while claiming place as a kind of object, they treat it as disposable, as fungible excess, like the money they make. As against this self-aggrandizing accumulation, Chrystos articulates the principle that "it is not right to take without giving," emphasizing that "hungry / people need the food they could be growing That spirituality / is not separate from food or wildness or respect or giving." The poem imaginatively reoccupies this privatized territory, situating it within a symbolic economy ordered around a "spirituality" of "respect" and "giving."

Though that gesture could be taken as confirming her role as a provider of Indian spiritual wisdom, Chrystos here indicates that the sensibility nonnatives wish to purchase as a reified product instead inheres in a network of material relations with the land and other living beings, one that not only can be realized outside of legally recognized Indian spaces but whose internal logic repudiates the arbitrary and violent containments produced through such official demarcations. If the text in some sense traffics in the stereotypical, that effect can be understood less as a capitulation to an invented, generic Indianness than the cocirculation of Indigenous potentialities alongside circuits of capitalist extraction, the possibility of realizing the former within the very places claimed as "Private Property." She notes that she saves the wings and, by extension, writes the poem, "because ignorance must be remembered," but such memory indicates the copresence of a knowledge waiting to be materialized. Chrystos's sensations of disgust and outrage at the family's *waste*, her affective labor in the face of it, index such knowledge—its virtual presence alongside current enactments/literalizations of settler "ignorance."

Even more directly and forcefully than "Wings of a Wild Goose," "Crazy Grandpa Whispers" insists that space deemed non-Indian should be indigenized, in ways that have nothing to do with federal acknowledgment of Native politics but that still productively might be characterized as sovereignty. The figure of the title

> tells me: take a pick ax to new car row hack & clear the land
>   plant Hopi corn down to the sea
> tells me: break open that zoo buffalo corral
>   chase them snorting through the streets
> tells me: put up tipis in every vacant lot
>   shelter the poor without rent

The space she describes here clearly is urban, and this voice from the past incites her to (re)claim it. Although the text codes the various modes of reoccupying the land as Indian ("corn," "buffalo," "tipis"), the altered sense of place that emerges does not emphasize the construction of new Native enclaves. These images indicate a repurposing of the territory to make it more available to all its inhabitants. She adds, "Grandpa tells me: take back these cities / live as your ancestors Sew up the mouth of the enemy / with their damn beads," suggesting that the projects she envisions arise out of a sense of connection to her "ancestors." Yet even as it reconnects with history in ways that reverse the settler economy—the reference to "beads" alluding to the asymmetry of land purchases (as in the tales told of the selling of Manhattan) and/or to the circulation of Indianness as a reified commodity (beads, feathers, buckskin, etc.)—the injunction to "take back" settler-occupied space seems less about a particular people reexerting jurisdictional authority over their traditional homelands than about the dissemination and materialization of principles understood as Indigenous—live *as* your ancestors.

The expansive possibilities addressed here do not relate to any particular Native nation, but neither are they simply reducible to the genericizing imaginary of stereotype. Chrystos's depiction here of Indigenous potential, notably the first poem in a collection entitled *Not Vanishing*, depends upon positing a broad-based priorness that serves as the basis for leveraging existing geographies of ownership. The very insistence on the continuing relevance of indigeneity as an unextinguishable and ongoing presence in places from which Indians supposedly were cleared long ago provides a way of marking the collusion between Indian policy and the stereotypes of Indian containment (also suggested by Chrystos's use of the term "treaty" discussed earlier). While incoherent and ridiculous when viewed through the prism of existing bureaucratic structures of tribal sovereignty, these *whisperings* raise questions about what gets to count as a viable claim. What institutional procedures and mappings shape the possibilities for defining and enacting sovereignty? How is that framing, as well as the materialities it engenders, made self-evident through the long-standing extraction of Indianness from indigeneity, the reification of the latter within an economy of rarity, authenticity, and disappearance (which attends and supplements the economy of dispossession, dislocation, and exploitation of Native resources and labor)? Chrystos notes, "if I obey you they'll lock me up again / like they did you / Grandpa it's such a fine / fine line / between my instincts & their sanity laws." To attend to the "whispers," and their call for a reorganization of the political economy of land tenure, is "crazy"; the attempt to realize such visions violates "their sanity laws."

The living words of the ghost ("Crazy Grandpa supposed to be dead") point to the process by which the potential for an expansive Indigenous remapping of social space is *ghosted,* cast as an inability to grasp the real. This settler common sense emerges in the relay among various state-endorsed institutions—the phrase "locked up" indicating and connecting the prison and the asylum. In *Tribal Secrets* Robert Warrior describes sovereignty as "a decision—a decision we make in our minds, in our hearts, and in our bodies—to be sovereign and to find out what that means in the process," adding, "The value of our work then expresses itself in the constant struggle to understand what we can do" (123). Chrystos explores the ways institutionalized settler expectations constitute the terrain of that "struggle," the existing conditions and geographies in which such "a decision" can be made, while simultaneously indicating that incipient possibilities— if officially and popularly disavowed—remain, contained within the unrecognized materiality of Native people inhabiting spaces that are not (legally) theirs. The poem ends with the observation, "Grandpa I'm still learning how to walk in this world / without getting caught." Depicting being Native in unsanctioned places and ways as a kind of crime for which one could be "caught," these lines suggest that the act of *walking*—the quotidian inhabitance of urban space—functions as something like an assertion of sovereignty, providing an anchor for Indigenous imaginings (whispers) awaiting the possibility of fulfillment.

While tracing the spectralized presence of Indigenous persons, memories, and potentials that exceed the space of the reservation and the symbolic economy of Indianness, Chrystos does not portray herself as writing from outside the circuit of dominant modes of exploitation. Rey Chow has argued that people of color not only are subjected to a "coercive mimeticism" that demands they enact stereotype in the flesh but are called on to perform resistance to racist frameworks in ways that still accord with dominant images of them.[51] I have argued that Native people(s) have a different relation to stereotype in that they are presumed gone or in the process of quickly becoming so, and thus, nonnatives serve as the proper agents of *Indian* subjectivity, including its ostensibly naturalist/spiritualist opposition to capitalist modernity. By emphasizing her labor—working as a poorly paid maid, emotionally coping with the erasure of indigeneity (including her own), negotiating the institutionalized logics by which she appears "crazy"—Chrystos locates herself within extant economies, using her embodied experience as a means of both mapping and leveraging the commonsense materiality of settlement in non-Indian spaces. If her poetry can be characterized as resistance, it does not function, as in Chow's account, as a confirmation of type masquerading as the possibility of speaking from a position of political purity. In "She Said They Say," Chrystos mocks the idea of such a position.[52] Responding to the claim she has "sold out," she "roar[s] laughing," insisting:

> I want to be shown
> the unlikely one person who
> given our lives
> hasn't sold something to get by
> one time or another

She adds, "This IS the united states. This IS capitalism / even when we have other ideas / We're all selling out to stay alive." While seeking to imagine otherwise, as in the memories of dislocated peoples or envisioning an expansive Indigenous kind of occupancy, she recognizes the networks of "selling" that structure everyday life. As noted in the previous section, she suggests that to live in the United States is to be caught up within the system of reification and exchange through which the United States is (re)produced. The situation of having to try "to wash my name clean" from the charge of selling out suggests that her poetry is doing important work: "insults are how you know / you've got them where it hurts." The notion of a place outside existing dynamics of domination and exploitation does not "hurt," because it cannot grasp the concrete conditions of "our lives," including the labor of trying "to stay alive."

Chrystos's poetry navigates among spectacles of Indianness and attendant naturalizations of settler inhabitance as "property" in order to trace the itinerary of Native lives lived in non-"Indian" ways. She attends to their extrusion from nonnative accounts of indigeneity and the sensations generated by that erasure—or ghosting. In this way, her work might be said to manifest contemporary indigeneity by tracking the kinds of Native *hurt* that are endemic to settler systems of value and are unintelligible within their terms. Doing so, she invests the labor of survival with Indigenous meanings denied in official and popular narratives.

The Space of Desire

If Indianness operates as a symbolic economy that casts as unreal the materialities of contemporary Native life (particularly in nonreservation places), Chrystos's collection of lesbian erotic poems *In Her I Am* emphasizes the immediacy of sensation and uses that experience of fleshliness to highlight the presence of Native people in the present. Yet often indigeneity is indicated in these poems through what might be termed nature metaphors (rivers, woods, animals, topographical features of the landscape), and that mode of marking Native identity could be interpreted as stereotypical, recirculating images that simultaneously ghost and commodify in ways discussed in the previous sections. In "Dildos, Hummingbirds, and Driving Her Crazy," Deborah Miranda observes, "Indian writing has often been stereotyped as 'nature poetry,' leaving Indian poets to wrestle with this problematic imagery. We know that if we use natural landscape as metaphor, we are being predictable, but on the other hand, these are not 'just' natural images to us" (144).[53] The use of "natural images" in Native poetry exceeds the stereotypical meanings attributed to them by nonnatives, but can they be understood as simply other than stereotype? As noted earlier, stereotype does not simply falsify; its reifications help produce and circulate forms of value, connecting to other long-standing modes of appropriation, extraction, and exploitation. However, just as Native people cannot will themselves free from the system of "selling," neither can the experience of Native selfhood be utterly distinguished from the stereotypical dissemination of Indianness. As discussed in chapters 2 and 3, interpersonal interactions and erotic life in the present remain suffused by settler ideologies—in particular of possession and purity. Rather than decrying the affective traces of such legacies as a kind of false consciousness, though, they can be engaged as part of the archaeology of contemporary Indigenous identities, the ways indigeneity actually is lived in the present. Recognizing the operation of settler-initiated frameworks in fantasy and emotional life enables both a reckoning with the multivectored, intimate effects of ongoing imperial histories and an exploration of how those very dynamics can be made the vehicle for (re)opening possibilities for peoplehood and self-determination. In this vein, Chrystos's erotic poetry dwells within and distends the stereotype. She addresses how conventional images of Indianness work as part of Native affective formations, but in doing so, she endows the image with a sensuous physicality that exceeds the terms of settler value while making "nature," and an attendant sense of an Indigenous connection to the landscape, achingly proximate within urban space, suggesting an extension of the possibilities for envisioning sovereignty as a kind of lived practice.

In Her I Am explores the complicated ways that desire recirculates the terms of oppression and the affective labor entailed in transforming them into a vehicle of Indigenous self-expression. Chrystos indicates the necessity of acknowledging how such dynamics inform individual structures of feeling. Further, registering the ways histories of settlement take part in Native emotional and erotic experience provides an alternative to stereotypical portraits of Indians as wooden warriors, harmonious ecologists, and/or spiritual informants while also suggesting the intimate impact of such popular images on Native self-understandings. In "Against," she remarks, "your skin red under my hand against every / political principle we both hold you want / me to spank you & I do" (24). This desire seems particularly problematic in light of the fact that they are "survivors of childhood violence with black eyes / in common from mothers who hated our difference." Given that Chrystos's mother is nonnative (as noted in the biographical note that accompanies all of her books), that "difference" for her includes her Menominee lineage. She adds, "Your people as well as mine slaughtered in millions / Queer we're still open season." From this perspective the sexual scene of spanking appears to repeat the dynamics of "childhood violence," which itself can be understood as animated by broader legacies of genocidal assault. Chrystos offers an implicit connection between such "slaughter" and the fact that "queer[s]" are "still open season." She intimates that the effort to police and discipline non(hetero)normative desire itself can function as a mode of violence, possibly serving as an extension of the collective trauma suffered by oppressed and colonized peoples.

Noting that "it's wrong / to do this," she expresses a reticence that could be read either as confirming that the act indicates a pathological relation to prior violence or as suggesting that her sense of its "wrong[ness]" emerges out of the pathologization of "queer" pleasure. While insisting that "Out of our bruised lives should come some other way," the poem turns the recognition of continuity between the spanking and prior woundings (individual and collective) into the potential for an acknowledgment and reworking of that history through erotic play:

> This forbidden hand this deep memory this connection
> for which I've no explanation against a wall of right
> that would define us as victim/ aggressor

This "forbidden" fantasy becomes a way of realizing a "deep memory," providing a "connection" to past brutality. In contrast to her impression of spanking as "wrong," she offers the "wall of right," which offers only two, frozen options—"victim/ aggressor"—and in which *survivor* does not appear as an option distinguished from the former. In *Between the Body and Flesh*, Lynda Hart argues with respect to lesbian sadomasochism that fantasy, desire, and erotic pleasure function as more than a mere repetition of acts and relations of dominance that occur in other spaces, instead creating conditions through which painful and traumatic memories can be conjured and reworked. Doing so opens up new possibilities for subjectivity by both acknowledging the presence of violence (as past event, as well as present feature, of psychic/emotional life) and reconfiguring it in affectively enabling ways—facilitating a redefinition of one's experience as other than a passive object of others' aggression. Similarly, Veena Das suggests with respect to those who have endured systemic violence, "The zone of the everyday . . . [can] be recovered by reoccupying the very signs of injury that had been marked to forge continuity in that space of devastation" (74), "embracing the signs of injury and turning them into ways of becoming subjects" (215). The poem ends by observing, "Desire red & raw as wounds we disguise / we're open season." The "wounds" are present, whether discussed or not, and in the absence of a way of addressing them, they can become sources of shame, signs of a failure to be proper subjects. To act out processes of wounding through the use of spanking in erotic play makes "desire" into a vehicle for acknowledging the emotional consequences of being "open season" and for grappling with, rather than disguising, them.

This representation of and challenge to the supposed "wrong[ness]" of certain kinds of fantasy provides a frame for her invocation of more stereotypical images of Indianness in narrating her erotic connections with other women. "Dare" addresses her relationship with a Native woman. In marking both her jealousy and her deep suspicion of monogamy, Chrystos remarks, "She asks me to build her a white picket fence, a home, a forever, to love her & no other   I despise fences and climbed over them as soon as I could walk   Fences are psychosis, unreal   I know that she wants me to build the fence so she can jump over it, to watch what I'll do," adding, "I want us to live in a wide place, where all our canyons & arroyos are known, respected   I want to live with her in a spring wash of desire   I want our wanderings to cross & recross each other with a wind blowing away our tracks" (27–28). Rejecting idealized middle-class American domesticity, she alternately figures she and her lover as the landscape and as *wanderers* lacking any particular domicile, images redolent with an *Indian* naturalness and nomadism. In a journal entry included toward the end of the collection, she insists, "I'm tired of the dead roses of heterosexual romance & marriage which we ourselves slop over Lesbian sexuality and power" (79), suggesting that the earlier image of Indian "wandering" gains meaning within a refusal of heteronormative notions of privatized homemaking. The stereotype, then, provides a means of leveraging a vision of conjugal union presumed to be the organizing framework for social life in the United States. Additionally, Chrystos suggests the connection between this image of sexual/familial normality and the "tools & wreckages of the conquistador patriarch," noting that with respect to evaluating others' sexual choices, "we are in the very murky waters of how a colonized people could claim that consensuality or freedom are even possible" (80–81). The notion of the settledness of marital domesticity as a healthier option for Native people, therefore, runs up against the ways it takes part in larger structures of settlement. In "Stolen from Our Bodies," Driskill observes that Chrystos's "unapologetic Lesbian erotica [in *In Her I Am*] threatens heteropatriarchal culture, but also because the Sovereign Erotic set forth in her book deals with histories of abuse and colonization that deeply complicate the text" (59). Here, as in Deborah Miranda's work addressed in chapter 2, the ordering of putatively private life indexes and helps realize broader imperial principles and dynamics, like the "pleasure" of white children in their ownership and mastery of "natural" spaces, as discussed in the previous section. Thus, more than recycling conventional tropes of Indianness, the juxtaposition of "a white picket fence" with "wide place[s]" and "wanderings" in "Dare" marks the resistance to monogamous intimacy as part of a broader refusal of settler colonial mappings of social and emotional life, suggesting that potentially stereotypical imagery can provide a resource for naming alternative, Indigenous ways of being in the world.

Moreover, the depiction in "Dare" of both women as "canyons & arroyos" draws on the connection of Indianness with landscape to signal that they are equally Native, itself a point of tension in the relationship. Chrystos observes:

> This is one of the canyons between us, her traditions of a
> lifeline, grandmothers, ceremonies tended   She looks over at
> my back door banging in the wind, where I pray without a
> language, sitting on the steps, watching leaves move   I don't
> belong in her ceremonies; she thinks I do   Stubborn, I cling
> to the prayers I made up myself as a child of tenements, alone
> with drugs, violence, boozy wind of neglect (26)

Her lover has more direct connections to a given people and greater familiarity with their "traditions." Also, the mention of "tenements" as a point of contrast suggests that her lover's "lifeline" arises out of a childhood of geographic proximity to a reservation, as well. The differences between them, then, map onto those of stereotypical legitimacy—between proper Indianness and inauthentic urbanity. Part of the struggle occurs over inclusion into "ceremonies" that could signal indigeneity. In insisting she doesn't "belong," Chrystos both distinguishes her background from that of her lover—different peoples, different ceremonies—while also raising questions about what it means to "belong" to the category *Indian*. She has her own prayers and ceremonies, but they do not occur in a "language" marked as Native. Notably, though, the phrase "without a language" suggests that the prayers occur in English (as opposed to, say, Menominee) but also that there is not "language" through which to mark the ways that such feeling and practice are Native. In this way, her portrayal of herself through a seemingly generic invocation of Indian relation to the land functions as a means of expressing a sense of indigeneity for which there is not an available public discourse. Stereotype, then, operates not merely as an external imposition but as a vocabulary through which to negotiate intimate relationships.

Even as she elsewhere critiques the circulation of stereotype, *In Her I Am* explores how it can provide a medium for Native self-representation. More specifically, mobilizing such figures in depictions of her own desire invests them with a tactile, sensuous immediacy that gives them a materiality in the present that they otherwise lack—or actively erase by turning indigeneity into a remnant for nonnative use or rendering it ephemeral as generically spiritual wisdom. It becomes a vehicle for marking *as Native* experiences not officially or popularly acknowledged as such, connecting pleasure to a sense of place while opening the former to feelings beyond those of conjugal normality. In "Tenderly Your" she draws on conventional tropes of Indianness to depict her erotic relationship with another Native woman as part of the continuum of Indigenous history. The title runs into the opening line: "Tenderly Your / hands open me into the drum of my heart" (67). Especially when read alongside later images, like "your fingers twined in leather," which is immediately followed by the command to "Ride me now," this initial description clearly alludes to lesbian lovemaking, but rather than euphemizing the act of vaginal penetration, the portrayal of it as like striking a drum presents women's homoerotic desire and pleasure as of a piece with indigeneity.[54] Given the common association of Indian drumming with ritual, this linkage further presents their sexual expression as containing a kind of spiritual understanding, although quite different from the disembodied and commodified kind sought by inquisitive nonnatives. Her lover's "hands" allow her access to "the drum" of her own "heart," suggesting not only that their erotic relation itself is spiritual but that it enables a reconnection with an Indigenous sensibility she carries within her (in ways reminiscent of Driskill's "Back to the Blanket" or Miranda's "From a Dream, I Wake to Tender Music"). Their passion further transports them through time: "We're in the grass of prairies our grandmothers rode / Sweet smell of distant cookpots edges the blue / Your kisses are a hundred years old & newly born / rich as the red earth where you straddle a pinto." These images of land gesture toward the specificity of genealogical connection to place while doing so in fairly generic terms—"grandmothers" referring to actual ancestors or functioning as a broad figure for indigeneity. Moreover, is this connection an implicit simile (where they are becomes like the "prairies"), or is it more descriptive (they actually are located in the same space once occupied by their "grandmothers")? Rather than resolving these tensions, the poem plays on them, deferring the distinction between the literal and the conventional in ways that expands the possibility for envisioning what counts as both real Native place and proper means of marking it as such. If settler jurisdiction deterritorializes Indigenous peoples only to reterritorialize them as Indians in U.S. domestic space, Chrystos here reterritorializes the image of Indianness, using it as a means of presenting lesbian pleasure as a mode of Indigenous inhabitance—a sensual reclaiming of space that reaches across "a hundred years" in ways that make the connection to "red earth" "newly born."

This invocation of the past through the deployment of stereotype depicts desire as a central part of the labor of opening up the present to Indigenous meaning, to possibilities of perception and sensation that can shift the lovers' relation to their own personal histories. After presenting their passion as a drumming that evokes cooking grandmothers on the prairies, Chrystos commands, "Ride me now as your hungry lips blow me softly / Flaming ride us past our rapes our pain / past years when we stumbled lost." The shift from "a hundred years ago" to being "newly born" leaps over the "years when we stumbled lost," but the description of her lover's kisses and hands in terms of a kind of generic Indianness also suggests that the feelings expressed through such figures opens avenues for recontextualizing "our rapes." Those violations appear located in time, and the poem correlates mobility with the possibility of a new way of experiencing the rapes in relation to the rest of their lives. Anchored by the connection to grandmothers of a century ago, though, the imagination of such a change does not suggest a decisive break with what has come before. Rather, the doubling of "ride" as both traversing the prairies on horseback and lovemaking depicts their erotic joy ("This / is why we were made by creation") as containing within it the potential for emotional movement, reconnecting she and her lover to the "past" while simultaneously portraying it as a capacious place that enables them to travel "past" their "pain." As opposed to figuring a unidirectional, linear development, in which the "rapes" must shape everything that comes after, time opens up as space, their passion suggesting a new way of occupying this terrain—less as a reified, contained, owned space than through a visceral form of transmotion. In this way, their vulnerability to each other, as well as the resulting pleasure, enacts a form of sovereignty, a reclaiming of their bodies from the effects of possessive assault which both is like an Indigenous reclaiming of the "rich . . . red earth" and is a means of enacting that very process. Stereotypical images of Indianness, then, serve here as a way of indexing how erotic relations can function as a way of realizing a regenerative sense of Native presence—providing a means of marking a sensation latent within the experience itself while doing the work of making that feeling publicly intelligible as such.

Many of the images Chrystos uses can be seen as somewhat generically Indian, offering a vision of Native people(s) that draws on features expected by nonnatives due to their conventional role in popular narratives. Though perhaps somewhat more directly echoing familiar tropes of Indianness, this invocation of indigeneity resembles those discussed in Driskill's and Miranda's work. I did not address their works as stereotypical, instead reading them as indicative of an attempt to mark how unrecognized histories live on as structures of feeling in ways that allow them to be (re)actualized as experiences of embodiment. Rather than distinguishing between those representations and Chrystos's, I want to suggest that the stereotypical cast of the latter also applies to the former, but such an attribution is not meant to delegitimize either. As Chrystos observes, as discussed in the previous sections, stereotype operates as part of a settler system of value, ghosting Native people and places that do not fit the type. In this way, figurations of Indianness generate reality-effects that affect the extent to which experiences can be understood *as Native,* including potentially by Indigenous people. If stereotype can be juxtaposed with the "tribal real," in Vizenor's terms, how does one come to know that "real"? Or more to the point, following the questions raised throughout this study, how do particular, institutionalized conceptions of the "tribal" shape the possibility for acknowledging forms of indigeneity as "real"—as authentic and/or existent? I have argued that metaphor functions less in contrast to the literal than as a way of leveraging processes of literalization, marking forms of contemporary Native being from which there is not a public language—and which are denegated within available discourses—while seeking to create conditions for the acknowledgment of forms of indigeneity disparaged, denied, and dismissed as inauthentic. The principal critical figures in each chapter—haunting, melancholy, genealogy—mark this complex relation between residuality and emergence and the role of figuration in enabling the movement from one to the other. As mobilized by Chrystos in her erotic poems, stereotype does similar work, providing a way of representing quotidian sensations as expressions of Indigenous continuity while simultaneously indicating how such Indigenous being is affected by the ongoing experience of settler occupation. If her poetry portrays the labor of survival as a Native person in non-Indian space, it also enacts the labor of transforming stereotype into a means of marking Native presence amid its containment, commodification, and erasure.

In "Disobedience (in Language) in Texts by Lesbian Native Americans," Janice Gould asks, "Is there not any place that is sacred, that is safe from violation?" She adds, "Perhaps there are spaces within the psyche that can and must remain beautifully inarticulate and mute. I would like to think there is a vast reserve of silence that can never be taught to speak" (43). Part of the struggle both thematized and enacted in Chrystos's poetry is how to understand such silence as the ongoing presence of Native pasts despite their erasure and in spaces other than those officially demarcated as Indian. The tension between manifesting indigeneity and becoming an icon of Indianness intersects with that between making visible one's own life as an example of Indigenous survival and subjecting intimate sensations of selfhood to the violations of settler-dominated public discourses. The deployment of stereotype as a kind of metaphor entails both drawing on and suspending its referential potential, maneuvering within existing discursive and institutional fields while marking the violence enacted by their literalizations. The danger lies in treating stereotype as transparently referential rather than as a critical, tactical inhabitance of available modes of signification. Thus, part of the labor Chrystos performs lies in not only using stereotype to index indigeneity but simultaneously signaling its insufficiency to that project, alluding to the "silence" it cannot capture and thereby marking the unspoken presence of a "reserve" irreducible to figurations of Indianness.

"In the Wild River of Your Arms" illustrates that taxing negotiation (75–76). The poem suggests how Chrystos's erotic relations enable such mediation, giving play to feelings unintelligible within the conventional tropes of Indianness. She observes in the middle of the poem:

> In the wild river of your tongue
> I travel light years away from everyone
> who has lain with me claiming
> some corner of my spirit as their own
> read meanings into me
> without my knowledge or consent
> made me afraid of my own desire
> ploughed me with confusion
> as they called arid sand a verdant bank
> tried to kill all
> that surges clear in me
> a wild river uncontained
> without a name

As in "Tenderly Your," pleasure transports her, but here her lover's "tongue" leads her away from a past of attempted possession. The desire to "read meanings into [her]" is an integral part of a process of "claiming," a term that suggests the correspondence between the reification of Indianness and the seizure of Native land and resources explored more fully elsewhere in her work (as discussed earlier). She juxtaposes these efforts to appropriate her by those who have "lain" with her—as a kind of conduit through which Indianness can become "their own"—with the "wild river" of orgasmic sensation which expresses the sensations within her. That invocation of "wild[ness]" marks how fully experiencing and fulfilling her "desire" runs against and overflows imposed "meanings" and acts of "claiming."

Yet the image of the river and the trope of wildness appear of a piece with the kind of Indian attribution she uses it to repudiate. The river, however, is both "uncontained" and "without a name," implying that the effort to designate what "surges" in her as a "wild river" does not in fact capture the feelings. The text here employs a potentially stereotypical formulation, which seems aligned with the very sort of "meanings" she refuses, and highlights its inadequacy—the failure of any available "name" to reflect the experience of herself since that sensation exceeds acts of "claiming." She positions her "desire" as itself defying *containment* by the available means she has to name it—specifically, to name it as an expression, embodiment, and experience of indigeneity. The turning of the figure of the river in the first line of each stanza further underlines the problem of reference: "wild river of your arms," "wild river of your laughter," "wild river of your tongue," "wild river of your cunt," "wild river of your soul," and "wild river of your eyes." This running reference to aspects of her lover as a "wild river" can appear as consonant with the attempt by others to "claim" her, but the characterization of her own desire as a "wild river" produces a similarity and sympathy between herself and her lover, positioning "wild" as an effort to mark a kind of engagement and continuity rather than as an innate quality. To see her "wild[ness]" as a thing to be possessed means that she bears it as if it were a resource that could be extracted, and in this way, the attribution of wildness to her functions as a projection through which she appears as an object of value in ways that disown the exploitative dynamics that shape the relationship ("read ... into me," "made me afraid of my desire," "ploughed me with confusion"). Notably, she speaks not of prior lovers but of "everyone / who has lain with me," a fairly broad phrasing that potentially encompasses romantic partners, tricks as part of sex work, and even those by whom she was raped. In this way, she suggests that intimate forms of contact and violation occur within the symbolic economy of settler "meanings," which reifies Indianness in ways that make it accessible/appropriable by nonnatives. By contrast, in characterizing her connection with her current lover as "wild," she speaks less of particular qualities or attributes than of a shared refusal to be *killed,* itself a condition for others' "claiming" of (invented/projected) Native *wildness.* The term, then, marks survival, one that is made possible through an erotic relation that accesses the very feelings displaced and disavowed by those who would "read" her as a wild Indian.

In that transposition, the image also shifts in terms of the kind of spatiality to which it alludes. The phrase "wild river" suggests a rushing stream outside the boundaries of *developed* areas—in a more pristine state of nature. In this sense "wild" designates the opposite of *civilized,* a location in which settlers can experience a sort of primal ferocity ostensibly freed from all social constraints. Such "meanings," though, have little relation to the poem's way of narrating place. In the first stanza she describes her lover's arms as "Bear[ing her] through nightmares" "in darkness I didn't know was my home / until you held me & would not / let go," and later she notes, "In the wild river of your soul" "I remember the child I was before / my uncle sliced her to debris / I see a long ribbon of our lives / flashing with the hope of home / I thought couldn't be." As opposed to viewing the "wild" as the antithesis of the domestic(ated), it serves here as a way of marking possibilities for "home." In doing so, though, it also exceeds normative narratives of the latter. Not only is it associated with "darkness," rather than a simple and uncomplicated sense of comfort, but it comes through an experience of intimacy with another woman and stands in stark contrast to the household of her childhood, in which she was not protected from repeated incestuous assault. Additionally, their desire helps her lover to move on from an abusive marriage and another failed relationship: "In the wild river of your cunt / where I am first to shake you free & screaming wildly / I swim against the tide of brutal discarded husband / shame & rocks of regret for a woman / who would not give you this water." The directness in the discussion of their pleasure presents the "hope of home" as one beyond conjugal couplehood, which as noted, Chrystos describes as "the dead roses of heterosexual romance & marriage" (79). Further, in the collection's final piece, "Night Gown," she observes that her objections to monogamy come from the fact that "I want neither to be owned nor to own anyone," and she adds, lesbianism "is a radical act" in that it expresses a "reverence for pleasure over procreation" (84–85). In this way, *wildness* speaks to an experience of embodiment that alters how one inhabits the ordinary geography of daily life, an opening of erotic potential that prompts a remapping of relations to people and places, both past and present. Accessing "this water" makes possible the envisioning of a kind of "home" based on a mutual recognition of trauma and vulnerability, where joy emerges out of a refusal of possession. From this perspective, "wild" indexes a process of becoming whole, but through sensual connection. In its use of this term, the poem suggests that the feeling of becoming located in oneself and in relation to one's own history defies the objectifications of others' claimings, while also bespeaking an enmeshment in Indigenous histories that do not fit into a narrative of untamed nature as the space of Indian home. The conjunction of "wild" and "home" gestures toward stability and instability simultaneously, portraying desire as both "uncontained" and as a mode of habitation. The attendant sensation and conceptual oscillation, like Vizenor's notion of transmotion, refuses the distinction between mobility and occupancy.

While not simply a negation of available markers of Indianness, Chrystos's poetry deforms them, outlining the space of what is "without a name" within them. In *The Cunning of Recognition,* Elizabeth Povinelli argues with respect to Aboriginal identity(/ies) in Australia, "Inspection always already constitutes indigenous persons as failures of indigeneity as such" (39), adding, "The very discourses that constitute indigenous subjects *as such* constitute them as failures *of such*" (48). Chrystos does not fit the model of spiritual guide, nor of the wooden Indian with the "headdress from hell" in the storefront window, and she explores how, from such perspectives, she cannot signify as other than a failure, as the absence of real Indianness inasmuch as books and representations by nonnatives constitute the principal archive for such determinations. Yet she further chronicles the series of interests at stake in that process of "inspection," including the ways it effaces legacies and ongoing trajectories of wounding that are crucial to the (re)production of U.S. political economy. Moreover, Chrystos plays on her apparent inability to signify properly as Indian, marking how the figure of the Indian has failed Native people(s). Her work pushes conventional tropes past their point of failure in ways that highlight the *work* of signifying contemporary Native presence—particularly in places that do not get to count in dominant form(ul)ations as authentically *wild* or *Indian*. That strategy less refutes or deconstructs the stereotype than highlights how the broader system of value and possession that it expresses and facilitates helps form the reality in which nonreservation Natives negotiate the experience of, and possibilities for articulating, indigeneity. Through connecting settler reifications to her embodied experience—of erasure, labor, and desire and the complex interweavings among them—she finds a means of expressing structures of feeling that literally have no place in official geographies of Native territoriality. Consequently, if as Gould suggests, there may be "spaces within the psyche" that provide a bulwark against ongoing histories of "violation," Chrystos's poetry turns emotional and erotic response into a vehicle for remapping the space of Native occupancy as it occurs in the context of institutionalized economies of state-sanctioned meanings and containment.

Conclusion

I have been addressing Native inhabitance of nonreservation space and the labor of survival amid institutional erasure and the fetishistic circulation of Indianness, and I have suggested such labor, and the enfleshment of stereotype, can be understood as an act of sovereignty. In prior chapters I also suggest at various points that sexual pleasure, ghostly remembrances, melancholic identification, and stories of Native endurance through ongoing patterns of settler abjection all could signify as sovereignty—an erotics of sovereignty as an embodied and affective matrix. In such a formulation, though, is "sovereignty" a metaphor? This question might mean that the term "sovereignty" works to transfer a sense of political import to the nonpolitical (nongovernmental, nonjursidictional, nonstrictly geopolitical) relations these writers address. From that perspective the domain of politics clearly is distinct from the something else at play in these texts and my analysis, with the topos of sovereignty providing a conceptual link through which to endow nonpolitics with a sense of import—with the gravity of issues that truly pertain to sovereignty.

However, that same question—is it a metaphor?—might be taken quite differently in ways I have sketched throughout this book. To answer yes need not entail seeing sovereignty as a way of figuring structures of feeling, as opposed to its literal, real, true, authentic meaning. Rather, to see sovereignty as a metaphor enables an understanding of the varied forms and networks of sensation these texts explore as bound up in, while also largely effaced by, the processes through which officially recognized modes of governance are (re)produced. Moreover, as opposed to contradistinguishing the figurative and the real, this (mis)use of "sovereignty" highlights how the real is *realized* through repeated institutionalized acts of figuration, which create and sustain the material conditions in which peoplehood can be signified and lived. What kinds of experiences, relations, histories are effaced or deemed irrelevant within legal discourses of sovereignty? How does stretching the topos of sovereignty to cover that which does not properly belong to the category work as a means of acknowledging how peoplehood may operate as an improper mode of being—one that lacks the kind of materiality endowed by state-sanctioned bureaucratic frames and apparatuses? Moreover, how might the characterization of such being *as sovereignty* insist on the ongoing, irreducible relation between such residual/potential relations of peoplehood and the legacies and effectivities of settler-state processes of literalization?

The texts I address do not posit a version of Indigenous authenticity—one that exists prior to, beyond, utterly distinct from the dynamics of settlement—that can be juxtaposed to existing tribal governance and substituted for it. Rather, they trace the ways the possibilities for envisioning and performing Native sovereignty remain overdetermined by the legacies and continuing imperatives of settler governance. As against an official story of redemption from past wrongs in which the recognition of self-determination exonerates or transcends the history of violence, exploitation, and displacement, these texts tell more complicated stories of collective selfhood. These are stories in which feelings point to kinds of experience that do not get to count as relevant in the legal and administrative discourses of Indian policy, while simultaneously indexing potential ways of being that might yet be realized as sovereignty. Those forms of memory and sensation emphasize continuity amid catastrophe, but these writings depict and enact modes of survival that are less focused on bodily/territorial insularity and normative reproduction than on vulnerability, an openness to other people, to place, to ancestors. Although not dismissing all sense of boundaries, the texts less prioritize marking and patrolling the borders of Native national identity than they outline capacious principles that can acknowledge both wounding and pleasure, histories of impression through which peoplehood continually is reconstituted as an active process—one also open to the future instead of one organized around the threat of declension from a purer past. While they do not suggest the desirability of foregoing the legal acknowledgment of Native nations by the United States, these authors do propose what I have termed an ethics of sovereignty, suggesting ways of imagining indigeneity less beholden to the fetishizing, anachronizing, amnesiac, racializing, and heteropatriarchal narratives that tend to shape the metaphorics, bureaucratics, and trajectories of U.S. Indian affairs. The texts here do not speak the language of public policy, but they do consider the embodied and emotional effects of policy, suggesting the latter be tempered by such an awareness.

Foregrounding queer Native people further centralizes within discussion of the contours and content of sovereignty experiences that often are cordoned off as "sexuality." Usually cast as properly private, erotics can serve as a site for addressing social dynamics that often are not deemed political or that are disowned and disavowed as merely the pathologies of given persons. These creative works take up what initially may appear as individual, idiosyncratic, and/or perverse as a way of illustrating how heteronormative definitions of Indian and tribal identity not only cast out LGBT, two-spirit persons from their peoples but materialize a disciplinary vision of peoplehood in which failure to meet the institutionalized ideal makes one either a threat to tribal legitimacy and respectability or a fake against which the conservation of real Indianness must be protected. This kind of reifying enclosure can be registered in violence done to sexually nonnormative persons, yet its effects extend beyond such instances, engendering a hostility toward other deviations from the straight line of Indian genealogy and an attendant constriction of whose bodies, lives, and memories can signify contemporary indigeneity. The authors here suggest that the continuing survival and well-being of Native nations is only strengthened by queering the terms of U.S. recognition: acknowledging the existence and value of queer Natives but also refusing settler logics of authenticity as the literal truth of Indigenous peoplehood. Such work functions less as a bid for inclusion than as a means of opening indigeneity and Native collective selfhood to other pasts, presents, and futures on land claimed by the United States.

Notes

Introduction

1. Prucha, 258. On Nixon's message, see Bruyneel, 157–59; Castile, *To Show,* 91–98.

2. On the termination program, see Deloria, *Custer;* Fixico, *Termination;* Philp, *Termination;* Wilkinson.

3. On rituals of national shame by settler-states, see Ahmed, *Cultural;* Povinelli, *Cunning.*

4. Moreton-Robinson, Introduction, 4

5. Castile, *To Show,* 67, 69

6. Castile, *To Show,* 73–74

7. Purcha, 275–77. The purview of Native governments in terms of managing themselves has expanded since the passage of the first self-determination statute in 1975, particularly in terms of deciding how to allocate federal funds. See Harvard Project, 17–36. The scope of self-determination still remains limited, however, in ways discussed later in this section.

8. On the importance of scale in U.S. Indian policy and Native nationality, see Silvern.

9. Prior to this change, tribes were getting around the BIA by using block grants from the Office of Economic Opportunity, created as part of President Johnson's Great Society initiative. See Castile, *To Show,* 23–42; Smith and Warrior; Wilkinson, 127–28, 191–94.

10. On the Trail of Broken Treaties, see Bruyneel, 163–67; Castile, *To Show,* 118–29; Smith and Warrior, 141–68; Wilkinson, 139–43.

11. The document is reprinted in Josephy, Nagel, and Johnson, 45–47.

12. See Niezen, 31–36.

13. For this sketch of Indigenous internationalism, I am drawing on a range of sources, including the following: Anaya, *Indigenous Peoples;* Brysk; Charters and Stavenhagen; Engle; Ivison, Patton, and Sanders; Lâm; Nelson; Niezen; Morris; Quesenberry; Trask.

14. Four countries voted against its adoption, the United States, Canada, Australia, and New Zealand—all Anglophone settler-states. All have subsequently reversed their position. For the U.S. statement of its, rather qualified, acceptance of the declaration, see "Announcement of U.S. Support for the United Nations Declaration on the Rights of Indigenous

< 267 >

Peoples," U.S. Department of State, http://www.state.gov/documents/ organization/153223.pdf.

15. The declaration is reprinted in its entirety in Charters and Stavenhagen, 378–90.

16. On contemporary U.S. Indian policy, see Aleinikoff; Barker, *Native;* Biolosi, *Deadliest;* Bruyneel; Castile, *Taking;* Cattelino; Cheyfitz, "Navajo"; Coffey and Tsosie; Deloria and Lytle; Fletcher; Frickey; Garroutte; Getches, Wilkinson, and Williams; Goldberg; Goldberg-Ambrose; Gover; Gunter; Harvard Project; LaDuke; Lawlor; Lemont; Lyons; Miller, *Forgotten;* Pommersheim; Richland and Deer; Riley, "Good"; Ruppel; Singer; Wilkins and Lomawaima; Wilkinson; Williams, *Like.*

17. In 1988, Congress changed the law such that amendments to tribal constitutions and amendments to them cannot be denied by the secretary of the interior unless their provisions violate federal law, but the BIA still has authority to make that determination. See Goldberg, 448–50. Furthermore, in 2004 Congress amended the existing provisions around tribal constitution making, adding that "each Indian tribe shall retain inherent sovereign power to adopt governing documents under procedures other than those specified in this section" (25 U.S.C. § 476 H.). However, even when tribal constitutions and amendments are not subject to oversight by the Department of the Interior, the BIA can exercise significant influence when offering "technical assistance" or in cases of procedural controversies, such as elections. See Gover.

18. He claims, "The idea of the nation is universal and modern; there are not radically different kinds of nations in the world" (135). He later states, "Citizenship is a universal (not Western) concept" (171). For contrary perspectives, see Biersteker and Weber; Brown, *Walled;* Chatterjee; Cheah; Kazanjian; Mehta; Nelson; Spivak, *Critique.*

19. See Barker, *Native;* Cheyfitz, "(Post)colonial"; Garroutte; Saunt; Sturm, *Blood;* TallBear; Thorne.

20. See also Bern and Dodds.

21. This relationship long has been a topic of concern within Marxian frameworks. For varied versions of the relation between the contours of institutionalized speech and possibilities for organizing, institutional access, distribution of resources, and embodied habit, see Bourdieu, *Logic;* Gramsci; Pietz; Spivak, *Critique.*

22. For creative use of existing statutory and judicial frameworks by Native nations, see Coffeey and Tsosie; Lemont; Pommersheim; Richland; Richland and Deer; Riley, "Good."

23. Though seeking to indicate the ability of the state to realize its terms/representations in material ways that shape possibilities for identification, relation, and action, I am also aware of the problems of treating the state as if it were a stable, unified entity rather than itself a nexus of

potentially competing discourses, practices, institutional entities, agendas, and interests. See Alonso; Das; Gramsci; Hall; Joseph and Nugent; Mitchell; Nelson; Taussig. Rather than emphasizing the dynamics of negotiation through which state effects are achieved and through which various social actors and groups engage with the variegated aspects of the state to their own ends, I am trying to mark the influence of state processes on the ways Indian and tribal identity are lived, the potential disjunction between forms of Indigenous selfhood in some way present in state discourses and practices and others that are not, and the difficulties and significance of acknowledging the latter as forms of Indigenous being.

24. In Cathy Caruth's terms, "a literary dimension . . . bear[s] witness to some forgotten wound" (5) due to the fact that trauma by its very nature cannot be represented in language. Instead, it preserves a literal encounter with the event that as a result of the shock of that encounter, is unnarratable, manifesting as forms of repetition whose patterns are allusively "literary." As against this model, I am suggesting metaphor registers that which cannot readily be represented, because it falls outside existing, institutionalized processes of literalization. The problem is not physiological but sociopolitical—what can function as *the real*. On the conceptual problems of Caruth's notion of the literal, see Leys, 266–97. On the problem of Caruth's notion of the literary, see LaCapra, 181–219.

25. In discussing "the spirit of the state" (148), and the operation of state power as a kind of spirit possession, Michael Taussig emphasizes the "ghost-like presence haunting the realness of reality" (175), "giving birth to literality whose realness achieves its emphatic force through being thus haunted" (186).

26. See Ricoeur, *The Rule*, 43.

27. Yet even while repeatedly suggesting this possibility, Ricoeur seeks to back away from its implications. He tries to differentiate his position from the "vitalist tendency," or the "ontological *naïveté*," that "abuses" metaphor by treating it as "literal" (251–52). Put succinctly, he tries to distance himself from *savage philosophy*, an anxiety suggested by the seemingly odd (although perhaps utterly predictable, in light of Cheyfitz's analysis) description of metaphor as like territorial conquest (236–37). To take metaphor "literally" threatens to disrupt the existing (geopolitical) order of things— or the literalizations on which that order rests.

28. I'm not trying to sever the relation between emotion and the senses, a connection central to many theorizations of affect. See Brennan; Gallagher; Massumi; Protevi. Instead, I'm alluding to the absence of a phenomenologically clear physical locus for emotion as a way of suggesting the potential effectivity of other kinds of experience not immediately understood as emanating from a distinguishable physical cause/site.

29. Within Native studies the "oral tradition" has served as a master

trope for marking intergenerational connection, as well as the simultaneity of continuity and adaptation. For examples, see Basso; Cruikshank; Cheyfitz, "(Post)Colonial"; Denetdale, *Reclaiming;* Justice, *Our Fire;* Ortiz; Sarris, *Keeping;* Teuton. Yet the turn to such tradition can implicitly presuppose a vision of collective identity that effaces the struggles around authenticity and literalization I have been discussing. Approaching the transmission of peoplehood through sensation, as memory, opens up a possibly less unifying sense of collectivity that also addresses legacies of trauma and rupture.

30. See Moya and Hames-García.

31. In addressing this model, I implicitly draw on the thoroughgoing critique of the politics of immediacy and adequation that Theodor Adorno offers in *Negative Dialectics,* as well as the ethics of marking the relation between knowledge production and political systems of domination that is central to that critique. See also Varadharajan.

32. For examples, see Teuton, 7–9, 22–23, 178–79, 200–202.

33. Here, I am understanding empiricism as a particular set of knowledge-producing practices and strategies having to do with the notion that a fact is a documentable kind of information (usually achieved through observation) that is both outside extant social systems of meaning and not bearing a contingent relation to any specific system of claims making. See Poovey. In this way, it functions as what Ian Hacking in *Historical Ontology* has described as a "style of reasoning" that generates particular kinds of truth rather than simply reflecting a preexistent entity. For discussion of how the tools of empiricism might be redirected toward kinds of analysis that do not fit the domain and protocols of conventional empiricism, see Latour.

34. These points not only are consistent with the productive goals articulated by Teuton and Womack, as noted in the previous paragraph, but arise as tensions within Teuton's and Womack's arguments, where a commitment to realism seems to constrain rather than facilitate the intellectual and political vision they offer.

35. Teuton, 9, 16.

36. Teuton, 207.

37. I am not positioning literary discourses as having a more privileged relation to the authentic truth of indigeneity than legal discourses. Though I am not focusing on such dynamics, issues of genre, publication, and the production of these texts as mass-circulated commodities cannot be bracketed entirely as part of the ways these texts engage with Native histories, identifications, and possibilities for Indigenous self-representation. On the complex relations between affect, genre, and the transnational modes of intertextuality that influence poetic articulations of local or vernacular identity, see Cavitch; Hart, *Nations;* Ramazani. Reciprocally, I am aware of the ways that presenting literary discourses as representative can efface

not only class-inflected access to various forms of literacy and publication but the ways such class difference may also index distinctions in ways of understanding what constitutes peoplehood and politics (the difference between elite and subaltern formations/formulations). On this issue, see Beverley, *Subalternity;* Guha; Rifkin, *Manifesting;* Spivak, *Critique.* Bearing these problems in mind, I focus on how these literary texts seek to register and create room in public discourse for forms of Native reality not easily accommodated, or actively effaced/disavowed, in existing legal and administrative frameworks.

38. In a seminal essay for postpositivist critics, Satya P. Mohanty makes just such an argument. He asserts that "we can distinguish legitimate identities from spurious ones" based on how "adequate" they are "to the reality they share" and "how adequately they explain" reality, given that "different experiences and identities refer to different aspects" of the same world (56–57). Thus, identities can be treated like propositional statements about the world that may be falsified.

39. Work in subaltern studies extensively has explored how forms of anticolonial political opposition can rely on the ideologies of what constitutes "politics" institutionalized by the colonizer. For examples, see Beverley, *Subalternity;* Chatterjee; Guha; Guha and Spivak; Rodríguez, *Latin.* The issue, then, is not whether such modes of governance are authentically Native but the ways they maintain forms of governance instituted under the colonial system that do not treat alternative modes of decision making, collective organization, land tenure, etc. as potentially valid.

40. For similar feminist questioning around the ways "tradition" gets mobilized to validate sexism, see Barker, "Gender"; Denetdale, "Chairmen"; Smith, "Queer Theory."

41. See also Teuton, 27, 183.

42. All of the writers I address in some fashion turn back to the work of Audre Lorde, particularly her essay "Uses of the Erotic" (in *Sister Outsider*). In addition to the work discussed below, see also Driskill, Finley, Gilley, and Morgensen; Justice and Cox; Justice, Rifkin, and Schneider; Kenny; Warrior, "Your Skin."

43. Driskill prefers gender-neutral pronouns.

44. The category of two-spirit has emerged since the early 1990s as a means of addressing Native sexuality and gender in ways that mark a continuity between traditional social roles and contemporary identities, but as some have noted, this concept can emphasize gender variation in ways that references to "sexuality" cannot. For discussion of two-spirit identity, politics, and self-representations, see Driskill, "Stolen"; Driskill, Finley, Gilley, and Morgensen; Jacobs, Thomas, and Lang; Mayer; Miranda, "Extermination."

45. See Foucault, *History.*

46. See Denetdale, "Chairmen"; Justice, "Go Away"; Rifkin, *When;* Smith, *Conquest.*

47. Native feminist scholarship has explored how a heteropatriarchal imaginary initially imposed by the settler-state has been crucial in defining Indigenous political identity and sovereignty in the United States and Canada in ways that subordinate the interests, voices, and needs of Native women and that end up weaving sexism into Native peoples' own institutionalized conceptions of indigeneity. For examples, see Barker, "Gender"; Denetdale, *Reclaiming;* Denetdale and Goeman; Lawrence; Ramirez; Ross, *Inventing;* Smith, *Conquest;* Smith and Kauanui.

48. On such rejection, see Gilley; Jacobs, Thomas, and Lang; Tatonetti, "Visible"; Womack, "Suspicioning."

49. Recent work on affect has suggested the need to attend to forms of collective feeling that do not resolve into kinds of articulations easily intelligible as political claims. In Anne Cheng's terms, we need to examine kinds of "grief" that do not articulate well as "grievance." See also Cvetkovich; Eng and Kazanjian; Love; Muñoz, *Cruising;* Nealon; Ngai; Scott.

50. See Driskill, "Doubleweaving"; Driskill, Finley, Gilley, and Morgensen; Morgensen, "Settler"; Nealon, *Foundlings;* Rifkin, *When;* Schneider, "Oklahobo"; Smith, "Queer Theory."

51. In *Trauma: A Genealogy,* Ruth Leys argues that the notion of trauma oscillates somewhat incoherently between two models: mimetic (affectability, suggestability, and identification between the sufferer of the trauma and external forces) and antimimetic (a relation in which a fully external source impacts a coherent self, leaving a literal mark of one kind or another). While using the term "trauma" somewhat colloquially in addressing the violence of settlement, I also seek to understand the texts' representation of contemporary indigeneity as the experience of forms of collective selfhood that exceed the imposed terms of settler policy (antimimetic) and are affected and influenced by those terms (mimetic), refusing both the idea of the maintenance of a pure Indigenous essence and the notion of a clear break in which indigeneity is lost/vanished/extinguished. Tracking the complex braidings of continuity and affectability under settler occupation, as well as thinking that conceptual and historical knot as the basis for an ethics, is the work of this study in its engagement with queer Native writing. Scholars have addressed "affectability" as a mode of racialization through which nonwhite peoples are contrasted to the transparent "I" of whiteness. See Rodríguez; Silva; Smith, "Queer." I am suggesting that affectability might be reclaimed as a way of thinking about interdependence and the permeation of collective identity by legacies of the past.

52. See also Blackhawk; Den Ouden; Hoxie; Mandell; Ostler; Rifkin, *Manifesting.*

53. See Deloria and Lytle; Ruppel; Wilkins and Lomawaima.

54. This essay is currently unpublished but is in the author's possession. For studies addressing the representation of land within contemporary Native literature, see Adamson; Allen; Schweninger; Teuton.

55. To clarify, I am not presenting the erotic as a *cultural* alternative or supplement to the *political* sphere of sovereignty. The very distinction between cultural and political in this way runs into at least two problems: (1) it implicitly can accept the metapolitical authority of the settler-state to define what counts as politics, putting anything else that seems significant for Native peoples into the category of culture, and (2) settler-state definitions of what counts as Indian *culture* have been a way of regulating Native authenticity while subjecting Indigenous sovereignty to conformity to such (settler-defined) notions of culture. See Cattelino; Engle; Niezen; Povinelli, *Cunning*; Raibmon; Rifkin, "Indigenizing"; Rifkin, *When*; Simpson, "Subjects." For an effort to rethink modes of Native national governance in light of alternative values, characterized as "cultural sovereignty," see Coffey and Tsosie.

56. See also Biolosi, "Imagined"; Bruyneel; Pommersheim.

57. On the relay between conceptions of insulated political sovereignty and isolated individual subjectivity, see Brown, *Walled*; Clifford, *Political*; Cohen; Elmer; Foucault, *"Society"*; Povinelli, *Cunning*.

58. In "The Devil in the Details: Controverting AlieNation in Indian Conversion Narratives," Vera Palmer draws on the work of Merleau-Ponty to suggest ways land is experienced as part of Native embodiment, such that its loss can generate feelings comparable to a phantom limb. (The essay is unpublished and in the author's possession.)

59. My account resonates with Chadwick Allen's blood/land/memory complex, while focusing on later texts and, more specifically, on the nexus of sensation, sexuality, and sovereignty. In "Theorizing American Indian Experience," Womack insists that he is not "a secular critic," because he believes in the necessity of being open to various kinds of spirit as animating forces in the world (366–67). Similarly, Teuton's chapters are organized around such felt relations to place and ancestors that would not likely be considered in most realist accounts.

60. The idea is taken from Hacking's text of the same name.

61. See Brickman; Khanna; Povinelli, *Empire*; Seshadri-Crooks; Viego.

62. I also do not see a conflict between the notion of socially and historically distinct modes of affective relation and scholarly work that draws on scientific research on the physical capacities, limits, and dynamics of human affect. Though often pitched in universalizing ways, such work does in fact make room for varied formations while also providing quite cogent and compelling ways of negotiating the relation between individuals as distinct bodily entities and the patterned connections to other people, and one's

environment, that function in physical and primary ways. For examples of such work, see Brennan; Gallagher; Massumi; Protevi.

63. On the "straight line" versus "queer" deviations, see Ahmed, *Queer.*

64. For examples, see Berlant and Warner; Ferguson; Freeman, *Wedding;* Gopinath; Puar.

65. On this latter concept, see also Duggan; Manalansan.

66. For an articulation of such a critical position within a broader support for projects that might occur under the banner of nationalism, see Warrior, "Native Critics."

1. The Somatics of Haunting

1. Here, I am addressing the Cherokee Nation, rather than the Eastern Band or Keetowah Band.

2. On this series of events, see Barker, *Native,* 189–216; Jacobi; Justice, "Notes"; Kannady.

3. Jacobi, 828.

4. See Cheyfitz, "(Post)Colonial"; Garroutte; Justice, "Go Away"; Saunt, *Black;* Sturm, *Blood;* TallBear.

5. See Byrd, "Been"; Ray, 388–94; Rubio. For discussion of the history of people of African descent in the Cherokee Nation, see McLoughlin; Mankiller; Miles; Perdue, *Slavery;* Sturm, *Blood.*

6. On the anthropological notion of substance, see Carsten, 109–35; Strathern, 111–33.

7. See Carsten, 136–62; Rifkin, *When;* Schneider, *Critique;* Stevens, *Reproducing;* Weinbaum.

8. Such questions about Cherokee jurisdiction have been raised quite vocally about the exclusion of the Freedmen, particularly in the efforts of the Congressional Black Caucus to deny federal funding to the Cherokee Nation until it reverses this policy. See Byrd, "Been"; Jerry Reynolds, "Freedmen Status at Issue in Washington," *Indian Country Today,* June 29, 2007; Eric Cheyfitz, "The Historical Irony of H.R. 2824," *Indian Country Today,* August 10, 2007; "Race, Not Citizenship, Informs Watson's Cherokee Bill," *Indian Country Today,* August 24, 2007; Jerry Reynolds, "Congressional Black Caucus Hosts Rally against Cherokee Nation," *Indian Country Today,* October 5, 2007. On the possibility of Cherokee Freedmen seeking redress within international fora, see Rubio.

9. For overviews of the allotment period, see Adams; Burton; Hoxie.

10. "Cherokees Vote for Indian Blood," *Indian Country Today,* March 9, 2007

11. For a similar critique, see Byrd, "Been"; Scott Richard Lyons, "Cherokee by Text," *Indian Country Today,* October 18, 2007.

12. See Marx, *Capital*. See also Derrida, *Specters*, 149–52; Pietz; Spivak, "Scattered Speculations."

13. Jacobi, 829. Even if Reynolds and McKinley each possibly could bear Cherokee children, the inability to imagine a direct symmetry between the marital unit and the reproductive one threatens to unhinge the process by which that heteronormative fusion can naturalize social identities as biologically given, including the concreteness/endurance of Cherokee identity as racial blood. Thanks to Bethany Schneider for helping me clarify this point.

14. See Hoxie; Pfister; Rifkin, "Romancing Kinship."

15. On the exploration of the abject as a key modality for producing and rethinking racialized subjectivity, see Scott.

16. On the use of "tropes of substance" to signify political identity as an innate quality of embodiment, see Alonso. On the racialization of "cultural" or "ethnic" formations, see Balibar; Brown, *Regulating;* Chow, *Protestant;* Silva; Stevens, *Reproducing;* Visweswaran.

17. I should clarify, though, that I am not suggesting that the legal and policy frameworks of tribal nations in the contemporary United States *necessarily* bear such a reactive relation to the history and structures of federal Indian policy. For a critique of the underexamined notions of authenticity that would support such a claim, as well as an excellent discussion of the ways tradition gets envisioned and deployed in Hopi courtrooms, see Richland.

18. In *Blood Politics* Circe Sturm quotes Cherokees who express the fear that the absence of sufficient amounts of "Indian" blood among citizens of the Cherokee Nation will lead the U.S. government to refuse to continue to recognize it as a distinct polity (99), replaying concerns over detribalization and political recognition that can be traced to U.S. policy beginning in the late nineteenth century. In "Genealogy as Continuity," Kirsty Gover observes that tribal membership requirements based on blood quantum of Indianness are not equivalent to requirements based on tribally specific blood quantum and/or lineal descent from a tribal member in that the latter do not work from a generic, racial Indianness. She notes, however, that the use of blood requirements is still crucial in maintaining a sense of collective identity as a "tribe" from the perspective of U.S. officials, so the other forms of descent that she notes not only still tend to operate in heteronormative ways but also appear to be ways for Native peoples to protect themselves against the settler assumption that they have ceased to be really Indian.

19. Since Driskill has expressed a preference for gender-neutral pronouns, I will use "ze" and "hir" when referring to Driskill.

20. I should note that my account of Driskill's text will not return to

the topic of the Cherokee Freedmen per se, dwelling on ways of reckoning Native embodiment other than racial Indianness rather than addressing the place of racially "black" persons in Cherokee nationhood. Driskill's portrait of preremoval Cherokee life also tends not to speak to patterns of slave-holding. The movement ze encourages away from reproductive genealogy/substance and toward the generational transmission of sensations of touch, desire, and dependency as experiences of Cherokeeness, however, speaks to the long, layered, and complicated history of people of African descent as part of Cherokee socialities—perhaps offering a way of thinking of that relation that also provides an alternative to the juridical emphasis on the treaty of 1866 as the moment of (forced) inclusion of blacks as members of the Cherokee Nation.

21. See also Dinshaw et al.; Freeman, *Time;* Goldberg and Menon; Nealon, *Foundlings.*

22. See Bergland; Deloria, *Playing;* Elmer.

23. Derrida's investment in a future that breaks with the past is shared by scholars who draw on a Deleuzian notion of the virtual as a way of thinking temporality, and the critique and shift I offer is applicable to that work, as well. See Grosz; Massey; Massumi; Oksala. For an outstanding analysis of the ways contemporary theory, particularly that of Deleuze and Guattari, depends on turning Native people(s) into a pastless trace, see Byrd, *Transit.*

24. See Benjamin.

25. See the Introduction for discussion of Williams's notions of *residual, emergent,* and *structures of feeling.*

26. See also Chakrabarty. For a different account of colonial haunting, focusing on the ways postcolonial national identification is structured by the residual effects of structures of feeling under formal colonial control, see Khanna.

27. On the relation between the literal and the figurative and the work of metaphor, see the discussion in the Introduction. On the assessment of claims to Cherokee *realness,* see Sturm, *Becoming.*

28. Although I encountered it after writing this chapter, Lisa Tatonetti's "Indigenous Fantasies and Sovereignty Erotics" offers a reading of "Beginning Cherokee" that resonates with my own.

29. See Holmes and Smith.

30. For a discussion of "translation" in the context of Indigenous lega-cies of trauma, see Kaplan, 101–21. She describes it as a communication occurring across a "cultural divide" in the present, even if the participants are both Indigenous, but in this case I am addressing a relation across time in which the aim is to articulate the devastating fallout of settler policy as experiences that remain Indigenous. For discussion of the complex role of the Cherokee language (particularly the syllabary invented by Sequoyah in

the 1820s) in processes of cultural retention and ways of envisioning relations between a collective past and present, see Bender.

31. For comparative discussion of contemporary Cherokee representations of the Trail of Tears, see Justice, *Our Fire*, 155–203; Krupat. I address the Trail of Tears in greater detail in the next section.

32. On the emergence of the Eastern Band of Cherokees, including the combination of those who fled from removal with those Cherokees who already had secured a separate existence as individual propertyholders under the U.S.–Cherokee Treaty of 1819, see Finger, *Eastern Band*. On the later history of the band, see Finger, *Cherokee Americans*.

33. On the reunion of the Eastern Band of Cherokees with the Cherokee Nation of Oklahoma in April 1984, see Finger, *Cherokee Americans*, 180–81; Mankiller, 47–48.

34. On the ways in which language, land, and memory are intertwined in Native poetry, see Fast, *Heart*, 85–123.

35. As Joni Adamson notes in her reading of Joy Harjo's work, "What happens if the only language in which you can articulate this vision is the colonizers' language? For the dispossessed and marginalized, the difficulty of transforming English is not only that it has been used to pave over a landscape alive with myth and event, but that it is a language used to perpetuate a deadly silence that veils the incredible destruction and horrifying bloodshed of the last five hundred years" (125–26).

36. In *Our Elders Lived It*, Deborah Davis Jackson offers a similar observation about the relation of urban-raised Anishinaabe to their reservation-raised parents: "Their parents' silences are transformed from absences into powerful presences, 'fully palpable, and sometimes consuming.' . . . Far from being unconditionally empty or silent, these absences, as dynamic semiotic signs, are filled with a cacophony of competing messages—a mix of pride and shame, acceptance and rejection, whispering of something lost but not saying what it was" (113). Understanding silence in this way, as a shared context from which meaning emanates rather than what has been structurally foreclosed from speech, runs against the grain of Cathy Caruth's theorization of trauma as literally generating unspeakability. She argues that the immensity of trauma means that it escapes conscious knowledge and thus remains unnarratable except as flashback and fragment. See Caruth. For challenges to this account that rethink the meaning of "trauma" and of the social (rather than psychoanalytic/physiological) character of what can be narrated, as well as the possibilities of narration/engagement, see Ahmed, *Cultural*; Cvetkovich; Das; Fassin and Reichtman; Hart; Leys.

37. See Vizenor, *Manifest*, 70.

38. On the presence of similar narratives among other unenrolled people claiming Cherokee ancestry, see Sturm, *Becoming*.

39. For an exploration of the notion of catastrophe, especially as contrasted with genocide, see Kazanjian and Nichanian; Nichanian.

40. Several times, the text references the story of how spider brought fire to the other creatures. See Justice, "Go Away."

41. In a similar vein, Das refers to collective trauma that remains individually unspeakable as a kind of "poisonous knowledge" for which the body of the victim/witness becomes the "container" (52–58).

42. On the traditional importance of the tongue for Cherokees, as signifying one of the four "life forces that emanated from the human body," see Kilpatrick, 392–93.

43. As noted in the Introduction, this sense of the material effectivity of immaterial or ephemeral forces conventionally has been dismissed within post-Enlightenment Euro-American discourses as a fallacy of "savage" thought. See Bracken.

44. This moment resonates with Keith Basso's description of the work of memory in Native languages: "The place-maker's main objective is to speak the past into being, to summon it with words and give it dramatic form, to *produce* experience by forging ancestral worlds in which others can participate and readily lose themselves . . . , creating in the process a vivid sense of what happened long ago—right here, on this very spot, could be happening *now*" (32).

45. See also Tatonetti, "Indigenous," 161.

46. This male birth of stories echoes a similar image in the opening pages of Leslie Marmon Silko's *Ceremony*.

47. See Perdue, *Cherokee Women*.

48. See Butler, *Gender;* Ingraham.

49. The last council held prior to removal was in what is now the Red Clay Historic Park in Tennessee. See Awiakta, "Daydreaming," 70. Since the poem covers only two pages (56–57), I will forego parenthetical citations.

50. On the role of removal as a policy tactic from Jefferson onward, see Wallace.

51. For the text of the Indian Removal Act, see Prucha, *Documents*, 52–53.

52. On preremoval Cherokee governance, the conflict with Georgia, policy surrounding and in the wake of the Indian Removal Act, and the Trail of Tears, see Garrison; McLoughlin; Norgren; Perdue, *Cherokee;* Rifkin, *Manifesting;* Thornton; Wilkins, *Cherokee.*

53. "Beloved," 75. See also Anderson, "Situating"; Fast, *Heart.*

54. See Brown, *Walled;* Cohen, *Body*, 32–129; Collier, Maurer, and Suárez-Navez; Elmer; Foucault, *"Society";* Frost; Hirsch; Macpherson; Taussig.

55. For a later finding to the same effect under the Fourteenth Amendment, see *Santa Clara County v. Southern Pacific Railroad* (1886).

56. James Thomas Stevens has made something like the obverse of this

point, that quotidian logics and practices of desire in the United States are inseparable from the ongoing history of settler colonialism. See Dowling; Stevens, "Poetry."

57. The poem is a single page (66), so page numbers for quotations are unnecessary.

58. See Adams; Hoxie; Pfister.

59. "Stolen," 51–52.

60. On the "intimate event," the centrality of romantic couplehood in liberal notions of personhood, see Povinelli, *Empire*.

61. The image of Native or, more specifically, Cherokee remains surfacing on traditional land borne by flood (here, of lava) may be an allusion to the construction and operation of the Tellico Dam. See Awiakta, *Selu*, 41–64.

62. On such baskets and their import, see Awiakta, *Selu*; Driskill, "Doubleweaving"; Hill.

63. This idea resonates with Sean Teuton's notion of "somatic place."

64. This way of conceptualizing intergenerational trauma differs greatly from those that draw on Nicholas Abraham and Maria Torok's notion of the "phantom" passed from one generation to the next. Noting "that the 'phantom' . . . is nothing but an invention of the living" (171), they argue that treating this kind of inherited psychological effect proves quite difficult because the patient's "construction" that the analyst studies "bears no direct relation to the patient's own [psychic] topography but concerns someone else's": "The phantom will vanish only when its radically heterogeneous nature with respect to the subject is recognized" (174). In other words, whatever previous trauma is transmitted to the current generation remains only an alien imposition to be excised rather than a formative aspect of subjectivity or a marker of belonging to a supraindividual collective.

65. For discussion of the history and ideological work of map making and particularly its role in Euro-colonization of the Americas, see Brückner; Mignolo; Sparke; Warhus.

66. On the history of connecting New World land and Native bodies, usually supine women, see Carr; Kolodny; Kupperman; Shoemaker.

67. On the violation of Native women's bodies as a key technology of settler rule in the United States, see Smith, *Conquest*.

2. Landscapes of Desire

1. On being "disappeared," see Gordon, 63–135. See also Taylor, 161–89.

2. On the acknowledgment process, see Cramer; Field; Garroutte; Gunter; Klopotek; Laverty, "Ohlone"; McCullough and Wilkins; Miller, *Invisible*, 68–112; Miller, *Forgotten*; Ramirez, 102–25; Slagle; Tolley.

3. See Miller, *Forgotten*.

4. Cramer, 37–38. On the change to the regulations in 1994, see Cramer, 95; McCullough and Wilkins, 363–64; Miller, *Invisible*, 107–10; Miller, *Forgotten*, 75; "Procedures."

5. Field, 85; Gunter, 107. The BAR has been changed to the Office of Federal Acknowledgment (OFA) (Laverty, "Recognizing," 342).

6. McCulloch and Wilkins, 368. The criteria for determining "tribal" identity largely are drawn from those articulated in *Montoya v. U.S.* (1901), which were picked up by Felix Cohen and others in the Indian service in conceptualizing and implementing the Indian Reorganization Act (1934). See Cramer, 34; Field, 85; Miller, *Forgotten*, 28–29.

7. This process of authentication/gatekeeping, though, is not simply an invention of the settler-state but actively supported by many federally recognized tribal governments in ways that other Native intellectuals and activists have critiqued. See Klopotek, 32–36; Miller, *Invisible*, 16–17, 68–112; Miller, *Forgotten*, 40–41, 70–71. Moreover, a number of tribes, particularly in California, have engaged in processes of disenrollment in which people are stripped of tribal citizenship due to a determination by the tribal government that they are not actually descendants of people who belonged to the tribe—a decision that sometimes appears to be due to the fact that those disenrolled engaged in public forms of dissent. See Barker, *Native*, 146–85; Riley, "Good," 1113–16; Ramirez, 161–69. As Sara-Larus Tolley suggests, though, "The original and continuing state violence toward Native peoples" serves as a "catalyst" for "what is sometimes reputed to be [the] notorious factionalism" within and among Native peoples in California (195).

8. On the weighting of evidence, despite official claims to the contrary, see Garroutte, 70–73; Miller, *Invisible*, 108–11; Tolley.

9. Miller, *Forgotten*, 14; Laverty, "Ohlone," 41. See also Garroutte, 27–29.

10. In an interesting twist on this difficulty, David Johnson asks with respect to the limits of the South African Truth and Reconciliation Commission's ability to restore tribal lands taken during Apartheid, "Is it possible to mourn something that you want back?" (293).

11. Miller, *Forgotten*, 3. See also Cramer, 6.

12. On this formulation, see Spivak, *Outside*. As Greg Sarris notes, "Federally recognized tribes eat, those not recognized don't—at least not at the table of government helpings. Only federally recognized tribes are allowed a land base, trust land that is held by the government, which means that non-recognized tribes don't have the means for shelter and sustenance from a collective land base either" (Foreword, xii–xiii).

13. However, on the possibilities for collective identification and cohesion outside of or beyond the recognition process, see Klopotek. Due to the particular history of colonization and erasure in California, which I further address later in this chapter and the next, Native peoples in California have

a larger number of groups seeking recognition than elsewhere. As of 2004, 64 of the 235 groups seeking federal acknowledgment were in California (Tolley, 19).

14. On emotion as a form of critical knowledge and mapping, see also Ahmed, *Cultural,* 168–90; Das.

15. Her father is Chumash through his mother and Esselen through his father. See Miranda, *Indian Cartography,* x–xii. The Ohlone/Costanoan-Esselen Nation (OCEN) was organized as such in 1992 and currently is seeking federal acknowledgment. See Laverty, "Recognizing." He notes that the choice to use the term "nation" instead of "tribe" "particularly underscores the organizers' sense that the families the political organization was to represent were descended from a diverse group of amalgamated indigenous peoples," later adding that "the Esselen Nation organization was entirely new and formed as a rather alien if not altogether artificial construct" ("Recognizing," 40, 62).

16. On the relationship between erotic wholeness and the broader healing of Native peoples, see also Brant; Driskill, "Stolen"; Gould, "American Indian"; Warrior, "Your Skin."

17. The treaties made in 1851–52 with Native peoples in California, which were never ratified by Congress, did not include Esselen and other coastal groups considered to have been fully assimilated by the mission system. Esselen people did, however, maintain sites of communal solidarity. See Laverty, "Recognizing."

18. On this distinction, see Eng and Kanzanjian.

19. On racial melancholia, see also Eng, "Transnational"; Eng and Han; Muñoz, *Disidentifications.*

20. For more on this particular torsion, and the racist call to perform stereotypical modes of cultural difference, see Chow, *Protestant;* Silva. For a specifically Lacanian approach to these same issues, see Viego.

21. For a fascinating discussion of the ways bodily self-understanding could be understood to emerge out of social relations of memory and desire, as well as the ways the state exerts ownership over the sexed body as a kind of property, see Salamon.

22. In *Talkin' Up to the White Woman,* Aileen Moreton-Robinson argues, "The life writings of Indigenous women are an extension of Indigenous relationality in that they express the self as part of others and others as part of the self within and across generations" (2). For a differently configured discussion of melancholia as a framework for understanding Native self-representation, see Lawlor. She focuses on the ways Native nations' portrayal of themselves within various public venues can draw attention to the past, of both settler violence/displacement and Indigenous tradition, as still active in the present.

23. Cheng, 80.

24. For discussion of the work of imagination in (re)creating place in other Native poets, see Fast, 85–162; Goeman, "Notes"; Gould, "Poems." Miranda's depiction of an internal(ized) landscape resonates with N. Scott Momaday's much-discussed notion of blood memory, though Miranda's image does not draw on terminologies often associated with racial identity. On Momaday's formulation and its relation to Native landedness, see Allen, 178–92; Lawrence, 199–201; Schweninger, 131–48; Strong and Winkle; Teuton, 43–78.

25. The following historical sketch has been drawn from Bean; Bouvier; Castillo; Costo and Costo; Field; Goldberg-Ambrose; Haas; Heizer and Almquist; Hurtado; Jackson and Castillo; Laverty, "Recognizing"; Miranda, "Extermination"; Phillips; Pitt; Sandos; Shipek; Slagle; Tolley.

26. See *Cherokee Nation v. Georgia;* Norgren.

27. On this point in particular within federal findings on parts of the Esselen petition, see Lavery, "Recognizing," 446–49.

28. Laverty, "Ohlone," 67.

29. On this dynamic and the ways it can position indigeneity as negative or anachronistic entrapment, see Niezen; Povinelli, *Empire;* Tully. For a very different account of how collective belonging shapes subjectivity through the circulation of affect, see Ahmed, *Cultural.*

30. On the tendency to understand memory as "mine" in a way that duplicates notions of possessive individualism, see Ricoeur, *Memory,* 96–119.

31. On the ways post-Enlightenment Euro-American notions of the "literal" depend on treating a culturally specific sensory epistemology as if it were the ontological basis/nature of all human perception, see Seremetakis.

32. Here, I cannot help but note that when Cheng seeks to describe the coercive imposition of group membership, her word of choice repeatedly is "tribal" (21, 192, 195).

33. On the ways concepts of individual physical interiority and the self-enclosed body emerge out of struggles in Europe to conceptualize and defend the sovereignty of emergent states in the seventeenth century, see Cohen. On the relation between the development of a notion of psychic interiority and the consolidation of bourgeois political economy in the United States in the nineteenth century, see Castiglia; Merish; Rifkin, *When.*

34. On the legacy of primitivism (in which non-European groups are seen as possessing an unindividuated form of collectivity) and the ways the texts in this study (including Miranda) avoid this evolutionist paradigm, see the Introduction.

35. Butler, *Psychic,* 183.

36. Butler, *Psychic,* 170, 179, 181.

37. On the ways "savage" thinking has been charged with illogically

personifying abstract ideas and social processes, endowing them with sentience and will, see Bracken.

38. For a similar account of the need to work through loss, see LaCapra.

39. Even as she makes this argument, though, Butler's work continues to be shaped by a commitment to individualism and an inability to think forms of collectivity other than those defined by citizenship. On this dynamic, see Smith, "American Studies."

40. On this relation, see Smith, *Conquest.* For the connection between sexual violence and the political economy of colonization in California, see Bouvier; Castañeda, "Sexual Violence"; Hurtado.

41. I am using "myth" in the ways Sheila Marie Contreras does in *Blood Lines,* to indicate iconic narratives and tropes.

42. On La Malinche, see Alarcón, "Traddutora"; Contreras, 105–32; Esquibel; Gonzalez; Límon; Moraga, "A Long Line." On *mestizaje,* or the mixture of Spanish and Indian cultures and blood, see Alarcón, *Aztec;* Anzaldúa; Pérez-Torres; Saldaña-Portillo.

43. For a discussion of La Llorona's murder of her children as a figure of resistance, see Límon; Perez, *There Was,* 71–107.

44. On the proliferation of versions of La Llorona, see Límon; Perez.

45. On this process, see Rifkin, *Manifesting,* chapter 3.

46. See Castillo; Haas; Hurtado; Monroy; Shipek, "California." On the ways recognition is complicated by the nonnative assumption that Native people are really Mexicans, see Lavery, "Recognizing"; Ramirez.

47. See Ross, *Inventing.*

48. On the mission system in California, see Bouvier; Castañeda, "Engendering the History"; Castañeda, "Sexual Violence"; Castillo, "The Impact"; Costo and Costo, 155–99; Haas, 1–44; Hackel, "Land, Labor, and Production"; Hurtado, 33–102; Monroy, 51–162; Phillips, *Indians and Intruders;* Sandos, "Between"; Shipek, "California."

49. Since the poem is one page, further citations are unnecessary.

50. Since the poem is one page, further citations are unnecessary.

51. Here, I am suggesting an alternative to "working through," often used to describe the resolution of mourning.

52. In this way, her work both resembles and differs from Driskill's, which casts desire deemed deviant within a heteronormative frame as a means of reclaiming a sense of indigeneity but which tends to suggest the retention of a more specific set of traditions (as in "Love Poems: 1838–1839" and "Back to the Blanket").

53. Since the poem is one page, further citations are unnecessary.

54. On the relation between the rhetoric of ownership in romance and the history of Euro-colonization in the Americas, see Dowling; Stevens, "Poetry."

55. Miranda, *Indian Cartography*, 82.

56. In this way, Miranda's discussion of birth and creation resonates with José Muñoz's project in *Cruising Utopia* of turning to the past as a means of opening up potentialities for the future that bypass the pragmatic (neoliberal) framing of (gay and lesbian) politics in the present. However, Muñoz's work tends to take citizenship as an a priori frame, rather than investigating how social formations cast as ephemeral and nonpolitical generate alternative kinds of collectivity that are askew with respect to membership in the nation-state.

57. Since the poem is one page, further citations are unnecessary.

58. For other accounts of the limits of the discursive and legal frameworks in the South African hearings, see Johnson; Sanders; Wilson, *Politics*.

59. Though I focus on John Beverley's work, see also Arias; Gugelberger; Rodríguez, *Latin;* Saldaña-Portillo.

60. For efforts to define subalternity, see Beverley, *Subalternity;* Guha; Prakash; Rifkin, *Manifesting*, Introduction; Spivak, "Subaltern."

61. "Notes," 184.

62. Miranda's text also remains askew with respect to prominent efforts to reconceptualize testimony that distinguish it from processes of state adjudication. Giorgio Agamben's *Remnants of Auschwitz* often is cited as one of the most important recent efforts to address the effort to speak the unspeakable by those who have survived systems of devastating oppression and genocide. For Agamben testimony less references particular state logics or processes than reveals the ontological character of subjectivity as predicated on the possibility of its dissolution, refusing the categorical distinction between the human and the inhuman generated within systems of violence. To bear witness to the Holocaust is less to document particular events for an archive of one kind or another—to testify as in a court case— than to refuse to define what it means to be human through reference to the forms of self-presence and speech systematically denied those subjected to genocidal violence. "Testimony takes place where the speechless one makes the speaking one speak and where the one who speaks bears the impossibility of speaking in his own speech, such that the silent and the speaking, the inhuman and the human enter into a zone of indistinction" (120). From this perspective, to testify to state violence insists on the impossibility of an absolute distinction between those who can speak and those who cannot, pointing to the "remainder" of the subject that persists in even the most extreme experiences of dehumanization. Yet Agamben's efforts to theorize testimony run into a similar problem as existing critical efforts to reconceptualize melancholy. There is no place for thinking a substantive connection to collectivity, one that is not simply draped over the primacy of isolated/insulated individuality. If testimony entails indexing the inherent potential for desubjectification, how can we analyze sociohistorically

contingent processes of subjectification—the impress of alien forms of subjectivity? The text suggests an imperial inscription of one system of subjectivity over another. *The Zen of La Llorona* does not so much testify to the (ever-present possibility for the) dissolution of a generically human—or specifically Indigenous—subjectivity as seek to express and enact modes for (re)creating indigeneity in the current moment amid continuing legacies of loss, less gesturing toward something outside itself than positioning its own act of speaking as also a performance of the process about which it speaks.

63. Since the piece is only one page, further citations are unnecessary.

64. Ellipses present in the original.

65. The use of the Day of the Dead as the setting for the last piece reflects this dynamic. Although often described as traceable to Aztec traditions, Stanley Brandes argues that the ritual dynamics of this annual fall celebration bear a striking resemblance to those surrounding All Souls' Day in early-modern Iberia, suggesting a recontextualization of southern European Catholicism in the wake of the Spanish conquest, but he also suggests that the distinctive use of sugar (as in the skulls Miranda mentions), as well as the continuing overwhelming popularity of the event in greater Mexico, partially can be explained by reference to the mass death that followed for more than a century in the wake of Euro-contact and the importance of the emergent sugar industry in the political economy of eighteenth- and nineteenth-century Mexico. Though not original to the Americas, the Day of the Dead takes on a distinctive shape due to the particular contours and consequences of Spanish colonization, is animated by the horror that provides the implicit symbolic context for its ritual dimensions, and is transformed into a joyous occasion that simultaneously functions as commemoration—never escaping the orbit of the legacy of imperial assault even as its affect speaks to survival rather than to mourning. (The phrase "greater Mexico" is borrowed from the work of José E. Limón.)

66. See Gunter.

67. In Miranda's work, dancing often serves as a figure for the retention and/or reclamation of Native community. In particular, see "First Step" (*Zen*, 34–35) and "Gone Dancing" (*Indian Cartography*, 86–87).

3. Genealogies of Indianness

1. "Procedures," 83.7.

2. "Procedures," 83.1.

3. "Procedures," 83.7.

4. For examples of such scholarship, see Barker, *Native;* Brownwell; Cheyfitz, "(Post)Colonial"; Garroutte; Gover; Penn, *As We Are Now;* Rifkin, *When;* Saunt; Tolley, 167–72.

5. In *Reproducing the State*, Jacqueline Stevens argues that race can be

defined as "a subpopulation of human beings with observed or imagined physical characteristics understood to correspond with a geographical territory of origins. Presently the geographical territory or racial origins is understood as a continent" (191). From this perspective the "racial origin" that is Indianness cannot be separated from the "geographical territory" understood as the basis of tribal identity.

6. On the ways U.S. officials tend to equate high blood quantum with sociopolitical cohesion, see Gover.

7. In particular, see Justice, "Go Away."

8. See Collier and Yanagisako; Povinelli, *Empire;* Schneider, *Critique.*

9. Sarris is currently tribal chairman of the Federated Indians of Graton Rancheria, a group that was federally recognized by Congressional act in 2000 after having been terminated by congressional act in 1958. See http://www.gratonrancheria.com/timeline.htm. See also H. Rpt. 677, 106th Cong., 2d sess.; Sarris, Foreword, xiii–xiv. Previously, Sarris also had identified as southern Pomo and coast Miwok. See Sarris, *Mabel.* The differences in name do not represent separate groups but the complex, overlapping, and inconsistent ways Native populations to the north of San Francisco have been named by officials and nonnative experts. On the complex political economy of Native land tenure and self-governance in the region, see Bauer; Goldberg-Ambrose; Laverty, "Recognizing"; Slagle; Tolley.

10. The people in the novel call themselves Waterplace Pomo, but I use Pomo as a shorthand for convenience. As an official and ethnographic term, Pomo designates a variety of peoples conventionally understood as part of a shared linguistic/cultural group.

11. While extending beyond state citizenship to the performance of sovereignty and collective Native identity, this dynamic resembles the ideal of the "good straight ethnic." See Puar.

12. As Laura Furlan Szanto argues, the attention to "mixed-blood origin stories" "changes the focus of Indian identity . . . away from authenticity in favor of detailing the geographic and economic circumstances that are the cause of racial mixing" (83). I develop this analysis further by attending to other deviations from (hetero)normative Indianness.

13. This vision of resistance as "dispersion" can reiterate the same problems noted in the last chapter with respect to theories of melancholy, in that it can presume the individual as the site of such an undoing of identity/subjectivity. Doing so ontologically can presuppose the individual as the atom of social dynamics in ways that leave aside collectivity as a primary aspect of human sociality. For an example of this problem within a Foucaultian genealogical paradigm, see Clifford, *Political,* 125–47.

14. For "reprosexuality," see Luciano. While I came across this source after writing the chapter, Sara-Larus Tolley also draws on Foucault's notion

of genealogy in addressing the kinds of proof demanded of Native peoples for recognition (190).

15. See Brownwell, 301–5; Cramer, 137–62; Garroutte, 19–25; Justice, "Go Away"; Klopotek; Miller, *Forgotten*, 11–12.

16. While in no way autobiographical, and not about the Federated Indians of Graton Rancheria, the novel does echo many of the elements of that people's history, including residence of a majority in Santa Rosa, the loss of a BIA-provided reservation in the vicinity of Graton due to termination, and the effort to receive federal acknowledgment in the 1990s—a process occurring as Sarris was writing the novel. See H. Rpt. 677, 106th Cong., 2d sess.; 1998 H.R. 4434; Sarris, *Keeping*, 11–12, 92–94.

17. Though I later draw on Sarris's scholarly account of the Bole Maru religion, I should note that the impression conveyed of it in *Watermelon Nights* differs greatly from that in *Keeping Slug Woman Alive*, described in the latter as "inculcat[ing] an impassioned Indian nationalism in the homes and roundhouses" (67).

18. On the ways Sarris's fiction casts the urban environment of Santa Rose as legitimately Native space, rather than as merely a placeholder for the ostensibly true indigeneity of a recognized reservation, see Rice, 170–93; Szanto, 88–95.

19. The novel does not address the need to prove their worthwhileness to other Native peoples, but in *Mabel McKay*, Sarris notes that Violet Chappel (the daughter of Essie Parrish, a Kashaya Pomo Bole Maru dreamer) once said to him about the people living in Santa Rosa, "Oh, *those* people! Greg, you know all the gutter snipe, the lost Indians" (57).

20. Not all genealogical modes of reckoning are heteronormative or implicitly predicated on race. For a particularly evocative discussion of the distinction between traditional Hawaiian genealogies and notions of racial bloodedness, see Kauanui. For discussion of the history of inserting Native peoples into settler discourses of sexuality, see Rifkin, *When*.

21. Lawrence, 25.

22. If as Sara-Larus Tolley suggests, "Federal Recognition represents a refutation of genocide" (19), the novel suggests that apparent official engagement with the history of settler violence does not necessarily ameliorate the pervasive insecurity following genocide, given that the United States does not necessarily acknowledge such devastation in extending recognition and can just as easily *change its mind.*

23. Notably, Lena and Mona also refer to Zelda Toms and Nellie Copaz as "whores that stole our land" (60). Later, I address how the novel presents "whore" as a kind of identity category and the ways it marks sorts of social relations among Pomos that do not get to count as tribal.

24. I note these relationships not only to help keep track of how characters

are connected but to suggest the ways Sarris calls on readers to reconstruct intergenerational familial networks that exceed the terms of the nuclear family and its lineage and that have direct effects on the lives of the characters and the plot of the novel. One way of "cheating" in figuring out who is related to whom is to use the genealogical chart Sarris provides in *Grand Avenue*, his first novel that concerns members of this same community and these families. It is notable that he does not include such a chart for *Watermelon Nights*, putting greater pressure on the reader to find the connections, as well as implicitly questioning the implications and stakes of the logic of the genealogical chart.

25. Laura Furlan Szanto notes that Johnny and Felix's sexual encounter occurs in the same creek Nellie Copaz describes as "sacred" in *Grand Avenue* (74).

26. In *Writing History, Writing Trauma*, Dominick LaCapra seeks to distinguish between "absence" and "loss." Although he is addressing a more theoretical point with respect to deconstructive methodologies, his characterization of the effects of conflating the one with the other seems quite apt for thinking about the role of proper genealogy in the recognition process: "In converting absence into loss, one assumes that there was (or at least could be) some original unity, wholeness, security, or identity that others have ruined, polluted, or contaminated and thus made 'us' lose. Therefore, to regain it one must somehow get rid of or eliminate those others—or perhaps that sinful other in oneself" (58).

27. On songs and baskets in Pomo life, see Sarris, *Mabel*; Sarris, *Keeping*, 51–62.

28. Mabel McKay was a widely known and respected medicine person among the Pomos and adjacent peoples. In *Mabel McKay*, Sarris notes that people often confused her for a poisoner and that she repeatedly was told during her training that she needed to know how poisoning works in order to counter it. See also Loeb, 329–34.

29. On the roundhouse as a spiritual center present in each Pomo village, see Loeb, 159–63, 338, 354; Parkman. On the presence of roundhouses elsewhere in the region, see Bauer.

30. On the Bole Maru, see Bauer; Du Bois; Loeb, 394–97; Meighan and Riddell; Sarris, *Mabel*, 1–34; Sarris, *Keeping*, 63–76.

31. Sarris, *Keeping*, 67. Big Sarah seems to be based on Annie Jarvis, the dreamer on the Kashaya Reservation who proceeded Essie Parrish (to whom Sarris was related and of whom he often has written). See Du Bois, 231–32; Sarris, *Keeping*, 10. Important to note, Sarris distinguishes Jarvis from Parrish in their attitudes toward Pomo interaction with whites, indicating that the latter "favored open relations with non-Indian communities."

32. Sarris, *Keeping*, 67.

33. In *The History of Sexuality*, vol. 1, Foucault characterizes normalization as "a power whose task is to take charge of life[,] need[ing] continuous regulatory and corrective mechanisms": "distributing the living in the domain of value and utility" (144).

34. On the individualization of broader political conflicts, such that they are narrated as inherent qualities of certain bodies in ways that efface their macrological dimensions, see Cohen; Das.

35. In suggesting that the revivalism of the Bole Maru incorporates the heteronormative logics of the surrounding Euramerican society, I am not suggesting such borrowing makes it less authentically Pomo. Many scholars have noted the possibility for forms of Native social change and reinvention that adopt element of Euramerican practices, principles, languages, technologies, media without merely assimilating to Euramerican social formations. For examples, see Bauer; Ortiz; Nelson; Raibmon; Usner. In the case of Native American revivalism, this case has been made perhaps most strongly by Gregory Dowd. Rather than locating a traditionalist origin from which to cast the Bole Maru as a falling away, which would repeat the very kind of narration I've been critiquing, I am tracing the questions Sarris's novel raises about the effect of employing normative genealogy in efforts to protect Pomo peoplehood, not as against some truer version of Pomo identity but in terms of its consequences for Pomo people and the alternative possibilities for living community that doing so forecloses.

36. The Pomos are thrown off the ranch by Benedict after Chum kills herself, presumably due to both the fact that he has refused to allow her to see his son Westin anymore and that she is pregnant with Westin's child, after which the community moves to land near Sebastopol that had been reserved for a different people, but only one member of that group—known only as Reginald—remains. The Bureau of Indian Affairs officially recognizes their right to reside on this reservation until it is lost several decades later.

37. On the legacy of (the absence of) federal Indian policy in California, see Castillo; Costo and Costo; Hurtado; Ramirez; Rifkin, *Manifesting*, 149–96; Shipek, *Pushed*; Slagle; Tolley.

38. She says, "We forgot Creation, which is why Creation forgot us.... It's why we're hungry" (152).

39. In particular, on the long-standing, nonstigmatized presence of homoeroticism, as well as more varied forms of gender expression, among Pomos, see Lang, 91–92, 182–83, 204–5, 215–16, 221–22; Loeb, 248; Roscoe, 16, 235, 240. On prior forms of polygamy, see Loeb, 198, 243–44.

40. This incident may be drawn from the thwarted effort by Mabel McKay's mother to sell her into marriage (Sarris, *Mabel*, 28).

41. See note 36.

42. Philip Laverty notes that one of the ways Native people could gain

access to property in the nineteenth and early twentieth centuries was through marriage to nonnatives ("Recognizing," 365, 443), so the vehemence of Benedict's and others' response may have been animated by anxiety over the possibility of Indians gaining legally legitimated access to land through marital union.

43. Sarris, *Keeping,* 68.

44. Such a depiction resonates with certain theories of trauma. In particular, see Caruth.

45. Within Pomo traditions, and those of other adjacent peoples in Northern California, songs, dances, and ceremonial paraphernalia, while used for community rituals, all belong to particular persons and can be transferred to others, although not necessarily following the legal logics of inheritance. See Du Bois; Loeb, 199; Sarris, *Mabel.*

46. See Rifkin, "Indigenizing"; Rifkin, *When.*

47. The notion of "biopolitics" is drawn from Foucault's work. In *The History of Sexuality,* vol. 1, he juxtaposes it with the "right of death" that inhered in monarchical sovereignty: "This death that was based on the right of the sovereign is now manifested as simply the reverse of the right of the social body to ensure, maintain, or develop its life" (136). See also Clifford, *Political;* Nealon, *Foucault;* Puar; Stoler.

48. Work in subaltern studies extensively has explored how forms of anticolonial political opposition can rely on the ideologies of what constitutes politics institutionalized by the colonizer. For examples, see Beverley; Chatterjee; Guha, *Dominance;* Guha and Spivak; Rodríguez, *Latin.* On the "bribe of straightness," see Rifkin, *When* (particularly chapters 3 and 6).

49. See Du Bois, 302; Loeb, 161, 290, 300.

50. In her account of the spread of the 1870 Ghost Dance and the emergence of the Bole Maru, Cora Du Bois observes, "It cannot be stressed too strongly that dancing was the preeminent form of religious expression to these central Californian Indians" (308).

51. Various claims by the narrators, particularly their reflections on other characters, are revealed to be faulty or at least skewed by the provision of additional information or perspective elsewhere in the novel. The absence of a later qualification can be taken, then, as a form of authorization on the novel's part, displacing the binary of flawed first-person narration versus that of an omniscient narrator. In the final section of the chapter, I address how the novel ties personal acts of storytelling to the potential for generating truth claims about Pomo peoplehood.

52. Thanks to Mishuana Goeman for calling on me to consider more carefully these aspects of the text.

53. "Procedures," 83.7.

54. Povinelli presents the intimate event as gaining meaning through contradistinction from the extended genealogical ties attributed to Indige-

nous peoples, but I have been arguing that part of the recognition of *tribal* identity for Native peoples in the United States depends on demonstrating an *Indianness* that fundamentally relies on the intimate event as its condition of (racial) intelligibility.

55. On the danger of the pursuit of a nondefiled image for colonized peoples, see Chow, "Where."

56. Foucault, "Two Lectures," 83–85.

57. In *Assuming a Body,* Gayle Salamon argues that the documentary "fact" of the sex one is assigned at birth functions as a kind of state property claim, and in this vein, I am suggesting that claims to biological Indianness, as well as the heterogenealogy on which such claims rest, operate as a kind of property that provides access to the property that is reservation land.

58. See Smith, *Conquest.*

59. For a very evocative account of the dangers of accepting settler modes of mapping as the truth of Native inhabitance and identity, see Goeman, "Notes."

60. Veena Das describes a similar process, although with respect to rumor rather than to storytelling, as one in which "the signature of the state can detach itself from its origin and be grafted onto other structures and other chains of signification" (177).

61. On Sarris's depiction of this dynamic in *Grand Avenue,* see Rice, 191–92. In *Mabel McKay,* he says of the tale of Mabel McKay's life, "Her story, the story, our story. Like the tiny basket in my shirt pocket, different threads, sedge and redbud, woven over one willow rod into a design that went round and round, endless" (164–65). On weaving as a model for producing knowledge, see also Driskill, "Doubleweaving."

62. On the process of engaging state archives in service of researching a recognition petition, and the frustrated desires generated by the archive, see Tolley, 148–91.

63. On the ways genocide gives rise to collective forms of subjectivity that extend beyond the immediate space of death, see Rodríguez, *Suspended.* Whereas he suggests that in the case of Filipinos and Filipino Americans the legacy of genocide makes such identity(/ies) inherently incoherent, Sarris's novel addresses ways that the legacy of sadness and spite can be recognized and rewoven as a basis for collective solidarity and kindness.

4. Laboring in the City

1. Cheyfitz, "(Post)Colonial," 5; Prucha, *Documents,* 233, 364–65.

2. According to the 2000 census, 4.3 million people self-identified as American Indian or Alaska Natives and about 64 percent lived outside legally recognized Native territory (U.S. Census Bureau, "We the People," 14). That often-cited calculation, though, only applies to "American Indians

and Alaska Natives who reported only one race and one tribe," excluding people who checked boxes for belonging to multiple races and/or to multiple tribes (U.S. Census Bureau, "We the People," 3).

3. See American Indian Policy Review Commission, 23–45; Fixico, *Termination*, 134–57; Metcalf; Philp, "Stride."

4. As Vine Deloria Jr. suggested in 1969, "Many tribes have said that there is no incentive in building up their reservations if there is a chance they will be sold out unexpectedly in the near future" (136).

5. On termination more broadly, see Deloria, *Custer*; Fixico, *Termination*; Philp, *Termination*; Rosier; Wilkinson, *Blood Struggle*. On Menominee termination and restoration, see Beck, 129–78; Peroff. Given that Chrystos was born in San Francisco in 1946, her father had left the Menominee reservation prior to this period. On the role of off-reservation Menominee in aiding the restoration effort, see Beck, 159–61. Some scholars have warned against understanding movement to the city only as a result of terminationist policies, a view that leaves aside some people's decision to embrace urban life. See Lobo, "Urban"; Ramirez.

6. See Danzinger; Harvard Project, 351–67; National Urban Indian Family Coalition. On the difficulty of locating aggregate information on federal funding and programs for nonreservation-based Native people, see National Urban Indian Family Coalition (esp. 14–15).

7. In *The Cunning of Recognition*, Elizabeth Povinelli observes of that same process, "Shame's political pleasure, its sublime politics, lies in conjuring an experience 'beyond ideology' in a moment saturated with ideological readjustments of state discrimination" (183).

8. On the difficulties posed for Native peoples when they pursue modes of sovereignty not perceived by nonnatives as authentically Indian, see Bruyneel, 171–205; Cattelino; Engle; Lawlor; Niezen; Povinelli, *Cunning*; Raibmon; Simpson, "Subjects."

9. For discussion of how cities can serve as "hubs" in which individuals from different peoples can engage with each other while still maintaining enduring relationships with their own peoples, see Ramirez. For discussion of Native life in urban areas, see Danzinger; Fixico, *Urban*; Jackson, *Our Elders*; Lawrence; Lobo, "Urban"; Metcalf; Straus and Valentino; Thrush.

10. See also Biolosi, "Imagined."

11. In *The Protestant Ethnic*, Ray Chow argues, "What the successful use of stereotypes by political regimes has proved is not simply that stereotypes are clichéd, unchanging forms but also—and much more importantly— that stereotypes are capable of engendering realities that do not exist" (59). The scholarship on Indian stereotype is quite extensive; for examples, see Deloria, *Indians*; Deloria, *Playing*; Goeman, "Disrupting"; Green, "Pocahontas"; Huhndorf; Mithlo; Ross, *Inventing*. In drawing on this work, I

seek to track the ways Chrystos explores the extractive dynamics of stereo-type, its function as a form of fetish within settler political economy, and the labor entailed in reproducing one's existence as a Native person in the wake of the erasures stereotype performs.

12. On congressional plenary power, see Harring; Pommersheim; Wilkins; Wilkins and Lomawaima.

13. On the use of racist stereotype in U.S. Supreme Court decisions, see Coffey and Tsosie; Williams, *Like*.

14. Even when the government does not do so, it remains a possibility. As Jessica Cattelino observes, "Recent Supreme Court rulings suggest that indigenous commercial success threatens to undermine the basic tenets of sovereign immunity [tribes' right to refuse to be sued, just as states can] in the eyes of the court," adding, "A closely related joke circulating around Indian Country is that while it used to be that 'the only good Indian is a dead Indian,' a phrase associated with nineteenth-century military conquest, now it's that 'the only good Indian is a poor Indian'" (101–2). See also Bruyneel, 171–205; Cramer; Simpson, "Subjects." The acquisition of wealth by Native nations also remains continually haunted by the threat of a renewed move toward termination, especially given that the self-determination policy itself often has been articulated and justified as a process of freeing tribes from federal superintendence in rhetoric that echoes that used during the termination period. See Castile, *Taking*.

15. For a reading of Native writing, particularly Native women's erotic poetry, as rhizomatic, see Miranda, "In My Subversive Country."

16. On the ways reified forms of identity (including stereotype) might provide a window onto the political economy that generates such reification, see Floyd.

17. In *Talkin' Up to the White Woman*, Aileen Moreton-Robinson notes, "The traditional woman is the woman against whom all Indigenous women are measured, yet in her pristine state she does not exist" (89).

18. On the notion of the assemblage, see Deleuze and Guattari; Protevi; Puar.

19. This opening note is only one page but is not paginated.

20. She observes at many points in her work that she is the child of a Menominee father and a Euramerican mother but that she has never resided in officially recognized Menominee territory. On the history of the Menominees, including their termination and subsequent restoration, see Beck; Peroff.

21. Chrystos, *Fire Power*, 63. Since I have chosen poems from different volumes, I will indicate the collection and page number when I begin discussing each. They all are only a page or two, so I will forego page citations for each quote. For discussion of *Dances with Wolves*, see Huhndorf, 1–5.

22. While Anne Cheng addresses how racialized types can serve as sites of white identification and fantasy, I want to suggest that Indianness uniquely functions in the contemporary United States as a racialized figuration meant to be taken up by those outside the population it ostensibly designates and that serves as a sign of the actual absence from contemporary life of that population.

23. *Fugitive,* 23.

24. Huhndorf marks a distinction between "going native" and "playing Indian," suggesting the former has more long-term aims, but I read them as more or less synonymous.

25. For discussion of the varied ways Native nations may draw on stereotype in their public displays, see Lawlor. For a discussion of the complexities of notions of fungibility in relation to Native nations' participation in capitalist networks, see Cattelino. I should note that I am not, nor is Chrystos, suggesting that connection to capitalism is somehow contaminating of a pure Native identity. As I will illustrate in the next section, Chrystos addresses the inevitability of "selling out" in light of Native people's (and peoples') actual positions within settler political economy. However, I seek to emphasize the ways Chrystos explores stereotype as a kind of extraction/exploitation connected to larger forms of seizure and exchange in U.S.–Native history.

26. *Fugitive,* 38.

27. For an account that approaches similar issues around sexual identity, but through Lukács and Foucault, see Floyd.

28. For discussion of the relation between the circulation of capital and the (spirit) power of the state, see Taussig, 119–45.

29. Fugitive, 66–67.

30. See Green, "Pocahontas."

31. See Hoxie; Robertson; Winnemucca. I should note, though, the complexity of fry bread as both signifier and practice, in that it cannot and should not be taken merely as a symbol of oppression, while it also points to kinds of material deprivation and lack of access to prior modes of subsistence that characterized the reservation system. Thanks to Tol Foster for suggesting the need for such clarification.

32. *Fire,* 122–23.

33. He was a Lakota warrior who took part in the fight against General George Armstrong Custer in 1876 and who was killed while held in U.S. custody the following year. See Ostler.

34. For discussion of the contemporary politics of energy extraction on Native land, see Cheyfitz, "Navajo"; Harvard Project, 159–75.

35. The essay is unpublished and in the author's possession.

36. For discussion of the ways other kinds of histories can persist alongside and within those of capitalism, see Chakrabarty.

37. *Fire*, 69–70.

38. For discussion of this dynamic, see Thrush.

39. For a wonderful essay that uses Chrystos's figuration of the absence of a "treaty" as the jumping off point for considering the role of Native people in the academy as shuttled between the roles of native informant and vanishing Indian, see Barker and Teaiwa.

40. On the Ghost Dance, see Ostler. The figure of the Ghost Dance is a significant one in contemporary Native literature. See Gould, "American"; Huffstetler.

41. See Ostler.

42. See Deloria, *Indians*, 15–51.

43. *Not*, 7.

44. Jean O'Brien has described the repeated process of declaring the incipient accomplishment of Native extermination (specifically in nineteenth-century New England) as "lasting."

45. *Fugitive*, 15.

46. *Fire*, 56.

47. In *Writing as Witness*, Beth Brant notes that romanticizing, stereotypical representations of Native people leave aside questions of labor: "No one discusses the issue of class in the same breath with Native writers," "we are never considered to be workers, and never is it mentioned what we have to endure to bring a pay cheque home" (79). On histories of effacing and anachronizing Native labor, see also Usner.

48. In addressing the role of capitalist value in making "the nonsensuous sensuous," see Derrida.

49. *Not*, 1, 34–35.

50. Chow, *Protestant Ethnic*, 95–127.

51. *Fugitive*, 23.

52. On "affective histories," see Chakrabarty, 18.

53. For an extended consideration of this problematic, see Schweninger. Here, I am more concerned, however, with the difference between reservation and nonreservation spaces and the role of stereotype in managing and negotiating that relation.

54. On the long-standing popular cultural association of Indians with drumbeats, see Deloria, *Indians*, 183–223.

Bibliography

Abraham, Nicholas, and Maria Torok. *The Shell and the Kernal.* Vol. 1. Edited and translated by Nicholas T. Rand. Chicago: University of Chicago Press, 1994.

Adams, David Wallace. *Education for Extinction: American Indians and the Boarding School Experience, 1875–1928.* Lawrence: University Press of Kansas, 1995.

Adamson, Joni. *American Indian Literature, Environmental Justice, and Ecocriticism: The Middle Place.* Tucson: University of Arizona Press, 2001.

Adorno, Theodor W. *Negative Dialectics.* 1966. Translated by E. B. Ashton. 1973. Reprint, New York: Continuum, 1987.

Agamben, Giorgio. *Homo Sacer: Sovereign Power and Bare Life.* 1995. Translated by Daniel Heller-Roazen. Palo Alto, Calif.: Stanford University Press, 1998.

———. *Remnants of Auschwitz: The Witness and the Archive.* 1999. Translated by Daniel Heller-Roazen. New York: Zone Books, 2002.

Ahmed, Sara. *The Cultural Politics of Emotion.* New York: Routledge, 2004.

———. *Queer Phenomenology: Orientations, Objects, Others.* Durham, N.C.: Duke University Press, 2006.

Akiwenzie-Damm, Kateri. "Erotic, Indigenous Style." In *(Ad)dressing Our Words: Aboriginal Perspectives on Aboriginal Literatures,* edited by Armand Garnet Ruffo, 143–51. Penticton, British Columbia: Theytus Books, 2001.

Alarcón, Daniel Cooper. *The Aztec Palimpsest: Mexico in the Modern Imagination.* Tucson: University of Arizona Press, 1997.

Alarcón, Norma. "Traddutora, Traditora: A Paradigmatic Figure of Chicana Feminism." *Cultural Critique* 13 (Fall 1989): 57–87.

Aleinikoff, T. Alexander. *Semblances of Sovereignty: The Constitution, the State, and American Citizenship.* Cambridge, Mass.: Harvard University Press, 2002.

Alexander, Jeffrey C. "Toward a Theory of Cultural Trauma." In *Cultural Trauma and Collective Identity,* edited by Jeffery C. Alexander, et al., 1–30. Berkeley: University of California Press, 2004.

Allen, Chadwick. *Blood Narrative: Indigenous Identity in American Indian and Maori Literary and Activist Texts.* Durham, N.C.: Duke University Press, 2002.

< 297 >

Alonso, Ana María. "The Politics of Space, Time, and Substance: State Formation, Nationalism, and Ethnicity." *Annual Review of Anthropology* 23 (1994): 379–405.

American Indian Policy Review Commission (Task Force Eight). *Report on Urban and Rural Non-reservation Indians: Final Report to the American Indian Policy Review Commission.* Washington, D.C.: U.S. Government Printing Office, 1976.

Anaya, S. James. *Indigenous Peoples in International Law.* New York: Oxford University Press, 1996.

Anderson, Eric Gary. "Situating American Indian Poetry: Place, Community, and the Question of Genre." In *Speak to Me Words: Essays on Contemporary American Indian Poetry,* edited by Dean Rader and Janice Gould, 34–55. Tucson: University of Arizona Press, 2003.

Anzaldúa, Gloria. *Borderlands/La Frontera: The New Mestiza.* 2nd ed. San Francisco: Aunt Lute Books, 1999.

Arias, Arturo, ed. *The Rigoberta Menchú Controversy.* Minneapolis: University of Minnesota Press, 2001.

Arondekar, Anjali. *For the Record: On Sexuality and the Colonial Archive in India.* Durham, N.C.: Duke University Press, 2009.

Awiakta, Marilou. "Daydreaming Primal Space: Cherokee Aesthetics as Habits of Being." In *Speak to Me Words: Essays on Contemporary American Indian Poetry,* edited by Dean Radar and Janice Gould, 56–70. Tucson: University of Arizona Press, 2003.

———. *Selu: Seeking the Corn-Mother's Wisdom.* Golden, Colo.: Fulcrum Publishing, 1993.

Balibar, Etienne. "Is There a 'Neo-Racism'?" In *Race, Nation, Class: Ambiguous Identities,* edited by Etienne Balibar and Immanuel Wallerstein and translated by Chris Turner, 17–28. New York: Verson, 1991.

Barker, Joanne. *Native Acts: Law, Recognition, and Cultural Authenticity.* Durham, N.C.: Duke University Press, 2011.

———. "Gender, Sovereignty, and the Discourse of Rights in Native Women's Activism." *Meridians: Feminism, Race, Transnationalism* 7, no. 1 (2006): 127–61.

Barker, Joanne, and Teresia Teaiwa. "Native InFormation." In *Reading Native American Women: Critical/Creative Representations,* edited by Inés Hernández-Avila, 107–27. New York: Altamira Press, 2005.

Basso, Keith. *Wisdom Sits in Places: Language and Landscape among the Western Apache.* Albuquerque: University of New Mexico Press, 1996.

Bauer, William J., Jr. *We Were All Like Migrant Workers Here: Work, Community, and Memory on California's Round Valley Reservation, 1850–1941.* Chapel Hill: University of North Carolina Press, 2009.

Bean, Lowell John, ed. *The Ohlone, Past and Present: Native Americans of the San Francisco Bay Region.* Menlo Park, Calif.: Ballena Press, 1994.

Beck, David R. M. *The Struggle for Self-Determination: History of the Menominee Indians since 1854.* Lincoln: University of Nebraska Press, 2005.

Bender, Margaret. *Signs of Cherokee Culture: Sequoyah's Syllabary in Eastern Cherokee Life.* Chapel Hill: University of North Carolina Press, 2002.

Benjamin, Walter. "Theses on the Philosophy of History." In *Illuminations,* edited by Hannah Arendt and translated by Harry Zohn, 253–64. New York: Shocken Books, 1969.

Bergland, Renée L. *The National Uncanny: Indian Ghosts and American Subjects.* Hanover, N.H.: University Press of New England, 2000.

Berlant, Lauren, and Michael Warner. "Sex in Public." *Critical Inquiry* 24, no. 2 (1998): 548–66.

Bern, John, and Susan Dodds. "On the Plurality of Interests: Aboriginal Self-Government and Land Rights." In *Political Theory and the Rights of Indigenous Peoples,* edited by Duncan Ivison, Paul Patton, and Will Sanders, 163–80. New York: Cambridge University Press, 2000.

Beverley, John. *Subalternity and Representation: Arguments in Cultural Theory.* Durham, N.C.: Duke University Press, 1999.

———. *Testimonio: On the Politics of Truth.* Minneapolis: University of Minnesota Press, 2004.

Biersteker, Thomas J., and Cynthia Weber, eds. *State Sovereignty as Social Construct.* Cambridge: Cambridge University Press, 1996.

Biolosi, Thomas. *"Deadliest Enemies": Law and the Making of Race Relations On and Off Rosebud Reservation.* Berkeley: University of California Press, 2001.

———. "Imagined Geographies: Sovereignty, Indigenous Space, and American Indian Struggle." *American Ethnologist* 32, no. 2 (2005): 239–59.

Blackhawk, Ned. *Violence over the Land: Indians and Empires in the Early American West.* Cambridge, Mass.: Harvard University Press, 2006.

Bourdieu, Pierre. *The Logic of Practice.* 1980. Translated by Richard Nice. Palo Alto, Calif.: Stanford University Press, 1990.

———. "Social Space and Symbolic Power." In *In Other Words: Essays toward a Reflexive Sociology,* translated by Matthew Adamson, 122–39. Palo Alto, Calif.: Stanford University Press, 1990.

Bouvier, Virginia Marie. *Women and the Conquest of California, 1542–1840.* Tucson: University of Arizona Press, 2001.

Bracken, Christopher. *Magical Criticism: The Recourse of Savage Philosophy.* Chicago: University of Chicago Press, 2007.

Brandes, Stanley. "Sugar, Colonialism, and Death: On the Origins of Mexico's Day of the Dead." *Comparative Studies in Society and History* 39, no. 2 (1997): 270–99.

Brant, Beth. *Writing as Witness: Essay and Talk.* Toronto: Women's Press, 1994.

Brehm, Victoria. "Urban Survivor Stories: The Poetry of Chrystos." *Studies in American Indian Literatures* 10, no. 1 (1998): 73–82.

Brennan, Teresa. *The Transmission of Affect.* Ithaca, N.Y.: Cornell University Press, 2004.

Brickman, Celia. *Aboriginal Populations in the Mind: Race and Primitivity in Psychoanalysis.* New York: Columbia University Press, 2003.

Brown, Wendy. *Regulating Aversion: Tolerance in the Age of Identity and Empire.* Princeton, N.J.: Princeton University Press, 2006.

———. *Walled States, Waning Sovereignty.* New York: Zone Books, 2010.

Brownwell, Margo S. "Who Is an Indian? Searching for an Answer to the Question at the Core of Federal Indian Law." *University of Michigan Journal of Law Reform* 34 (2000–2001): 275–320.

Brückner, Martin. The Geographic Revolution in Early America: Maps, Literacy, and National Identity. Chapel Hill: University of North Carolina Press, 2006.

Bruyneel, Kevin. *The Third Space of Sovereignty: The Postcolonial Politics of U.S.–Indigenous Relations.* Minneapolis: University of Minnesota Press, 1997.

Brysk, Alison. *From Tribal Village to Global Village: Indian Rights and International Relations in Latin America.* Palo Alto, Calif.: Stanford University Press, 2000.

Burton, Jeffrey. *Indian Territory and the United States, 1866–1906.* Norman: University of Oklahoma Press, 1995.

Butler, Judith. *Frames of War: When is Life Grievable?* New York: Verso, 2009.

———. *Gender Trouble: Feminism and the Subversion of Identity.* New York: Routledge, 1990.

———. *The Psychic Life of Power.* Palo Alto, Calif.: Stanford University Press, 1997.

Byrd, Jodi. "'Been to the Nation, Lord, but I Couldn't Stay There': American Indian Sovereignty, Cherokee Freedmen and the Incommensurability of the Internal." *interventions* 13, no. 1: 31–52.

———. *The Transit of Empire: Indigenous Critiques of Colonialism.* Minneapolis: University of Minnesota Press, 2011.

Carr, Helen. *Inventing the American Primitive: Politics, Gender, and the Representation of Native American Literary Traditions, 1789–1936.* New York: New York University Press, 1996.

Carsten, Janet. *After Kinship.* New York: Cambridge University Press, 2004.

Caruth, Cathy. *Unclaimed Experience: Trauma, Narrative, History.* Baltimore: Johns Hopkins University Press, 1996.

Castañeda, Antonia I. "Engendering the History of Alta California, 1769–1848." In *Contested Eden: California before the Gold Rush,* edited by

Ramón Gutiérrez and Richard J. Orsi, 230–59. Berkeley: University of California Press, 1998.

———. "Sexual Violence in the Politics and Policies of Conquest: Amerindian Women and the Spanish Conquest of Alta California." In *Building with Our Hands: New Directions in Chicana Studies,* edited by Adele De la Torre and Beatríz M. Pesquera, 15–33. Berkeley: University of California Press, 1993.

Castiglia, Christopher. *Interior States: Institutional Consciousness and the Inner Life of Democracy in the Antebellum United States.* Durham, N.C.: Duke University Press, 2008.

Castile, George Pierre. *Taking Charge: Native American Self-Determination and Federal Indian Policy, 1975–1993.* Tucson: University of Arizona Press, 2006.

———. *To Show Heart: Native American Self-Determination and Federal Indian Policy, 1960–1975.* Tucson: University of Arizona Press, 1998.

Castillo, Edward D. "The Impact of Euro-American Exploration and Settlement." In *Handbook of North American Indians: California,* vol. 8, edited by Robert F. Heizer, 99–127. Washington, D.C.: Smithsonian Institution, 1978.

Cattelino, Jessica. *High Stakes: Florida Seminole Gaming and Sovereignty.* Durham, N.C.: Duke University Press, 2008.

Cavitch, Max. *American Elegy: The Poetry of Mourning from the Puritans to Whitman.* Minneapolis: University of Minnesota Press, 2007.

Chakrabarty, Dipesh. *Provincializing Europe: Postcolonial Thought and Historical Difference.* Princeton, N.J.: Princeton University Press, 2000.

Charters, Claire, and Rudolfo Stavenhagen, eds. *Making the Declaration Work: The United Nations Declaration on the Rights of Indigenous Peoples.* Copenhagen: IWGIA, 2010.

Chatterjee, Partha. *The Nation and Its Fragments: Colonial and Postcolonial Histories.* Princeton, N.J.: Princeton University Press, 1993.

Cheah, Pheng. *Inhuman Conditions: On Cosmopolitanism and Human Rights.* Cambridge, Mass.: Harvard University Press, 2006.

Cheng, Anne Anlin. *The Melancholy of Race: Psychoanalysis, Assimilation, and Hidden Grief.* New York: Oxford University Press, 2000.

Cherokee Nation v. Georgia, 30 U.S. 1 (1831).

Cheyfitz, Eric. "The Navajo-Hopi Land Dispute: A Brief History." *interventions* 2, no. 2 (2000): 248–75.

———. *The Poetics of Imperialism: Translation and Colonization from "The Tempest" to "Tarzan."* Philadelphia: University of Pennsylvania Press, 1997.

———. "The (Post)Colonial Construction of Indian Country: U.S. American Indian Literatures and Federal Indian Law." In *The Columbia Guide to American Indian Literatures of the United States since 1945,* edited by Eric Cheyfitz, 1–124. New York: Columbia University Press, 2006.

Chow, Rey. *The Protestant Ethnic and the Spirit of Capitalism.* New York: Columbia University Press, 2002.

———. "Where Have All the Natives Gone?" In *Writing Diaspora,* 27–54. Bloomington: University of Indiana Press, 1993.

Chrystos. *Fire Power.* Vancouver: Press Gang Publishers, 1995.

———. *Fugitive Colors.* Cleveland: Cleveland State University Poetry Center, 1995.

———. *In Her I Am.* Vancouver: Press Gang Publishers, 1993.

———. *Not Vanishing.* Vancouver: Press Gang Publishers, 1988.

Clifford, James. "Varieties of Indigenous Experience: Diasporas, Homelands, Sovereignties." In *Indigenous Experience Today,* edited by Marisol de la Cadena and Orin Starn, 197–223. Oxford: Berg, 2007.

Clifford, Michael. *Political Genealogy after Foucault: Savage Identities.* New York: Routledge, 2001.

Coffey, Wallace, and Rebecca Tsosie. "Rethinking the Tribal Sovereignty Doctrine: Cultural Sovereignty and the Collective Future of Indian Nations." *Stanford Law and Policy Review* 12 (2001): 191–210.

Cohen, Ed. *A Body Worth Defending: Immunity, Biopolitics, and the Apotheosis of the Modern Body.* Durham, N.C.: Duke University Press, 2009.

Colás, Santiago. "What's Wrong with Representation? Testimonio and Democratic Culture." In *The Real Thing: Testimonial Discourse and Latin America,* edited by Georg M. Gugelberger, 161–71. Durham, N.C.: Duke University Press, 1996.

Collier, Jane F., Bill Maurer, and Liliana Suárez-Navaz. "Sanctioned Identities: Legal Constructions of Modern Personhood." *Identities* 2, nos. 1–2 (1997): 1–27.

Collier, Jane Fishburne, and Sylvia Junko Yanagisako. *Gender and Kinship: Essays Toward a Unified Analysis.* Palo Alto, Calif.: Stanford University Press, 1987.

Contreras, Sheila Marie. *Blood Lines: Myth, Indigenism, and Chicana/o Literature.* Austin: University of Texas Press, 2008.

Costo, Rupert, and Jeannette Henry Costo. *Natives of the Golden State: The California Indians.* San Francisco: The Indian Historian Press, 1995.

Cramer, Renée Ann. *Cash, Color, Colonialism: The Politics of Tribal Acknowledgment.* Norman: University of Oklahoma Press, 2005.

Cruikshank, Julie. *The Social Life of Stories: Narrative and Knowledge in the Yukon Territory.* Lincoln: University of Nebraska Press, 2000.

Cvetkovich, Ann. *An Archive of Feelings: Trauma, Sexuality, and Lesbian Public Cultures.* Durham, N.C.: Duke University Press, 2003.

Danzinger, Edmund Jefferson, Jr. *Survival and Regeneration: Detroit's American Indian Community.* Detroit: Wayne State University Press, 1991.

Dartmouth College v. Woodward, 17 U.S. 518 (1819).

Das, Veena. *Life and Words: Violence and the Descent into the Ordinary.* Berkeley: University of California Press, 2007.

Deleuze, Gilles, and Felix Guattari. *A Thousand Plateaus: Capitalism and Schizophrenia.* 1980. Translated by Brian Massumi. Minneapolis: University of Minnesota Press, 1987.

Deloria, Philip J. *Indians in Unexpected Places.* Lawrence: University Press of Kansas, 2004.

———. *Playing Indian.* New Haven, Conn.: Yale University Press, 1998.

Deloria, Vine, Jr. *Custer Died for Your Sins: An Indian Manifesto.* 1969. Norman: University of Oklahoma Press, 1988.

Deloria, Vine, Jr., and Clifford M. Lytle. *The Nations Within: The Past and Future of American Indian Sovereignty.* Austin: University of Texas Press, 1998.

Denetdale, Jennifer Nez. "Chairmen, Presidents, and Princesses: The Navajo Nation, Gender, and the Politics of Tradition." *Wicazo Sa Review* 21, no. 1 (2006): 9–28.

———. *Reclaiming Diné History: The Legacies of Navajo Chief Manuelito and Juanita.* Tucson: University of Arizona Press, 2007.

Denetdale, Jennifer Nez, and Mishuana Goeman, eds. "Native Feminisms: Legacies, Interventions, and Indigenous Sovereignties." *Wicazo Sa Review* 24, no. 2 (2009).

Den Ouden, Amy E. *Beyond Conquest: Native Peoples and the Struggle for History in New England.* Lincoln: University of Nebraska Press, 2005.

Derrida, Jacques. *Specters of Marx: The State of the Debt, the Work of Mourning, and the New International.* Translated by Peggy Kamuf. Routledge: New York, 1994.

Dinshaw, Carolyn, Lee Edelman, et. al. "Theorizing Queer Temporalities: A Roundtable Discussion." *GLQ* 13, nos. 2–3 (2007): 177–95.

Dowd, Gregory Evans. *A Spirited Resistance: The North American Struggle for Unity, 1745–1815.* Baltimore: Johns Hopkins University Press, 1992.

Dowling, Sarah. "'And through Its Naming Become Owner': Translation in James Thomas Stevens's *Tokinish.*" *GLQ* 16, nos. 1–2 (2010): 191–206.

Driskill, Qwo-Li. "Doubleweaving Two-Spirit Critiques: Building Alliances between Native and Queer Studies." *GLQ* 16, nos. 1–2 (2010): 69–92.

———. "Stolen from Our Bodies: First Nations Two-Spirits/Queers and the Journey to a Sovereign Erotic." *SAIL* 16, no. 2 (2004): 50–64.

———. *Walking with Ghosts.* Cambridge, UK: Salt Publishing, 2005.

Driskill, Qwo-Li, Chris Finley, Brian Joseph Gilley, and Scott Lauria Morgensen, eds. *Queer Indigenous Studies: Critical Interventions in Theory, Politics, and Literature.* Tucson: University of Arizona Press, 2011.

Du Bois, Cora. *The 1870 Ghost Dance.* 1938. Lincoln: University of Nebraska Press, 2007.

Duggan, Lisa. "The New Homonormativity: The Sexual Politics of Neo-liberalism." In *Materializing Democracy: Toward a Revitalized Cultural Politics*, edited by Russ Castronovo and Dana D. Nelson, 175–94. Durham, N.C.: Duke University Press, 2002.

Elmer, Jonathan. *On Lingering and Being Last: Race and Sovereignty in the New World.* New York: Fordham University Press, 2008.

Eng, David L. "Transnational Adoption and Queer Diasporas." *Social Text* 21, no. 3 (2003): 1–37.

Eng, David L., and Shinhee Han. "A Dialogue on Racial Melancholia." In *Loss: The Politics of Mourning*, edited by David L. Eng and David Kazanjian, 343–71. Berkeley: University of California Press, 2003.

Eng, David L., and David Kazanjian. "Introduction: Mourning Remains." In *Loss: The Politics of Mourning*, edited by David L. Eng and David Kazanjian, 1–28. Berkeley: University of California Press, 2003.

Engle, Karen. *The Elusive Promise of Indigenous Development: Rights, Culture, Strategy.* Durham, N.C.: Duke University Press, 2010.

Esquibel, Catriόna Rueda. *With Her Machete in Her Hand: Reading Chicana Lesbians.* Austin: University of Texas Press, 2006.

Fassin, Didier, and Richard Rechtman. *The Empire of Trauma: An Inquiry into the Condition of Victimhood.* Princeton, N.J.: Princeton University Press, 2009.

Fast, Robin Riley. *The Heart as a Drum: Continuance and Resistance in American Indian Poetry.* Ann Arbor: University of Michigan Press, 1999.

Felman, Shoshana. *The Juridical Unconscious: Trials and Traumas in the Twentieth Century.* Cambridge, Mass.: Harvard University Press, 2002.

Ferguson, Roderick A. *Aberrations in Black: Toward a Queer of Color Critique.* Minneapolis: University of Minnesota Press, 2004.

Field, Les W. "Unacknowledged Tribes, Dangerous Knowledge: The Muwekma Ohlone and How Identities Are 'Known.'" In collaboration with the Muwekma Ohlone Tribe. *Wicazo Sa Review* 18, no. 2 (2003): 79–94.

Finger, John R. *Cherokee Americans: The Eastern Band of Cherokees in the Twentieth Century.* Lincoln: University of Nebraska Press, 1991.

———. *The Eastern Band of Cherokees, 1819–1900.* Knoxville: University of Tennessee Press, 1984.

Fixico, Donald L. *Termination and Relocation: Federal Indian Policy, 1945–1960.* Albuquerque: University of New Mexico Press, 1986.

———. *The Urban Indian Experience in America.* Albuquerque: University of New Mexico Press, 2000.

Fletcher, Matthew L. M. "The Insidious Colonialism of the Conqueror: The Federal Government in Modern Tribal Affairs." *Washington University Journal of Law and Policy* 19 (2005): 273–311.

Floyd, Kevin. *The Reification of Desire: Toward a Queer Marxism*. Minneapolis: University of Minnesota Press, 2009.

Foucault, Michel. *The History of Sexuality*. Vol. 1. 1976. Translated by Robert Hurley. 1978. Reprint, New York: Vintage Books, 1990.

———. "Nietzsche, Genealogy, History." In *The Foucault Reader*, edited by Paul Rainbow and translated by Donald F. Bouchard and Sherry Simon, 76–100. New York: Pantheon Books, 1984.

———. *"Society Must Be Defended": Lectures at the Collége de France, 1975–1976*. Translated by David Macey. New York: St. Martin's Press, 2003.

———. "Two Lectures." In *Power/Knowledge: Selected Interviews and Other Writings, 1972–1977*, edited by Colin Gordon and translated by Alessandro Fontana and Pasquale Pasquino, 78–108. New York: Pantheon Books, 1980.

Freccero, Carla. *Queer/Early/Modern*. Durham, N.C.: Duke University Press, 2006.

Freeman, Elizabeth. *Time Binds: Queer Temporalities, Queer Histories*. Durham, N.C.: Duke University Press, 2010.

———. *The Wedding Complex: Forms of Belonging in Modern American Culture*. Durham, N.C.: Duke University Press, 2002.

Frickey, Philip P. "(Native) American Exceptionalism in Federal Public Law." *Harvard Law Review* 119 (2005): 431–90.

Frost, Samantha. "Fear and the Illusion of Autonomy." In *New Materialisms: Ontology, Agency, and Politics*, edited by Diana Coole and Samantha Frost, 158–77. Durham, N.C.: Duke University Press, 2010.

Gallagher, Shaun. *How the Body Shapes the Mind*. New York: Oxford University Press, 2005.

Garrison, Tim Alan. *The Legal Ideology of Removal: The Southern Judiciary and the Sovereignty of Native American Nations*. Athens: University of Georgia Press, 2002.

Garroutte, Eva Marie. *Real Indians: Identity and the Survival of Native America*. Berkeley: University of California Press, 2003.

Getches, David H., Charles F. Wilkinson, and Robert A. Williams Jr., eds. *Cases and Materials on Federal Indian Law*. St. Paul, Minn.: West Group, 1998.

Gilley, Brian Joseph. *Becoming Two-Spirit: Gay Identity and Social Acceptance in Indian Country*. Lincoln: University of Nebraska Press, 2006.

Goeman, Mishuana R. "Disrupting a Settler Grammar of Place in the Visual Memoir of Hulleah Tsinhnahjinnie." Unpublished manuscript.

———. "Notes toward a Native Feminism's Spatial Practice." *Wicazo Sa Review* 24, no. 2 (2009): 169–87.

Goldberg, Carole. "Members Only? Designing Citizenship Requirements for Indian Nations." *Kansas Law Review* 50 (2002): 437–71.

Goldberg, Jonathan, and Madhavi Menon. "Queering History." *PMLA* 120, no. 5 (2005): 1608–17.

Goldberg-Ambrose, Carole. *Planting Tail Feathers: Tribal Survival and Public Law 280.* Los Angeles: American Indian Studies Center, University of California, 1997.

Gonzalez, Deena J. "Malinche as Lesbian: A Reconfiguration of 500 Years of Resistance." *California Sociologist* 14, nos. 1–2 (1991): 91–97.

Gopinath, Gayatri. *Impossible Desires: Queer Diasporas and South Asian Public Cultures.* Durham, N.C.: Duke University Press, 2005.

Gordon, Avery F. *Ghostly Matters: Haunting and the Sociological Imagination.* Minneapolis: University of Minnesota Press, 1997.

Gould, Janice. "American Indian Women's Poetry: Strategies of Rage and Hope." *SIGNS* 20, no. 4 (1995): 797–817.

———. "Disobedience (in Language) in Texts by Lesbian Native Americans." *ARIEL* 25, no. 1 (1994): 32–44.

———. "Poems as Maps in American Indian Women's Writing." In *Speak to Me Words: Essays on Contemporary American Indian Poetry,* edited by Dean Radar and Janice Gould, 21–33. Tucson: University of Arizona Press, 2003.

Gover, Kirsty. "Genealogy as Continuity: Explaining the Growing Tribal Preference for Descent Rules in Membership Governance in the United States." *American Indian Law Review* 33 (2008–9): 243–309.

Gramsci, Antonio. *Selections from the Prison Notebooks.* Edited and translated by Quintin Hoare and Geoffrey Nowell Smith. New York: International Publishers, 1971.

Green, Rayna. "The Pocahontas Perplex: The Image of Indian Women in American Culture." *The Massachusetts Review* 16, no. 4 (1975): 698–714.

Grey, Jackie. "The 'Labor' of Belonging." *International Journal of Critical Indigenous Studies* 3, no. 1 (2010): 2–14.

Grosz, Elizabeth. *Time Travels: Feminism, Nature, Power.* Durham, N.C.: Duke University Press, 2005.

Gugelberger, Georg M., ed. *The Real Thing: Testimonial Discourse and Latin America.* Durham, N.C.: Duke University Press, 1996.

Guha, Ranajit. *Dominance without Hegemony: History and Power in Colonial India.* Cambridge, Mass.: Harvard University Press, 1997.

Guha, Ranajit, and Gayatri Chakravorty Spivak, eds. *Selected Subaltern Studies.* New York: Oxford University Press, 1988.

Gunter, Dan. "The Technology of Tribalism: The Lemhi Indians, Federal Recognition, and the Creation of Tribal Identity." *Idaho Law Review* 35 (1998): 85–123.

Haas, Lisbeth. *Conquests and Historical Identities in California, 1769–1936.* Berkeley: University of California Press, 1995.

Hackel, Steven W. "Land, Labor, and Production: The Colonial Economy of Spanish and Mexican California." In *Contested Eden: California before the Gold Rush,* edited by Ramón Gutiérrez and Richard J. Orsi, 111–46. Berkeley: University of California Press, 1998.

Hacking, Ian. *Historical Ontology.* Cambridge, Mass.: Harvard University Press, 2002.

Hall, Stuart. "Gramsci's Relevance for the Study of Race and Ethnicity" In *Stuart Hall: Critical Dialogues in Cultural Studies,* edited by David Morley and Kuan-Hsing Chen, 411–40. New York: Routledge, 1996.

Harring, Sidney L. *Crow Dog's Case: American Indian Sovereignty, Tribal Law, and United States Law in the Nineteenth Century.* New York: Cambridge University Press, 1994.

Hart, Lynda. *Between the Body and the Flesh: Performing Sadomasochism.* New York: Columbia University Press, 1998.

Hart, Matthew. *Nations of Nothing but Poetry: Modernism, Transnationalism, and Synthetic Vernacular Writing.* New York: Oxford University Press, 2010.

Harvard Project on American Indian Economic Development. *The State of the Native Nations: Conditions under U.S. Policies of Self-Determination.* New York: Oxford University Press, 2008.

Heizer, Robert F., ed. *The Eighteen Unratified Treaties of 1851–1852 between the California Indians and the United States Government.* Berkeley: Archaeological Research Facility, Department of Anthropology, University of California, 1972.

Heizer, Robert F., and Alan J. Almquist. *The Other Californians: Prejudice and Discrimination under Spain, Mexico, and the United States to 1920.* Berkeley: University of California Press, 1971.

Hill, Sarah H. *Weaving New Worlds: Southeastern Cherokee Women and Their Basketry.* Chapel Hill: University of North Carolina Press, 1997.

Hirsch, Eric. "Property and Persons: New Forms and Contests in the Era of Neoliberalism." *Annual Review of Anthropology* 39 (2010): 347–60.

Holmes, Ruth Bradley, and Betty Sharp Smith. *Beginning Cherokee.* 2nd ed. Norman: University of Oklahoma Press, 1977.

Hoxie, Frederick E. *A Final Promise: The Campaign to Assimilate the Indians, 1880–1920.* 1984. Reprint, Cambridge: Cambridge University Press, 1992.

Huffstetler, Edward. "Spirit Armies and Ghost Dancers: The Dialogic Nature of American Indian Resistance." *SAIL* 14, no. 4 (2002): 1–17.

Huhndorf, Shari M. *Going Native: Indians in the American Cultural Imagination.* Ithaca, N.Y.: Cornell University Press, 2001.

Hurtado, Albert L. *Indian Survival on the California Frontier.* New Haven, Conn.: Yale University Press, 1988.

Ingraham, Chrys. "The Heterosexual Imaginary: Feminist Sociology and Theories of Gender." *Sociological Theory* 12, no. 2 (1994): 203–19.

Ivison, Duncan, Paul Patton, and Will Sanders, eds. *Political Theory and the Rights of Indigenous Peoples.* Cambridge: Cambridge University Press, 2000.

Jackson, Deborah Davis. *Our Elders Lived It: American Indian Identity in the City.* DeKalb: Northern Illinois University Press, 2002.

Jackson, Helen Hunt, and Abbot Kinney. *Report of Mrs. Helen Hunt Jackson and Abbot Kinney on the Mission Indians in 1883.* Boston: Stanley and Usher, 1887.

Jackson, Robert H., and Edward Castillo. *Indians, Franciscans, and Spanish Colonization: The Impact of the Mission System on California Indians.* Albuquerque: University of New Mexico Press, 1995.

Jacobi, Jeffrey S. "Two Spirits, Two Eras, Same Sex: For a Traditionalist Perspective on Native American Tribal Same-Sex Marriage Policy." *University of Michigan Journal of Law Reform* 39 (Summer 2006): 823–50.

Jacobs, Sue-Ellen, Wesley Thomas, and Sabine Lang, eds. *Two-Spirit People: Native American Gender Identity, Sexuality, and Spirituality.* Urbana: University of Illinois Press, 1997.

Johnson, David. "Theorizing the Loss of Land: Griqua Land Claims in Southern Africa, 1874–1998." In *Loss: The Politics of Mourning,* edited by David L. Eng and David Kazanjian, 278–99. Berkeley: University of California Press, 2003.

Joseph, Gilbert M. and Daniel Nugent, eds. *Everyday Forms of State Formation: Revolution and the Negotiation of Rule in Modern Mexico.* Durham, N.C.: Duke University Press, 1994.

Josephy, Alvin M., Jr., Joane Nagel, and Troy Johnson, eds. *Red Power: The American Indians' Fight for Freedom.* 2nd ed. Lincoln: University of Nebraska Press, 1999.

Justice, Daniel Heath. "Beloved Woman Returns: The Doubleweaving of Homeland and Identity in the Poetry of Marilous Awiakta." In *Speak to Me Words: Essays on Contemporary American Indian Poetry,* edited by Dean Radar and Janice Gould, 71–81. Tucson: University of Arizona Press, 2003.

———. "'Go Away, Water!' Kinship Criticism and the Decolonization Imperative." In *Reasoning Together: The Native Critics Collective,* edited by Craig S. Womack, Daniel Heath Justice, and Christopher B. Teuton, 147–68. Norman: University of Oklahoma Press, 2008.

———. "Notes toward a Theory of Anomaly." *GLQ* 16, nos. 1–2 (2010): 207–42.

———. *Our Fire Survives the Storm: A Cherokee Literary History.* Minneapolis: University of Minnesota Press, 2006.

Justice, Daniel Heath, and James Cox, eds. "Queering Native Literature,

Indigenizing Queer Theory." Themed cluster in *SAIL* 20, no. 1 (2008): xiii–xiv, 1–75.

Justice, Daniel Heath, Mark Rifkin, and Bethany Schneider, eds. "Sexuality, Nationality, Indigeneity: Rethinking the State at the Intersection of Native American and Queer Studies." Special issue, *GLQ* 16 nos. 1–2 (2010).

Kannady, Christopher L. "The State, Cherokee Nation, and Same-Sex Unions: In Re: Marriage License of McKinley and Reynolds." *American Indian Law Review* 29 (2004–5): 363–81.

Kaplan, E. Ann. *Trauma Culture: The Politics and Terror of Loss in Media and Literature.* New Brunswick, N.J.: Rutgers University Press, 2005.

Kauanui, J. Kēhaulani. *Hawaiian Blood: Colonialism and the Politics of Sovereignty and Indigeneity.* Durham, N.C.: Duke University Press, 2008.

Kazanjian, David, and Marc Nichanian. "Between Genocide and Catastrophe." In *Loss: The Politics of Mourning,* edited by David L. Eng and David Kazanjian, 125–47. Berkeley: University of California Press, 2003.

Kenny, Maurice. "Tinselled Bucks: A Historical Study in Indian Homosexuality." In *Living the Spirit: A Gay American Indian Anthology,* edited by Will Roscoe, 15–31. New York: St. Martin's Press, 1988.

Khanna, Ranjana. *Dark Continents: Psychoanalysis and Colonialism.* Durham, N.C.: Duke University Press, 2003.

Kilpatrick, Alan. "A Note on Cherokee Theological Concepts." *American Indian Quarterly* 19, no. 3 (1995): 389–405.

Klopotek, Brian. *Recognition Odysseys: Indigeneity, Race, and Federal Tribal Recognition Policy in Three Louisiana Indian Communities.* Durham, N.C.: Duke University Press, 2011.

Kolodny, Annette. *The Lay of the Land: Metaphor as Experience and History in American Life and Letters.* Chapel Hill: University of North Carolina Press, 1975.

Krupat, Arnold. "Representing Cherokee Dispossession." *SAIL* 17, no. 1 (2005): 16–41.

Kupperman, Karen Ordahl. *Indians and English: Facing Off in Early America.* Ithaca, N.Y.: Cornell University Press, 2000.

LaCapra, Dominick. *Writing History, Writing Trauma.* Baltimore: Johns Hopkins University Press, 2001.

LaDuke, Winona. *All Our Relations: Native Struggles for Land and Life.* Cambridge, Mass.: South End Press, 1999.

Lâm, Maivân Clech. *At the Edge of the State: Indigenous Peoples and Self-Determination.* Ardsley, N.Y.: Transnational Publishers, 2000.

Lang, Sabine. *Men as Women, Women as Men: Changing Gender in Native American Cultures.* Translated by John L. Vantine. Austin: University of Texas Press, 1998.

Latour, Bruno. *Reassembling the Social: An Introduction to Actor-Network-Theory.* New York: Oxford University Press, 2005.

Laverty, Philip Blair. "The Ohlone/Costanona-Esselen Nation of Monterey, California: Dispossession, Federal Neglect, and the Bitter Irony of the Federal Acknowledgment Process." *Wicazo Sa Review* 18, no. 2 (2003): 41–77.

———. "Recognizing Indians: Place, Identity, History, and the Federal Acknowledgment of the Ohlone/Costonoan-Esselen Nation." PhD diss., University of New Mexico, 2010.

Lawlor, Mary. *Public Native America: Tribal Self-Representation in Museums, Powwows, and Casinos.* New Brunswick, N.J.: Rutgers University Press, 2006.

Lawrence, Bonita. *"Real" Indians and Others: Mixed-Blood Urban Native Peoples and Indigenous Nationhood.* Lincoln: University of Nebraska Press, 2004.

Ledesma, Rita. "The Urban Los Angeles American Indian Experience: Perspectives from the Field." *Journal of Ethnic and Cultural Diversity in Social Work* 16, nos. 1–2 (2007): 27–60.

Lemont, Eric D., ed. *American Indian Constitutional Reform and the Rebuilding of Native Nations.* Austin: University of Texas Press, 2006.

Leys, Ruth. *Trauma: A Genealogy.* Chicago: University of Chicago Press, 2009.

Limón, José E. "La Llorona, the Third Legend of Greater Mexico: Cultural Symbols, Women, and the Political Unconscious." In *Between Borders: Essays on Mexicana/ Chicana History,* edited by Adelaida R. Del Castillo, 399–432. Encino, Calif.: Floricanto Press, 1990.

Lobo, Susan. "Is Urban a Person or a Place? Characteristics of Urban Indian Country." *American Indian Culture and Research Journal* 22, no. 4 (1998): 89–102.

———. "Urban Clan Mothers: Key Households in Cities." *American Indian Quarterly* 27, nos. 3–4 (2003): 505–22.

Loeb, Edwin M. *Pomo Folkways.* Berkeley: University of California Press, 1926.

Lomawaima, K. Tsianina. "Domesticity in the Federal Indian Schools: The Power of Authority over Mind and Body." *American Ethnologist* 20, no. 2 (1993): 227–40.

Lorde, Audre. *Sister Outsider: Essays and Speeches.* Freedom, Calif.: The Crossing Press, 1984.

Love, Heather. *Feeling Backward: Loss and the Politics of Queer History.* Cambridge, Mass.: Harvard University Press, 2007.

Luciano, Dana. *Arranging Grief: Sacred Time and the Body in Nineteenth-Century America.* New York: New York University Press, 2007.

Lyons, Scott Richard. *X-Marks: Native Signatures of Assent.* Minneapolis: University of Minnesota Press, 2010.

Macpherson, C. B. *The Political Theory of Possessive Individualism: Hobbes to Locke.* New York: Oxford University Press, 1962.

Manalansan, Martin F., IV. "Race, Violence, and Neoliberal Spatial Politics in the Global City." *Social Text* 84–85, nos. 3–4 (2005): 141–55.

Mandell, Daniel R. *Tribe, Race, History: Native Americans in Southern New England, 1780–1880.* Baltimore: Johns Hopkins University Press, 2008.

Mankiller, Wilma, and Michael Wallis. *Mankiller: A Chief and Her People.* New York: St. Martin's Griffin, 1993.

Marx, Karl. *Capital.* Vol. 1. 1867. Translated by Ben Fowkes. 1976. Reprint, New York: Penguin Books, 1990.

Massey, Doreen. *For Space.* London: Sage, 2005.

Massumi, Brian. *Parables for the Virtual: Movement, Affect, Sensation.* Durham, N.C.: Duke University Press, 2002.

Mayer, Sophie. "This Bridge of Two Backs: Making the Two-Spirit Erotics of Community." *SAIL* 20, no. 1 (2008): 1–24.

McCulloch, Anne Merline, and David E. Wilkins. "'Constructing' Nations within States: The Quest for Federal Recognition by the Catawba and Lumbee Tribes." *American Indian Quarterly* 19, no. 3 (1995): 361–88.

McLoughlin, William G. *Cherokee Renascence in the New Republic.* Princeton, N.J.: Princeton University Press, 1986.

Mehta, Uday Singh. *Liberalism and Empire: A Study in Nineteenth-Century British Liberal Thought.* Chicago: University of Chicago Press, 1999.

Meighan, Clement W., and Francis A. Riddell. *The Maru Cult of the Pomo Indians: A California Ghost Dance Survival.* Los Angeles: Southwest Museum, 1972.

Merish, Lori. *Sentimental Materialism: Gender, Commodity Culture, and Nineteenth-Century American Literature.* Durham, N.C.: Duke University Press, 2002.

Metcalf, Ann. "Navajo Women in the City: Lessons from a Quarter-Century of Relocation." *American Indian Quarterly* 6, nos. 1–2 (1982): 71–89.

Mignolo, Walter D. *The Darker Side of the Renaissance: Literacy, Territoriality, and Colonization.* Ann Arbor: University of Michigan Press, 1995.

Miles, Tiya. *Ties That Bind: The Story of an Afro-Cherokee Family in Slavery and Freedom.* Berkeley: University of California Press, 2006.

Miller, Bruce Granville. *Invisible Indigenes: The Politics of Nonrecognition.* Lincoln: University of Nebraska Press, 2003.

Miller, Mark Edwin. *Forgotten Tribes: Unrecognized Indians and the Federal Acknowledgment Process.* Lincoln: University of Nebraska Press, 2004.

Million, Dian. "Felt Theory: An Indigenous Feminist Approach to Affect and History." *Wicazo Sa Review* 24, no. 2 (2009): 53–76.

Miranda, Deborah. "Dildos, Hummingbirds, and Driving Her Crazy." *Frontiers* 23, no. 2 (2002): 135–49.

———. "Extermination of the *Joyas:* Gendercide in Spanish California." *GLQ* 16, nos. 1–2 (2010): 253–84.

———. *Indian Cartography.* New York: Greenfield Review Press, 1999.

———. "'In My Subversive Country': Searching for American Indian Women's Love Poetry and Erotics." PhD diss., University of Washington, 2001.

———. *The Zen of La Llorona.* Cambridge, UK: Salt Publishing, 2005.

Mitchell, Timothy. "Society, Economy, and the State Effect." In *State/Culture: State Formation after the Cultural Turn,* edited by George Steinmetz, 76–97. Ithaca, N.Y.: Cornell University Press, 1999.

Mithlo, Nancy Marie. *"Our Indian Princess": Subverting the Stereotypes.* Santa Fe, N.M.: School for Advanced Research Press, 2008.

Mohanty, Satya P. "The Epistemic Status of Cultural Identity: On *Beloved* and the Postcolonial Condition." In *Reclaiming Identity: Realist Theory and the Predicament of Postmodernism,* edited by Paula M. L. Moya and Michael R. Hames-García, 29–66. Berkeley: University of California Press, 2000.

Monroy, Douglas. *Thrown among Strangers: The Making of Mexican California in Frontier California.* Berkeley: University of California Press, 1990.

Moraga, Cherríe L. "A Long Line of Vendidas." In *Loving in the War Years: Lo que nunca pasó por sus labios,* 82–133. Cambridge, Mass.: South End Press, 2000.

Moreton-Robinson, Aileen. Introduction to *Sovereign Subjects: Indigenous Sovereignty Matters,* edited by Aileen Moreton-Robinson, 1–11. Crows Nest, New South Wales: Allen and Unwin, 2007.

———. *Talkin' Up to the White Woman: Indigenous Women and Feminism.* St. Lucia: University of Queensland Press, 2000.

Morgensen, Scott Lauria. "Settler Homonationalism." *GLQ* 16, nos. 1–2 (2010): 105–31.

Morris, Glenn T. "International Law and Politics: Toward a Right to Self-Determination for Indigenous Peoples." In *The State of Native America,* edited by M. Annette Jaimes, 55–86. Cambridge, Mass.: South End Press, 1992.

Moulton, Gary E., ed. *The Papers of Chief John Ross: Volume I, 1807–1839.* Norman: University of Oklahoma Press, 1985.

Moya, Paula M. L., and Michael R. Hames-García, eds. *Realist Theory and the Predicament of Postmodernism.* Berkeley: University of California Press, 2000.

Muñoz, José Esteban. *Cruising Utopia: The Then and There of Queer Futurity.* New York: New York University Press, 2009.

———. *Disidentifications: Queers of Color and the Performance of Politics.* Minneapolis: University of Minnesota Press, 1999.

Nandy, Ashis. *The Intimate Enemy: Loss and Recovery of Self under Colonialism.* New York: Oxford University Press, 1983.

National Urban Indian Family Coalition. "Urban Indian America: The Status of American Indian and Alaska Native Children and Families Today." 2008. http://www.aecf.org/~/media/Pubs/Topics/Special%20 Interest%20Areas/SW%20border%20and%20American%20Indian%20 Families/UrbanIndianAmericaTheStatusofAmericanIndianan/ Urban%2020Indian%2020America.pdf.

Nealon, Christopher. *Foundlings: Lesbian and Gay Historical Emotion before Stonewall.* Durham, N.C.: Duke University Press, 2001.

Nealon, Jeffrey T. *Foucault beyond Foucault: Power and Its Intensification since 1984.* Palo Alto, Calif.: Stanford University Press, 2008.

Nelson, Diane M. *A Finger in the Wound: Body Politics in Quincentennial Guatemala.* Berkeley: University of California Press, 1999.

Ngai, Sianne. *Ugly Feelings.* Cambridge, Mass.: Harvard University Press, 2005.

Nichanian, Marc. "Catastrophic Mourning." In *Loss: The Politics of Mourning,* edited by David L. Eng and David Kazanjian, 99–124. Berkeley: University of California Press, 2003.

Niezen, Ronald. *The Origins of Indigenism: Human Rights and the Politics of Identity.* Berkeley: University of California Press, 2003.

Norgren, Jill. *The Cherokee Cases: The Confrontation of Law and Politics.* New York: McGraw Hill, 1996.

O'Brien, Jean M. *Firsting and Lasting: Writing Indians out of Existence in New England.* Minneapolis: University of Minnesota Press, 2010.

Oksala, Johanna. "Anarchic Bodies: Foucault and the Feminist Question of Experience." *Hypatia* 19, no. 4 (2004): 97–119.

Ortiz, Simon. "Towards a National Indian Literature: Cultural Authenticity in Nationalism" *MELUS* 8, no. 2 (1981): 7–12.

Ostler, Jeffrey. *The Plains Sioux and U.S. Colonialism from Lewis and Clark to Wounded Knee.* New York: Cambridge University Press, 2004.

Palmer, Vera. "The Devil in the Details: Controverting AlieNation in Indian Conversion Narratives." Unpublished manuscript.

Parkman, E. Breck. "Community and Wilderness in Pomo Ideology." *Journal of California and Great Basin Anthropology* 16 no. 1 (1994): 13–40.

Patton, Paul. *Deleuze and the Political.* New York: Routledge, 2000.

Penn, William S. "Tradition and the Individual Imitation." In *As We Are Now: Mixblood Essays on Race and Identity,* edited by William S. Penn, 87–114. Berkeley: University of California Press, 1997.

Penn, William S., ed. *As We Are Now: Mixblood Essays on Race and Identity.* Berkeley: University of California Press, 1997.

Perdue, Theda. *Cherokee Women: Gender and Cultural Change, 1700–1835.* Lincoln: University of Nebraska Press, 1998.

————. *Slavery and the Evolution of Cherokee Society, 1540–1866.* Knoxville: University of Tennessee Press, 1979.

Perez, Domino Renee. *There Was a Woman: La Llorona from Folklore to Popular Culture.* Austin: University of Texas Press, 2008.

Pérez-Torres, Rafael. *Mestizaje: Critical Uses of Race in Chicano Culture.* Minneapolis: University of Minnesota Press, 2006.

Peroff, Nicholas C. *Menominee Drums: Tribal Termination and Restoration, 1954–1974.* Norman: University of Oklahoma Press, 1982.

Pfister, Joel. *Individuality Incorporated: Indians and the Multicultural Modern.* Durham, N.C.: Duke University Press, 2004.

Phillips, George Harwood. *Indians and Indian Agents: The Origins of the Reservation System in California, 1849–1852.* Norman: University of Oklahoma Press, 1997.

————. *Indians and Intruders in Central California, 1769-1849.* Norman: University of Oklahoma Press, 1993.

Philp, Kenneth R. "Stride toward Freedom: The Relocation of Indians to Cities, 1952–1960." *Western Historical Quarterly* 16, no. 2 (1985): 175–90.

————. *Termination Revisited: American Indians on the Trail to Self-Determination, 1933–1953.* Lincoln: University of Nebraska Press, 1999.

Pietz, William. "Fetishism and Materialism: The Limits of Theory in Marx." In *Fetishism as Cultural Discourse,* edited by Emily Apter and William Pietz, 119–51. Ithaca, N.Y.: Cornell University Press, 1993.

Pitt, Leonard. *The Decline of the Californios: A Social History of the Spanish-Speaking Californians, 1846–1890.* Berkeley: University of California Press, 1966.

Pommersheim, Frank. *Braid of Feathers: American Indian Law and Contemporary Tribal Life.* Berkeley: University of California Press, 1995.

Poovey, Mary. *A History of the Modern Fact: Problems of Knowledge in the Sciences of Wealth and Society.* Chicago: University of Chicago Press, 1998.

Porcello, Thomas, Louise Meintjes, Ana Maria Ochoa, and David W. Samuels. "The Reorganization of the Sensory World." *Annual Review of Anthropology* 39 (2010): 51–66.

Povinelli, Elizabeth A. *The Cunning of Recognition: Indigenous Alterities and the Making of Australian Multiculturalism.* Durham, N.C.: Duke University Press, 2002.

————. *The Empire of Love: Toward a Theory of Intimacy, Genealogy, and Carnality.* Durham, N.C.: Duke University Press, 2006.

Powell, Malea. "The X-Blood Files: Whose Story? Whose Indian?" In *Native Authenticity: Transnational Perspectives on Native American Literary Studies,* edited by Deborah L. Madsen, 87–102. Albany: SUNY Press, 2010.

Prakash, Gyan. "Subaltern Studies as Postcolonial Criticism." *The American Historical Review* 99, no. 5 (1994): 1475–90.

"Procedures for Establishing That an American Indian Group Exists as an Indian Tribe." 25 CFR Part 83 (1994).

Protevi, John. *Political Affect: Connecting the Social and the Somatic.* Minneapolis: University of Minnesota Press, 2009.

Prucha, Francis Paul, ed. *Documents of United States Indian Policy.* 3rd ed. Lincoln: University of Nebraska Press, 2000.

Puar, Jasbir K. *Terrorist Assemblages: Homonationalism in Queer Times.* Durham, N.C.: Duke University Press, 2007.

Quesenberry, Stephen V. "Recent United Nation Initiatives concerning the Rights of Indigenous Peoples." *American Indian Culture and Research Journal* 21, no. 3 (1997): 231–60.

Radar, Dean, and Janice Gould, eds. *Speak to Me Words: Essays on Contemporary American Indian Poetry.* Tucson: University of Arizona Press, 2003.

Raibmon, Paige Sylvia. *Authentic Indians: Episodes of Encounter from the Late-Nineteenth-Century Northwest Coast.* Durham, N.C.: Duke University Press, 2005.

Ramazani, Jahan. *A Transnational Poetics.* Chicago: University of Chicago Press, 2009.

Ramirez, Renya K. *Native Hubs: Culture, Community, and Belonging in Silicon Valley and Beyond.* Durham, N.C.: Duke University Press, 2007.

Ray, S. Alan. "A Race or a Nation: Cherokee National Identity and the Status of Freedmen's Descendants." *Michigan Journal of Race and Law* 12 (2007): 387–463.

Rice, David A. "Mediating Colonization: Urban Indians in the Native American Novel." PhD diss., University of Connecticut, 2004.

Richland, Justin. *Arguing with Tradition: The Language of Law in Hopi Tribal Court.* Chicago: University of Chicago Press, 2008.

Richland, Justin B., and Sarah Deer. *Introduction to Tribal Legal Studies.* 2nd ed. New York: Rowman and Littlefield, 2010.

Ricoeur, Paul. *Memory, History, Forgetting.* Translated by Kathleen Blamey and David Pellauer. Chicago: University of Chicago Press, 2004.

———. *The Rule of Metaphor: Multi-disciplinary Studies of the Creation of Meaning in Language.* Translated by Robert Czerny, with Kathleen McLoughlin and John Costello. Toronto: University of Toronto Press, 1979.

Rifkin, Mark. "Indigenizing Agamben: Rethinking Sovereignty in Light of the 'Peculiar' Status of Native Peoples." *Cultural Critique* 72 (Fall 2009): 88–124.

———. *Manifesting America: The Imperial Construction of U.S. National Space.* New York: Oxford University Press, 2009.

———. "Romancing Kinship: A Queer Reading of Indian Education and Zitkala-Sa's *American Indian Stories," GLQ* 12, no. 1 (2006): 27–59.

————. *When Did Indians Become Straight? Kinship, the History of Sexuality, and Native Sovereignty.* New York: Oxford University Press, 2010.

Riley, Angela. "(Tribal) Sovereignty and Illiberalism." *California Law Review* 95 (2007): 799–848.

Robertson, Paul. *The Power of the Land: Identity, Ethnicity, and Class among the Oglala Lakota.* New York: Routledge, 2002.

Rodríguez, Dylan. *Suspended Apocalypse: White Supremacy, Genocide, and the Filipino Condition.* Minneapolis: University of Minnesota Press, 2010.

Rodríguez, Ileana. *The Latin American Subaltern Studies Reader.* Durham, N.C.: Duke University Press, 2001.

Roscoe, Will. *Changing Ones: Third and Fourth Genders in Native North America.* New York: St. Martin's Griffin, 1998.

Rosier, Paul C. "'They Are Ancestral Homelands': Race, Place, and Politics in Cold War Native America, 1945–1961." *Journal of American History* 92, no. 4 (2006): 1300–1326.

Ross, Fiona C. *Bearing Witness: Women and the Truth and Reconciliation Commission in South Africa.* Sterling, Va.: Pluto Press, 2003.

Ross, Luana. *Inventing the Savage: The Social Construction of Native American Criminality.* Austin: University of Texas Press, 1998.

Rubio, Greg. "Reclaiming Indian Civil Rights: The Application of International Human Rights Law to Tribal Disenrollment Action." *Oregon Review of International Law* 11 (2009): 1–41.

Ruppel, Kristin L. *Unearthing Indian Land: Living with the Legacies of Allotment.* Tucson: University of Arizona Press, 2008.

Salamon, Gayle. *Assuming a Body: Transgender and Rhetorics of Materiality.* New York: Columbia University Press, 2010.

Saldaña-Portillo, María Josefina. *The Revolutionary Imagination in the Americas and the Age of Development.* Durham, N.C.: Duke University Press, 1993.

Sandos, James A. "Between Crucifix and Lance: Indian–White Relations in California, 1769–1848." In *Contested Eden: California before the Gold Rush,* edited by Ramón Gutiérrez and Richard J. Orsi, 196–229. Berkeley: University of California Press, 1998.

Santa Clara County v. Southern Pacific Railroad Company, 118 U.S. 394 (1886).

Sarris, Greg. Foreword to *Quest for Tribal Acknowledgment: California's Honey Lake Maidus,* by Sara-Larus Tolly, xi–xv. Norman: University of Oklahoma Press, 2006.

————. *Grand Avenue: A Novel in Stories.* New York: Penguin, 1994.

————. *Keeping Slug Woman Alive: A Holistic Approach to American Indian Texts.* Berkeley: University of California Press, 1993.

————. *Mabel McKay: Weaving the Dream.* Berkeley: University of California Press, 1994.

————. *Watermelon Nights*. New York: Penguin, 1999.

Saunt, Claudio. *Black, White, and Indian: Race and the Unmaking of an American Family*. New York: Oxford University Press, 2005.

Schneider, Bethany, "Oklahobo: Following Craig Womack's American Indian and Queer Studies." *SAQ* 106, no. 2 (2007): 599–613.

Schneider, David M. *A Critique of the Study of Kinship*. Ann Arbor: University of Michigan Press, 1984.

Schultheis, Alexandra W. *Regenerative Fictions: Postcolonialism, Psychoanalysis, and the Nation as Family*. New York: Palgrave Macmillan, 2004.

Schweninger, Lee. *Listening to the Land: Native American Literary Responses to the Landscape*. Athens: University of Georgia Press, 2008.

Scott, Darieck. *Extravagant Abjection: Blackness, Power, and Sexuality in the African American Literary Imagination*. New York: New York University, 2010.

Seremetakis, C. Nadia. "The Memory of the Senses, Part I: Marks of the Transitory." In *The Senses Still: Perception and Memory as Material Culture in Modernity*, edited by C. Nadia Seremetakis, 1–18. Chicago: University of Chicago Press, 1994.

Seshardi-Crooks, Kaplana. "The Primitive as Analyst: Postcolonial Feminism's Access to Psychoanalysis." *Cultural Critique* 28 (1994): 175–218.

Shipek, Florence Connolly. "California Indian Reactions to the Franciscans." In *Native American Perspectives on the Hispanic Colonization of Alta California*, edited by Edward D. Castillo, 174–86. New York: Garland Publishing, 1991.

————. *Pushed into the Rocks: Southern California Indian Land Tenure, 1769–1986*. Lincoln: University of Nebraska Press, 1987.

Shoemaker, Nancy. *A Strange Likeness: Becoming Red and White in Eighteenth-Century North America*. New York: Oxford University Press, 2004.

Silko, Leslie Marmon. *Ceremony*. 1977. Reprint, New York: Penguin Books, 2006.

Silva, Denise Ferreira da. *Toward a Global Idea of Race*. Minneapolis: University of Minnesota Press, 2007.

Silvern, Steven E. "Scales of Justice: Law, American Indian Treaty Rights and the Political Construction of Scale." *Political Geography* 18 (1999): 639–68.

Simpson, Audra. "On Ethnographic Refusal: Indigeneity, 'Voice' and Colonial Citizenship." *Junctures* 9 (2007): 67–80.

————. "Subjects of Sovereignty: Indigeneity, the Revenue Rule, and Juridics of Failed Consent." *Law and Contemporary Problem* 71, no. 3 (2008): 191–216.

Singer, Joseph William. "Canons of Conquest: The Supreme Court's Attack on Tribal Sovereignty." *New England Law Review* 34 (2003): 641–68.

Slagle, Allogan. "Unfinished Justice: Completing the Restoration and Acknowledgement of California Indian Tribes." *American Indian Quarterly* 13, no. 4 (1989): 325–45.

Smith, Andrea. "American Studies without America: Native Feminisms and the Nation-State." *American Quarterly* 60, no. 2 (2008): 309–16.

———. *Conquest: Sexual Violence and American Indian Genocide*. Cambridge, Mass.: South End Press, 2005.

———. "Queer Theory and Native Studies: The Heteronormativity of Settler Colonialism." *GLQ* 16, nos. 1–2 (2010): 41–68.

Smith, Andrea, and J. Kēhaulani Kauanui. "Native Feminisms without Apology." *American Quarterly* 60, no. 2 (2008): 241–316.

Smith, Paul Chaat. *Everything You Know about Indians Is Wrong*. Minneapolis: University of Minnesota Press, 2009.

Smith, Paul Chaat, and Robert Allen Warrior. *Like a Hurricane: The Indian Movement from Alcatraz to Wounded Knee*. New York: New Press, 1996.

Sparke, Matthew. *In the Space of Theory: Postfoundational Geographies of the Nation-State*. Minneapolis: University of Minnesota Press, 2005.

Spivak, Gayatri Chakravorty. *A Critique of Postcolonial Reason: Toward a History of the Vanishing Present*. Cambridge, Mass.: Harvard University Press, 1999.

———. *Outside in the Teaching Machine*. New York: Routledge, 1993.

———. "Scattered Speculations on the Question of Value." In *In Other Worlds: Essays in Cultural Politics*, edited by Gayatri Chakravorty Spivak, 154–73. New York: Routledge, 1988.

———. "Subaltern Studies: Deconstructing Historiography." In *Selected Subaltern Studies*, edited by Ranajit Guha and Gayatri Chakravorty Spivak, 3–32. New York: Oxford University Press, 1988.

Stevens, Jacqueline. *Reproducing the State*. Princeton, N.J.: Princeton University Press, 1999.

Stevens, James Thomas. "Poetry and Sexuality: Running Two Rails." *GLQ* 16, nos. 1–2 (2010): 183–89.

Stoler, Ann Laura. *Race and the Education of Desire: Foucault's History of Sexuality and the Colonial Order of Things*. Durham, N.C.: Duke University Press, 1995.

Strathern, Marilyn. *Kinship, Law, and the Unexpected: Relatives Are Always a Surprise*. New York: Cambridge University Press, 2005.

Strauss, Terry, and Debra Valentino. "Retribalization in Urban Indian Communities." *American Indian Culture and Research Journal* 22, no. 4 (1998): 103–15.

Strong, Pauline Turner, and Barrik Van Winkle. "'Indian Blood': Reflections on the Reckoning and Refiguring of Native North American Identity." *Cultural Anthropology* 11, no. 4 (1996): 547–76.

Sturm, Circe. *Becoming Indian: The Struggle over Cherokee Identity in the Twenty-First Century.* Santa Fe, N.Mex.: SAR Press, 2010.

———. *Blood Politics: Race, Culture, and Identity in the Cherokee Nation of Oklahoma.* Berkeley: University of California Press, 2002.

Szanto, Laura Furlan. "'Like a Cannibal in Manhattan': Post-relocation Urban Indian, Narratives." PhD diss., University of California–Santa Barbara, 2006.

TallBear, Kimberly. "DNA, Blood, and Racializing the Tribe." *Wicazo Sa Review* 18, no. 1 (2003): 81–107.

Tatonetti, Lisa. "Indigenous Fantasies and Sovereign Erotics: Outland Cherokees Write Two-Spirit Nations." In *Queer Indigenous Studies: Critical Interventions in Theory, Politics, and Literature,* edited by Qwo-Li Driskill, Chris Finley, Brian Joseph Gilley, and Scott Lauria Morgensen, 155–71. Tucson: University of Arizona Press, 2010.

———. "Visible Sexualities or Invisible Nations: Forced to Choose in *Big Eden, Johnny Greyeyes,* and *The Business of Fancydancing.*" *GLQ* 16, nos. 1–2 (2010): 157–82.

Taussig, Michael. *The Magic of the State.* New York: Routledge, 1997.

Taylor, Diana. *The Archive and the Repertoire: Performing Cultural Memory in the Americas.* Durham, N.C.: Duke University Press, 2003.

Teuton, Sean Kicummah. *Red Land, Red Power: Grounding Knowledge in the American Indian Novel.* Durham, N.C.: Duke University Press, 2008.

Thorne, Tanis C. *The World's Richest Indian: The Scandal over Jackson Barnett's Oil Fortune.* New York: Oxford University Press, 2003.

Thornton, Russell. *The Cherokees: A Population History.* University of Nebraska Press, 1990.

Thrush, Coll. *Native Seattle: Histories from the Crossing-Over Place.* Seattle: University of Washington Press, 2007.

Tolley, Sara-Larus. *Quest for Tribal Acknowledgment: California's Honey Lake Maidus.* Norman: University of Oklahoma Press, 2006.

Trask, Haunani-Kay. *From a Native Daughter: Colonialism and Sovereignty in Hawai'i.* Honolulu: University of Hawaii Press, 1999.

Tully, James. *Strange Multiplicity: Constitutionalism in an Age of Diversity.* New York: Cambridge University Press, 1995.

U.S. Census Bureau. "We the People: American Indians and Alaska Natives in the United States." U.S. Department of Commerce, 2006.

Usner, Daniel H., Jr. *Indian Work: Language and Livelihood in Native American History.* Cambridge, Mass.: Harvard University Press, 2009.

Varadharajan, Asha. *Exotic Parodies: Subjectivity in Adorno, Said, and Spivak.* Minneapolis: University of Minnesota Press, 1995.

Viego, Antonio. *Dead Subjects: Toward a Politics of Loss in Latino Studies.* Durham, N.C.: Duke University Press, 2007.

Visweswaran, Kamala. *Un/common Cultures: Racism and the Rearticulation of Cultural Difference.* Durham, N.C.: Duke University Press, 2010.

Vizenor, Gerald. *Fugitive Poses: Native American Indian Scenes of Absence and Presence.* Lincoln: University of Nebraska Press, 1998.

———. *Manifest Manners: Postindian Warriors of Survivance.* Middletown, Conn.: Wesleyan University Press, 1994.

Wallace, Anthony F. C. *Jefferson and the Indians: The Tragic Fate of the First Americans.* Cambridge, Mass.: Harvard University Press, 1999.

Warhus, Mark. *Another America: Native American Maps and the History of Our Land.* New York: St. Martin's Press, 1998.

Warrior, Robert. "Native Critics in the World: Edward Said and Nationalism." In *American Indian Literary Nationalism,* edited by Jace Weaver, Craig S. Womack, and Robert Warrior, 179–224. Albuquerque: University of New Mexico Press, 2005.

———. *Tribal Secrets: Recovering American Indian Intellectual Traditions.* Minneapolis: University of Minnesota Press, 1995.

———. "Your Skin Is the Map: The Theoretical Challenge of Joy Harjo's Erotic Poetics." In *Reasoning Together: The Native Critics Collective,* edited by Craig S. Womack, Daniel Heath Justice, and Christopher B. Teuton, 340–52. Norman: University of Oklahoma Press, 2008.

Weinbaum, Alys Eve. *Wayward Reproduction: Genealogies of Race and Nation in Transatlantic Modern Thought.* Durham, N.C.: Duke University Press, 2004.

Wilkins, David. *American Indian Sovereignty and the United States Supreme Court.* Austin: University of Texas Press, 1997.

Wilkins, David E., and K. Tsianina Lomawaima. *Uneven Ground: American Indian Sovereignty and Federal Law.* Norman: University of Oklahoma Press, 2001.

Wilkins, Thurman. *Cherokee Tragedy: The Ridge Family and the Decimation of a People.* 1970. Reprint, Norman: University of Oklahoma Press, 1986.

Wilkinson, Charles. *Blood Struggle: The Rise of Modern Indian Nations.* New York: W. W. Norton & Company, 2005.

Williams, Raymond. *Marxism and Literature.* Oxford: Oxford University Press, 1977.

Williams, Robert A., Jr. *Like a Loaded Weapon: The Rehnquist Court, Indian Rights, and the Legal History of Racism in America.* Minneapolis: University of Minnesota Press, 2005.

Wilson, Richard A. *The Politics of Truth and Reconciliation in South Africa: Legitimizing the Post-Apartheid State.* New York: Cambridge University Press, 2001.

Winemucca, Sarah. *Life among Piutes: Their Wrongs and Claims.* 1883. Reprint, Reno: University of Nevada Press, 1994.

Womack, Craig. "Suspicioning: Imagining a Debate between Those Who Get Confused, and Those Who Don't, When They Read the Poems of Joy Harjo. Or What's an Old-Timey Gay Boy Like Me to Do?" *GLQ* 16, nos. 1–2 (2010): 133–55.

———. "Theorizing American Indian Experience." In *Reasoning Together: The Native Critics Collective,* edited by Craig S. Womack, Daniel Heath Justice, and Christopher B. Teuton, 353–410. Norman: University of Oklahoma Press, 2008.

Index

Abraham, Nicholas, 114, 279n64
Adamson, Joni, 277n35
Adorno, Theodor, 270n31
affect: in Chrystos's work, 43,
  237–63; collective feeling and,
  3, 19, 36–37, 272n49; in Driskill's
  work, 53, 76–77, 80, 87, 90; embodied spatiality and, 33–34,
  263–66; erotic and, 28, 31; locus
  of emotion and, 35, 269n28; in
  Miranda's work, 96, 100, 108–12,
  128, 132–34, 148; in Sarris's work,
  158–66, 169–71, 179, 186–87,
  197–214; scientific research on,
  273n62
African descent, peoples of: denial
  of tribal identity for, 40; rejection in Cherokee nation of,
  45–52, 274n8, 275n20
"After Colonization" (Miranda),
  99–100, 102–17
"After San Quentin" (Miranda),
  103–4, 115–17, 120–21, 125–29
"Against" (Chrystos), 251–52
Agamben, Giorgio, 284n62
Ahmed, Sara, 34–37, 195, 216
Akiwenzie-Damm, Kateri, 28–29,
  31–33
Allen, Chadwick, 273n59
allotment period: Cherokee invocation of, 49–52; dismantling of
  Native landholdings during, 7;
  Native nations disintegration
  under, 48–52

American Indian Policy Review
  Commission, 216
ancestors, Cherokee identity and
  loss of, 65–68
Anishinaabe people, 277n36
anthropological research, kinship
  concepts and, 154–59
Aristotle, on metaphor, 14
Arondekar, Anjali, 209
assimilation, melancholia of, 101–2
Assuming a Body (Salamon), 291n57
Australia, Aboriginal reconciliation in, 216
authenticity: in Chrystos's work,
  223–36; determinations of,
  13–25; genealogical purity
  and, 159–80; legacies of federal Indian policy and, 10–11,
  275n17; tribal identity and,
  102–3, 280n7. *See also* blood;
  racialization
autonomy, federal self-
  determination initiative and,
  1–2
Awiakta, Marilou, 73

"Back to the Blanket" (Driskill),
  69, 77–83, 256
Basso, Keith, 57, 278n44
"Beginning Cherokee" (Driskill),
  55–56, 68–69, 76, 84
Benjamin, Walter, 54
Between the Body and Flesh (Hart),
  252

< 323 >

Mark Rifkin is assistant professor of English at the University of North Carolina at Greensboro. He is the author of *Manifesting America: The Imperial Construction of U.S. National Space* and *When Did Indians Become Straight? Kinship, the History of Sexuality, and Native Sovereignty.*